DEBATING 21ST CENTURY NUCLEAR ISSUES

OWEN C.W. PRICE AND JENIFER MACKBY
EDITORS

CSIS

CENTER FOR STRATEGIC AND INTERNATIONAL STUDIES
WASHINGTON, D.C.

The Center for Strategic and International Studies (CSIS) seeks to advance global security and prosperity in an era of economic and political transformation by providing strategic insights and practical policy solutions to decisionmakers. CSIS serves as a strategic planning partner for the government by conducting research and analysis and developing policy initiatives that look into the future and anticipate change. Our more than 25 programs are organized around three themes:

Defense and Security Policy—With one of the most comprehensive programs on U.S. defense policy and international security, CSIS proposes reforms to U.S. defense organization, defense policy, and the defense industrial and technology base. Other CSIS programs offer solutions to the challenges of proliferation, transnational terrorism, homeland security, and post-conflict reconstruction.

Global Challenges—With programs on demographics and population, energy security, global health, technology, and the international financial and economic system, CSIS addresses the new drivers of risk and opportunity on the world stage.

Regional Transformation—CSIS is the only institution of its kind with resident experts studying the transformation of all of the world's major geographic regions. CSIS specialists seek to anticipate changes in key countries and regions—from Africa to Asia, from Europe to Latin America, and from the Middle East to North America.

Founded in 1962 by David M. Abshire and Admiral Arleigh Burke, CSIS is a bipartisan, nonprofit organization headquartered in Washington, D.C., with more than 220 full-time staff and a large network of affiliated experts. Former U.S. senator Sam Nunn became chairman of the CSIS Board of Trustees in 1999, and John J. Hamre has led CSIS as its president and chief executive officer since 2000.

CSIS does not take specific policy positions; accordingly, all views expressed herein should be understood to be solely those of the authors.

ISBN 978-0-89206-499-1

Center for Strategic and International Studies
1800 K Street, N.W., Washington, D.C. 20006
Tel: (202) 887-0200   Fax: (202) 775-3199   Web: www.csis.org
Information on the Project on Nuclear Issues may be found at www.csis.org/isp/poni

CONTENTS

ABBREVIATIONS AND ACRONYMS

AAAS	American Association for the Advancement of Science
ABM	Anti-Ballistic Missile [Treaty]
ACDA	Arms Control and Disarmament Agency
AEC	Atomic Energy Commission
AF&F	Arming, Fusing and Firing System
AP	Additional Protocol
APEC	Asia-Pacific Economic Cooperation
ARF	ASEAN Regional Forum
ASEAN	Association of Southeast Asian Nations
ASMP	*Air-Sol Moyenne Portée* – a French air-breathing missile
BMD	Ballistic Missile Defense
BWC	Biological Weapons Convention
C^2	Command and Control
C^3I	Command, Control, Communications, and Intelligence
CCP	Chinese Communist Party
CD	Conference on Disarmament
CMC	Central Military Committee
COAs	Courses of Action
CONOPS	Concept of Operations
CONUS	Continental United States

CTBT	Comprehensive Nuclear Test-Ban Treaty
CTM	Conventional Trident Modification —a conventional warhead for Trident ballistic missiles
DMZ	Demilitarized Zone
DOD	Department of Defense
DOE	Department of Energy
DPRK	Democratic People's Republic of Korea (North Korea)
DTRA	Defense Threat Reduction Agency
EADS	European Aeronautic Defence and Space Co.
EMP	Electromagnetic Pulse
EU	European Union
FMCT	Fissile Material Cutoff Treaty
GCC	Gulf Cooperation Council
GDP	Gross Domestic Product
HUMINT	Human Intelligence
IAEA	International Atomic Energy Agency
ICBM	Intercontinental Ballistic Missile
ICI	Istanbul Cooperation Initiative
INF	Intermediate Range Nuclear Force
IRCG	Islamic Revolutionary Guards Corp
JDEC	Joint Data Exchange Center
JSTPS	Joint Strategic Planning Staff
KPA	Korean People's Army
LANL	Los Alamos National Laboratory
LEP	Life Extension Program
LLNL	Lawrence Livermore National Laboratory
LMJ	*Laser Mégajoule*
LOW	Launch on Warning
MAD	Mutually Assured Destruction
MD	Missile Defense
MDA	U.S. Missile Defense Agency
MIRV	Multiple Independently Targetable Reentry Vehicle
MOD	Ministry of Defence
NATO	North Atlantic Treaty Organization
NCA	Nuclear Command Authority

NDS	National Defense Strategy
NFU	No First Use
NNSA	National Nuclear Security Administration
NPR	Nuclear Posture Review
NPT	Nuclear Non-Proliferation Treaty
NSG	Nuclear Supplier's Group
NSS	National Security Strategy
NWS	Nuclear Weapon State
OPLANs	Operations Plans
PAL	Permissive Action Link
PGS	Prompt Global Strike
PRPs	Personnel Reliability Programs
PSI	Proliferation Security Initiative
QDR	Quadrennial Defense Review
RNEP	Robust Nuclear Earth Penetrator
ROK	Republic of Korea (South Korea)
RRW	Reliable Replacement Warhead
RVSN	Russia's Strategic Missile Forces (*Raketniye voiska strategicheskogo naznacheniya*)
SAC	Strategic Air Command
SAIC	Science Applications International Corporation
SDR	Strategic Defence Review
SFIs	Significant Findings
SIOP	Single Integrated Operational Plan
SLBM	Submarine-Launched Ballistic Missile
SMF	Strategic Missile Forces
SNM	Special Nuclear Material
SORT	Strategic Offensive Reductions Treaty (Moscow Treaty)
SRF	Strategic Rocket Forces
SSBN	Strategic Ballistic Missile Submarine
SSP	Stockpile Stewardship Program
TA-55	Technical Area 55 —a plutonium facility at Los Alamos National Laboratory
TMD	Theater Missile defense
TMD AHWG	Theater Missile Defense Ad-Hoc Working Group

TNA	*Tête Nucléaire Aéroportée* — a French air-launched nuclear warhead
TNO	*Tête nucléaire océanique* - a new-generation French nuclear warhead
UN	United Nations
UNSC	United Nations Security Council
USN	United States Navy
USNORTHCOM	United States Northern Command
USSTRATCOM	United States Strategic Command
WMD	Weapons of Mass Destruction

ACKNOWLEDGMENTS

In Memoriam
Leon Sloss (1926–2006)

The late Leon Sloss, friend and mentor to PONI since its inception, acted as a senior editor for this book until his death on November 1, 2006. His parting is keenly felt by those whose lives he touched.

The editors and authors sincerely thank Dr. Michael Wheeler and Ambassador Linton Brooks for suggesting and encouraging the production of this text within the auspices of the Project on Nuclear Issues (PONI). Strong support was provided by Elaine Bunn, Frank Miller, Frank Moore, Tom Neary, George Quester, Brad Roberts, Paul Taylor, Victor Utgoff, and Christopher Williams, who helped shape the objectives of the book, mentored the authors, and reviewed their work. Roberta Howard, Divina Jocson, and Camille Sawak are thanked for shepherding the text through the publishing process, and Dr. Clark Murdock (director of PONI) is especially commended for giving the editors and authors both the freedom and support necessary for success.

FOREWORD

Linton Brooks and Michael Wheeler

I n the half century between the end of the Second World War and the collapse of the Soviet empire, nuclear weapons dominated American national security thinking. The prospect of a nuclear confrontation with the Soviet Union influenced American attitudes and actions throughout the globe. Starting with the early work of Bernard Brodie and with Albert Wohlstetter's seminal article "The Delicate Balance of Terror," American defense intellectuals developed a complex theory of nuclear deterrence. American officials spent time wrestling with such concepts as counterforce and counter value targeting, the importance of throw-weight, crisis stability, arms race stability, escalation control, extended deterrence, and, above all, with the difficult question, "how much is enough?" We argued over differences between deterrence and warfighting. We worried about maintaining a secure reserve to prevent global dominance by the Soviet Union after a nuclear exchange. We built NATO, the most successful peacetime alliance in history, around shared risks and responsibilities for nuclear operations. To help manage the nuclear confrontation, we led the way in developing bilateral and multilateral nuclear arms control regimes. So pervasive was the influence of nuclear weapons that, for many, the very word "strategic" lost its rich historic meaning and became simply a synonym for "nuclear."

Ambassador Linton Brooks was Administrator of the National Nuclear Security Administration, U.S. Department of Energy, from 2002 to 2007. Dr. Michael Wheeler is Director of the Advanced Systems and Concepts Office, Defense Threat Reduction Agency.

In hindsight, our theories were somewhat limited. Despite occasional entreaties to consider the impact of nuclear proliferation on stability, we largely failed to think strategically about nuclear weapons possessed by third countries, assuming they would somehow be subsumed in the US-Soviet confrontation. We paid no meaningful attention to nuclear terrorism. Although we studied the role of limited nuclear exchanges within a broad conflict with the Soviet Union, we acted as though nuclear weapons, once used in any fashion, would inevitably lead to a massive exchange.

With the collapse of the Soviet Union, this intellectual legacy quickly came to be seen as largely irrelevant. Nuclear weapons became, for many, a thing of the past, like the horse cavalry or the coast artillery—capabilities that once were important but that could now be safely ignored. Some ignored nuclear policy because they could not see any relevance for nuclear weapons in the post-Cold War world. Others saw the demise of the Soviet Union as an opportunity to reduce reliance on weapons they had always considered immoral. But most people didn't think about nuclear weapons at all, despite the wake-up call that international inspectors provided when they revealed the depth of the Iraqi nuclear weapons program after the First Gulf War. Throughout the 1990s, decision-makers and defense intellectuals turned their attention elsewhere.

A decade after the collapse of the Soviet Union the nuclear tests by India and Pakistan in 1998, growing concern about the future direction of China and the Russian Federation, the recognition that states like North Korea and Iran were seeking to develop nuclear weapons, and the threat of nuclear terror in the aftermath of September 11, 2001, combined to make it clear that, no matter what some individuals wished, nuclear weapons remained very much an important part of the post-Cold War world. Gradually, beginning with the 2001 Nuclear Posture Review, the policy community began to re-engage on the subject of nuclear weapons. Then came Iraq, which increasingly dominated national security thinking both inside and outside of government, driving out all other considerations. As a result, the stark reality is that while the world has changed dramatically since Christmas 1991 when General Secretary Gorbachev announced the end of the Soviet Union, nuclear thinking has not advanced to match those changes. Despite sporadic calls by lonely voices, there has been no national discussion or debate on this important topic outside the very small community of nuclear specialists.

In 2002, when it was still possible to believe that a national dialogue on the future of nuclear weapons and nuclear weapons policy was possible, a group of Cold War-era nuclear experts met at a dinner sponsored by Dr. John Hamre, President of the Center for Strategic and International Studies. The two of us were present. We had both spent the 1980s deeply enmeshed in nuclear issues from the different perspectives of the Navy and the Air Force and of the Joint Staff and the White House. Like virtually everyone at that dinner, we shared the view that renewed thinking on nuclear issues was crucial.

As the discussion proceeded, all of us recognized the complete absence of new participants in the debate. There were infrequent meetings and seminars to discuss nuclear issues, but the participants were, almost to a person, the same people we would have encountered at similar gatherings in the mid-1980s. This is a concern for two reasons, one obvious and one slightly less so. The obvious concern is that the individuals with experience in developing and articulating nuclear policy will inevitably be passing from the scene over the coming years and will need to be replaced. Indeed, one of our good friends present at that first dinner, Leon Sloss, has since departed. His wisdom and experience was a national treasure we no longer can reach out to. The less obvious—but more pressing—concern is that those of us with long experience during the Cold War were accustomed to thinking of nuclear issues only in the context of large-scale exchanges with a single superpower adversary. No matter how flexible and agile we think our minds are, a lifetime of dealing with one particular view of the nuclear problem may not be the best preparation for the challenges posed by nuclear weapons in the 21st century.

The Project on Nuclear Issues (PONI) grew out of these twin insights. It was designed to encourage younger scholars, practitioners and scientists to think deeply and carefully about the challenges of what Keith Payne has called "the second nuclear age." This book is the result of some of their thinking. The essays it contains are important for at least three reasons. First, they are important in themselves. Each deals with a significant issue where clear thinking backed by sound analysis is crucial. Second, they are important because they illustrate that diversity of issues with which the United States must grapple in the coming years. Finally, they are important as an opportunity for new voices to enter the discussion of nuclear issues. These new voices, like those of the authors in this volume, will come from national laboratories, think tanks, the academic community, the military, and elsewhere. Unburdened with the intellectual legacy of the Cold War, they will have a better chance of gaining the fresh insights we so desperately need.

The United States will face many challenges with regard to nuclear weapons in the coming decades. It will need to decide whether and how to modernize our aging nuclear weapons infrastructure. It will need to decide whether to embrace the opportunities posed by the Reliable Replacement Warhead. It will need to decide on what additional reductions in the stockpile are appropriate and how those reductions relate to the growing capability of a responsive infrastructure. It will need to decide the appropriate relationship between offense and defense and between nuclear and non-nuclear or non-kinetic capabilities. It will need to improve the linkage between our nuclear weapons policy and our nonproliferation policy. It will need to face the continuing challenge of preventing nuclear terrorism. It will need to address deterrence in a 21st century context.

All of these issues are important. Arguably, however, the most important question facing us is gaining and articulating a clearer understanding of the fundamental purpose or purposes of nuclear weapons in the 21st century. The essays in this volume, by helping to illuminate various aspects of the nuclear challenges we face, will help the United States as it gropes toward a consensus on these fundamental issues.

War and conflict have been with us as long as the human race has existed. Plato said that only the dead have seen the end of war. Similarly, however much we may wish it were otherwise, nuclear weapons and the challenges they pose will be with us for the foreseeable future. Failing to meet these challenges could have devastating consequences for the United States. Sound and diverse thinking on these issues will be crucial. This book is a good step in that direction.

PREFACE

Clark Murdock

There is little margin for error in nuclear deterrence in times of crisis. This is no less true for the United States today, with its asymmetric adversarial relationships with regional states having "rogue" regimes, than during the Soviet era. Although the U.S.-Soviet ideological struggle included infamous episodes such as the Cuban Missile Crisis—where the world held its breath for thirteen days on the brink of nuclear annihilation—there was a maturity in the relationship, along with the cold comfort of mutually assured destruction. There is no such mutual understanding in the relations between the U.S., Western countries and regional actors that have ambitions to acquire WMD. Potentially ambiguous threats of the use of nuclear weapons have been reported prior to Operation Desert Storm and through the ongoing tensions with Iran and North Korea. However, the credibility of such threats has eroded over time.

Former adversaries retain large nuclear stockpiles. Strategies to deter the use of WMD and dissuade the modernization or acquisition of these terrible weapons must now be carefully crafted for the new security environment. Compounding the problem, transformation of the large stockpiles of nuclear weapons will take a long time. The U.S. stockpile continues to reduce its warhead numbers to meet treaty obligations, but the infrastructure is barely capable of sustaining even a modest stockpile

---

Clark Murdock is a Senior Adviser at CSIS and Director of the Project on Nuclear Issues (PONI). Information on PONI may be found at www.csis.org/isp/poni.

of 1,700-2,200 operationally deployed warheads and a reserve stockpile without modernization and improved efficiencies.

Of more concern is that successive administrations have not been able to build political consensus or develop a compelling public narrative in order to support a coherent, overarching strategy necessary to support new deterrence policies, doctrine, required force structures, weapons, operational plans, the underpinning technologies and military industrial complex. Much of this can be attributed to a desire to reduce the relevance of nuclear weapons in national security strategy and the resultant lack of attention to them.

In 2002 Donald Winter, then a senior vice president at Northrop Grumman, and now Secretary of the Navy, Dr. Hamre, former Deputy Secretary of Defence and now President of CSIS, and, and Amb. Linton Brooks, then Administrator of the National Nuclear Security Administration, concluded that investment in human capital was the most pressing issue facing the U.S. nuclear weapons community. Further, it is the nuclear weapons policy community that seems to have suffered most by the benign neglect of the preceding decade. It was seen that many with an interest in and experience with nuclear matters were retired or soon retiring and the next generation was absent, whereas the military, national laboratories, and industry had continued to maintain a level of recruitment and programmatic effort to provide a foundation of intellectual capability. However, all will face the effects of the retirement of the baby boom generation over the next few years. Having made this stark observation, they established the CSIS Project on Nuclear Issues (PONI).

The goals of the project are twofold. First, PONI aims to build and sustain a networked community of young nuclear experts from the military, the national laboratories, industry, academia, and the policy community. Secondly, PONI works to contribute to the debate and leadership on nuclear issues by generating new ideas and discussions among both its members and the public at large.

From the first conference at U.S. Strategic Command (USSTRAT-COM) in November 2003, PONI members have been considering nuclear weapons-related matters and presenting their thinking to senior policy makers in the U.S. government. In recognition of the value provided by PONI, sponsors have institutionalized their support and are committed to continuous funding. At the third annual PONI conference, held at USSTRATCOM, Dr. Mike Wheeler and Ambassador Linton Brooks challenged the PONI membership to write a "seminal work"—an edited volume on contemporary nuclear issues. The 16 papers in this book are the result, having been selected from more than double the number of prospective authors. They have very much been written from the fresh perspective that the young PONI membership has brought to this critical area of policy analysis. True to the PONI model, the authors have enjoyed unique access to seasoned practitioners in the field from the National Nuclear Security Administration and the Defense Threat Reduction Agency. This group of senior scholars and former government officials has been invaluable in the process of shaping the guiding themes: U.S. nuclear weapons policy, the drivers, their contribution to deterrence and the challenges of ownership. They have offered priceless assistance to the authors through coaching and peer review.

Proliferation of weapons of mass destruction remains one of the most serious threats to the peace and security of the United States, its allies and the international community. Nuclear weapons offered a foundation to the relative peace of the Cold War. Since that era the U.S. nuclear deterrence policy has evolved to meet the new and less certain threats as part of national security and foreign policy. In addition to the shift of emphasis from a bipolar world of superpowers to a unipolar world, where regional tensions dominate the headlines and attention of the White House, this environment has been confused by the war on terror and the threat of WMD terrorism. *Debating 21ˢᵗ Century Nuclear Issues* deliberately excludes terrorism from its contents, although there was much interest from PONI members—prospective authors—on the basis that there is little role for nuclear weapons in deterring WMD terrorism. The one possible exception is state-sponsored WMD terrorism. Deterrence of such potential state adversaries requires robust attribution methods and intelligence—which are beyond the scope of this volume—and a coherent nuclear deterrence policy, posture, force structure, and infrastructure, which are very much the focus of this book.

In four sections, *Debating 21ˢᵗ Century Nuclear Issues* examines the threats (states with nuclear weapons and those with clear nuclear ambitions), considers recent developments and perspectives of the other nuclear-weapon states, analyses U.S. policy and strategies for putting into operation its nuclear deterrent and looks at the interplay between U.S. nuclear weapons and broader nuclear policies: civil energy cooperation and non-proliferation.

These topics are critical, but sometimes overlooked, aspects of U.S. security policy. It is clear that the U.S. Congress and administration will continue to develop and execute strategies to maximize the effectiveness of the nation's nuclear forces as part of what the 2006 Quadrennial Defense Review Report calls "tailored deterrence." That document, among other things, reinforced a policy of de-emphasis of nuclear weapons within the national security strategy, but this message is not the one taken by others. The George W. Bush administration has struggled to articulate an overall strategy that chimes with both the security needs of the nation and the concerns of Congress. Critics of the current execution of U.S. nuclear policy have highlighted perceptions of near-peer competitors. Accusations of strategies that seek nuclear, first strike, primacy over Russia—based on a mischaracterization of intent and incomplete analysis of the technical capabilities of the U.S. military and its development plans—have damaged the already fragile stockpile transformation plans that seek to move America away from a Cold War nuclear posture. A decade of relative neglect by successive administrations on nuclear weapons policy matters has no doubt contributed to this, at precisely the time when the changes in the international security environment demand attention to nuclear weapons, nuclear deterrence and non-proliferation policy. *Debating 21st Century Nuclear Issues* offers insights into many of the issues for policy makers, analysts and scholars.

INTRODUCTION

Though the threat of international terrorism has become the top priority of most policy makers, the legacy of the nuclear arms race leaves many important challenges unresolved. Nuclear stockpile matters receive little attention from senior members of the U.S. administration or the U.S. Congress when compared with their centrality in the second half of the 20th century. Neither stockpile issues nor nuclear power are likely to be key to political campaigns, however, future administrations will continue to grapple with the implications of possessing a nuclear force and the ever changing security environment with inexorable possibilities of nuclear proliferation.

The authors of *Debating 21st Century Nuclear Issues* are members of the Project on Nuclear Issues (PONI) who are in their early to mid-career years and who have debated some of the ideas that are presented in this volume. Interest was solicited from PONI members on topics such as the security environment, the role of U.S. nuclear weapons, developments in the other nuclear-weapon states, how the United States is developing and executing nuclear force policies and how these relate to nonproliferation. In approaching this generation, it is hoped that a fresh perspective will be valued by policy makers, and that writing the book will contribute to the aim of PONI, i.e. the creation of an informed cadre of young nuclear thinkers from which policy makers of the future can be drawn.

In part one, Michael Tkacik introduces one of the most vexing challenges faced by nuclear policy makers and planners: how the asymmetrical characteristics of potential regional nuclear adversaries complicate deterrence of such actors. He addresses the challenges through, among other things, improved understanding of other cultures. Jonathan Hagood, noting the emerging salience and emphasis of nuclear dissuasion in U.S. security policy, suggests three models that relate dissuasion to deterrence. In doing so, he offers tools that can aid policy makers and planners in both the development of security strategies and the communication of policy to the American public and U.S. allies. Written at a time of daily developments in the Six Party Talks and a tense U.S. relationship with Pyongyang, Dennis Shorts examines the North Korean example of how possession of nuclear capabilities, by an otherwise weak state, can limit U.S. options. This is a case study of coercion and nuclear blackmail by a "maddeningly resilient 'failed state' with weapons of mass destruction" for which he proposes remedies. In contrast to focusing on rollback strategies, David Palkki and Larry Rubin consider how to react to a future nuclear Iran. In doing so, they address the possibility that regional powers may well gain and deploy nuclear arsenals—as India, Pakistan and Israel have done before—despite coherent and prolonged international pressure to exercise restraint and to abandon programs. Drawing on regional field work, they appraise three multilateral approaches—regional collective security organizations, missile defense systems, and the Proliferation Security Initiative (PSI)—to determine how best to mitigate the effects of Iranian nuclear acquisition with the aim of avoiding secondary proliferation in the region. As a whole, the authors in part one illustrate the key nuclear deterrence challenges that the United States faces in the "second nuclear age."

In part two, Richard Weitz assesses the role, status, and planned developments of Russian strategic nuclear forces. In doing so, we are reminded that although President Bush declared that Russia is no longer America's enemy, it remains a significant nuclear power whose relationship with the United States has worsened in the early years of the 21st century. Against a backdrop of increasing Chinese defense budgets, Dakota Rudesill looks at China's nuclear posture and considers the implications of its nuclear modernization. Bruno Tertrais describes the recent modernization of French nuclear forces and the associated deterrence doctrine. He compares and contrasts the French posture with that of the United States and Britain, seeing some convergence. In their chapter, Michael Sulmeyer and Nick Ritchie analyze the British decision to replace its first generation Trident submarines and the debate surrounding this decision. Eric Miller catalogues the fortunes of U.S.-Russian missile defense cooperation, again recalling how good intentions—born after the break-up of the Soviet Union and the Warsaw Pact and in the immediate aftermath of 9-11—can be hampered by differing objectives, cultures and an absence of political support on both sides of a deteriorating relationship. Together these chapters draw our attention to the stark reality that the other nuclear weapon states are undertaking significant and costly modernization of their nuclear forces. In contrast, the United States has no comparable program and barely possesses the ability to manufacture nuclear warheads.

The chapters in part three examine the execution of current policy, the attendant climate, various administration proposals extant at the time of writing, and new ideas to foster debate. Owen Price suggests how non-nuclear warhead technology previously developed for the Prompt Global Strike mission could be integrated with a much reduced nuclear stockpile, while maintaining deterrence and military effects, augmenting force and infrastructure modernization centered on the Reliable Replacement Warhead (RRW). George Nagy considers how the U.S. military views nuclear weapons and how U.S. military culture has influenced nuclear planning. Jerome Conley describes contemporary nuclear command and control challenges and their implications for crisis stability and U.S. foreign policy. Lani Miyoshi Sanders sets out the challenges facing the Unites States in modernizing or otherwise recapitalizing its nuclear complex. Her chapter highlights the tensions between programmatic drivers, national policy, and domestic politics that have colored much of the limited congressional debate over recent years. Finally, Francis Slakey and Benn Tannenbaum share their analysis of two potential approaches to maintaining the U.S. nuclear arsenal for the long term--the RRW program and Life Extension Programs--and their effects on the nuclear production complex.

In part four, Whitney Raas reminds us that the U.S. leadership in cooperative nonproliferation efforts complements U.S. security programs in general and nuclear deterrence in particular to advance security objectives and assuage the censure of international critics for any proposed U.S. modernization, respectively. Her chapter is a timely reminder of the importance of this issue after many years of relative neglect for things multilateral. Mary Beth Nikitin contemplates the potential implications of the 2006 U.S. "nuclear deal." with India. Her chapter examines how the *real-politick* of the deal clashes with the idealism of the Nuclear Nonproliferation Treaty stalwarts and its likely effect on proliferation.

This collection of work represents a fresh perspective on some of the principal issues facing today's nuclear policy makers.

PART ONE

NEW AND EMERGING CHALLENGES
TO U.S. SECURITY POLICY

CHAPTER ONE

REGIONAL NUCLEAR POWERS AND U.S. POLICY: A STUDY IN ASYMMETRIES

Michael Tkacik

This chapter examines how possession of nuclear weapons by a regional adversary might affect U.S. deterrence options.[1] It first notes that although many believe U.S. nuclear forces are sufficient to deter any regional actor, this confidence relies on questionable assumptions. Next, it examines the characteristics of regional challenges. Having established likely regional contexts, the chapter investigates the likely objectives of regional adversaries during a crisis. The chapter then reviews ways to enhance the United States' ability to face a challenge by a nuclear-armed regional foe. Finally, it focuses on the difficulties of communicating with a culturally dissimilar regional adversary, to the detriment of deterrence, hinting at U.S. policy and strategy options for the future.

GENERAL PROBLEMS FOR DETERRENCE THEORY IN THE TWENTY-FIRST CENTURY REGIONAL CONTEXT

The extent to which nuclear deterrence theory is fungible across time and situation is not clear. Though many believe nuclear weapons have been de-emphasized, in fact the U.S. Strategic Command (STRATCOM) has seen both its nuclear and conventional missions expand. STRATCOM is expected, inter alia, to deter both conventional and nuclear aggression worldwide; to respond to asymmetric threats; to support other theaters of operation; and to assure friends while dissuading, deterring and, if necessary, defeating enemies.[2] Notwithstanding these new missions, many outside of STRATCOM view nuclear weapons as either deemphasized or their capabilities as easily fungible—that deterrence is "one-size-fits-all." Many seem to assume that because deterrence at large force levels worked against the Soviets, so too should it work against any future opponent.[3]

It is not clear that the assumptions of the Cold War remain fully applicable today for many reasons, two of which stand out.[4] First, the assumption of rationality may sometimes be misplaced.[5] What is rational in one culture at one point in time under one set of circumstances may appear less so in another time and place.

> [D]eterrence theory posits a rational, reasonable, and to a large extent predictable opponent. History demonstrates, however, that opponents often do not understand one another well and therefore behave in ways that appear 'senseless'—even when each party involved believes, by its own light, that it is calculating rationally and behaving reasonably. This can lead to costly misjudgments.[6]

And such misjudgments in the regional context may be complicated by problems of communications and false assumptions about one and other. Thus it is inappropriate to assume a regional opponent will act as the Soviet Union did.

Second, it should be noted that the intelligence gathering capabilities of the regional adversary are likely to suffer in comparison with Cold War capabilities. Intelligence is never perfect, but it may be even more flawed than in the past because regional adversaries simply lack the assets that were available to the superpowers. In some cases, such as North Korea, the United States is also operating from a severe intelligence deficit. This makes understanding and predicting an adversary's behavior more challenging and miscalculation more likely.

So then, a real challenge for the West in deterring regional adversaries is our inability to understand them and vice versa. Almost "all empirical assessments" of deterrence conclude "understanding the opponent, its values, motivation, and determination is critical to the success or failure of deterrence policies."[7] Although today we have more information than ever about other cultures, and we are able to communicate more quickly than in the past, our understanding of other cultures does not seem to have kept pace with security challenges. One need only take note of the seemingly intractable differences between Islamic and Western cultures to realize we still do not understand one another very well. It seems scholars and politicians who assure us that deterrence will work today as it worked in the past have not thought as deeply about the problem as they might.[8] Though many claim to know how deterrence works and how to make it keep working, in fact deterrence may be quite situation specific.[9] It is dangerous to speak blithely of America's ability to deter all comers, no matter what the situation. While deterrence may continue to function effectively in the 21st century regional context, that function is likely to be far more complex than in the past. In order to avoid these problems, analysis must begin with context. As Sun Tzu lectured 2,500 years ago, "Know your enemy."

CHARACTERISTICS OF REGIONAL CHALLENGES

Asymmetry of Interests

As noted above, regional nuclear challenges may look very different from Cold War challenges. One key difference in a conflict between a regional power and the United States is the asymmetry of interests involved. "To the extent a challenger perceives the defender's interests in a conflict to be low, the challenger will likely draw the conclusion that the defender's resolve to defend these interests will also be low... The regional crises with the greatest chance for misperceptions of U.S. resolve will be the ones in which the U.S. interests are ambiguous."[10]

In a regional conflict, anything over which the regional power is willing to challenge the United States is likely to be exceptionally important to the regional power. For example, when North Vietnam was willing to challenge the United States during the Cold War, it perceived the very independence of its nation at stake. In the twenty-first century, it is unlikely that a regional challenger to the United States will have superpower support, thus we can surmise that the adversary will perceive its interests as exceptionally important. Owing to such an asymmetry of interest, it is likely "that regional adversaries will have an advantage over the United States in a game of brinkmanship..."[11] Therefore, we might expect the regional adversary to be more willing to take risks and the United States to be more risk averse.[12] Even if U.S. interests are more than "peripheral," they are still not likely to rise to the level of the regional adversary.

Power Projection

WMD in the hands of a regional adversary is likely to make U.S. power projection much more difficult. And given the perception among certain adversaries that the United States can be driven off by an initial bloodletting, some could view a nuclear strike on U.S. power projection capabilities as sufficient to drive the United States away. Attempting to deter a regional power from using nuclear weapons while at the same time projecting U.S. power into that regional adversary's home area is therefore likely to be difficult. American strategy "will need somehow to free U.S. leaders from a challenger's threats of WMD escalation. Our policies will have to enable U.S. leaders to do what we assumed Soviet Cold War leaders would not: project overwhelming force into an opponent's territory without being deterred by the possibility of the opponent's escalation to WMD."[13]

This is all the more challenging when one realizes the opponent may not even have to target U.S. power projection forces directly. For instance, it may suffice to target a local port. Ports are especially vulnerable to WMD missile strikes and could make power projection at acceptable cost levels nearly impossible for the United States.

Authoritarian Challengers

It is likely that the regional adversary facing the United States in some future conflict will be authoritarian in nature. As such, threats that would deter a democratic form of government may not deter an authoritarian leadership, although personal safety and survival may act as credible motivators for regime leaders. In cases such as North Korea, the "threat of even massive societal change may not be an effective basis for deterrence of such leadership."[14] Authoritarian leaders therefore must be deterred by holding their vital interests at risk, not their people. Hence U.S. nuclear weapons are only a potential component of a U.S. response—an ultimate response (though with its own gradations and flexibility perhaps)—but not necessarily the first response, unlike the more certain escalation of the Cold War.

[Il]logic of Actors

Some argue the actors the United States is likely to face in the twenty-first century will be less logical than in the past. They point in particular to non-state actors, as well as to "rogue states." There are two potential problems when dealing with "illogical actors." First, they may simply not respond to cost/benefit analysis. Second, they may be unpredictable in their actions, even if they do engage in such analysis. This illogic is not necessarily posited to arise from some inherent pathology. Rather, it is that regional conflicts may be about issues that are so unfamiliar to the United States as to appear illogical. For example, myths about conflicts sometimes mean that the parties are fighting about things that never even happened. Conflicts in the former Yugoslavia follow this pattern, as arguably does the Arab/Israeli conflict.[15] The primary issues of dispute are often below the surface of logic, focusing on "fundamental values such as religion, often involving a matter of blood and flesh. In such a situation, [the] logic of mutual deterrence could be easily distorted and replaced by human factors such as distrust, wish of revenge, pride, miscalculation and misperception."[16] That is to say, psychological factors are likely to be even more relevant than in the Cold War, including psychological dysfunction and other realities that do not fit easily into the rational calculus of deterrence. Rationality is thus likely to suffer in regional conflict.

Asymmetric Taboos[17]

Given that nuclear weapons have not been used in anger since 1945, many assert that a taboo has grown up against their use. To the extent that such a taboo exists, it would appear more powerful in the Western democracies than elsewhere. This contention is supported by the fact that other WMD use such as chemical and biological warfare has occurred in non-Western authoritarian states including Iraq, Vietnam, and Afghanistan. Yet the United States has threatened nuclear use in the past and may have to again in order to deter first use by a regional power. Hence, friction exists "between the long-standing taboo against regional nuclear use and the possible U.S. need for credible nuclear threats in support of regional deterrence policies."[18] The plausible existence of a taboo is problematic enough, but U.S. actions have complicated the problem. Senior officials from the first Bush administration admitted in the aftermath of the 1991 Gulf War that, while they had strongly implied a nuclear response to Iraqi WMD use, in fact they never intended to carry out nuclear retaliation, even had the Iraqis used WMD.[19] So for observing regional adversaries, more credence is lent to the notion that the United States operates under a nuclear taboo and may not use nuclear weapons. U.S. threats therefore may lack credibility in a future regional contingency. But for the regional adversary, given the increased pertinence of psychological factors and given the perceived geographic confinement of the conflict, there may be fewer barriers to the use of nuclear weapons.[20]

Ultimately then, the question is whether local powers can deter U.S. entry into a regional conflict, or whether once involved in military action, the United States can deter nuclear use by the regional actor (so called intra-war deterrence). U.S. leaders must initially decide whether they think the regional adversary will use one or more nuclear weapons. If the United States believes the regional adversary will use nuclear weapons, the United States may choose not to intervene except in all but the most extreme cases. Therefore, the ability of the United States to use force is limited, often in the places it is most needed. It should be noted that this ignores security assurances given to U.S. regional allies.

The regional context may thus be unfavorable to the United States. In this environment, a regional adversary is likely to seek "(1) to deter U.S. intervention within the region, (2) to intimidate U.S. allies within the region, and (3) to ensure the survival of the state or regime from external threats, specifically to prevent the United States from seeking unconditional surrender or the ouster of leadership as the condition for an armistice."[21] Each of these objectives deserves further examination.

REGIONAL ADVERSARY OBJECTIVES

Preventing U.S. Intervention

The first goal of any regional adversary would be to prevent U.S. intervention in the region, thereby guaranteeing freedom to operate. The methods for preventing U.S. intervention are diverse. Yet, no matter what choice the regional actor makes, it must ultimately be willing to use nuclear weapons first against the United States. This point is paramount. No matter what threat is made, if the United States does not back down, the regional adversary must be willing to launch a nuclear weapon against the United States or its allies. The United States, conversely, has only to deter such first use by a far weaker regional adversary. The regional adversary is likely to have a very small arsenal, implying exceptionally "precious assets."[22] The United States, on the other hand, even after the Moscow Treaty, will have thousands of strategic nuclear weapons available, not to mention tactical weapons. Here, the asymmetries clearly favor the United States. Though this chapter has noted variables that favor the challenger, in this case, barring an extremely irrational foe and assuming the United States is willing to force the issue, it would be surprising to see the regional adversary launch a nuclear attack in the face of overwhelming U.S. response. A "U.S. deterrent strategy based on escalation dominance should" therefore be credible.[23] Moreover, if the United States has supplemented its strike capabilities with defenses, the United States might be able to significantly blunt or even eliminate the incoming attack. Consequently, putting the regional adversary in a position where it has to use nuclear weapons first is about as dominant a posture as the United States could hope for. A regional adversary threatening first use should not deter U.S. leaders. But for this approach to work, U.S. leadership must trust deterrence. If U.S. leaders fear first use by a regional adversary more than they trust deterrence, the United States may choose not to intervene.[24]

U.S. policy in the near term should thus seek to enhance its strike capabilities (both conventional and nuclear), to think more deeply about escalation dominance in the regional context, to improve its theater and national missile defenses, and to "enlighten" political leaders as to the sorts of threats they might face and the need to stand up to such threats.[25] Given all this, it is less likely that the opponent will risk nuclear attack against U.S. power projection forces. Instead, the regional adversary is likely to threaten U.S. allies.

Intimidating Allies

One of the most effective strategies a regional adversary could adopt in order to deter the United States would be to threaten U.S. allies in the region with nuclear attack.[26] U.S. allies are likely to be critical for basing purposes, over-flight rights, protecting sea-lanes of communication, providing logistical support, and providing other key benefits. In addition, U.S. assurances to such allies probably reduce incentives to proliferate.

It is, of course, ultimately in the interests of the ally to assist U.S. intervention. If the ally is no longer committed to protecting its interests, it is unlikely that the U.S. public or U.S. leadership will risk U.S. forces.

The threat by the regional adversary against U.S. allies need not be exceptionally imaginative. By threatening a nuclear attack on a key allied city, or even by simply being ambiguous in doctrine or targeting, the regional adversary will hope to deter the United States or coerce allies into denying support to the U.S. military.[27] Foiling such a threat will be more complicated than preventing first use against American targets, but the United States will still have key advantages, which often seem under-appreciated. U.S. responses should include a combination of the threat of retaliation (extended deterrence) and defenses. Of course, the United States' ability to offer such a response will be dependent in part on the allies' acceptance of certain risks.

The most basic threat a regional adversary could make would be to attack targets in allied states.[28] Here, the United can threaten retaliation with the assurance of clear escalation dominance.[29] Consequently, a regional adversary's attack would be suicidal, though to be sure the United States must communicate this in a culturally acceptable way such that the adversary understands the illogic of its nuclear preemption.

The problem with extended deterrence, of course, is making it credible. But assuming the regional adversary does not have the ability to threaten the U.S. homeland in a timely manner, one of the key difficulties of extended deterrence ("trading New York for Paris") is removed. Beyond this, however, the regional adversary must still be made to believe that the United States cares enough to retaliate against the regional adversary for any attack on a particular U.S. ally. This can be difficult if there is no history of U.S. commitment. But such a commitment can be built, if not historically, then empirically. "A U.S. strategy of extended deterrence should be credible if the U.S. commitment to the threatened ally is strong and clearly communicated. U.S. troops on allied soil are a classic way to communicate this commitment."[30] The presence of U.S. troops and other linking factors should be backed by declaratory statements that the United States will respond to the use of WMD against its ally in devastating fashion.

The common bond between the United States and its local ally can be strengthened if the United States can offer the ally defensive protection. If the ally has some reasonable assurance that its homeland will be defended, as well as the presence of U.S. troops in the homeland, it will be less likely to withdraw from its coalition commitments.[31] Theater defenses thus help not only to hold coalitions together, they can actually *help to build* coalitions and prevent proliferation. While reassuring allies in the face of regional nuclear threats is challenging, an adversary's actions when facing a threat to its own survival is probably the most difficult challenge facing the United States in the regional context.

Regime Survival

Regime survival is a shorthand reference to the difficulties of deterring a regional adversary while the adversary's regime perceives itself simultaneously to be under threat of destruction.[32] "U.S. protestations that its intentions are benign may fall on deaf ears."[33] The ability of the United States to influence this perception will be even more difficult in the face of cultural and other communication difficulties. "Under these circumstances, a regional adversary's threat to use nuclear weapons first is highly credible.[34]

Deterrence is so difficult in this situation because the regional adversary, especially if authoritarian, has little left to lose (except perhaps the lives of the its decision makers, which will be difficult to guarantee in the twenty-first century war environment).[35] As a result, adversary leadership may have little disincentive to withhold its nuclear use. Under such circumstances, "the United States essentially has two choices: Avoid placing regional opponents in this position or abandon deterrence in favor of strategies that emphasize damage limitation."[36]

The former strategy relinquishes any hope of regime change by force; it is a "limited-aims" strategy. Even if it chooses to follow that policy, however, the United States still must find a way to convince the regional adversary that the United States does not seek regime change or destruction. This would be difficult in any crisis, but even more so during war and more so yet in the face of cultural dissimilarity. Still, the alternative of an undeterrable nuclear strike against the United States or an ally is unacceptable.[37] Some claim, "a serious drawback, apart from the question of whether the adversary actually believes U.S. war aims are limited, is that this approach creates a strong incentive for regional states to acquire nuclear weapons."[38] This concern seems misplaced. Any other strategy by the United States will likely mitigate in favor of greater weapon development, not less development. In other words, the lesson from the strategy advocated below may be that the regime in question simply had too few nuclear weapons (or insufficient means to deliver them).

The alternative to a limited-aims strategy is to begin a conventional counterforce campaign against enemy WMD assets so that the enemy cannot launch an attack or the attack can be defended against if it is launched, i.e., a strategy of deterrence by denial, leaving U.S. nuclear counterforce strikes to provide some measure of intra-war deterrence and escalation dominance. The conventional nature of such a counter-force campaign, especially if begun well before the regime is actually under direct military threat, may reduce the justification for nuclear first use, no matter what the regional adversary's declaratory policy is.[39] But the sort of intelligence necessary to support conventional strikes with sufficient confidence would not appear to exist today. Furthermore, it is just as likely as not that a conventional counterforce campaign would, at some point, put the adversary regime in a "use them or lose them" position (intra-war deterrence thus becomes important). Under this strategy, it is hoped that nuclear retaliatory threats would deter the regional adversary from launching a nuclear attack while the conventional counterforce campaign is under way. If this strategy is to work then, any ground counteroffensive against the regional adversary's regime must wait until after the conventional counterforce campaign is successfully completed. And at that point U.S. battle damage assessment must be able to accurately conclude that all or most enemy WMD are eliminated. It would be imprudent to assume that intelligence could be this accurate. While U.S. political leadership may not demand 100 percent confidence that all enemy nuclear weapons have been destroyed, decision makers are likely to require very high levels of confidence. Regional adversaries may also have other options for inflicting costs on the United States or its allies (e.g., terrorism and the transfer of WMD materials or technology to terrorists or other states). Damage limitation risks nuclear use by the adversary, makes holding coalitions together more difficult in the face of this possibility, and may encourage proliferation among friendly states to offset any regional foe's nuclear weapons. However, such a conventional counterforce strategy could be most valuable as a U.S. tool of deterrence and dissuasion. Damage limitation approaches may be difficult to sell when a limited-aims strategy is offered as an alternative, but the deterrent value of the assets and accompanying declarations should not be ignored.

COMPLEMENTING NUCLEAR AND NON-NUCLEAR DETERRENCE

Nuclear deterrence can be complemented by preparing other options for a regional contingency. Multiple options provide the U.S. flexibility and allow it to take advantage of asymmetries. Moreover, additional options allow the United States to avoid being forced into nuclear use.[40] The capabilities most needed include robust, quickly deployable conventional forces (themselves a potential component of conventional deterrence and "tailored" deterrence strategies), as well as improved intelligence capabilities.

More broadly speaking, an understanding about the regional culture will be indispensable in any future conflict. The need for greater understanding of local cultures is especially true for Americans, who are renowned for their parochialism.

> Absent an adequate appreciation of the specific opponent's values, goals, determination, perceptions, risk propensities, and so forth, and absent the capacity to make the U.S. threat credible in the eyes of the opponent based on that knowledge, prediction of that challenger's likely response to U.S. threats under varying conditions will involve a considerable amount of speculation and guesswork.[41]

Continued investment in this sort of regional intelligence is therefore appropriate.

Understanding a regional adversary's culture and political system, as well as other traits of its leadership helps to improve the bargaining position of the United States in a crisis. Intangibles will also be important. The "challenger's actions can be shaped by pursuit of intangibles: 'great prestige, respect, and deference, in short, honor."[42] While the list is not complete, "adversary decision making in the face of U.S. deterrent actions is also influenced by their strategic culture, idiosyncrasies of decision mechanisms and the leader's decision style, and leadership risk of tolerance."[43] These differences "must limit the reliability of any generic formula for deterrence."[44] It is beyond the scope of this chapter to provide a detailed recommendation on how to obtain and make use of such information. But clearly,

> a multidisciplinary approach to such [regional] profiles would be necessary; included should be psychologists, cultural anthropologists, historians, political scientists, economists, regional specialists, and military specialists. The more comprehensive and accurate the characterization of the challenger, the better prepared should U.S. policymakers be to tailor deterrence to the opponent and context.[45]

One way to further enhance American understanding of a regional adversary's particular culture and values is to have allies in the region.[46]

It seems clear that the United States can and should do a better job of understanding the cultures of potential regional adversaries. Assuming that it understands the asymmetric advantages that inure it to regional foes, that it appreciates its own force structure advantages, that it moves to enhance certain capabilities including missile defense, conventional counterforce capabilities, and battlefield intelligence, and that it invests in better understanding potential regional foes, one key regional pitfall remains unexplored: communication. None of the understanding of the complexities of regional deterrence in the post-Cold War world matters if we cannot communicate effectively with regional opponents.

COMMUNICATIONS IN THE REGIONAL CONTEXT

The noticeable differences in culture between the United States and regional opponents can complicate deterrence. One especially significant complication may arise in communicating with a regional adversary. This is important because, for deterrence to work, threats must be effectively communicated.[47] Communication, however, may come under intense pressure in the regional context. For example, some contrast "Cold War strategies based on years of close interaction between the U.S. and Soviet leaders with multiple regional conflicts involving unfamiliar actors."[48]

> How messages are presented, when, and by whom can shape the opponent's response. For example, in some political cultures, greater significance would likely be placed on a message delivered by a close relative of the U.S. president then if it were delivered by a local U.S. official or even a senior official from Washington. And, as Alexander George has noted, in some cultures leaders respond 'very negatively indeed' to direct threats.[49]

Moreover, recipients of communications in any culture may misinterpret those messages. "Not only does selective attention distort a message, but selective interpretation further confuses the meaning."[50] So on top of not paying attention, sometimes recipients purposely ignore or reinterpret messages.[51] These problems of distortion may be heightened in the inter-cultural context. There will also be great asymmetries in intelligence capabilities that could otherwise be used to help interpret communications and U.S. intent, or, in the case of the DPRK, the reverse due to the dearth of U.S. human intelligence assets.

Communication is complicated when the parties have opposing interests. When these parties are also from different cultures, the difficulty of communication is further heightened. "As language and culture are inextricably bound, cross-cultural communication is complex and potentially problematic. Even speaking the same language does not guarantee effective intercultural communication."[52] In a regional crisis, opposing interests are likely to be extremely high value interests. The cultural differences will almost certainly be significant in the early twenty-first century when we are likely to see clashes between "the West and the rest." Communicators should "consistently bear in mind that the more substantial the differences in cultural background between the sender and receiver involved in the communicative process, the more substantial the differences in the meaning attached to the message and social behavior will be."[53] Beyond this contextual or background fog, conflict (and especially violent conflict) makes communication more difficult. "Different cultural assumptions toward conflict are one factor contributing to intercultural miscommunication and conflict."[54]

Although scholars of intercultural communication have identified numerous potential communication pitfalls, this chapter focuses on a few that seem especially relevant. These issue sets include whether a culture values individualism or collectivism, has independent or interdependent self-views, is low context or high context, and/or follows a monochronic or polychronic time schedule.

Individualism v. Collectivism

A key cultural difference that manifests itself in communications is whether individualism or collectivism is valued. Some cultures value independent identity, individual rights, and individual obligations. Others value collective identity (group identity, obligations, and concerns). Individualism and collectivism also manifest themselves in cultural views on conflict. Individual approaches toward conflict focus on personal accountability and allow for expressions of emotion (and these approaches, of course, color communication). Collective approaches put collective opinions forward, restrain emotions, and seek group accountability. The individual approach is found most often in the West, while the collective approach is more prevalent in Asia and the Middle East.[55] The sectarian killings tearing Iraq apart today may be viewed on one level as a manifestation of demands for collective revenge. "Individualists tend to hold the person accountable for the conflict; collectiv-ists tend to emphasize the context that contributes to the conflict."[56] It is therefore apparent that in the context of a regional conflict between states of different cultures, there will be ample room for misunderstand-ing about the causes of the conflict and that communication between the parties will reflect different assumptions. Not only will it be difficult to resolve the conflict as a consequence, but deterrent threats are likely to be misinterpreted by the collectivist and viewed as more aggressive than they are in fact meant to be. Rather than be seen as an attempt to prevent some activity, they may be viewed as an attempt to intimidate and place collective blame, which in turn may lead to intransigence or even additional aggression on the part of the culturally dissimilar re-gional adversary.[57]

Another potential problem between an individualist actor (e.g., the United States) and a collectivist regional adversary is that the acceptable solutions to conflict may be very different. The collectivist may seek to resolve the situation by minimizing dangers to whatever status quo has developed. And in attempting to minimize dangers, the regional adver-sary may have very different methods of communication. The United States is likely to attempt to place blame and seek direct redress of griev-ances and to do so through direct, perhaps blunt, communication. The regional adversary may instead seek to play down differences. For the collectivist, the "underlying assumption is that the function of language as a means of social communication is not to state facts and opinions, but to maintain the feeling of harmonious relationships."[58] These vary-ing assumptions and forms of communication may lead to misunder-standing. In the context of nuclear deterrence, such misunderstanding can have disastrous results.

Independent v. Interdependent Self-Views

Another key communicative factor is whether a culture emphasizes in-dependent or interdependent self-views. "Independent-self individuals tend to worry about whether they present their individualistic self cred-ibly and completely in front of others. Interdependent-self individuals tend to be more reflective of what others think of their projected face image in the context of in-group/out-group relations."[59] Once again, there is ample room for misunderstanding because of differences in un-derlying understandings about the very purpose of communication. The independent-self individual will tend to be as clear as possible in communication. The interdependent-self individual though, will be more concerned with how his communication reflects back on his own image and role within his "in-group" This individual may perceive slights to his "face" that are especially disturbing to him because he feels he has been humiliated before his own group (perhaps by a threat). But for the independent-self individual, such threats are part and parcel of the larger ongoing conflict and are seen as valuable in making clear the action he seeks to deter. In attempting to make clear his threats, the Westerner may in fact humiliate and antagonize his culturally dissimilar regional adversary.

The communication problems of the independent and interdependent self-views extend to the way in which they communicate. So "while independent-self individuals tend to practice direct verbal communications, expressing their own thoughts and feelings, interdependent-self individuals tend to practice responsive communication, anticipating the thoughts and feelings of the other person."[60] Again, there is room for misunderstanding here. The Westerner will communicate a threat directly and expect it to be taken as such. But the interdependent-self individual will search for deeper meaning, possibly misunderstanding the communication. This misunderstanding may be complicated by frustration on the part of the Westerner, who cannot understand why his clear signals are not responded to, and who may begin to suspect deceit on the part of the interdependent-self individual. In the end, the independent-self view tends to dovetail with individualism, while the interdependent-self view tends to dovetail with collectivism. Independent-view people see themselves as autonomous, rational, and unencumbered agents of change. Interdependent-view people see themselves as group-bound, role-based, and harmony-seeking individuals. This approach may bring into question some of the fundamental assumptions about communications on which deterrence relies, such as rational actors seeking to achieve clear goals. It would be too strong to say these cultures are irrational, but it would not be too strong to note that there exists room for misunderstanding. Nuclear deterrence in the regional context may be more difficult than first thought. Not only are asymmetric interests problematic, but communication is beginning to appear problematic as well.

Low-Context v. High-Context Communication

Low-context and high-context forms of expression complicate the problems of communication discussed above. "Low-context communication
emphasizes expressing intention or meaning through explicit verbal
messages. High-context communication emphasizes conveying intention or meaning through the context (for example, social roles, positions) and the nonverbal channels (for example, pauses, silence, tone of
voice) of the verbal message."[61]

Certainly the low-context communicator (the Westerner) views
communication more simply than his high-context counterpart. The
low-context communicator misses much both in context itself and also
in nonverbal clues.[62] The misunderstanding of context means the Westerner will fail to notice subtleties such as importance attached to the
person selected to negotiate by the high-context culture. It may be that
this person is not important enough to make decisions or that this person, though lacking rank, is very close to the adversary's leadership and
thus more important than the Westerner realizes. The impact of nonverbal clues is unclear. On the one hand, communications during crisis
may not take place in person, making nonverbal context less important.
On the other hand, nonverbal clues will be important during face-to-
face communication, and could retain importance in the way public
statements are issued and perceived. The nonverbal clues may take on
importance during signaling as well and signaling might reinforce (or
detract from) written and verbal communication. Nonverbal signaling
that might be clear to another culture could be unclear, ignored, or even
completely missed by the West.[63]

The expectations for communicators also differ in low context and
high context situations.

> In low-context communication, the speaker is expected to construct
> a clear persuasive message that the listener can decode easily. In con-
> trast, high-context communication refers to communication patterns
> of indirect verbal mode, ambiguous talk, nonverbal subtleties, and
> interpreter-sensitive value… In high-context communication, the lis-
> tener or interpreter of the message is expected to read 'between the
> lines,' to infer accurately the implicit intent of the nonverbal message,
> and to observe the nonverbal nuances and subtleties that accompany
> the verbal message.[64]

These differing expectations complicate a bargaining game already characterized (on the Western side) as one in which it is acceptable to make "threats that leave something to chance," where appearing insane (or at least unpredictable) is sometimes valued, and where ultimately one is threatening to use the most powerful weapons known to human-kind.[65] There may be ample opportunity for a high-context listener to see something between the lines that the low-context speaker did not intend, or for the low-context listener to miss completely something the high-context speaker intended to carry great import. The appreciation of "background" issues is far greater in high-context communication than low-context communication, making Westerners (and probably Americans even more so) especially vulnerable to missing important clues. The complexity of high-context communication is completely foreign to most Americans who, of course, prize directness. "High-context communication emphasizes the importance of multilayered contexts (for example, historical context, social norms, roles, situational and re-lational contexts) that frame the interaction."[66] Multilayered contexts are alien concepts to the untrained American.

The difficulties between low-context and high-context communi-cation are familiar to those who have had dealings with the Japanese. For example, there is "the Japanese culture of *sasshi* (conjecture or tacit understanding). Japanese people generally believe that it is pointless to speak precisely and explicitly with one another because we are expected to read between the lines."[67] So not only is communication pursuant to the Western model difficult to establish, in fact it is "pointless."

Monochronic v. Polychronic Time

Monochronic (Western) and polychromatic time refer to the differ-ent ways that cultures understand and use time. "Some cultures follow monochronic time schedules and use time in linear ways, whereas peo-ple in polychronic cultures tend to engage in multiple activities simul-taneously."[68] This is problematic insofar as the United States is likely to approach the crisis on one timetable, while a polychronic culture may approach the crisis on another schedule. This may cause the Unit-ed States to believe the adversary does not view the crisis as seriously as it might, thereby possibly leading to miscalculation. Alternatively, the United States might see the adversary as inattentive thus provok-ing action by the United States to "get the adversary's attention." Or the adversary might see the United States as pushing too hard and react unnecessarily out of fear. In all of these cases the different views of time could negatively affect managing a crisis in the regional context.

Another way of thinking about these differences in approaches to time is to think in terms of "conflict rhythms."

> People move in different rhythms in conflict negotiations. Intercultural communication between individualists and collectivists is magnified when the implicit rhythm of time plays a decisive role in the encounter. M-time [monochronic] individuals want to move faster to address substantive problems and resolve the conflict. P-time [polychronic] individuals prefer to deal with relational and context issues before concrete, substantive negotiation.[69]

So then, when time plays a key role, as it must in any regional crisis, other culturally defined communication differences, such as the difference between individualists and collectivists, take on greater import. When the United States differs markedly from a potential regional foe on almost all indices of culturally relevant communication variables, we are likely to see a negative synergistic effect where miscommunication and misunderstanding lurk around every corner.[70] And given that deterrence is really just a method of bargaining during crisis, we may see the United States attempting to resolve issues before other cultures are ready to discuss them, further antagonizing each side.

There are other opportunities for frustration when M-time and P-time individuals conflict.

> For M-time individuals, conflict management time should be filled with problem-solving or decision-making activities. For P-time individuals, time is a 'being' idea governed by the smooth implicit rhythms in the interactions between people. When two P-time individuals come into conflict, they are more concerned with restoring disjunctive rhythms in the interaction than with dealing head-on with substantive issues.[71]

So again, P-time individuals, who presumably spend more time in contact with other P-time individuals, have certain assumptions about the resolution of conflict. Those assumptions are not likely to apply when in conflict with the United States. And the United States is sure to become frustrated with an adversary who appears to be delaying, ignoring deadlines, and avoiding resolution of key issues. The behavior is likely to be perceived as evidence of an underlying agenda characterized by dishonesty. This is a recipe for the United States to move more aggressively, pushing the regional adversary into a corner, and adding fuel to whatever fire sparked the conflict. At the very least, the parties have different understandings about what the appropriate timeline for conflict resolution is, as well as what the resolution itself looks like. Frustration on both sides may be added into an already difficult conflict.

Other Difficulties in Cross-Cultural Communications

Beyond these cultural values and assumptions, cultures tend to approach nonverbal communication very differently. Note that these differences do not just exist between the West and the rest, but also among the "rest" as well (e.g., Pakistan and India also have different values and assumptions).

Although discussed in various places above, emotions and nonverbal communications are handled differently by different cultures. For example, "for collectivists, the masking of negative emotions is critical to maintaining a harmonious front during conflict. When collectivists feel embarrassed or perceive face threat in conflict, they may sometimes smile to cover up their embarrassment or shame."[72] Yet in Western culture, smiling in time of crisis can sometimes indicate a cavalier attitude or possibly even a challenge. Again, the opportunity for misreading communications is clear.

Silence also has different meanings in different cultures. In particular, individualist and collectivist cultures differ on the meaning of silence. "Silence is a critical strategy in dealing with both in-group and out-group conflicts in collectivist cultures. Silence may signal approval or disapproval in collectivist conflict interaction."[73] It is initially noteworthy then that the United States will need a level of sophistication not just to recognize that silence has meaning, but also to identify whether silence is positive or negative. "In silence, the conflict parties incur no obligations. Silence may also be interpreted as an ambiguous 'yes' or 'no' response. On the other hand, silence may be viewed as an admission of guilt or incompetence in an individualistic culture."[74] And of course, failure to correctly interpret the meaning of silence may lead to more than a failure to fully understand an adversary; it may lead to exactly the opposite conclusion from what it was intended to convey.

When one aggregates the problems discussed above, the great difficulty in managing a regional crisis with a culturally dissimilar adversary becomes clear. "The lack of specific information about each other's conflict assumptions or styles often creates negative interaction spirals that deepen the cultural schism. The lack of communication skills to handle such problematic intercultural episodes appropriately and effectively also compounds the miscommunication chasm."[75] The already present mistrust is intensified. When one combines a number of Western cultural communication features on one side of a conflict, and sets them against a combined number of non-Western features on the other side, one might refer to these differing types of conflict and communications approaches as the outcome oriented-model (Western) and the process-oriented model (non-Western). [76]

> An outcome-oriented model emphasizes the importance of asserting individual interests in the conflict situation and moving rapidly toward the phase of reaching tangible outcomes or goals. A process-oriented model emphasizes the importance of managing mutual or group face interests in the conflict process before discussing tangible outcomes or goals. 'Face,' in this context refers to upholding a claimed sense of positive public image in any social interaction...[77]

Here, one can imagine the complications that might arise in a regional crisis where the United States makes threats that are viewed as damaging to face by the leader or negotiator of the regional adversary. One area where these interactions might combine is on the Korean peninsula. Though a detailed discussion of a Korean scenario is beyond the scope of this chapter (see chapter 3 by Dennis Shorts), it is appropriate to briefly examine communication peculiarities of Koreans.

Although Koreans are not necessarily the most dissimilar of cultures, their culture clearly combines many attributes that stand in juxtaposition to American culture and communication patterns.

> Korean perception of communication is anchored in Buddhist philosophy, which is characterized by the inarticulate or prelinguistic process of the mind... Truth must be gained without trying and in every spoken truth the unspoken has the last word; words are approximations, sometimes helpful, sometimes misleading... In Western culture, however, people believe that words do, in fact, mean what they say. Aristotle insisted that clarity is the first virtue of good style.[78]

Many of the previously discussed concepts are clearly reflected in this description of the Korean approach to language. Koreans have an interdependent self-view and focus on high-context communications. Reading between the lines is as important if not more important than what is actually said. This approach is to be contrasted with an American view that stresses clarity and especially in the context of a crisis typically seeks to avoid multiple meanings to the same message. Facial expressions, hand and arm gestures, eye behavior, and clothing all send different messages in American and Korean cultures, thus opening the way for misinterpretation. For example, "Koreans who are angry try not to express their anger outwardly... Adults, especially men are not expected to smile frequently; it is a sign of weakness."[79] Thus an American who smiles may have that smile misinterpreted, and at the same time may not be able to spot anger on behalf of a Korean.

To complicate things further, even among cultures that are collectivist, specifics often differ. So Arabs touch while Asians do not. Arabs focus eyes on the speaker while Asians look indirectly at the speaker.[80] While there is room for miscommunication for an American in either context, that miscommunication may have different causes in each region. Of course, a nuclear crisis could occur in either region. Moreover, the way one interprets messages occurs in a pre-existing worldview.[81] Thus, decision-makers in an authoritarian, closed regime may distort communications in ways outsiders cannot predict. This is especially so for almost pathological regimes such as the DPRK.

CONCLUSION

Communication problems, along with the potential asymmetry of interests, are among the greatest challenges faced by the United States in a regional crisis when reliant on deterrence. This chapter argues that deterrence (especially nuclear deterrence) is likely to be more difficult to achieve in the regional context when confronting a nuclear-armed adversary than in the Cold War context, but that regional adversaries can be deterred in most instances if care is taken to acknowledge the uniqueness of each regional situation. The chapter initially critically examined the view that regional deterrence differs little from Cold War deterrence. The chapter then examined important differences that are likely to exist in the regional context. The chapter next discussed possible regional adversary objectives and some U.S. capabilities that might be enhanced pre-crisis in order to strengthen its position. Finally, the chapter analyzed difficulties in communications that might arise in the regional context, and how these difficulties might complicate deterrence.

Notes

The author would like to thank Frank Miller, Frank Moore, and Owen Price for their insightful comments on this chapter. The author remains solely responsible for any inaccuracies contained herein.

1. Deterrence is used in this chapter in a broader sense than strategic nuclear deterrence during the Cold War. Rather, deterrence here reflects the Deterrence Operations Joint Operating Concept 2.0 (August 2006). Deterrence is tailored, adversary specific, includes both nuclear options and conventional options, and otherwise integrates "all elements of national power." *Deterrence Operations Joint Operating Concept 2.0* (August 2006), 7–8.

2. See generally, *Deterrence Operations Joint Operating Concept 2.0*. See also, *Nuclear Posture Review* (Washington, D.C.: Office of the Secretary of Defense, 2001).

3. Even here, some argue that we have overestimated how similar the Soviets were to the West. See, John A. Battilega, *Soviet Views of Nuclear Warfare: The post Cold War Interviews* (Carlisle, PA: Strategic Studies Institute, 2004).

4. Keith B. Payne, *Deterrence in the Second Nuclear Age*, (Lexington, KY: The University Press of Kentucky, 1996), 92.

5. Many have noted the problem of imperfect information for rational actor models. See for example, Graham Allison, *Essence of Decision: Explaining the Cuban Missile Crisis* (Boston: Little, Brown, 1971). See also, Charles Lindblom, "Still Muddling, Not Yet Through," *Public Administration Review* 39 (November–December, 1979).

6. Payne, *Deterrence in the Second Nuclear Age*, 56. See also, Owen Price, "Preparing for the Inevitable: Nuclear Signaling for Regional Crises," in this volume.

7. Payne, *Deterrence in the Second Nuclear Age*, 117.

8. Ibid., 46.

9. Ibid., 45–6.

10. Dean Wilkening and Kenneth Watman, *Nuclear Deterrence in a Regional Context* (Santa Monica, CA: RAND, 1995), 15.

11. Ibid., 11.

12. Ibid., ix.

13. Payne, Deterrence in the Second Nuclear Age, 34.

14. Ibid., 131. However, the dominance of the military in such societies could be a useful lever point. Military planners of a threshold state might spend more time thinking about nuclear deterrence than previously. Targeting of military assets and personnel—as in the Cold War—may well be effective countervalue targeting as well as deterrence by denial of military capability. I am indebted to Owen Price for this point.

15. Masako Ikegami, *Missile Defense and Nuclear Deterrence in post–Cold War Regional Conflicts* (paper presented at the 24th ISODARCO Summer Course on Nuclear Weapons in the New International Context, 16–26 June 2003) 1, http://www.isodarco.it/courses/candriai03/candrai03-papers.html.

16. Ibid.

17. See also, Thomas Schelling, An Astonishing Sixty Years: The Legacy of Hiroshima (lecture presented on receiving the 2005 Nobel Prize in Economics, 8 December 2005), http://nobelprize.org/nobel-prizes/economics/laureates/2005/schelling-lecture.pdf.

18. Payne, Deterrence in the Second Nuclear Age, 140.

19. See, for example, Colin Powell, *A Soldier's Way* (London: Hutchinson, 1995), 324.

20. Masako Ikegami, Missile Defense and Nuclear Deterrence, 1.

21. Wilkening and Watman, Nuclear Deterrence in a Regional Context, 32.

22. Ibid., xi.

23. Ibid., 53.

24. The decision on whether to intervene in the face of regional nuclear threats is more complex and depends on the nature of the regional crisis. For example, the U.S. might need to honor its positive security assurances and ensure that its nuclear umbrella remains a credible escalation option. My point here is that U.S. leadership must be willing to engage in brinkmanship and trust that U.S. forces will deter an adversary's first use.

25. On the value of defenses, see Wilkening and Watman, *Nuclear Deterrence in a Regional Context*, 55–6.

26. See generally, Robert Critchlow, "Whom the Gods Would Destroy," *Naval War College Review* (Summer 2000) vol. LIII, no. 3.

27. Wilkening and Watman, Nuclear Deterrence in a Regional Context, 34.

28. Ibid., 56.

29. Though of course such dominance can still risk unacceptable losses for

allied and adversary populations.

30. Wilkening and Watman, *Nuclear Deterrence in a Regional Context*, 56–7.

31. Ibid., 58.

32. I have often wondered if Saddam did not use WMD (and released his Western hostages) during the first Gulf War because his personal safety and that of his regime were guaranteed. It may be that even regime change can occur and regional nuclear use can be deterred if the U.S. guarantees the safety of the pertinent dictator. Of course, the 2003 invasion of Iraq and the subsequent execution of Saddam Hussein may call U.S. credibility on such guarantees into question.

33. Wilkening and Watman, *Nuclear Deterrence in a Regional Context*, 35. The DPRK is an example of a regime that seems convinced the U.S. seeks its destruction. Such a perception would be heightened during major hostilities, no matter what the U.S. claimed.

34. Wilkening and Watman, *Nuclear Deterrence in a Regional Context*, xiii.

35. Again, it may be possible to "make a deal with the devil" by guaranteeing the well-being of regime leadership (including exile with a generous living stipend to a third country). But there may be significant difficulty in reaching such an agreement during ongoing hostilities. And opposition leadership will have little incentive to reach such an agreement until the military situation has turned sufficiently sour. Finding the "sweet spot" whereby regional leadership realizes it must negotiate for personal survival, yet they are not so distressed that they order the use of nuclear weapons, would be challenging. Furthermore, it is unclear whether adversary commanders in authority might take matters into their own hands. Owen Price has suggested that there may be other "public disgraces" that could be used to deter regional leadership.

36. Wilkening and Watman, *Nuclear Deterrence in a Regional Context*, 60.

37. It is noteworthy that reassuring allies becomes more difficult if the United States adopts a policy of regime change.

38. Wilkening and Watman, *Nuclear Deterrence in a Regional Context*, 60.

39. Ibid., 60.

40. Robert L. Brown, "21st Century Deterrence: Punishment versus Denial and the Demand for U.S. Nuclear Weapons," in *The Future Security Environment and the Role of U.S. Nuclear Weapons in the Twenty-First Century* (Washington, D.C.: Center for Strategic and International Studies, 2005), 34.

41. Payne, *Deterrence in the Second Nuclear Age*, 75.

42. Ibid., 111 (quoting Donald Kagan).

43. Doctrine for Joint Nuclear Operations, Joint Publication 3–12 (15 March 2005) (Department of Defense), viii.

44. Payne, *Deterrence in the Second Nuclear Age*, 127.

45. Ibid., 128.

46. Robert Oakley, "Deterrence: Clash and Utilization of Value Systems," *Appendix I to Post–Cold War Conflict Deterrence,*_http://fermat.nap.edu/html/pcw/Dt-i.htm.

47. On miscommunication, especially in the nuclear context, see Robert Jervis, *Perception and Misperception in World Politics* (Princeton, NJ: Princeton University Press, 1976).

48. Jonathan Hagood, "Dissuading Nuclear Adversaries: The Strategic Concept of Dissuasion and the U.S. Nuclear Arsenal," in *The Future Security Environment and the Role of U.S. Nuclear Weapons in the Twenty-First Century* (Washington, D.C.: Center for Strategic and International Studies, 2005), 24–26.

49. Payne, *Deterrence in the Second Nuclear Age*, 124 (footnote omitted).

50. Brett Seabury, "Communication Problems in Social Work Practice," *Social Work* (January 1980), 41.

51. On "bounded rationality," see Herbert Simon, *Models of Bounded Rationality* (Cambridge, MA: MIT Press, 1997).

52. Johann Le Roux, "Effective Educators are Culturally Competent Communicators," *Intercultural Communication* 13, no. 2 (March 2002): 41–42.

53. Ibid., 38.

54. Stella Ting-Toomey, "Intercultural Conflict Competence," in eds. Judith Martin, et al., *Readings in Cultural Contexts* (Mountain, View, CA: Mayfield Publishing Company, 1998), 404.

55. On individualism and collectivism in communication, conflict, and culture, see Ting-Toomey, "Intercultural Conflict Competence," 403.

56. See Ibid., 409.

57. Professional Notes, *World Englishes* (Aug 2005), vol. 24, Issue 3, 405.

58. World Englishes, 405.

59. Ting-Toomey, "Intercultural Conflict Competence," 403.

60. Ibid., 403–404.

61. Ibid., 404.

62. For more on the importance of nonverbal clues, see Peter Andersen and Hua Wang, "Unraveling Cultural Cues: Dimensions of Nonverbal Communication Across Cultures," in *Intercultural Communication: A Reader*, eds., Larry

Samovar et al., (Belmont, CA: Thomson Wadsworth, 2006) (11th ed.), especially 254–5.

63. See, for example, Owen Price, "Preparing for the Inevitable: Nuclear Signaling for Regional Crises," *Comparative Strategy* 26: 2, 103–115.

64. Ting-Toomey, "Intercultural Conflict Competence," 404.

65. On "threats that leave something to chance," see Thomas C. Schelling, *The Strategy of Conflict* (Cambridge: Harvard University Press, 1960).

66. Ting-Toomey, "Intercultural Conflict Competence," 404.

67. "Professional Notes," 405.

68. Andersen and Wang, "Unraveling Cultural Clues," 252. It is conceivable that increased "multi-tasking" on the part of Americans is moving us, if only slightly, toward a more polychronic understanding of time. But even if this is the case, the underlying philosophy toward problem solving in American remains distinctly monochronic.

69. Ting-Toomey, "Intercultural Conflict Competence," 406.

70. As Donald Rumsfield might say, the "unknown unknowns" become more troublesome.

71. Ting-Toomey, "Intercultural Conflict Competence," 406.

72. Ibid., 407.

73. Ibid., 408.

74. Ibid., 409.

75. Ibid., 409.

76. Ibid., 405 (citation omitted).

77. Ibid., 405 (citation omitted).

78. Min-Sun Kim, "A Comparative Analysis of Nonverbal Expressions as Portrayed by Korean and American Print-Media Advertising," in eds., Judith Martin, et al., *Readings in Cultural Contexts* (Mountain View, CA: Mayfield Publishing Company, 1998), 207–8 (citations omitted).

79. Kim, "A Comparative Analysis," 208.

80. Ibid., 209.

81. Seabury, "Communications Problems," 41.

CHAPTER TWO

TOWARDS A POLICY OF NUCLEAR DISSUASION

HOW CAN DISSUASION IMPROVE U.S. NATIONAL SECURITY?

Jonathan Hagood

Since the formal introduction of the term *dissuasion* by the 2001 Quadrennial Defense Review Report (QDR), its practical meaning has remained in doubt—especially as *deterrence* evolves into a post-Cold War, post-9/11, "tailored" security strategy.[1] Although defense strategists have invested a significant amount of effort in recent years into understanding the relevance of deterrence to contemporary and future security environments, dissuasion remains a poorly understood and little researched strategy. Nevertheless, official defense policy continues to highlight both dissuasion and deterrence as methods by which the United States can accomplish its security objectives.[2] How dissuasion helps the United States meet these goals and improve its national security is left unexplored. The dearth of interest in dissuasion implies either its lack of practical utility or the belief that the United States can effectively "dissuade future military competition" by continuing to focus on its ability to deter and defeat adversaries.

Both of these beliefs sidestep an important opportunity to craft a comprehensive strategy of dissuasion that incorporates elements of deterrence and its traditional counterpart, *compellence*. This is clearest when examining strategies of *nuclear dissuasion*, the subject of this chapter. A successful strategy of nuclear dissuasion convinces a state to refrain from acquiring or expanding nuclear weapons capabilities. The United States has a long history of successes and failures in the area of nuclear dissuasion, and the salient feature of this history is that elements of deterrence and compellence in the guise of promises of punishment and reward featured prominently in these situations. In the end, successful strategies of nuclear dissuasion influenced the decision calculus of states by making one choice (nuclear rollback) more attractive than another (nuclear proliferation). That is, the United States successfully compelled states to undertake one set of actions that improved the national security of the United States while deterring other acts that potentially harmed U.S. national security.

Today, with the risk of proliferation to non-, sub-, or "rogue" state actors for whom strategies of deterrence may not be effective at the forefront of military and security planning, the United States is transforming its nuclear strategy but imprecisely reforming its doctrine and mission. In particular, while most policymakers and the general public agree that nuclear deterrence remains a critical bulwark of national security, its applicability to specific cases is murky; and the 2001 Nuclear Posture Review (NPR) even downplays the relative importance of nuclear weapons themselves.[3] Indeed, it's not uncommon to hear the phrase: "Where deterrence works you don't need it, and where you need deterrence it doesn't work." The need to dissuade nuclear competition further confuses the issue because the efficacy of deterrence and its relationship to dissuasion are in doubt and their portfolios appear to overlap.

In this context, the easiest way to deter a nuclear adversary would appear to be dissuading the acquisition of such weapons in the first place. However, such a crude formula obscures the need for research into the nature of dissuasion and deterrence—both conventional and nuclear—and the ways in which these strategies complement and interact with one another. Although such a task has yet to be undertaken in any systematic fashion, this chapter begins the process by identifying clear differences between dissuasion and deterrence, drawing understandable distinctions between the two, and modeling their relationship. While a clarification of differences and distinctions suggests the need to apply *either* dissuasion *or* deterrence to a given adversary, this chapter employs models to demonstrate how *both* dissuasion *and* deterrence may apply to questions of nuclear strategy. Indeed, we have an opportunity today to craft a policy of nuclear dissuasion that leverages the tools and strengths of nuclear deterrence inherited from the Cold War. A focus on countering and preventing nuclear proliferation means that the strategic goals of the United States are best met by strategies of nuclear dissuasion rather than those purely focused on deterrence. To be sure, deterrence is not an outdated concept from a bygone age. Quite the contrary, nuclear deterrence was, is, and will continue to be a critical component of a policy of nuclear dissuasion. Yet the added dimension of U.S. conventional superiority over potential adversaries (or competitors) such as relatively weak states or "rogue" regimes with nuclear capability must be considered when evaluating dissuasion and deterrence strategies.

A BRIEF HISTORY OF DISSUASION

Thomas Schelling credits J. David Singer with proposing the term *dissuasion* in an article published in 1963. Singer created a model to demonstrate the possible combinations of influence situations in a bilateral system. The model labeled situations in which "A prefers that B *do* a certain act (X)" as cases of *persuasion* while situations in which "A prefers that B *not* do a particular act, but do almost anything else (non-X or O) instead" were cases of dissuasion.[4] In *Arms and Influence* (1966), Schelling built upon this idea by distinguishing between "a threat intended to keep from starting something" (dissuasion) and "a threat intended to make an adversary do something" (persuasion).[5] Schelling preferred "deterrence"—a term already in common use despite Singer's interpretation of it as a subset of dissuasion—and "compellence," which, as Schelling noted, was the best term available to him.[6]

The French use of *dissuasion nucléaire* notwithstanding, the term *deterrence* maintained its hegemonic status as the term applied to strategies designed to prevent particular acts of aggression. The concept of dissuasion first re-appeared in a meaningful way in the 1998 study entitled "U.S. Nuclear Policy in the 21st Century: A Fresh Look at National Strategy and Requirements."[7] Its use foreshadowed the term's inclusion in the defense and security strategies of the Bush Administration, which began with the 2001 QDR. However, dissuasion as introduced in "A Fresh Look" is a confusing concept. It is at times: (a) a component of deterrence—"the three traditional elements of deterrence [are] retaliation, denial, and dissuasion"; (b) a product of deterrence—"dissuasion is… the impact of the total U.S. deterrent posture, including infrastructure, in shaping the security environment, and specifically in shaping the calculations of potential adversaries"; and (c) a way through which deterrence can be achieved—"the United States can place greater emphasis on… deterrence through dissuasion."[8]

As a next step, the 2001 QDR significantly clarified the relationship between dissuasion and deterrence. The report identified four primary defense goals for the United States: "assuring allies and friends; dis-suading future military competition; deterring threats and coercion against U.S. interests; and, if deterrence fails, decisively defeating any adversary."[9] These four concepts infused the defense and security policy documents of the Bush administration. For example, the 2002 National Security Strategy (NSS) restated verbatim the defense goals from the 2001 QDR and specifically argued that the United States could "dissuade those who seek to acquire [WMD] by persuading enemies that they can-not attain their desired ends."[10]

By 2005, the goals of assurance, military-centric dissuasion, deter-rence, and defeat completed a rhetorical shift toward being understood as means to an end. The National Defense Strategy (NDS) placed them in the category of "How We Accomplish Our Objectives," which the NDS identified as the need to "secure the United States from direct attack, se-cure strategic access and retain global freedom of action, strengthen al-liances and partnerships, and establish favorable security conditions."[11] The NDS also noted that the United States "will place greater emphasis on those capabilities that enable us to dissuade others from acquiring catastrophic capabilities (WMD) [and] to deter their use."[12] The 2006 QDR highlighted dissuasion-in-action, stating, "forward-deployed forc-es and flexible deterrent options have successfully dissuaded potential enemies and assured allies and partners."[13] More importantly, the 2006 QDR introduced the priority of "Shaping the Choices of Countries at Strategic Crossroads" as a way to operationalize the NDS. This goal was closely linked to strategies designed to dissuade "a major or emerging power [from choosing] a hostile path in the future," while also persuad-ing allies and partners to make choices that "foster cooperation and mu-tual security interests."[14]

The NSS, the NDS, and the 2006 QDR embrace dissuasion and deter-rence as concepts critical to the nation's defense and security. However, these documents transformed both dissuasion and deterrence from the strategic goals of the 2001 QDR to the means to achieve those goals. This is an important shift because it explains dissuasion and deterrence as *tools* of strategy rather than *objectives* themselves. From this, I argue that nuclear weapons policy should not focus on the question: How do we achieve dissuasion and deterrence? Instead, policy formation should begin by asking: How can dissuasion and deterrence improve U.S. na-tional security?[15]

MODELING DISSUASION AND DETERRENCE

Despite the Bush Administration's relatively consistent use of the terms dissuasion and deterrence, doubt and disagreement as to how the two concepts relate to one another remain.[16] In what follows, I propose three dissuasion-deterrence models, which I label the Nonproliferation Model, the Continuum Model, and the Comprehensive Dissuasion Model. I use the term "model" in a modest sense: more than a conceptual framework but less than a theory. These models are not consistently empirical generalizations with descriptive, predictive, and explanatory power. Instead, they are analytical exercises within the context of the "doubt and disagreement" surrounding the relative meanings of deterrence and dissuasion. However, these models do carry normative and prescriptive implications, and I propose them as methods for communicating policy intentions and as potential aids to the development of "tailored" strategies of deterrence and dissuasion.

A second caveat is that these models do not result from any systematic historical investigation. Such an analysis would be valuable but is beyond the task I have set myself here. Furthermore, such empirical and historical investigations are best not undertaken until we have a clearer understanding of the conceptual differences between deterrence and dissuasion. Historical analysis might produce some interesting anecdotes and valuable insights, but it would not lead to logically consistent and reliable propositions, in large part because the practical meanings and uses of deterrence and dissuasion have changed so much over time.[17] Nevertheless, historical examples are necessary when illustrating arguments and conclusions about strategy, and I do make use of historical cases when discussing the models that follow.

The *Nonproliferation Model* is the least complicated dissuasion-deterrence model to understand and apply. It is based upon the idea that deterrence prevents the *use* of nuclear weapons while dissuasion inhibits the *acquisition, expansion, improvement or proliferation* of nuclear arsenals. Under this model, the *actions* being proscribed drive the choice of an appropriate strategy (see Table 1).

For example, a policy designed to prevent the use of nuclear weapons by North Korea (DPRK) would rely upon deterrence, while policies designed to prevent an increase in the size of the DPRK's arsenal and/or the export of nuclear weapons technology by the regime would include strategies of dissuasion. The response to a strategy of nuclear blackmail

Table 2.1: The Nonproliferation Model

Nuclear Strategy	Examples of Proscribe Actions (achieved through assurance, compellece, persuasion, threats)
Dissuasion	Export of Nuclear Weapons Technology and/or Materials Acquisition of Nuclear Arsenal Increase in Arsenal Size Additional Arsenal Capabilities
Deterence	Use of Nuclear Weapons

by North Korea would be one of deterrence if the DPRK is threatening a nuclear strike and dissuasive if proliferation to terrorist groups is threatened. As a result, the Nonproliferation Model implicitly allows both dissuasion and deterrence to operate at the same time against the same adversary if, for example, the United States wanted to prevent both the use of a North Korean nuclear weapon and the spread of nuclear technology from the DPRK at the same time. In addition, while both strategies make use of incentives or disincentives, a precise interpretation of the Nonproliferation Model means that the nuclear strategy in question depends upon the proscribed action and not the policy tools involved in implementation.

The increased complexity of the Continuum Model derives from understanding that practical strategies can make use of multiple approaches that include both deterrence and dissuasion. As Figure 2 illustrates, the model places the 2001 QDR's original defense goals of assurance, dissuasion, deterrence, and defeat on a continuum that spans allies, potential competitors, and enemies. A key feature of this model is the clear relationship between dissuasion and assurance through the promise of diplomatic and economic solutions to the problems that the potential adversary believes proliferation will resolve. As Alexander Montgomery notes after reviewing the history of U.S. nonproliferation efforts, "offering benefits that closely mirror some of the core motivations of these states to proliferate has met with some success." [18] For example, the extension of U.S. nuclear deterrence resolved the need by East Asian allies to deter effectively nuclear aggression. In addition, the creation of the Nuclear Suppliers Group provided a marketplace for nuclear technology industries for nations without complete nuclear capabilities.[19] Finally, isolation from the international system has also been "identified as a possible correlate of nuclear weapons programs," and the United States should not overlook the value of helping to normalize a state's international status.[20] Although, Libya would seem to be the most recent and clearest example of this policy at work, there are mixed results from the ongoing DPRK example.

Figure 2.1: The Continuum Model

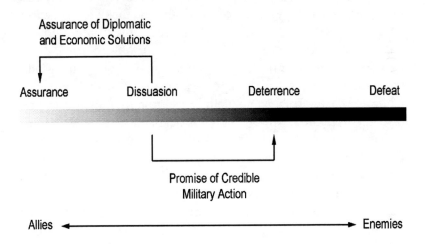

A second feature of the Continuum Model is the clear relationship between dissuasion and deterrence through the promise of credible military action (e.g. nuclear and non-nuclear strikes). While assurance increases the benefits of choosing not to proliferate, credible military threats decrease the possible benefits of proliferation (dissuasion by denial). However, the issue is one of credibility; and deterrence complements dissuasion to the degree that adversaries do not perceive the United States as self-deterred. For example, the United States could develop a nuclear weapon tailored to destroy effectively underground biological and chemical weapons bunkers. This is a credible deterrent that aids WMD dissuasion only if potential proliferators believe that the United States favors the benefits of a nuclear strike over the costs of collateral damage and international opprobrium.

A final and critical component of the Continuum Model is the identification of the object of nuclear strategy as an ally, potential competitor, or enemy. Policymakers who see the world through this model first ask about the relationship between the two states of interest. On the one hand this makes sense, the Pentagon does not need to waste time developing plans to defeat or deter the nuclear forces of allies like the United Kingdom or France, although it does wish to dissuade proliferation by allies such as Japan, Saudi Arabia, Turkey, etc., owing to the potential destabilizing effects and the consequent threats to the interests of the United States and its allies. Any shift in relations between the United States and its allies will be a slow process. However, at the other extreme, a focus on defeating potential enemies runs the risk of neglecting strategies of assurance and dissuasion for states that currently threaten national security. It is also true that the Continuum Model ignores the potential need to dissuade allies from acquiring, expanding, or enhancing their nuclear arsenals. Using the Continuum Model to make a cost-benefit calculus on proliferation, we have an intuitive sense of how to track states that gradually move from friendly regional rivals to potential enemies. However, it is less clear how the model illuminates U.S. policy towards existing extended deterrence clients that face new regional nuclear powers and the question of developing their own indigenous nuclear programs.[21]

The Comprehensive Dissuasion Model makes explicit the relationship between dissuasion, deterrence, and assurance implied by the Continuum Model by proposing a comprehensive view of dissuasion that contains elements of deterrence and compellence. Consequently, *comprehensive* dissuasion does not lie on a continuum at the same level as deterrence and assurance but exists in a hierarchical relationship with these strategies.

This third model begins with the idea that dissuasion is fundamentally a strategy intended to influence the choices of an adversary. Unlike a strict interpretation of deterrence as a strategy calculated to convince an adversary to do anything *other* than the proscribed action, comprehensive dissuasion is a strategy designed to channel adversary choices toward actions that improve U.S. national security. Successful deterrence of a potential security threat maintains the status quo, which has a neutral effect on national security (granted that maintaining the stability of national security is itself a positive development). Successful dissuasion goes a step further than deterrence by also compelling an adversary to select from its range of policy choices an action that improves U.S. national security. Figure 2 graphically portrays the manner in which dissuasion through deterrence and compellence acts upon the decision calculus of an adversary contemplating a range of choices that can be placed on a sliding scale indexed to the effects of these choices on U.S. national security.

Figure 2.2: The Comprehensive Dissuasion Model

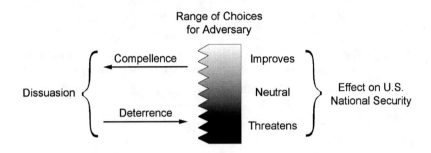

Channeling an adversary towards a particular area of its range of choices accounts for the underlying reasons why an adversary would contemplate acquiring, expanding, or improving its nuclear arsenal. Historically, we know that choices about nuclear proliferation are not made in a vacuum, and the United States has a long history of influencing how other nations interpreted the range of choices available to them. In the past, the United States has repeatedly been willing to offer diplomatic and economic incentives to compel states to roll back their nuclear programs and not simply freeze them, and these incentives often engaged the reasons that underlay the state's initial interest in proliferation.[22]

A comprehensive strategy of nuclear dissuasion would build upon informal yet successful strategies that combined elements of compellence and deterrence in a new and interesting way. In a recent essay on the historical differences between the two terms in the academic literature, Maria Sperandei highlights deterrence and compellence as "distinctive-and-linked strategies" and argues that:

An actor who engages in a deterrent policy should already have an idea of his possible compellent replies in case the opponent refuses to behave as the deterrer desires. The deterrer's idea will obviously change across time... The smoother the linkage and the less abrupt the passage from a compellent to a deterrent policy, the better for the side planning and executing them.[23]

Sperandei's conception of deterrence and compellence as "sequential policies" is an important step towards unifying them in policy and in practice, but I argue that doing so stops short of seizing the opportunity—perhaps limited to nuclear strategy—to combine deterrence and compellence in a synchronous and comprehensive strategy.[24] That is, there is no theoretical or practical reason why the United States cannot pursue strategies of deterrence and compellence *at the same time* in order to influence the decision calculus of a current or potential nuclear adversary (or competitor). Labeling such comprehensive strategy "dissuasion" leverages contemporary interest in the term, allows deterrence to maintain its traditional role of directly preventing military action against the United States, and emphasizes that a policy based on nuclear dissuasion ultimately *prevents* actions that would threaten U.S. national security.[25]

TOWARD A COMPREHENSIVE POLICY OF NUCLEAR DISSUASION

Each of these three models of dissuasion and deterrence could be used to develop nuclear policy. Use of the Nonproliferation Model – the most basic of the three—would be restrictive because of its *either/or* approach to strategies of dissuasion and deterrence. The second model, that of the Continuum, could aid in the development of strategies that are at least aware of the linkages between dissuasion, deterrence, and assurance; but I argue that simple awareness of the ability to construct an overall policy that includes each of these strategies and calculates their relative weight in a given scenario is not enough. Instead, a comprehensive nuclear policy that emerges from the Comprehensive Dissuasion Model promises to incorporate pro-actively strategies of deterrence and compellence as critical and equally important parts of a policy of nuclear dissuasion, while at the same time allowing for its tailored application.

There are different kinds of nuclear relationships for which deterrence must be individually tailored, and it follows that the same must be true for dissuasion. It is one thing to dissuade a threshold state and another to dissuade a nuclear near-peer. Clearly, the stability of deterrence depends upon many factors, and therefore dissuasion necessarily engages each potential adversary or competitor differently. For example, the United States may dissuade a threshold state by resolving regional security tensions diplomatically, providing economic outlets for domestic nuclear technology industries, and incorporating the state into regional and international institutions. When trying to dissuade an existing nuclear power, similar tactics may not work because the state already enjoys some deterrent benefit from its nuclear arsenal, might already be engaged in regional and international organizations, and may seek to expand its self-perception as a regional hegemon. In this case, the nuclear near-peer competitor may be dissuaded by downplaying the possible benefits of nuclear expansion in light of the current benefits the state enjoys.

As a result of the tailored nature of nuclear dissuasion, any general policy should allow for the flexibility to accommodate different and changing regional (and sometimes domestic) security and political environments. However, I propose that a comprehensive strategy of nuclear dissuasion can be framed in general terms as follows:

Compellence

- *General Assurance:* e.g., the United States assures states of existing diplomatic and economic solutions to perceived security problems. These solutions raise the benefits of choosing not to proliferate. For example, this can be achieved by the appropriate selections of targets and careful communication with the adversary.

- *Tailored Compellence:* e.g., the United States identifies within the entire range of choices available to an adversary a small number that will improve U.S. national security. The U.S. tailors a package of incentives and solutions that compel an adversary to choose from these alternatives.

Deterrence

- *Affirming the Credibility of the U.S. Deterrent:* e.g., the United States promises that any nuclear or WMD strike against the U.S., its allies, or its military forces will result in a response, which may include, but not be limited to, the use of nuclear capabilities. Furthermore, this general deterrence is tailored to the type of state and the actions being deterred.[26]

- *Negating the Credibility of the Adversary's Deterrent:* e.g., the United

States clearly states that nuclear or WMD threats by an adversary against the U.S., its allies, or its military forces will be met by overwhelming U.S. response that includes nuclear and conventional capabilities to preserve the security interests of the United States.

- *Deterrence by Denial:* e.g., the United States promises the following actions against states that threaten the security of the U.S., its allies, or its military forces (with conventional escalation and U.S. nuclear forces providing the intrawar deterrence against nuclear or WMD use):

  - Threshold states that choose to proliferate will provoke a preventive military strike designed to cripple permanently the nuclear or WMD program before it can reach fruition.[27]

  - The United States will interdict illegal nuclear technology transfer involving threshold or "rogue" states. This involves the movement of people, knowledge, materials, or equipment to or from states of security concern.

  - When possible, a preemptive U.S. military strike designed to neutralize permanently WMD capabilities before they can be used or proliferated will be directed at nuclear "rogues" that choose to make such capabilities operational.[28]

This would or could be adopted as a policy of comprehensive nuclear dissuasion: channeling the decision calculus of a state contemplating the range of choices surrounding the acquisition, expansion, or improvement of nuclear capabilities. If successfully applied, a policy of nuclear dissuasion provides a beneficial alternative to proliferation that improves the national security of the United States, underscores the self-evident costs of nuclear use, lowers the likelihood of successful nuclear or WMD development, and clearly removes any potential deterrent effects of nuclear capabilities.

How would such a policy of nuclear dissuasion be put into operation? Apart from clearly announcing this policy in general terms, it should be articulated in detail and periodically updated for specific potential adversaries. However, the policy would also need to be sufficiently ambiguous on specifics of response or the conditions that would trigger a nuclear response (i.e., tailored) to avoid unnecessary commitment traps. During this process, economic and diplomatic benefits tied to compelling a particular choice by an adversary would need to be clearly expressed, negotiated in good faith, and delivered after agreements were secured. In terms of the nation's nuclear posture, the "old triad" makes capabilities clear, reliable, and survivable; demonstrably effective defenses raise the likelihood that a limited nuclear strike would not succeed or at least would limit the consequences of a nuclear salvo; and the responsive infrastructure establishes the ability to anticipate and react to changes in the security environment.

Furthermore, the United States military contributes to a policy of dissuasion by establishing its ability to carry out preventive and preemptive strikes as well as operate effectively on a nuclear battlefield (another form of deterrence by denial). Although there are no near-term needs for new nuclear or conventional weapons to successfully intervene and neutralize nuclear or WMD programs, future events and developments may change military needs and popular perception of new weapons. Making the entire range of military capabilities—not just new nuclear weapons systems—available to counter proliferation will offset anything a potential adversary may do.

CONCLUSIONS

The central tenet of a policy of comprehensive nuclear dissuasion would be to manipulate the costs and benefits of the entire range of choices available to an adversary—not just the course of action the United States seeks to deter. That is, borrowing from the 2006 QDR, comprehensive nuclear dissuasion can effectively "shape the choices of countries at strategic crossroads" precisely because it accounts for and engages *all* of the choices available to the country in question. A decision by an adversary that would improve U.S. national security—rather than maintain the status quo—is possible when the comprehensive goal of dissuasion through deterrence *and* compellence is taken into account. In addition to deterring action, the United States needs to compel favorable choices by adversaries, competitors, friends and allies that will improve U.S. national security.

The way in which dissuasion can improve the national security of the United States is clear. Comprehensive dissuasion strategies seek to reduce the likelihood that adversaries will obtain nuclear or WMD arsenals and may well slow any progress of those determined to acquire them. In addition, effective dissuasion also increases the likelihood that potential adversaries will choose to reduce their dependence on military solutions to their security and economic problems. Finally, comprehensive nuclear dissuasion is a strategy designed to channel the energy and resources of adversaries into policies that improve U.S. national security—both in direct relation to the adversary in question and on a regional or global scale. The United States can indeed—through comprehensive dissuasion—shape the choices of countries to the benefit of the United States. and its allies. There is an opportunity in today's strategic environment to emphasize such a comprehensive policy for combating proliferation, one that does not rely solely upon military efforts or new nuclear weapons. I argue that comprehensive nuclear dissuasion is that policy.

Notes

1. "Quadrennial Defense Review Report" (2001 QDR), September 2001, www.defenselink.mil/pubs/qdr2001.pdf.

2. See "The National Defense Strategy of the United States of America" (NDS), March 2005, http://www.defenselink.mil/news/Mar2005/d20050318nds1.pdf, iv.

3. See Donald H. Rumsfeld, Secretary of Defense, "Nuclear Posture Review Report: Foreword," January 9, 2002, http://www.defenselink.mil/news/Jan2002/ d20020109npr.pdf; J.D. Crouch, Assistant Secretary of Defense for International Security Policy, "Special Briefing on the Nuclear Posture Review," January 9, 2002, http://www.defenselink.mil/transcripts/2002/t01092002_t0109npr.html; and "Findings of the Nuclear Posture Review," January 9, 2002, http://www. defenselink.mil/DODCMSShare/briefingslide/ 120/020109-D-6570C-001.pdf.

4. J. David Singer, "Inter-Nation Influence: A Formal Model," *The American Political Science Review*, Vol. 57, No. 2 (June 1963), 424.

5. Thomas Schelling, *Arms and Influence* (New Haven: Yale University Press, 1966), 69.

6. Ibid., 71.

7. "U.S. Nuclear Policy in the 21st Century: A Fresh Look at National Strategy and Requirements," July 1998, http://www.ndu.edu/inss/books/Books_2001/ US%20Nuclear%20Policy%20-%20Nov%2001/USNPAF.pdf.

8. Ibid., 1.5.

9. 2001 QDR, 11.

10. "The National Security Strategy of the United States of America" (2002 NSS), September 2002, www.whitehouse.gov/nsc/nss.pdf, p. 14.

11. NDS, iv.

12. NDS, 3.

13. "Quadrennial Defense Review Report" (2006 QDR), February 2006, http://www.defenselink.mil/qdr/report/Report20060203.pdf, p. 14. In this instance, dissuasion helped maintain favorable security conditions while also retaining global freedom of action. We could also add other tools commonly portrayed by their proponents as aids to nuclear dissuasion such as the Proliferation Security Initiative (PSI), the Megaport Initiative, and continued work on National Missile Defense (NMD). See Andrew C. Winner, "The Proliferation Security Initiative: The New Face of Interdiction," *The Washington Quarterly*, Vol. 28, No. 2 (Spring 2005), 129-143; Steven Aoki, Deputy Undersecretary of Energy for Counterterrorism, "Testimony on 'Detecting Smuggled Nuclear Weapons' before the Senate Judiciary Subcommittee," July 27, 2006, http://www.nnsa.doe.gov/docs/congressional/2006/2006-07-27_SJC_Nuclear_Detection_Hearing_(Aoki).pdf; and Robert Powell, "Nuclear Deterrence Theory, Nuclear Proliferation, and National Missile Defense," *International Security*, Vol. 27, No. 4 (Spring 2003), 86-118.

14. 2006 QDR, 27-28.

15. The 2001 QDR's definition of dissuasion as an objective, dissuading competition with the United States left the means by which the U.S. could achieve this goal unclear. Rethinking dissuasion as a policy tool further broadens its meaning. Nuclear dissuasion encompasses tools that seek to prevent horizontal and vertical proliferation, sponsorship of nuclear terrorism, deterrence of nuclear threats, and potentially even competition by offering positive security assurances to U.S. adversaries or allies.

16. The Administration itself has added to the confusion. For example, The National Strategy for Combating Terrorism (September 2006, available at http://www.whitehouse.gov/nsc/nsct/2006/index.html) states that one of the major objectives of the strategy is to "deter terrorists and supporters from contemplating a WMD attack and, failing that, to dissuade them from actually conducting an attack" (p. 14). In this instance, the administration reverses deterrence and dissuasion from the otherwise consistent usage seen in earlier documents.

17. Singer makes a similar argument about his persuasion-dissuasion model in "Inter-Nation Influence: A Formal Model," although he also suggests that much could be learned from the literature of psychology, sociology, or anthropology.

18. Alexander H. Montgomery, "Ringing in Proliferation: How to Dismantle an Atomic Bomb Network," *International Security*, Vol. 30, No. 2 (Fall 2006), 179.

19. This is true for both buyers and sellers. Because of entities like the NSG

and the Zanger Committee, a nation need not have a complete nuclear fuel cycle in order to participate as a supplier on the world market. Similarly, a nation may exercise its right to nuclear technology under the NPT without maintaining all (or even any) parts of the fuel cycle.

20. Montgomery, 180.

21. See David Yost, "Dissuasion and Allies," *Strategic Insights*, Vol. 4, No. 2 (February 2005), http://www.ccc.nps.navy.mil/si/2005/feb/yostfeb05.pdf.

22. See Ariel E. Levite's discussion of "the threat (or promise) of denying (or providing) economic and technological assistance [as] another tool commonly (and successfully) used by the United States to encourage nuclear nonproliferation," in "Never Say Never Again: Nuclear Reversal Revisited," *International Security*, Vol. 27, No. 3 (Winter 2002/03), 78-79.

23. Maria Sperandei, "Bridging Deterrence and Compellence: An Alternative Approach to the Study of Coercive Diplomacy," *International Studies Review*, Vol. 8 (2006), 277.

24. Ibid., 279.

25. One could conceivably take the perspective of a comprehensive strategy of "persuasion" that combines compellence and dissuasion and would emphasize compellence. I argue for dissuasion in large part because of the large body of military and academic literature that explores how to use military force and technology to prevent adversary actions that threaten the national security of the United States.

26. USSTRATCOM's current Joint Operating Concept on Deterrence Operations (DO JOC) already incorporates many elements of a policy of comprehensive nuclear dissuasion (See the "Deterrence Operations Joint Operating Concept: Version 2.0," August 2006. http://www.dtic.mil/futurejointwarfare/concepts/do_joc_v20.doc).

27. The U.S. strike on a pharmaceuticals factory in Sudan on August 20, 1998, although in large part retaliation for bombings of U.S. embassies in Kenya and Tanzania, was nevertheless a military strike designed to prevent the production of chemical weapons that could be used against the United States.

28. It may seem that imperfect intelligence and U.S. risk intolerance would reduce the credibility of such an option, especially as part of a declaratory policy. However, while missile defense may be a more credible policy of denial from a declaration perspective, the point here is to declare the intention of the United States to deny actively the ownership of WMD.

CHAPTER THREE

NORTH KOREA AND IMPLICATIONS FOR U.S. NATIONAL SECURITY POLICY

Dennis Shorts

America faces few national security challenges as enduring or as difficult to resolve as the Democratic Peoples Republic of Korea (DPRK), or North Korea. Pyongyang's October 2006 underground nuclear test was the most dramatic event in a saga marked by mutual distrust and frightening brinkmanship. With a standing army of more than one million—70 percent of which is deployed near the demilitarized zone (DMZ)—DPRK is a brutal police state perpetually on a war footing. The government's *songun* (military first) ethos characterizes an isolated totalitarian regime where the oppression of millions is fashioned through propaganda as a glorious military struggle against Western "imperialists."

In contrast to its espoused national ideology of *juche*, or extreme self-reliance, the regime has depended upon the aid and largesse of other nations to meet the basic needs of its citizens. With a population of just over 23 million and an economy smaller than New Hampshire's,[1] North Korea's modest experiments with market reform and limited economic cooperation (mainly with Chinese and South Korean partners) have done little to alleviate the profound suffering of its citizens. In the end, the scant resources available are channeled to military endeavors as well as to luxury items for the power elite.

What continues to astonish the international community is the ability of this "failed state" to muddle on with a "cult of personality" leader at its helm. Although he is portrayed as being a madman, Kim Jong-il's actions over the course of his leadership have been largely calculating, albeit eccentric. Despite ruling a backward economy with few national assets, the so-called "Dear Leader" has leveraged threats and managed crises remarkably well over the years. However, the 2006 nuclear test marked a new era in North Korean brinkmanship politics, and seriously undermines global nuclear nonproliferation efforts.[2]

This chapter will begin by exploring possible drivers for North Korea's pursuit of nuclear arms—namely, developing a credible deterrent, raising the value of its bargaining chips, managing internal political exigencies, and generating hard currency through illicit weapons sales (including ballistic missile technologies as well as potential nuclear materials). The discussion will then move to an analysis of U.S. national security priorities in light of these drivers. How can the United States convincingly draw red lines while seeking to negotiate toward peace?

STRATEGIC INTENTIONS

Validating the capability assessments of U.S. intelligence agencies over the previous several years, North Korea's underground nuclear test on October 9, 2006 removed any lingering doubt that fashioning and detonating a crude nuclear device lay within the ambit of North Korea's technical expertise.[3] (More worrying, its burgeoning stockpile of plutonium grants it continued resources to refine its bomb-making, and its ballistic missile technology would give it the ability to strike Seoul or Tokyo, and could pose a future threat to the continental United States as well.) With this development, it is crucial to consider what North Korea's intentions are in terms of its nuclear program. Given the opaqueness of the regime and the difficulty of obtaining intelligence (especially human intelligence), this question is nearly impossible to answer with full confidence.[4] There are several possible ways to interpret the motivations behind Pyongyang's actions to date. It is important to note, however, that these possibilities are in no way discrete—these factors, along with others, interact in a complex calculus that one could only know were one to be privy to Kim Jong-il's thoughts. What can be known is that power elite decision-making is driven by pressing imperatives for regime survival: North Korea and Mr. Kim want a guaranteed future.

Creating a Credible Deterrent

Since the Korean War (1950-1953), North Korea has consistently pointed to a security threat emanating from the United States as the central rationale for developing its military arsenal. Although the state is incredibly militarized, much of its forces are antiquated and poorly maintained, and there is little doubt that North Korea recognizes the steadily declining nature of its conventional capabilities. The DPRK is far outstripped by the combination of U.S. and South Korean forces faced off against it across the DMZ (however, its artillery batteries aimed at Seoul remain a powerful deterrent to the United States and its allies). Accordingly, Pyongyang has focused on weapons such as ballistic missiles and artillery aimed at civilian targets and has allegedly pursued chemical and biological arms.[5]

The July 4th 2006 launch of a long-range Taepo-dong 2 missile, coupled with the 2006 nuclear test, shows the DPRK actively seeking to develop a credible deterrent to ward off what it calls "the U.S. imperialists' aggression and war moves."[6] In addition, it can certainly be argued that the war in Iraq reinforced the calculation among U.S. adversaries that nuclear weapons are needed for deterrence.[7] Nuclear armed states do not get invaded.

However, a sub-kiloton explosion does not constitute automatic nuclear deterrence. There are several components to presenting a credible deterrent. As Siegfried Hecker, the former head of Los Alamos National Laboratory and one of the few American nuclear physicists to visit North Korea's Yongbyon reactor complex explained to his DPRK hosts, a true deterrent has three parts: the ability to make plutonium metal, the ability to design and build a nuclear device, and the ability to integrate the device into a delivery system.[8]

By most accounts, Pyongyang's 2006 test signaled the near accomplishment of the first two. This is a qualified statement given the explosion's low yield.[9] However, this low yield did not necessarily constitute a failure, but can be more accurately characterized as a lack of success.[10] Most judge that North Korean scientists will have gleaned much from the test and will most likely "test again to assert the credibility of its nuclear arsenal."[11] Indeed, we might also expect a missile test in conjunction with another nuclear detonation to demonstrate that the nation might one day be capable of marrying a nuclear warhead onto a ballistic missile (although warhead miniaturization seems still to present a daunting hurdle). To this end, Pyongyang's actions may be seen as a quest to satisfy all three conditions for achieving true nuclear deterrence in the foreseeable future.

The Ultimate Bargaining Chip

With a decrepit national economy based on illicit arms sales and state sponsorship of criminality (counterfeiting and drug smuggling, among other activities), nuclear crises might be used as a tool to periodically extract aid from the international community. Through this brinkmanship, Kim Jong-il might have tested in order to increase the value of the benefits package to be offered for freezing and forgoing nuclear weapons development. North Korea's typical negotiating strategy has sought to ratchet up crises, regularly going into modes that step to and back away from drastic actions. As it has done so, the United States (and indeed the international community as a whole) has looked upon the antics of North Korea with concern, tempered in some cases with a certain crisis fatigue. Pyongyang can be counted on to provoke a perennial crisis when doing so serves its needs and wins it benefits. This is an intrinsically dangerous strategy and, as many experts argue, increasingly limits North Korea's range of choices as the talks carry on. In this regard, maintaining leverage in negotiations entails "show[ing] that not all threats are bluffs."[12] To this end, given its vitriolic statements, the DPRK might have tested a nuclear weapon in order to save "face" and maintain credibility.

It might seem counterintuitive for Pyongyang to risk broad-ranging UN sanctions in order to seek more economic benefits from the international community. However, the North has done just this over the years and, up until the 2006 nuclear test, Beijing and Seoul have accommodated an intransigent DPRK by providing money and aid while six-party talks floundered. Ostensibly this was done largely out of fear of risking total economic (and regime) collapse in the North, which would inevitably lead to floods of refugees over the Chinese and South Korean borders.

The October 9, 2006 test might also be a response to the comprehensive financial sanctions executed by the U.S. Treasury Department on Banco Delta Asia, a Macao-based bank with extensive North Korean dealings in counterfeit U.S. currency. In the crackdown, the DPRK claimed that $24 million in assets were unjustly frozen.[13] For the cash-strapped North, this action certainly hurt their vulnerable coffers, and may have played a part in North Korea's return to the six-party talks in November 2006.

There is great debate over whether North Korea would actually bargain away something as precious as their nuclear program, an endeavor in which they have invested much of their scarce resources over the past several decades. However, some point to North Korea's statement that it would still seek a nuclear-free Korean peninsula as a future goal as evidence of Pyonyang's willingness to negotiate a dismantlement.[14] There is no way of knowing now if this will take place; and the historical record for countries voluntarily relinquishing nuclear arms is not encouraging.[15]

Internal Political Intrigue

Internal political intrigue having to do with challenges to the legitimacy of Kim Jong-il's leadership, as well as uncertainty surrounding the implementation of a succession plan, might drive the North's leader to parry threats from within through the credibility that nuclear arms might offer (especially from the perspective of the hard-line military cadre). While there is no question that Kim wields absolute power within his regime, what is less clear is the extent to which his power remains unassailable as he seeks to pass leadership of the country to a member of his family (possibly one of his sons).[16]

The late Kim Il-sung, the founding father of North Korea (enshrined as the leader of the nation in perpetuity), spent decades preparing the way for his son, the "Dear Leader." And, though largely seen during the early years of his ascent as a playboy cinephile with a penchant for cognac, Kim Jong-il has succeeded in consolidating power and co-opting the power elite in government—mainly by shifting political influence from the Korean Workers' Party to the National Defense Commission (of which he is chairman) and, by extension, the Korean Peoples' Army (KPA).[17] Unlike his father, who was considered a war hero for having fought the Japanese in Manchuria, the younger Kim has no military experience. Accordingly, some posit that he has compensated for this by instituting *songun* policies. Although there is debate as to the ultimate influence the military elite have in Pyongyang, there is no question that they "on many issues have what amounts to veto authority."[18]

As in most totalitarian countries, the North's nuclear program is largely managed by the military. Because of the KPA's influence in decision making, it is a safe assumption that military advisers to Kim Jong-il saw a detonation as an opportunity to demonstrate the military's and scientific communities' accomplishments. This is clear in the Korean

Central News Agency statement following the test: "Both to the people and military, who have always yearned for the strength to defend the nation, this day brings joy and encouragement."[19]

POLICY IMPLICATIONS AND RED LINES

At the time of writing, more than a year after substantive meetings in six-party talks, there is little doubt that the North's 2006 test killed most hopes that this format would yield results in the next round of talks (and this has been borne out by the conclusion of talks that began on December 18, 2006).[20] However, not all is lost. The six-party structure has allowed the United States to coordinate policies with China, Japan, South Korea, and Russia—countries with much at stake for maintaining stability in Northeast Asia. This six-party framework also goes some way toward building a nascent security structure that could be expanded in future years to address a host of issues that are important for preserving peace in the region.[21]

The End of Ambiguity

North Korea's 2006 test is a clear departure from its previous tactic of maintaining ambiguity over its nuclear capabilities. Before the test, this ambiguity allowed South Korea and China to play down estimates of the scope and pace of Pyongyang's nuclear weapons program. China could dodge international (namely U.S.) pressure to punish North Korea for its intransigence. Uncertainty over North Korea's programs allowed a continued South Korean diminution in threat perception precipitated by years of the "Sunshine Policy" and its follow-on versions carried out by the liberal President Roh Moo-Hyun. South Korea's economic ventures such as the Kaesong Industrial Zone as well as joint tourism ventures to Mt. Kumkang continued apace. Why would North Korea jeopardize substantial material support from Seoul and Beijing by proceeding with the nuclear test? More important, why would North Korea risk offending its sympathetic neighbors, making them lose face by ignoring their entreaties not to test missiles or a nuclear device?

The answer might lie in the simple explanation that acquisition of a nuclear bomb is its overriding objective. Beijing and Seoul's distaste for interdiction of North Korean vessels and their softer interpretations of UN Security Council Resolution 1718 suggest difficulty in creating a true "coalition for punishment." Pyongyang might have made the gamble that, though sanctions would follow, South Korea and China would never risk precipitating the North's collapse. The humanitarian emergency that would ensue, along with the enormous economic burden that would be required to bring the backward North into the modern era, certainly give the two bordering nations pause.[22] Indeed, South Korea announced that economic ventures with the North will continue in the wake of their nuclear test.[23] Moreover, in terms of Chinese calculations, a united Korea presents problems of its own. There is no question that a unified and nationalistic Korea would complicate China's rise as a major power in the region. One attendant problem is the issue of history and geography. The Koguryo dispute in 2002 exposed China's fear of future territorial disputes and showed Beijing's attempts to preempt them.[24]

A second nuclear test would be a true gamble for the Northern regime. If this were to take place, the coalition built around U.S. and Japanese efforts would coalesce further and more closely coordinate a tough response. And, here, South Korea would have little choice but to suspend economic cooperation at the risk of tearing asunder an already wobbly U.S.-ROK alliance.[25] Although North Korean nuclear arms "would presumably invalidate the ROK's belief that the DPRK weapon's potential should not preclude the steady progression of inter-Korean relations," the converse currently seems to be true.[26]

Most important to the allies in the region in the wake of the test was the U.S. reassurance that the U.S. security umbrella is robust, and that Washington is committed to maintaining its alliance obligations in the region. Although some have posited that a nuclear breakout by North Korea would set off an arms race in the region, with Seoul and Tokyo seeking capabilities of their own, most experts (as well as those countries' leaders) have dismissed such thoughts.[27]

Red Lines

In the course of attempting to achieve its nuclear ambitions, North Korea has taken every opportunity to cross "red lines" that have been drawn. In the spring of 1994, North Korea crossed a red line by unloading the 5-megawatt reactor at Yongbyon. Conflict was avoided by the high-level trip of former President Jimmy Carter to Pyongyang. In subsequent years, withdrawal from the Nuclear Nonproliferation Treaty (NPT), eviction of International Atomic Energy (IAEA) inspectors from

Yongbyon, removal of the 8,000 spent fuel rods, and stated reprocessing of those rods show a North Korean pattern of behavior that seeks opportunities to cross red lines.[28] Doing so ratchets up crises in the hopes of winning larger "carrots," and reinforces Kim Jong-il's domestic image as a strong leader able to flout the constraints of the international community.

In one such instance, just days after Assistant Secretary Christopher Hill made the statement, "The United States will not live with a nuclear North Korea," Pyongyang detonated its first nuclear device. This was an embarrassment for Washington, but more significantly, North Korea had "publicly and very clearly thumbed its nose at China, which is no small feat, and it has significant implications for Chinese power and wherewithal."[29]

The most pressing threat in the current situation is not that North Korea will commit a suicidal act by launching a nuclear-tipped ballistic missile (a capability some years away) at the United States, but that the accumulation of fissile material the country is stockpiling is transferred or sold to a state or entity bent on violence.[30] By all accounts, this is the one red line that, if crossed, would lead to a firm U.S. response.[31] Most worrying, North Korea has hinted in the past that it would transfer fissile material if "the United States drives [it] into a corner."[32]

THE WAY FORWARD

What might the future hold? Even with subsequent rounds of six-party talks, there is a real possibility that North Korea will proceed with the development of its nuclear and missile programs in order establish a credible nuclear deterrent. Kim Jong-il might find it possible to suffer through sanctions (even if they are tightened), knowing that China and South Korea will not want his regime to collapse. Having "given up on the Bush administration as a negotiating partner," a demonstrated nuclear deterrent might give the North a more powerful negotiating position as the regime "waits for another American administration two years down the pike."[33]

In many ways, the timing of events during the period of October 9 encompasses the stark contrasts of the two Koreas. While North Korea detonated a nuclear bomb and hunkers down for another winter of famine and "struggle," South Korea's foreign minister was confirmed as the next UN Secretary General. "The appointment is seen as the supreme embarrassment for North Korea."[34] North Korea's burgeoning nuclear program is, in some ways, an attempt to hold on to the notion that North Korea is the real "Korea," the guardian of what truly comprises valid Korean culture and pride.[35]

As discussed in Michael Tkacik's chapter, Korea experts who have worked in Republican and Democratic administrations see the utility of appointing a high-level envoy to tackle the North Korean challenge. To this end, in consultation with six-party partners, the United States should appoint a presidential envoy to go to Pyongyang with real power to negotiate a settlement.[36] Other members of the six-party talks have advocated this. The appointment of Ban Ki-moon as UN Secretary General presents an opportunity to bring the resources of the UN more fully into the equation on this issue as well.

However, it is important to disavow regime change as an intention of Washington as it carries out further negotiations. In recent years, U.S. officials have done this by recognizing the sovereignty of the North. Whether Pyongyang accepts these statements as sincere is debatable. It is obvious that Kim Jong-il presides over a reprehensible regime and, understandably, many world leaders (President Bush chief among them) express a visceral hatred of the way things are run in Pyongyang. But, "we must deal with North Korea as it is, not as we want it to be."[37]

In many ways, the United States has tried to fit North Korea into the Libyan model of nuclear disarmament. During his trip to Pyongyang in January 2005, Representative Curt Weldon impressed upon the North Korean leadership the example of Libya.[38] He detailed how Libya, after relinquishing its nuclear ambitions, received comprehensive aid and an opening of ties with the West. He emphatically pointed out that North Korea could make the same decision and see the same benefits. In response, the North Korean officials stated, "We are not Libya. Don't compare us to Libya. We're a nuclear-capable country ready for war."[39]

Working toward resolving the North Korean nuclear problem should be the first step in addressing more fundamental issues in the regime at a later point. Trying to tackle all of Pyongyang's transgressions—from drug trafficking and missile sales to human rights abuses and abductions—is tantamount to seeking regime change. It is counterproductive and does nothing to diminish the threat of North Korea's nuclear weapons. The bottom line is that "you cannot have regime change and a deal."[40]

While North Korea increases the robustness of its current nuclear program, and suffers more isolation and suffering, the average North Korean citizen, especially those outside of Pyongyang, is in danger of starvation. Yet the destitute populace adheres to government exhortations urging: "Let's Eat Two Meals per Day, Not Three!"[41] Indeed, they have little other choice save for making the treacherous trip out of the country.[42]

Some argue that sending a presidential envoy to Pyongyang rewards North Korea and grants it a legitimacy that it does not deserve. Although there is a danger that Iran and other potential proliferators could see a precedent in this, it is the president's responsibility to deal with pressing national security concerns by seeking to solve them with all the tools available.[43]

It is important to note that concessions North Korea might make in its nuclear weapons program could be part of a strategy to stall before engaging in another cycle of belligerence and obstinacy. However, close coordination in the six-party format gives Pyongyang much less room in which to do this. In addition, reputational costs for North Korea would eventually become too high, especially in terms of Beijing's tolerance.

North Korea, a maddeningly resilient "failed state" with weapons of mass destruction, poses one of the most enduring and problematic international security threats to the United States. Concerted, focused attention, along with close coordination with regional allies, holds the best chance for solving the problem.

Notes

1. *CIA World Fact Book: North Korea*, December 19, 2006 and Victor Cha and David Kang, *Nuclear North Korea: A Debate on Engagement Strategies*, (New York: Columbia University Press, 2003) p. 43.

2. North Korea's withdrawal from the Nuclear Nonproliferation Treaty (NPT) came into effect on April 10, 2003. For more information on its withdrawal from the NPT, see Paul Kerr, "North Korea Quits NPT, Says Will Restart Nuclear Facilities," *Arms Control Today*, January/February 2003.

3. Larry K. Niksch, "North Korea's Nuclear Weapons Program," *Congressional Research Service Report for Congress*, October 5, 2006, pp. 10-15.

4. Ambassador Donald Gregg, a former CIA station chief in Seoul, has called North Korea "the longest-running intelligence failure in the history of U.S. espionage." See "Kim's Nuclear Gamble," *Frontline*, February 20, 2003. http://www.pbs.org/wgbh/pages/frontline/shows/kim/interviews/gregg.html

5. Jonathan Pollack, "The Strategic Futures and Military Capabilities of the Two Koreas," *Strategic Asia 2006-06: Military Uncertainty in an Era of Uncertainty*, National Bureau of Asian Research (Seattle Washington: 2005), p. 137.

6. "Concession and Submission to Imperialism Mean Death," *Korean Central News Agency*, October 23, 2006.

7. "The Future Nuclear Landscape: New Realities, New Responses," *Center for the Study of WMD 2006 Symposium Summary*, National Defense University, May 2006. Available at http://www.ndu.edu/WMDCenter/docUploaded//Symposium%202006%20-%20Key%20Themes.pdf.

8. See "Visit to the Yongbyon Nuclear Scientific Research Center in North Korea," *Testimony before the Senate Committee on Foreign Relations*, January 21, 2004, p.5. http://www.lanl.gov/orgs/pa/newsbulletin/2004/01/22/Hecker_Testimony_012104.pdf. Although Dr. Hecker's opinion of deterrence is valid, it is also important to note that classical definitions of minimal deterrence would set the bar much lower.

9. There have been several interesting propositions as to why North Korea's test had such a low yield: 1) A "fizzle" due to a design flaw in the implosion device; 2) A "test of principle design" that uses minimal fissile material in an effort to conserve a limited stockpile; 3) Test of material that is short of weapons grade; 4) Test of a core assembly for a boosted weapon (too advanced, very unlikely). These explanations come from Anthony Cordesman, "The Meaning of the North Korean Nuclear Weapons Test," *CSIS Commentary*, October 9, 2006.

10. Ambassador Charles "Jack" Pritchard remarks, Sigur Center for Asian Studies, George Washington University, October 17, 2006 and Owen Price, "Kim's Intentions Unclear in Return to Six-Party Talks," *World Politics Watch*, November 1, 2006, http://www.worldpoliticswatch.com/article.aspx?id=305#

11. Jungmin Kang and Peter Hayes, "Technical Analysis of the DPRK Nuclear Test," *Nautilus Institute Special Report*, October 20, 2006. Ambassador Charles "Jack" Pritchard remarks at George Washington University, October 17, 2006, echoed this sentiment.

12. Scott Snyder, *Negotiating on the Edge: North Korean Negotiating Behavior*, (Washington. D.C.: U.S. Institute of Peace Press, 1999) p. 81.

13. "After North Korea's Missile Launch: Are the Nuclear Talks Dead?" *Asia Briefing* Number 52, International Crisis Group, August 9, 2006, p. 3.

14. "North Korea's Nuclear Gamble," *Jane's Intelligence Digest*, October 13, 2006.

15. Jon Wolfstahl remarks, CSIS Press Briefing: North Korea's Nuclear Test, October 11, 2006.

16. "The lack of a known succession plan speaks to some uncertainty regarding leadership transition in the North." Remarks by Bruce Kligner, at "North Korea: 2007 and Beyond," Brookings-Center for Northeast Asian Policy Studies and Stanford-Asia Pacific Research Center Joint Conference, Washington, D.C., September 13, 2006.

17. For an interesting look into possible bureaucratic rivalry within North Korea, see Robert Carlin, "Wabbit in Freefall," *Policy Forum Online*, The Nautilus Institute, Sept. 21, 2006

18. Ken Gause, "North Korean Civil-Military Trends: Military Politics to a Point," *Strategic Studies Institute*, U.S. Army War College, September 2006, p. VI. Mr. Gause goes on to point out that Kim Jong-il has promoted a large number of military loyalists to the rank of general officer over the years in order to secure and consolidate his power.

19. "North Korea Conducts Nuclear Test," *Chosun Ilbo*, October 9, 2006.

20. Because the bulk of this paper was written before the breakthrough agreement reached on February 13, 2007, it does not adequately address early 2007 Six Party Talks and DPRK-U.S. developments. Suffice it to say that the tentative agreement—encompassing working groups to address issues that should eventually bring North Korea into the international community—is an extremely positive development and a cause for real hope.

21. For an in-depth look at the prospects for transforming the six-party process into an enduring security structure in the region, see, "Building Multi-Party Capacity for a WMD-Free Korea," *Institute for Foreign Policy Analysis Workshop*, Shanghai, China, March 16-17, 2005.

22. Russia also shares a five-mile border with North Korea, but it is heavily guarded; thus, Moscow would not be significantly affected by refugee outflows.

23. Thomas Shanker, "South Says it will Continue Projects in the North," *New York Times*, October 19, 2005. http://www.nytimes.com/2006/10/19/world/asia/19cnd-korea.html?_r=1&oref=slogin.

24. The Koguryo dynasty was an ancient kingdom of Korea that extended from present-day North Korea across the Tumen and Yalu rivers into China. Unbiased scholarly research confirms that the dynasty once ruled on Chinese land. China, however, began a campaign to discredit this notion and designate Koguryo as an ancient Chinese Kingdom—angering Koreans on both sides of the DMZ. See Park Sang-wu, "China Stirs History Furor," *The Korea Times*, September 12, 2006.

25. Where the United States sees Kim Jong-Il's regime as an international security concern and global threat to nonproliferation, South Koreans see the DRPK in peninsular terms. This is further exacerbated by South Korea's par-

ticipation in the global war on terror, which seems to be predicated on ROK pursuit of its own national interests rather than sentiments of alliance obligation. Indeed, by its non-participation in the Proliferation Security Initiative, there are signs that it is wavering between cooperating with the United States, seeking to accommodate China and not angering North Korea. See Victor Cha in Ellings and Friedberg ed., *Strategic Asia 2004-2005* (Seattle, Washington: The National Bureau of Asian Research, 2004).

26. Jonathan Pollack, "The Strategic Futures and Military Capabilities of the Two Koreas," *Strategic Asia 2006-06: Military Modernization in an Era of Uncertainty*, The National Bureau of Asian Research (Seattle Washington: 2005), p.163.

27. Although there have been some Japanese statements by members of the Diet to express such a reevaluation of Japan's non-nuclear stance, these seem to be more for domestic consumption that serious policy proposals.

28. For more information on this series of events, see Joel Wit et al., *Going Critical: The First North Korean Nuclear Crisis* (Washington, D.C.: Brookings Institution Press), 2004.

29. Kurt Campbell remarks, CSIS Press Briefing: North Korea's Nuclear Test, October 11, 2006.

30. Ambassador Robert Gallucci remarks, Center for Peace and Security Studies Lecture, Washington, DC, July 25, 2006.

31. Dr.park Hyeon-jung has suggested that over the course of the current crisis the United States has had no real red lines. North Korea has consistently stepped over any limitation the United States (or international community) has set. Author interview with Dr.park Hyeong-jung, Senior Fellow, Korean Institute for National Unification, and Visiting Fellow, Brookings Institution, October 23, 2006.

32. DPRK's Vice Foreign Minister, Kim Gye Gwan, as quoted by Selig Harrison upon their meeting on April 9, 2005. For more, see Paul Kerr, "U.S. Pushes to Restart North Korea Talks," *Arms Control Today*, May 2005. http://www.armscontrol.org/act/2005_05/NK_Talks.asp.

33. Ambassador Morton Abramowitz, Testimony before the Senate Foreign Relations Committee, July 20, 2006.

34. Author interview with Dr.park Hyeong-jung, Senior Fellow, Korean Institute for National Unification, and Visiting Fellow, Brookings Institution, October 23, 2006.

35. Speaking about North Korea's possible reaction to Foreign Minister Ban Ki-moon's appointment as UNSG: "No, he's not the legitimate leader of Korean pride. He shouldn't be the repository of our nationalism. It should be us. We're

the ones with nuclear weapons." Derek Mitchell remarks, CSIS Press Briefing: North Korea's Nuclear Test, October 11, 2006.

36. "We need someone of President Carter's stature (someone like Jim Baker). Give this person the challenge of talking as a presidential envoy to Kim Jong-il." Ambassador Charles "Jack" Pritchard, Sigur Center for Asian Studies, George Washington University, October 17, 2006. Also: "The North Koreans fear us. The North Koreans don't trust us. The North Koreans are offended by our rhetoric, and they have no stake in their relationship with the Bush administration. That could be changed, however, if a high-level emissary were sent to North Korea with a presidential letter indicating our interest in working towards a better relationship..." Ambassador Donald Gregg, "Kim's Nuclear Gamble," *Frontline*, February 20, 2003.

37. Ambassador Charles "Jack" Pritchard remarks, Sigur Center for Asian Studies, George Washington University, October 17, 2006.

38. Rep. Weldon met with DPRK's Vice Foreign Minister, Kim Gye-gwan, and Li Gun, Deputy Director for American Affairs at the Foreign Ministry. Rep. Weldon spent a total of 10 hours with these two officials. On the final day of his trip, he spent 90 minutes with Kim Jong-il himself.

39. Representative Curt Weldon's remarks, World Affairs Council of DC event, Cosmos Club, April 5, 2005.

40. Ambassador Robert Gallucci remarks, Center for Peace and Security Studies Lecture, Washington, DC, July 25, 2006.

41. Orville Schell, "In the Land of the Dear Leader," *Harper's*, July 1996. http://www.pbs.org/wgbh/pages/frontline/shows/kim/them/schell.html.

42. For a detailed look into the struggles of North Korean refugees, see "Perilous Journeys: The Plight of North Koreans in China and Beyond," *Asia Report No. 122*, International Crisis Group, October 26, 2006.

43. "...diplomacy is really designed for dealing with bad people on issues that you care about...I think value-neutral diplomacy is something we should seek to restore." Kurt Campbell remarks, CSIS Press Briefing: North Korea's Nuclear Test, October 11, 2006.

CHAPTER FOUR

DEALING WITH THE DAMAGE

HOW TO MANAGE A NUCLEAR IRAN

David Palkki and Lawrence Rubin

Iran is determined to acquire an independent nuclear fuel cycle, apparently paving the way for acquisition of nuclear weapons. Barring U.S. or Israeli military action or a surprising change of heart in Tehran, Iran could acquire the capability to produce nuclear weapons within a matter of years.[1] A nuclear Iran would profoundly alter the military balance in the region and might cause states such as Egypt, Saudi Arabia, Turkey, and Iraq to pursue nuclear weapon programs of their own. Many of these countries have considered developing nuclear weapons in the past, and some have significant financial means or scientific infrastructure to acquire nuclear weapons.[2] The risks are serious.

Most analysis of the Iranian nuclear threat focuses on how to prevent Iranian acquisition, primarily with sanctions or air strikes. By contrast, strategists have devoted considerably less attention to what the United States should do to prepare to live in a world with a nuclear Iran. Many Arab states have announced their desire to either restart or establish nuclear energy programs, which raises considerable fear that these programs could be used one day for military purposes.[3] How could the United States best pursue its goals of fostering stability in the region, preventing further proliferation from occurring, and ensuring that Iranian possession of nuclear weapons will not lead to increases in Iranian sponsored terrorism or successful coercive threats against the U.S. or its allies?

This chapter describes the likely costs and benefits of three different U.S.-led, multilateral responses to Iranian acquisition of nuclear weapon capabilities; we urge policymakers to quietly devote more attention to how to live with a nuclear Iran by making U.S. participation in the Proliferation Security Initiative (PSI) a top priority.[4] The first option we consider is to create a U.S.-led regional security organization, similar to the North Atlantic Treaty Organization (NATO) or the Association of Southeast Asian Nations (ASEAN). Second, the United States could continue to develop and deploy missile defense (MD) systems in an attempt to strengthen the credibility of U.S. extended deterrence and current U.S. alliances in the region. Third, we argue that the United States should expand Proliferation Security Initiative (PSI) efforts in the region because, of these options, PSI offers the greatest benefits at the lowest costs.

REGIONAL SECURITY REGIME

The first option is to pursue a regional security regime. Since the 1990s, individuals have exerted considerable effort in non-official foreign policy circles (Track 2) to establish a regional security regime.[5] More recently, there has been increasing discussion about extending NATO to protect key U.S. interests in the Persian Gulf and Middle East. Both of these multilateral options suffer from some of the same costs and are motivated by similar benefits. This section will review and assess key arguments for and against these two variations of a regional security system.

To begin, we must define the term "regional security regime." A regional security regime is a type of cooperative security architecture around which states agree to defend member states against external threats. The logic behind this security system is that long-term peace is better ensured within a comprehensive multilateral framework.[6]

There are a number of strong arguments supporting this type of security architecture. In balance of power terms, large defensive forces against impending threats lower the chance of an outbreak of hostilities. At the domestic level, a regional security regime in the Middle East may reduce internal pressure on regimes whose foreign policy interests are allied with the United States. Currently, bilateral relations with the United States dominate the Persian Gulf's security architecture. Despite deterring regional aggressors, however, security cooperation with the United States has fueled internal threats. The most notable example of such internal pressure is the withdrawal of U.S. forces from Saudi Arabia in 2003. Thus, to mitigate internal pressures on Gulf States, a regional security regime would replace non-Arab, non-Muslim, western forces with Arab and Muslim troops. This defense arrangement should appeal to local pan-Arab and pan-Islamic sympathies.

A third benefit for the United States is that a regional security system could have an effect on partner states' military doctrines, weapons programs, and military training,[7] each of which are areas where the United States has tried to push reform among its Arab allies.[8] The current system creates dependence on a great power, such as the United States, and removes the incentives for local actors to deal with external security threats themselves. Changing this bilateral framework to a multilateral one may reduce this dependency.

A fourth benefit is that a regional security system would help prevent a "cascade of proliferation" in the Middle East. Including powerful states such as Egypt and Saudi Arabia in a security regime would remove some of the incentives for these countries to develop their own nuclear weapons programs. Although a number of Middle Eastern countries have announced their intentions to develop or restart such programs, it is not predetermined that these countries will use the programs for military purposes.[9] Creating a regional security organization in an attempt to assuage states' feelings of vulnerability might help.

Despite the perceived benefits of such an arrangement, a regional security regime would have to overcome the enormous problem of deciding whom to include and exclude. Including Israel would carry with it a host of problems. Not including Iran would create problems with those states that favor a more cooperative arrangement with Iran, yet are key allies of the United States.

The first problem related to membership is how to deal with Israel. If the regional security regime were just limited to the Gulf, the Israel issue would be less important. However, Gulf security is inherently linked to broader Arab security, especially Egypt's security.[10] Since many Arab states lack diplomatic relations with Israel, proposing that they join a security regime with Israel before official diplomatic recognition is granted is far from realistic. Furthermore, even states that have diplomatic relations with Israel would not want to join a security regime with Israel due to domestic pressures. Open military cooperation with Israel would be unacceptable domestically to a population that still debates "normalization" and harbors strong dislike of Israel. While some elite decision-makers in Egypt and Jordan may be amenable to more quiet strategic cooperation, these regimes know the domestic realities and risks of aligning with Israel publicly.

Arab states would also find Israel's participation extremely problematic because of its unacknowledged possession of nuclear weapons. These states, led by Egypt, have maintained that they will pursue a nuclear-weapon-free zone in the Middle East, even at the expense of potential progress on related issues.[11] Institutionally based security cooperation would contribute to the *de facto* acceptance of Israel's nuclear weapons and severely reduce the ability of Arab states to pressure Israel to give up its weapons in the future.

Finally, inter-Arab security cooperation has failed in the past and the presence of the United States would do little to mitigate some of the suspicions and hostilities between Arab states. The military component of the Gulf Cooperation Council (GCC), originally created in response to security threats from the Iranian revolution and the Iran-Iraq war, has been largely ineffective due to concerns about military interoperability, considerable political disagreements and historic grievances, and a general preference for American military effectiveness. The Gulf War showed that GCC states were incapable of achieving regional security by themselves.[12] Attempts at intra-Arab regional security after the Gulf War failed as well, even as the United States recommended a GCC + 2 security arrangement known as the Damascus Declaration.[13] This idea proposed that GCC states with Egyptian and Syrian troops serve as an Arab deterrent against external threats. But this proposal never developed, due to the objections of Saudis and Kuwaitis, who feared Arab armies on their soil getting involved with internal politics.[14] The political problems within and outside the Persian Gulf show no sign of abating during the current crisis with Iran, suggesting that these intra-Arab disputes would create grave difficulties for a regional security regime.

On a related note, resistance in the United States and among regional allies might arise in response to movement from a bilateral to a multilateral framework. First, U.S. partners will likely oppose yielding the special status they have with the United States and will consider joining a regime in which they do not deal directly with the United States for their security as more of a loss than a gain. The United States, on the other hand, may not want to remove the leverage it possesses with respect to its bilateral partners.

A second option within the context of a security regime, which has received serious attention recently, is expanding NATO into the Middle East, specifically the Gulf.[15] Following the Mediterranean Dialogue (1994), the first important step to bring NATO to the Middle East occurred at the Istanbul Cooperation Initiative (ICI) in 2004. The ICI launched serious discussions about NATO's role in the Middle East. Since then, NATO has focused on Gulf relations, considering a formal relationship where none had existed. Thus far, NATO has cautiously approached its future involvement in the Middle East and has emphasized that it also has components that focus on reform and development in addition to the security dimension. In the security realm, the ICI outlines cooperation with Middle East states on such issues as proliferation, counterterrorism, financing, interoperability, and border security. At the Riga Summit in November 2006, NATO leaders inaugurated a Training Cooperation Initiative whereby NATO would offer training and education to participants of the Mediterranean Dialogue and the Istanbul Conference Initiative.

Expanding NATO into the Middle East has a number of the same pitfalls and benefits as creating a regional security organization. At the international level, NATO involvement might eventually mean that NATO's nuclear umbrella would openly protect Middle Eastern states. This would decrease the demand of member states to pursue nuclear weapons programs of their own as well as deter potential aggressors such as Iran. Yet, NATO's increasing role in the Gulf might be interpreted as a "surrogate operation" of the United States.[16] According to some scholars from the region, the public perceives NATO negatively because of its association with the United States and its foreign policy.[17] In addition, states with regional leadership roles at stake, such as Egypt, might see NATO's increased involvement as diminishing their influence in institutions such as the Arab League. This might help explain some of Egypt's perceived reluctance to engage in the Mediterranean Dialogue.[18]

Only Kuwait, Bahrain, and Qatar have joined the ICI. Saudi Arabia, the Gulf's most influential and important state, has serious reservations about joining the ICI. Saudi skepticism possibly stems from concerns over access to U.S. weaponry due to the close bilateral relationship, the fact that elite decision-makers prefer the military efficiency of the United States, and the ICI's requirements dealing with transparency of foreign military sales and reforming military doctrine. Furthermore, Saudi

Arabia will almost surely not join an organization in which it cannot maintain a powerful, if not hegemonic role, as it does in the GCC. Saudis might see the ICI as leading toward a diminution of their power.

The problems over which countries an expanded NATO would include and exclude are similar to those found in the proposed regional security regime mentioned above. The possibility of Israeli inclusion[19] would dissuade some states from participating in such a NATO-led security arrangement.[20] Another problem is how such an arrangement might interfere with bilateral ties with the United States. Finally, NATO also has its own internal problems, which might encumber operations in the region. In particular, NATO members disagree as to what the alliance's role should be. NATO, involved in its second mission outside its traditional area of operations, is currently at a crossroads. Its success or failure in Afghanistan will have a large effect on its future relationship with the Middle East. NATO's expansion into the Middle East could risk seriously increasing tensions within an organization that is already struggling to define its proper geo-political role

What are the prospects for the future? Will potential member states abandon bilateral relations with the United States to join a U.S.-led regional security regime? This scenario is unlikely, given the current benefits the partner states already receive from bilateral relations with the United States. Creation of a new regional security regime is, therefore, a highly unlikely solution to ensure the security of Gulf States. The NATO option is much more promising but it is still too early to tell if this framework will be successful. While there does not seem to be an immediate institutional solution to ensure the security and stability of the Gulf States, this analysis has suggested that multilateral frameworks have a number of advantages over bilateral ones. With the threat of a number of Middle East states developing nuclear weapons programs, it is important for policymakers to consider how to encourage states to join a multilateral framework while guaranteeing that the United States will not lose leverage over security arrangements.

MISSILE DEFENSE (MD)

The second option is to continue to develop and deploy missile defense systems in an effort to defend against missile-delivered WMD. U.S. intelligence analysts believe that Iran is attempting to build a compact nuclear warhead that it could deliver on Shahab-3 missiles.[21] Iran has announced that it has successfully extended the range of the Shahab-3 to 1,200 miles, which would enable it to hit much of Southeastern Europe, including U.S. bases in Turkey.[22] Israel's chief of military intelligence has claimed that Iran received North Korean BM-25 missiles capable of flying 1,550 miles and delivering nuclear warheads,[23] and Vice Admiral Lowell Jacoby, a former Director of the Defense Intelligence Agency, has testified that Iran could acquire ICBMs by 2015.[24]

The United States is currently researching, developing, and even deploying a number of different types of MD, including ground-based terminal phase interceptors in Alaska and California and theater missile defenses (TMD), in response to the Iranian and North Korean threats. The following discussion focuses only on TMD systems, since they are the most technologically feasible near-term options. Moreover, TMD systems are the most multilateral in the sense that the United States can most easily place them under the operational control of allies.

TMD systems provide a number of benefits for the United States. As with other forms of MD, TMD enables the United States to intervene in regional conflicts at a lower risk of having WMD used against U.S. military personnel or allies.[25] TMD strengthens U.S. extended deterrence, lessens security-based pressures on other states in the region to acquire WMD, bolsters U.S. allies' resolve and vitiates incentives for them to bandwagon with Iran. Deploying MD to GCC states constitutes deterrence by denial in that it raises Iran's costs of attacking Gulf states while lessening the likelihood that the attacks will be successful. TMD also protects U.S. allies and troops in the region from the types of missile launches that are most difficult to deter, such as irrational or accidental launches.

One form of TMD is the sea-based Aegis MD system, which the U.S. Navy certified for combat in September 2006. This system's SM-3 missiles are capable of intercepting rockets launched from up to 800 miles away, and the United States and Japan are developing an improved interceptor to hit ICBMs up to 6,200 miles away. SM-3s target incoming ballistic missiles in their mid-course in the upper atmosphere. If the SM-3s miss, land-based Patriots (PAC-2 and PAC-3) can attack the incoming missiles in their terminal phase.[26]

Whereas tests of other forms of MD have encountered considerable testing difficulties, Patriot TMD batteries have proven to be quite effective. Critics argue that in the Gulf War the Patriot batteries succeeded in shooting down Iraqi rockets only between 40 and 70 percent of the time, yet the roughly $3 billion spent on Patriots' tracking and missile improvements helped them to perform spectacularly during the 2003 invasion of Iraq.[27] U.S. Patriot missiles (a combination of PAC-2s and PAC-3s) shot down all Iraqi missiles that they targeted. U.S. forces took down six Iraqi missiles, and Kuwaiti-manned batteries an additional three. Between six and nine Iraqi missiles were not targeted, since they were heading harmlessly for the desert or sea.[28]

While the performance of Patriot batteries during Operation Iraqi Freedom was spectacular, it was actually a bit too good. Patriots also shot down two friendly fighter jets, one British and one U.S., probably due to electromagnetic interference caused by overlapping Patriot radars. The British plane's transponder that identified the aircraft as friendly was also damaged, though, and the plane flew outside of its designated travel route for friendly aircraft.[29]

Additionally, though patriots can strike down short-range ballistic missiles, cruise missiles, aircraft, and unmanned vehicles,[30] they have had problems with cruise missiles. Cruise missiles fly more erratically and lower to the ground than ballistic missiles, thus making them more difficult to track. In the 2003 war with Iraq, U.S. patriot systems successfully destroyed Iraqi ballistic missiles, but failed to detect a CSSC-3 Seersucker cruise missile that skimmed across the water from the Faw Peninsula on its way to a seawall in Kuwait City.[31]

Another potential problem with MD systems is that while they will help dissuade additional countries in the region from developing WMD, they could lead countries that already have WMD to expand their arsenals. If states such as Israel or Iran fear that potential opponents could deploy effective missile defense systems, they will likely feel the need to enlarge their nuclear arsenals and employ other countermeasures accordingly.

Investments in MD will increase U.S. bargaining leverage vis-à-vis Iran, yet for a variety of reasons such leverage will be minimal. First and foremost, as critics of MD rightly remind, MD cannot protect against WMD that are smuggled and released in the vicinity of the target. If the United States and our allies cannot keep drugs out of our countries, the argument goes, what makes us think we could detect and deny entrance of WMD?[32] Clearly, MD is unlikely to be effective in isolation; improved intelligence, detection devices, and border control will also be necessary.

PROLIFERATION SECURITY INITIATIVE (PSI)

PSI activities provide a third multilateral means available to the United States to stem the proliferation of WMD in the Middle East following Iranian acquisition of nuclear weapons. First announced in 2003, PSI is an international counterproliferation effort. PSI lacks a central organization or staff and member states only participate in activities of their choosing. In other words, membership generates no automatic commitments. States that accept the PSI Statement of Interdiction Principles agree to cooperate in interdicting suspected WMD-carrying ships in one's territorial waters and refusing overflights or grounding aircraft in one's airspace. Over 80 countries now participate in PSI, according to Secretary of State Condoleezza Rice. This participation has led to 11 instances of halted WMD-transfers since 2004.[33] In 2005-2006, PSI has reportedly led to the interdiction of roughly 24 vessels, some of which were carrying nuclear and missile related materials to Iran.[34]

The U.S. goals for PSI are three-fold: a) lengthen the time for proliferators to acquire new nuclear capabilities, b) increase the political and economic costs to the state seeking these capabilities, and c) demonstrate U.S. resolve to combat proliferation."[35] Interdictions, and the threat thereof, make it more difficult for Iran and other states to transit illicit weapons parts and materials. PSI activities also signal to other states that potential costs, including confiscated goods and reputational costs, accompany nuclear dealings with Tehran. The activities may also encourage a cascade of cooperation. As The Economist opines, the "PSI will work best by persuading more countries that don't have them to pass and enforce proper export-control laws."[36]

Such 'coalitions of the willing' allow for multilateral action without some of the constraints and problems that accompany more formal institutions. These ad hoc coalitions are attractive to states, such as the United States, that are hesitant to enter into formal agreements. In PSI activities, the mission determines the participants and no state has a veto over the action of another in an activity in which it is uninvolved. The Wall Street Journal has embraced PSI because it "doesn't give the feckless or evil a veto over what it does" as do other international agreements.[37]

Another benefit of such ad hoc coalitions is found in the area of intelligence sharing. By limiting intelligence sharing to participants of specific interdiction activities rather than a larger group of states, the

United States can share sensitive intelligence at a significantly lower risk of compromising sources and methods. This provides a great advantage over intelligence-sharing procedures in such institutions as the U.N. Security Council and NATO, where members have reportedly shared sensitive U.S. information with America's adversaries.[38]

Patrolling and interdicting ships in the Gulf with the help of regional partners and other PSI allies will also enable the United States to provide prolonged naval patrols in the Gulf at much lower costs than would be the case under a more unilateral approach. Multilateral naval groups, such as NATO's Task Force 150 and 151, have already greatly lessened the load for the United States in the Gulf.[39] GCC states' naval modernization programs over the past decade prepare them to take much of the load in patrolling and conducting interdictions in the Gulf. Each has developed either maritime patrol aircraft or naval helicopters, and most have invested in either upgraded or new fast patrol boats.[40] Joint PSI exercises could also foster more institutionalized security arrangements with Gulf States and expand the areas of military cooperation.

While PSI assistance from allies will lessen U.S. burdens, the Gulf States have generally been reluctant to engage in behavior considered antagonistic toward Iran. When a January 2004 PSI exercise tracked a shipment from the Northern Gulf through the Straits of Hormuz to the North Arabian Sea, GCC states and Iraq refused to participate, even as observers.[41]

This reluctance appears to be waning, however. In the fall of 2006, GCC states exhibited much more support when roughly 25 states practiced intercepting ships with nuclear materials as part of PSI naval exercises in the Gulf near major Iranian shipping lanes. Bahrain hosted the exercise and contributed three ships, thus becoming the first Arab state to participate in PSI training. Observers included Kuwait, Qatar, and the United Arab Emirates. Press reports indicate that the purpose of the Gulf exercise was to practice interdicting North Korean nuclear materials en route to Iran.[42] A few months earlier, Turkey, which is a PSI member and potential proliferator, sent ships to participate in similar PSI exercises in the Mediterranean.[43]

Indian participation in PSI could also prove valuable in patrolling and interdicting ships heading to and from Iran in the Arabian Sea, though it might be difficult to persuade India to participate in such actions given amicable Indian-Iranian relations.[44] Moreover, such participation could be very destabilizing. If India were to interdict ships containing WMD material involving Iran, it might be tempted to do so with Pakistan also, thus raising tensions between the two states. Indian policymakers are currently debating whether to participate in PSI-related activities. The navy has pushed strongly for such activities, and Naval Chief Admiral Arun Prakash has stated that "from if, it has become a question of when" for India to take a leading role.[45]

Questions about the legality of PSI activities could hinder states from cooperating with U.S. interdiction efforts. China, Russia, and a number of other states have expressed deep concerns about the legality of PSI activities. The U.N. Law of the Sea Convention (UNCLOS) states that "no state may validly purport or subject any part of the high seas to its sovereignty," thus restricting interdictions in international waters. It makes exceptions, though, for ships suspected of slave trade, piracy, illegal broadcasting, or refusing to show their flags.[46]

In recent years, a variety of changes has occurred to increase the legality of PSI activities. U.N. Security Council Resolution 1540, passed in 2004, obligates states to counter non-state actors in all aspects of WMD proliferation. It also requires states to monitor and control sensitive materials, technologies, and equipment that originate from, are in, or are passing through their territories.[47] In 2005, the Convention for the Suppression of Unlawful Acts against the Safety of Maritime Navigation was amended to prohibit involvement of civilian vessels from transporting illicit WMDs.[48] And finally, as states' interdiction behavior changes, so too will customary international law.

One danger of PSI is that enthusiasts will believe that interdiction activities can replace the traditional nonproliferation regime. Detecting concealed, softball-sized highly enriched uranium or plutonium on board planes or ships is (in technical terms) extremely difficult.[49] Much could slip through. PSI success will depend to a large degree on extraordinarily good intelligence. It appears that the interdiction of the *BBC China* did not reveal the extent of A.Q. Kahn's ties to Libya, as is widely asserted; rather such ties, and the role of the *BBC China*, came to light as a result of a successful CIA operation to turn in a key member of Kahn's group.[50] It seems very uncertain whether the United States will receive such high quality intelligence regarding Iranian transfers, though, particularly if James Risen's sources in the U.S. intelligence community are correct that Iran rolled up all U.S. agents in Iran in 2004.[51]

Perhaps the greatest difficulty with conducting interdictions of Iranian ships in the Gulf will be dealing with Iran's response. U.S. MD efforts may help reassure wavering allies against the threat of Iranian rockets, yet Iran's growing asymmetric warfare capabilities[52] and history of terrorism suggest that Iranian sponsored subversion and terrorist actions will pose a more difficult challenge.

CONCLUSIONS

As Iran gets closer to acquiring an independent nuclear fuel cycle, the United States must prepare for the eventuality that Iran will have a nuclear weapons program that can threaten U.S. foreign policy interests in the region. In addition, the United States must decide how best to allay allies' fears to make sure they do not develop nuclear weapons programs of their own. The United States should begin now to think about the best ways to manage its relationships with regional partners and to protect its interests.

This chapter has taken a different approach than previous studies about Iranian nuclear proliferation. Instead of focusing on how to prevent Iran from acquiring nuclear weapons, this article deals with the eventuality that Iran will acquire an independent fuel cycle and nuclear weapons. It urges policymakers to quietly devote more attention to how to live with a nuclear Iran and explores the costs and benefits of several multilateral approaches.

Our analysis suggests that despite considerable shortcomings, of the three options we assess the PSI offers the greatest benefits at the lowest costs. The other two options, however, also offer benefits that should and could be incorporated. First, the benefits of a regional security regime highlight the importance of multilateral cooperation. The advantages of this type of proposal are different from the other options because it creates more pressure on regional states to work together. Second, one of the most important benefits of MD is the enhanced ability of the United States to credibly threaten regional aggressors if U.S. regional allies are threatened. If TMD is effectively deployed, it could enable the United States to worry less about a regional launch against its forces or regional allies. MD would also reduce the desire of regional states to acquire WMD to defend themselves. While the U.S. should continue to consider ways to embrace the benefits of these options, the optimal approach is for the United States to bolster the PSI and make it a top priority to deal with a nuclear Iran.

Notes

1. For a persuasive argument that U.S. military strikes are unlikely, see Peter Beinart, "Deterrent Defect," *The New Republic*, May 8, 2006. For assessments on how long it might take Iran to acquire nuclear weapons, see Graham T. Allison, "How Good is American Intelligence on Iran's Bomb?," *Yale Global*, June 13, 2006; Thomas Omestad, "How Close is Iran to the Bomb?," *U.S. News & World Report*, January 23, 2006.

2. Kurt M. Campbell, Robert J. Einhorn, and Mitchell B. Reiss, eds., *The Nuclear Tipping Point: Why States Reconsider their Nuclear Choices* (Washington, D.C.: Brookings Institution, 2004).

3. "Egypt and Nuclear Power: Nuclear Succession", *Economist*, September 28, 2006.

4. Analysis in this chapter is limited to U.S. policy options once Iran has acquired nuclear weapons. We do not take a position in this essay on whether the United States should abandon or pursue counter-proliferation efforts.

5. See Michael D. Yaffe, "The Gulf and a New Middle East Security System," *Middle East Policy* Vol. XI, No. 3, Fall 2004, Michael Kraig, "Assessing Alternative Security Frameworks for the Persian Gulf," *Middle East Policy*, Vol. XI, No. 3, Fall 2004, Bruce Jentleson and Dalia Dassa Kaye, "Security Status: Explaining Regional Security Cooperation and its Limits in the Middle East," *Security Studies* Vol. 8, No.1, (Fall 1998), Steven L. Spiegel, "Regional Security and the Levels of Analysis Problem," *Journal of Strategic Studies*, Vol. 26, No. 3 (September 2003).

6. Michael Kraig, "Assessing Alternative Security Frameworks," 145.

7. Ibid, 150.

8. Interviews with U.S. State Department and Department of Defense officials, August 2006, Washington D.C.

9. Hassan M. Fattah, "Arab Nations Plan to Start Joint Nuclear Energy Program," *The New York Times*, December 11, 2006.

10. Interviews with senior Egyptian foreign ministry officials, November 2005, March 2006, and November 2006, Cairo, Egypt.

11. The issue of Israel's nuclear weapons has had other negative effects on arms control initiatives. For instance, the Egyptians move to place the nuclear issue on the agenda halted the Arms Control Regional Security Talks (ACRS) in 1995.

12. Joseph Kechechian, *Security Efforts in the Arab World: A brief examination of Four Regional Organizations*, RAND, N-3570-USDP (1994), v.

13. Ibid, 18.

14. Interviews with Saudi official, Washington D.C., August 2006.

15. There has been increasing discussion of NATO's future role in the Middle East since its involvement in Afghanistan. In particular, the possibility of NATO involvement in peacekeeping operations in Lebanon has been discussed as an option.

16. Riad Kahwaji, "NATO's Evolving Role in the Middle East: The Gulf Dimension," June 3, 2005, www.stimson.org/swa/pdf/NATOTranscriptPanel1Edited.pdf, 9, Accessed November 20, 2006.

17. "NATO needs to correct its distorted image in the GULF region", Kuwait News Agency, Sept 13, 2006, www.gulfinthemedia.com/index.php?m+global_search&id=243360&PHPSESSID=062

18. Interviews with U.S. Department of Defense officials, August 2006, Washington, D.C.

19. At the NATO public diplomacy conference held in Israel, Oct 23, 2006, Deputy Secretary General of NATO H.E. Ambassador Alessandro Minuto Rizzo said, "When I look more closely at the Mediterranean Dialogue and focus on the specifics of NATO-Israel cooperation, I am struck by how much we have achieved and how quickly things are now moving forward." http://www.nato.int/docu/update/2006/10-october/e1023a.htm

20. Series of interviews with Egyptian governmental and non-government officials (Cairo. October, November 2006)

21. William Broad and David Sanger, "Relying on Computer, U.S. Seeks to Prove Iran's Nuclear Aims," *The New York Times*, November 13, 2005.

22. Kenneth Katzman, et al. *Iran: U.S. Concerns and Policy Responses*, CRS Report for Congress, Updated October 4, 2006, 20.

23. Ibid.

24. Ibid, 13.

25. Lawrence F. Kaplan, "Offensive Line: Why the Best Offense is a Good Missile Defense," *New Republic*, March 12, 2001; Robert Powell, "Nuclear Deterrence Theory, Nuclear Proliferation, and National Missile Defense," *International Security* 27:4 (Spring 2003), 86–118.

26. David Wood, "N. Korea Adds Fuel to Asian Arms Race," *Baltimore Sun*, October 11, 2006; Nick Brown, "US Test Intercepts Ballistic Missile in Descent Phase," *Jane's Defence Weekly*, May 31, 2006; Peter Alford, "Japan to Speed up Missile Defence," *The Australian*, August 3, 2005; "New Missile Interceptors Slated for '07 Defenses Seen in Response to N. Korea Risk," *The Daily Yomiuri*, June 22, 2003; Nick Brown, "US Certifies First Active BMD Outfit," *Jane's Defense Weekly*, September 20, 2006.

27. Bradley Graham, "Radar Probed in Patriot Incidents: False Signals May have led to Downings," *Washington Post*, May 8, 2003; Ross Kerber, "War in

Iraq/Defense System/Patriot Missiles: Friendly-Fire Cases Draw New Scrutiny to System," *The Boston Globe*, April 16, 2003. The comparison in effectiveness is imperfect, though, since in the Gulf War Iraq launched longer-range Scuds while in 2003 it fired primarily shorter-range Al Samoud-2s and Ababil-100s. See Bradley Graham, "Radar Probed in Patriot Incidents: False Signals May have led to Downings," *Washington Post*, May 8, 2003.

28. Ross Kerber, "War in Iraq/Defense System/Patriot Missiles: Friendly-Fire Cases Draw New Scrutiny to System," *Boston Globe*, April 16, 2003; Tom Walsh, "Patriot Missile Facing Crucial Combat Test," *Boston Herald*, April 8, 2003.

29. Anne Marie Squeo, "Too Much Radar Bugs Patriots: Missile Battery Site Overlap is Studied," *The San Diego Union-Tribune*, May 24, 2003.

30. Michael Richardson, "US Missile Shield: Work in Progress," *The Straits Times* (Singapore), July 6, 2006.

31. Bradley Graham, "Radar Probed in Patriot Incidents: False Signals May Have Led to Downings," *Washington Post*, May 8, 2003.

32. Spencer S. Hsu, "GAO Calls Radiation Monitors Unreliable," *Washington Post*, October 18, 2006.

33. Thomas Orszg-Land, "Special Report: Free-for-all on the high seas," *Jane's Terrorism & Security Monitor*, November 1, 2003; Sharon Squassoni, "Proliferation Security Initiative," *CRS Report for Congress*, June 7, 2005; Jon Fox, "U.S. Seeks to Stop North Korean Nuclear Shipments" *Global Security Newswire*, October 26, 2006. Accessed November 1, 2006 at www.nti.org; Jofi Joseph, "The Proliferation Security Initiative: Can Interdiction Stop Proliferation," *Arms Control Today*, June 2004.

34. "Proliferation Security Initiative," Updated August 2006. Accessed on November 1, 2006 at www.nti.org.

35. Erin E. Harbaugh, "The Proliferation Security Initiative: Counterproliferation at the Crossroads," *Strategic Insights* 3:7 (July 2004), 1.

36. "Pakistan's Nuclear Services: The Dangers of Flat-Pack Proliferation," *The Economist*, February 7, 2004.

37. "Hot Topic: The Arms-Control Illusion," *Wall Street Journal (Eastern edition)*, October 14, 2006.

38. According to one of Saddam's key bomb makers, after Saddam had an Iraqi national placed at the IAEA, "classified information began to flow from our spy inside the IAEA." Evidence also suggests that Greece passed classified plans for NATO airstrikes to the Bosnian Serbs, and that Russia shared details of Contact Group meetings directly with Serbia during the war in Bosnia. See Khidhir Hamza with Jeff Stein, *Saddam's Bombmaker: The Terrifying Inside Story of the Iraqi Nuclear and Biological Weapons Agenda* (New York:

Scribner, 2000), 77; Takis Michas, *Unholy Alliance: Greece and Serbia in the Nineties* (College Station, Texas: Texas A&M University Press, 2002), 38–39; Richard Holbrooke, *To End a War* (New York: Random House, 1999), 84.

39. Michael Knights, "Maritime Interdiction in the Gulf: Developing a Culture of Focused Interdiction Using Existing International Conventions," Nonproliferation Policy Education Center, p10–11. February 7, 2006. Accessed at www.npec-web.org1.

40. Ibid, 12.

41. Ibid, 8, 13.

42. Sue Pleming, "Anti-nuclear Naval exercise due in Gulf on Monday," *Reuters*, October 28, 2006; "PSI Exercise Under Way in Persian Gulf," Accessed on November 1, 2006 at www.nti.org.

43. Ibrahim Al-Marashi and Nilsu Goren, "U.S.-Turkey Agreement Stirs Debate in Turkey, Sets Benchmarks for Anticipated U.S.-India Nuclear Accord," *WMD Insights*. Accessed on November 10, 2006, at www.wmdinsights.com/I10/I10_ME5_USTurkeyNuclear.htm

44. For a brief overview of Indian-Iranian relations, see Kronstadt, K. Alan and Kenneth Katzman. *India-Iran Relations with U.S. Interests*. CRS Order Code RS22486. Washington, DC: Congressional Research Service, August 2, 2006.

45. V. Jayanth, "Maritime Security: Preparing for the Unexpected," *The Hindu*, September 20, 2005.

46. Erin E. Harbaugh, "The Proliferation Security Initiative: Counterproliferation at the Crossroads," *Strategic Insights* 3:7 (July 2004), 3.

47. Andrew Semmel, "U.N. Security Council Resolution 1540: The U.S. Perspective," Remarks at Conference on Global Nonproliferation and Counterterrorism: United Nations Security Council Resolution 1540. Chatham House, London, October 12, 2004. Accessed on November 15, 2006 at http://usinfo.state.gov/is/Archive/2004/Oct/21-694223.html.

48. Thomas Land, "Kremlin Counters WMD Threat on the Seas," *Gale Group Inc*, February 1, 2006.

49. Spencer S. Hsu, "GAO Calls Radiation Monitors Unreliable," *Washington Post*, October 18, 2006.

50. Ron Suskind, *The One Percent Doctrine: Deep Inside America's Pursuit of its Enemies since 9/11* (New York: Simon & Schuster, 2006).

51. James Risen, *State of War: The Secret History of the CIA and the Bush Administration* (New York: Free Press, 2006), 193.

52. Anthony Cordesman and Nawaf Obaid, *National Security in Saudi Arabia: Threats, Responses, and Challenges* (Washington, DC: Center for Strategic and International Studies and Westport: Praeger Security International, 2005), 14.

PART TWO

THE STRATEGIES OF OTHER
NUCLEAR-WEAPON STATES IN A CHANGING
SECURITY ENVIRONMENT

CHAPTER FIVE

RUSSIA'S NUCLEAR FORCES AND THEIR PROBLEMS
Richard Weitz

The Russian government has declared maintaining a robust nuclear force a national priority. In a January 12, 2006, article entitled, "Military Doctrine: Russia Must Be Strong" published in the Russian *Vedomosti* newspaper, then Defense Minister Sergey Ivanov said Russia's primary defense task for the 2006-2010 period is "to sustain and develop strategic deterrent forces at the minimum level needed to guarantee that present and future military threats are deterred."[1] Russian President Vladimir Putin reportedly told Ivanov that Russia's nuclear forces account for 90% of the country's security.[2]

Russia possesses sizeable forces in all categories of the traditional offensive nuclear triad. In the most recent data exchange conducted through the START process, whose treaty-governed counting rules assume that each platform carries the maximum number of warheads tested with that system, the Russia Federation declared that it had 4,162 "warheads attributed to deployed intercontinental ballistic missiles (ICBMs), deployed submarine-launched ballistic missiles (SLBMs), and deployed heavy bombers" as of January 1, 2007. Of these, the Russian Air Force had 14 Blackjack and 64 Bear heavy bombers equipped with nuclear-armed long-range cruise missiles (ALCMs). The Russian Navy's fleet included a dozen nuclear-powered strategic ballistic missile submarines (SSBNs) carrying 272 SLBMs with at most 1,392 warheads on multiple independently targetable re-entry vehicles (MIRVs). Russia's Strategic Missile Forces (*Raketniye voiska strategicheskogo naznacheniya* or RVSN), which have always constituted the strongest leg of Russia's strategic nuclear triad, had 530 land-based ICBMs—243 SS-25, 136 SS-19,

104 SS-18 ICBMs and 47 new SS-27Ms—equipped with at most 2,146 nuclear warheads.[3] Scholars at the National Resources Defense Council estimated the actual number of Russia's operational nuclear warheads in the active stockpile at 3,340 in the strategic forces (ICBMs, SLBMs, and strategic bombers) and 2,330 "nonstrategic" warheads on naval platforms, land-based aircraft, and air and missile defense systems.[4] Whatever the precise quantity, the Russian government has initiated several major programs aimed at improving the quality of its nuclear forces.

This chapter begins by analyzing Russian nuclear doctrine and policy. After a vigorous debate in the 1990s, Russian military planners reaffirmed the importance of retaining a robust offensive nuclear strike force to execute a range of important missions that they feared the country's weakened conventional forces might prove unable to implement. The most important of these included deterring a large-scale U.S. attack against Russian territory, averting a Russian defeat in a conventional military conflict, and limiting the undesirable escalation of an incipient nuclear conflict. The following section analyzes each of the main components of Russia's strategic nuclear forces. The chapter then examines the challenges Russia faces in sustaining these forces given substantial budgetary pressures, limitations on nuclear testing, and other general difficulties that also confront other nuclear weapons states. The concluding section discusses the possible evolution of Russia's nuclear forces and policies.

DOCTRINE AND POLICY

Nuclear vs. Conventional

During the 1990s, Russian strategists vigorously debated the importance of maintaining a robust nuclear deterrent.[5] A minority argued that, in the post-Cold War world, nuclear weapons had lost much of their military utility and hence Russia should concentrate on developing its conventional forces. The majority, however, continued to view Russia's nuclear arsenal as an essential instrument for preserving its status as a great power. Such considerations still weigh heavily on Russian strategic thinking. When asked why Russia deserved to be in the G-8, Russian President Vladimir Putin told a January 31, 2006, press conference that, "the G-8 is a club which addresses global problems and, first and foremost, security problems. Can someone in this hall imagine resolving, shall we say, problems concerning global nuclear security without the participation of the largest nuclear power in the world, the Russian Federation? Of course not." [6]

Besides these considerations of prestige and status, many Russians argued that the unprecedented effectiveness of U.S. conventional precision strikes in the former Yugoslavia, Afghanistan, and Iraq demonstrated Russia's need to retain a strong nuclear arsenal to balance its conventional weaknesses. Moreover, they observed that upgrading Russia's conventional forces to American standards would entail considerably greater expenditures than maintaining even a large nuclear force. In April 2006 General Yuriy Baluyevskiy, head of the Russian General Staff and First Deputy Defense Minister, told a press conference: "We are not going to tighten our belts or take off our last pair of trousers to achieve parity in the number of aircraft and missiles with the United States or all of NATO. . . . [Russia] has and will have nuclear deterrent forces sufficient to bring to reason anyone who could try to test the strength of our borders or tap our natural resources."[7]

Russian Declaratory Doctrine

The most important Russian doctrinal statements explicitly recognize the necessity of employing nuclear weapons under certain conditions. For example, Russia's January 2000 National Security Concept emphasizes that, "The Russian Federation should possess nuclear forces that are capable of guaranteeing the infliction of the desired extent of damage against any aggressor state or coalition of states in any conditions and circumstances." The document adds that Russia should prepare to employ "all available forces and assets, including nuclear, in the event of need to repulse armed aggression, if all other measures of resolving the crisis situation have been exhausted and have proven ineffective."[8]

Similarly, Russia's April 2000 Military Doctrine maintains that, "The Russian Federation reserves the right to use nuclear weapons in response to the use of nuclear and other types of weapons of mass destruction against it and (or) its allies, as well as in response to large-scale aggression utilizing conventional weapons in situations critical to the national security of the Russian Federation." The document also declares that Russian military forces "should be prepared to repulse aggression, effectively engage any aggressor, and conduct active operations (both defensive and offensive) under any scenario for the unleashing and waging of wars and armed conflicts, under conditions of the massive use by the enemy of modern and advanced combat weapons, including weapons of mass destruction of all types."[9]

These declaratory statements still appear operationally relevant since Russian military forces continue to conduct large-scale exercises with scenarios involving possible nuclear use.[10] In February 2004, for example, the Russian government conducted "Bezopasnost 2004" ("Security 2004"), the largest strategic military exercise in the history of the Russian Federation. It involved all elements of Russia's strategic forces.[11] More recently, in September 2006, the Russian Air Force simulated a massive cruise missile strike involving 70 strategic bombers against potential targets in the vicinity of Japan and Alaska. At the same time, the RSVN conducted a major command post exercise that practiced mobilizing forces from a peacetime to a wartime posture.[12]

Deterring a Direct Attack

At a minimum, Russian nuclear forces and strategy aim to prevent the United States or any other country from launching a major attack against Russian territory. In late 2006, Putin told Russian military leaders that the country's "deterrent forces should be able to guarantee the neutralization of any potential aggressor, no matter what modern weapons systems he possesses."[13] Russian nuclear planners most likely concentrate their planning and resources on surviving a war with the United States, since such a capability should provide the assets that Russia would need to defeat weaker nuclear adversaries (e.g., Britain, China, or France).

The worst-case scenario for Russian strategists would be an American attempt to decapitate the Russian leadership through a surprise attack involving U.S. nuclear and conventional attacks against Russian nuclear forces at their peacetime alert status. According to this logic, American leaders might anticipate crippling the Russian military response by incapacitating Russia's political and military decision makers before they could organize a coherent retaliatory strike. Such a hypothetical attack could employ SLBMs with depressed trajectories from U.S. SSBNs on patrol near Russia, or stealthy conventional weapons that would exploit weaknesses in Russia's early warning systems. U.S. ballistic missile and air defense systems would then attempt to intercept any Russian nuclear delivery platform that had survived an American first strike and been launched in reprisal.[14]

Russian military commanders are taking several steps to guard against a potential U.S. disarming attack. First, they continue to invest in mobile platforms such as nuclear submarines and special off-road vehicles capable of launching ICBMs. A moveable target is much more difficult to destroy than a stationary object, given the need to estimate its position at the time when the attacking warhead will arrive at its location. Second, the Russian government has retained a sizeable arsenal of nuclear warheads to increase the likelihood that a force of sufficient strength for retaliation would survive an American attack. Third, Russian officials continue to improve Russia's early warning systems and, to a much lesser degree, the country's ballistic missile defenses (BMD).

"De-Escalating" a Conventional Conflict.

Russian strategists have also indicated they might detonate a limited number of nuclear weapons—perhaps just one—to induce another country to end ("de-escalate" in Russian terminology) a conventional military conflict with Russia.[15] The selective strike would seek to exploit the inevitable "shock and awe" effect associated with nuclear use to cause the targeted decision makers to weigh the risks of nuclear devastation more heavily. This strategy exploits the fear that, after one nuclear explosion, the prospects of further detonations increase substantially. Initiating nuclear use would underscore the seriousness with which the Russian government viewed the situation and might encourage the other side to de-escalate the conflict and pressure its allies into making concessions.

The most commonly discussed contingency for a "de-escalation" mission is a NATO decision to intervene against a Russian military ally (e.g., Belarus) or on behalf of a non-member country (e.g., Georgia) in a conflict with Russia. The Russian military rehearsed such a scenario in their June 1999 "Zapad-99" ("West-99") exercises. After Russian conventional forces proved unable to repulse an attack on Russia and Belarus, Russian nuclear forces conducted limited strikes against the posited enemy.[16] During a subsequent command post exercise in October 2002, the military simulated launching nuclear strikes from strategic bombers and missiles.[17]

In 1993, the Russian government abandoned its declared pledge not to employ nuclear weapons first in a conflict, effectively establishing a justification in Russian doctrine for initiating nuclear use. The statement brought the declared strategic posture of Russia into line with that of the United States, Britain, and France (but not China). These NATO countries have never renounced the right to resort to nuclear weapons first in an emergency.

Actually exploding a nuclear device in a conflict would prove problematic. On the one hand, it could terminate the conflict in Russia's favor. On the other, it could lead to potentially, even large-scale, nuclear use if the other side considered the detonation a prelude to additional nuclear strikes and decided to escalate first. Russian officials would probably attempt to underscore the strike's limited nature to minimize the risks of further escalation. In conducting a nuclear strike for a "de-escalation" mission, for instance, Russian commanders could seek to minimize its opponent's civilian and perhaps even military casualties to discourage further nuclear use. For example, they could employ a low-yield tactical nuclear warhead against an adversary's military base, warship, or armored formation operating in a scarcely populated area. Alternately, Russian forces could detonate a high-altitude burst near an adversary's warships with the expectation that the explosion would not produce casualties or nuclear fallout, but would still devastate the fleet's sensors and communications due to its electro-magnetic pulse (EMP) and other effects.

Escalation Control

Russian strategists have long considered using limited nuclear strikes to alter the course of a conventional conflict that Russia risked losing. The January 2000 National Security Concept, for example, implied that Russia could use non-strategic nuclear forces to resist a conventional attack without engendering a full-scale nuclear exchange. A related function of Russian nuclear forces would be to prevent other countries from escalating a conventional conflict to a nuclear war. In such a scenario, Russia could threaten to retaliate disproportionately should an adversary employ nuclear weapons to try to alter a conventional battle in its favor. Even after one party has initiated a limited nuclear exchange, Russian commanders might attempt to control further escalation by issuing nuclear threats, showing restraint, or pursuing other "nuclear signaling."

The problem with attempting to exercise escalation control under combat conditions is that such tactics risk uncontrolled nuclear war. In theory, other possible firebreaks between non-nuclear operations and uncontrolled nuclear escalation might also exist. These could include attempts to enforce distinctions between strikes against either side's national homelands as opposed to less critical third areas, between strategic and tactical nuclear weapons, or even between nuclear strikes against military and civilian targets (i.e., "counterforce" vs. "countervalue" strikes). The most plausible line for limiting escalation, however, remains that between using and not using nuclear weapons at all.

RUSSIAN NUCLEAR FORCES

Like other nuclear weapons states, Russia has encountered challenges in maintaining robust nuclear forces in a post-Cold War environment characterized predominately by conventional and sub-conventional military threats. The Russian government currently pursues a multipronged approach toward sustaining its nuclear forces. It has been retiring older systems, extending the service life of existing systems, actively test launching delivery platforms in current operational status, and developing new nuclear weapons systems with advanced technologies.

Under the 2007-2015 State Armaments Program, the Russian government will provide the Ministry of Defense (MOD) with almost 5,000 billion rubles ($189 billion). According to Viktor Zavarzin, chair of the Duma's defense committee, the MOD has earmarked approximately one-fifth of this total for its strategic forces.[18] In assessing the viability of this plan, Ivanov correctly defined the supply side of the procurement equation as the main uncertainty: "The question now is whether the industries are capable of producing what the military needs."[19] Despite some progress, thus far the Russian military industrial complex has proven inadequate for this task.

Warhead Stockpiles

The Russian Federal Agency for Atomic Energy (Rosatom) develops and manufactures Russia's nuclear weapons. Russia has adhered to the global moratorium against nuclear weapons testing since 1990, but has conducted about a half dozen sub-critical explosions annually at the military's Central Testing Ground at the Novaya Zemlya range.[20] In July 2006, Ivanov visited the site and stressed that Russia kept it in a state of "permanent readiness for nuclear tests."[21] Besides the tests at Novaya Zemlya, the Ministry of Defense uses advanced computational techniques to simulate nuclear explosions.[22] In public, Russian officials express confidence in the capacity of the country's nuclear establishment to provide high-quality warheads.[23]

There are signs, however, that some Russian experts worry about their ability to certify warhead reliability without full-scale nuclear detonations. At the end of March 2006, Putin chaired a special meeting of about a dozen senior officials in charge of Russia's nuclear weapons infrastructure to assess how to sustain its health without weapons testing as Russia transforms its civilian nuclear energy industry. For the first time in Russian/Soviet history, Moscow has begun separating the civilian and military components of its nuclear complex.[24] Russian nuclear weapons designers also face successor-generation problems resulting from inadequate funding, attractive job opportunities in commercial high-technology industries, and other difficulties that have discouraged Russia's elite scientists and technicians from pursuing employment in the nuclear weapons sector.

Rosatom has sought to compensate for these problems by continuing to use warhead designs and materials certified by pre-moratorium testing. Since the mid-1980s, Russia has reduced its stock of intact warheads from approximately 35,000 to some 15,000 (of which some 9,300 are in reserve or awaiting dismantlement).[25] Nevertheless, the much shorter life of Russian warheads (estimated at 10-20 years, considerably less than U.S. warheads) means Russia remanufactures hundreds of warheads annually. Decommissioned warheads are shipped under guard to one of the two remaining large warhead assembly and disassembly facilities. Technicians there take them apart and replace components with limited service lives (e.g., plutonium pits). Surplus fissile material is stored for recycling or elimination.[26] Russian experts indicate that this frequent dismantling and remanufacturing process allows them to detect warhead problems without having to operate a U.S.-style scientific-based stockpile stewardship program—a system they could not afford in any case.[27]

To further ensure warhead sustainability, Ivanov announced in late April 2006 that all land and sea-based ballistic missiles entering service from the end of 2006 would be equipped with the same type of new warhead. Each missile will have either a single warhead or a MIRV cluster.[28] Russian designers hope to complete testing of such a common warhead in 2008. The Russian military intends to deploy these warheads, which supposedly have enhanced BMD penetrability, aboard both the new Topol-M ICBM (RT-2UTTH; designated by NATO as the

SS-27) and the Bulava SLBM (R-30 SS-NX-30), currently undergoing operational testing.[29]

Ground-Based Strategic Forces

While meeting with senior military officers in November 2006, Putin insisted that, "We must meet schedules to create new strategic weapons to secure a balance of forces in the world."[30] Arms control expert Alexei Arbatov calculates that Russia needs to produce approximately 30 ICBMs annually to maintain a strategic nuclear balance with the United States.[31] Until now, Russian defense firms have only built an average of half a dozen new ICBMs each year. This low production level, combined with the recent withdrawal from service of all rail-mobile SS-24 (RT-23UTTH; designated as the RS-22 under START I) missiles and the ongoing retirement of the road-mobile SS-25 (RT-2PM Topol RS-12M) ICBMs, has resulted in a gradual decline in the number of operational Russian ICBMs.

This decrease will become much more precipitous during the next few years since the RVSN will soon need to decommission almost all Soviet-built ICBMs, including the large liquid-fueled strategic missiles that carry most Russian strategic warheads. In January 2007, Lt. Gen Nikolai Solovtsev, RVSN commander, told the media that the RVSN would have to retire over two-thirds of Russia's fleet of 542 land-based ICBMs by 2015. He estimated that the RVSN would acquire only 62 new ground-launched strategic missiles by then. Solovtsev argued, however, that the superior quality of the new missiles, combined with Russia's strategic bombers and submarine-launched missiles, would still ensure that the country retained an adequate nuclear deterrent.[32] Some Russian experts estimate that the entire Russian strategic arsenal will soon possess only several hundred warheads on operational delivery systems.[33] Others worry that this preoccupation with strategic platforms is resulting in inadequate spending on supporting infrastructure for the ICBM fleet. One missile designer, for example, has argued that Russia has made insufficient progress in developing advanced command and communication networks for the new Topol-Ms.[34]

The mobile Topol-Ms represents the cornerstone of Russia's planned future ICBM arsenal. In early December 2006, the first three mobile Topol-Ms entered into operational deployment with the 54th RSVN missile division based in the town of Teikovo, about 250 km northeast of Moscow. On December 14, 2006, Putin called their newly operational status "a significant step forward in improving our defense capabilities."[35] Compared with the silo-based version of the Topol-M, which has been in service with the RSVN since late 1997, the mobile version is better protected against a potential adversary first strike since its location at any one time is less predictable. According to Russian sources, the Topol-M supposedly also has advanced technologies that enhance its ability to overcome hostile BMD systems.[36] In May 2007, Col. Gen. Nikolai Solovtsov, the RVSN commander, stated that Russia would stop deploying new silo-based Topol-Ms by 2010.[37] Nevertheless, Solomonov previously said that the Topol-M would remain Russia's main ICBM until 2045.[38]

Although both the silo- and the mobile-versions of the Topol-M presently carry only one warhead, many of Russia's other ICBMs have multiple warheads. After the United States withdrew from the Anti-Ballistic Missile (ABM) Treaty in June 2002, the Russian government declared itself no longer bound by the second Strategic Arms Reduction Treaty (START II), which prohibited MIRV-ed ICBMs. (The limitations embodied in START I will remain in effect until the accord expires in December 2009.) Russia's ability to retain its MIRV-ed missiles, which would have had to be discarded by 2007 if START II had come into effect, effectively solved the problem of how to sustain an extensive nuclear force, with thousands rather than hundreds of warheads, within the tight fiscal limits of the early years of the Putin administration. Had the START II prohibition come into force, Russia would have had to reconstruct its entire strategic arsenal to compensate for the lost MIRV-ed ICBMs. The demise of START II, combined with the equal and more permissive provisions of the 2002 Moscow Treaty (which does not prohibit MIRV-ed ICBMs) has allowed Moscow to maintain rough nuclear parity with Washington despite spending much less on its nuclear arsenal than the United States.[39]

The Russian military periodically test launches ballistic missiles to assess their operational viability. Russian policy makers assume that actual experience provides a more reliable measure of the missile's performance than the original "best-guess" estimates of their guaranteed service lives, which reflected the Soviet practice of developing a new generation of ICBMs every decade.[40] At present, Russia has extended the service lives of approximately 80% of the RVSN's ICBMs.[41] This figure is somewhat misleading since the Russian government, like that of the United States, is constantly upgrading these missiles' auxiliary systems, electronics, and computer programs.[42] Despite these extension programs, Solovtsov acknowledged in December 2006 that the RVSN expected to retire about 90% of its current ICBMs by 2016. In conformity with Russia's new emphasis on quality rather than quantity, he said that the Strategic Missile Forces plans to replace these missiles with a combination of silo- and mobile-based Topol-Ms.[43]

Sea-Based Nuclear Forces

If current trends continue, especially the ongoing retirement of Russia's oldest ICBMs, Russian Naval platforms will provide an increasing share of Russia's strategic nuclear warheads during the next decade. Russian SSBNs presently serve with both the Northern Fleet, based at the Kola Peninsula, and the Pacific Fleet, based in the Russian Far East. Navy commanders plan to continue this two-ocean deployment for their SSBNs, which have become the Navy's funding priority.[44] In February 2007, Admiral Vladimir Masorin, the Navy's commander in chief, stated that his service allocates approximately half its budget toward developing its strategic nuclear components.[45]

Despite this extensive funding, the Navy's ability to fulfill its increasingly important role in Russia's nuclear strategy remains in doubt. The most serious uncertainties relate to Russia's new "Bulava" missile ("Mace" in English). Three consecutive failed test launches—in September, October, and December 2006—have deepened concerns about this SLBM, which supposedly has advanced BMD-penetration capabilities.[46] In April 2007, Solomonov downplayed the problems with the Bulava, claiming they were expected and would soon be overcome.[47] That same month, Deputy Defense Minister Aleksei Moskovsky said that Russia would resume test launches of the Bukava by July 2007.[48]

The Bulava's problems call into question the military's plans to equip Russia's next (fourth) generation Project Mk 955 Borey-class nuclear-power submarines with a dozen of these missiles. In April 2007, the Russian Navy launched the first Borey-class submarine the *Yury Dolgorukiy*, by moving it to a dock at the Severodvinsk submarine base. The Navy plans to commission the ship next year after it completes construction and sea trials.[49] Putin himself observed that these submarines will represent Russia's first new SSBNs since the Soviet era.[50] The Navy plans to commission seven additional Borey-class submarines by 2017.[51] Russian military leaders eagerly await their entry into the Russian fleet since the existing 12 operational SSBNs, built before 1990, are becoming obsolete. Only one of Russia's Typhoon-class submarines, the recently refitted and renamed *Dmitriy Donskoy*, remains serviceable—currently as a test platform for launching the Bulava. The six Delta III-class (Project 667BDR) SSBNs will reach the end of their service lives within the next few years, along with their SS-N-18 (RSM-50) Stingray SLBMs. The six newer Delta-IV-class (Project 667BDRM Delfin) submarines assigned to the Northern Fleet are undergoing life-extension programs and upgrades to enable their continued service for at least another decade. They carry the liquid-fueled SS-N-23 (RM-54) SLBM. The latest version of the SS-N-23, the Sineva, can carry warheads that supposedly have enhanced BMD penetration capability.[52] The Russian defense industry, however, can currently produce at best a dozen of these SLBMs annually. In any case, the Sineva represents an insufficient substitute for the solid-fueled, longer-range, but troubled Bulava.[53]

The submarine leg of Russia's strategic triad suffers from other problems besides those plaguing the Bulava. In February 2004, the Navy experienced two other embarrassing failures, in Putin's presence, during tests of its older SLBMs. One missile failed to launch; a second exploded shortly after take-off. Furthermore, budgetary constraints and other complications have resulted in Russian military submarines conducting only a few patrols annually in recent years.[54] In 2002, it appears that the SSBN fleet did not perform even a single patrol.[55] In comparison, the Navy managed to conduct 30 patrols in 1991, and still about 10 annually by 1998.[56] This paucity of sea patrols has deprived Russian strategic submarine crews of opportunities to hone their operational and support skills. A September 2006 fire aboard the *Daniil Moskovskiy*, a Russian attack submarine, exposed serious maintenance problems.[57] Moreover, this lack of training may impede the SSBNs recent efforts to master new launch trajectories that could make their SLBMs less vulnerable to U.S. ballistic missile defenses.[58] Crews also lack opportunities to practice the skills they need to evade U.S. "hunter-killer" attack submarines. Finally, keeping submarines in port renders them more vulnerable since they become more detectable targets while immobile.

Strategic Bomber Fleet

Russia's strategic bomber fleet consists almost exclusively of Soviet-manufactured platforms capable of launching long-range air-launched cruise missiles (ALCMs) armed with nuclear warheads. Although Putin said in May 2006 that, "over the next five years we will have to significantly increase the number of modern long range aircraft, submarines and launch systems in our strategic nuclear forces," the Russian government has not yet committed to upgrading its strategic bomber fleet with a new generation of planes or cruise missiles.[59] During the Soviet period, the strategic bomber force constituted the weakest leg of the USSR's offensive nuclear triad. Since then, the Russian Federation has stopped building turboprop Tu-95MS (NATO-designated Bear) heavy bombers and only resumed production of the Soviet-designed supersonic Tu-160 (Blackjack) bomber in the last few years.

In January 2007, Vladimir Mikhailov, the commander-in-chief of the Russian Air Force, said Russia would commission approximately two new or modernized Tu-160 strategic bombers every three years. He added, however, that Russia would continue to upgrade the avionics and other components of the existing fleet as well as its support infrastructure.[60] For example, the Russian Air Force has begun upgrading the Tu-160s, which have a range of over 10,000 kilometers, to deliver conventionally armed missiles (typically 12 cruise missiles) or up to 40 tons of high-explosive gravity bombs.[61] Making them capable of employing conventional as well as nuclear weapons should help the planes to receive sufficient funding to keep them in a high state of readiness. In early December 2006, the Kazan aircraft production association completed upgrading the first Tu-160.[62] Lt. Gen. Igor Khvorov, the commander-in-chief of Strategic Bomber Aviation, insisted that modernized Tu-160s could remain the mainstay of Russia's strategic bomber force for decades: "Heavy aircraft are designed for the long term, so this aircraft will meet all the necessary requirements for at least another 30 years."[63]

In February 2007, Ivanov said that Russia's strategic bomber fleet would consist of at least 50 Tu-95 and Tu-160s through 2015.[64] The ability of Russia's strategic bombers to overcome adversarial air defenses is questionable, however, since they reportedly conduct infrequent training flights (though they do participate in major military exercises). The planes are also vulnerable to a first strike from fast-flying strategic missiles because they are normally stationed at only a small number of air bases in peacetime.[65] Plans to develop a new long-range cruise missile to replace the Kh-55, which could allow Russian planes to attack a target from safer distances, remain at an early stage.

Strategic Defenses

The Russian government is also upgrading the one strategic BMD complex currently operating around Moscow. Depending on how one characterizes the status of current U.S. BMD programs, this A-135 "Galosh" complex may represent the world's only operational national missile defense system.[66] On April 5, 2006, the government approved a plan to provide the A-135 with improved early-warning, reconnaissance, and telecommunications systems as well as advanced missile interceptors.[67] On February 27, 2007, Ivanov said that Russia should develop fifth-generation air defense, missile defense, and space defense systems by 2015.[68]

Besides restructuring its active defenses, the Russian government has begun to revitalize the country's early warning systems to thwart possible surprise missile attacks. The Russian Space Forces currently have two main ballistic missile detection systems. The first consists of a constellation of satellites with infrared sensors that can detect a missile's heat plume shortly after launch. The second element is a network of ground-based early-warning radars that can track incoming warheads. Having two means of detection, employing different physical principles, helps reduce the chances of error.

The Russian government has committed to supply Russia's Space Forces with a new, more advanced radar complex that aims to provide comprehensive coverage of all types of missile launches, including strategic and tactical ballistic missiles and cruise missiles.[69] The first new "Voronezh-M" radar station became operational in late December 2006 in the Leningrad Region, near St. Petersburg. It will close the gap in coverage of northwest Russia that arose in 1999 when Moscow abandoned its obsolete Dnestr-M Skrunde radar station in Latvia.[70] Col.-Gen. Vladimir Popovkin, the commander of Russia's Space Forces, announced in February 2007 that the government expects to complete construction of another Voronezh-type radar in southwest Russia in 2007.[71] Then Defense Minister Ivanov also indicated that Russia plans to build additional radar stations in order to end dependence on the stations located in the other former Soviet republics.[72]

The Russian government will soon take complementary steps to restore the country's debilitated constellation of early warning satellites. The Space Forces operate a first-generation network of Oko/US-KS satellites in highly elliptical Molniya-type orbits that constantly monitor the continental United States for possible launches of ICBMs. Russian authorities had planned to deploy a second generation of more advanced US-KMO satellites, some in geostationary orbits, to detect launches from foreign SSBNs deployed anywhere at sea, but this network for expanded coverage has yet to enter into service.[73] In February 2007, Ivanov said Russia would launch four more military satellites in 2007.[74]

Until these measures lead to a substantial improvement in the capacity of Russia's ground-based and space-based early-warning systems, Russian national security policy makers, like their Soviet predecessors, will probably continue to discount the credibility of any warnings these networks generate. Instead, they will likely still depend on broad strategic warning indicators (e.g., the overall state of Russian-American relations) in assessing the potential risks of an attack on Russia. They will also continue to rely primarily on the threat of military retaliation, especially with the country's offensive nuclear forces, to deter foreign aggression.[75]

FUTURE PROSPECTS

The Numbers Problem

Although Russia has more than enough nuclear weapons and constituent components, it has encountered problems deploying adequate numbers of strategic delivery platforms. Since the USSR's dissolution, Russian defense enterprises have manufactured far fewer new strategic ballistic missiles than required to replace the country's aging land- and sea-based strategic deterrents. As a result, the looming mass decommissioning of Soviet-era ICBMs (with as many as ten warheads each) will result in a precipitous decline in the relative contribution of Russia's land-based missiles to the offensive strategic triad. As Russia transitions from MIRV-ed ICBMs to single-warhead Topol-Ms, the number of nuclear warheads in its ICBM fleet is projected is forecast to decline from some 1,843 nuclear warheads today to 665 warheads by 2012. In contrast, the number of nuclear warheads deployed on SLBMs will decrease only slightly—from 624 warheads in 2007 to an estimated 600 warheads in 2012. The number of warheads aboard bombers could also decline somewhat from 872 warheads in 2007 versus a projected 788 warheads in 2015.[76]

For political and military leaders who have traditionally relied on land-based ICBMs for approximately 60-70% of their country's strategic nuclear warheads, Russia's growing dependence on its more vulnerable submarines and bombers must arouse a certain degree of anxiety among its strategists. In response, Russian designers might either develop a new MIRV-ed ICBM or, after the START I prohibitions against increasing the number of warheads attributed to an existing type of ICBM expire in December 2009, modify the Topol-Ms to carry multiple warheads. In May 2007, Solovtsov said that Russia would begin to equip the Topol-M mobile missile system with multiple re-entry vehicles in 2-3 years.[77]

Wildcards

Numerous external factors could affect the evolution of Russia's nuclear forces, especially their nuclear modernization plans. Despite many improvements, the nuclear weapons complex remains vulnerable to both safety concerns (e.g., accidents from aging equipment) and security breaches (e.g., terrorism or unauthorized thefts and diversions).[78] Russian nuclear plant managers also have inherited a host of expensive environmental problems from their Soviet predecessors. Cleaning up this mess could drain resources from military modernization.

Second, the Russian decision to reduce the variety of nuclear delivery platforms in service has already created crises whenever one type has experienced production (e.g., the Topol-M) or development (e.g., the Bulava) problems. The concomitant reduction in the types of nuclear warheads creates comparable risks from a failure of a particular warhead design. In particular, proposals to use a single warhead type on all future Russian ground-launched and submarine-launched ballistic missiles could prove disastrous should that design experience an irreparable technical fault—a development that could call into question the viability of Russia's entire strategic deterrent, given the weakness of the country's strategic bomber fleet.

Third, the Russian government might decide to allocate a greater share of defense spending to its conventional forces. Most military reform proposals envisage increasing the number of better-compensated professionals serving in the Russian armed forces, which remains largely an army of low-paid conscripts. The planned increase in the use of contract soldiers and other non-conscripts could entail substantially higher spending on human resources since attracting and keeping more volunteers will require providing them with better pay, housing, and food. In addition, Russian military commanders want to purchase many more advanced conventional weapons, such as expensive precision-guided munitions. Any fall in the government's energy exports, in combination with the competing demands of Russia's conventional forces, could further curtail spending on the country's nuclear forces.

Finally, Russia's future arms control environment remains extremely hard to predict. The process of implementing the May 2002 Russian-American Strategic Offensive Reductions Treaty (SORT) already entails uncertainties regarding the sustainability of the Russian nuclear arsenal. The treaty designates December 31, 2012, as the date by which the United States and the Russian Federation must reduce their offensive arsenals to between 1,700 and 2,200 "operationally deployed strategic warheads." Observers note that the absence of interim deadlines for reductions means that the SORT limits will both take effect and expire on the same day. Questions also exist about the treaty's lack of detailed verification procedures, the absence of a timetable and rules for warhead reductions, its 90-day withdrawal clause, and other issues associated with the three-page document.[79]

Thus far, both governments have affirmed their intention to cut their forces unilaterally to promised levels and have, accordingly, been removing them from operational deployment.[80] Between November 2000 and January 2005, Russia eliminated 1,740 nuclear warheads and 357 strategic delivery platforms.[81] The United States has also been reducing its forces in line with the SORT requirements.[82] In the absence of a new bilateral strategic arms control agreement, both governments might simply extend the SORT force-level limitations beyond 2012. Moscow and Washington could, however, negotiate a new strategic arms control agreement that would require changes in the number or deployment of Russian nuclear forces. Decrying what he termed the "stagnation" in Russian-American arms control, Putin in late June 2006 called for renewed bilateral dialogue with priority given to replacing the 1991 Strategic Arms Reductions Treaty (START) before it expires at the end of 2009.[83] Although neither government offered new proposals at the July G-8 summit in St. Petersburg, their foreign and defense ministries agreed to begin formally studying possible future strategic arms control measures. The first session of these talks occurred on March 29 in Berlin. Nevertheless, Russian and U.S. officials have not reached a consensus beyond a mutual agreement against simply extending the 1991 START accord beyond its scheduled expiration on December 5, 2009.[84]

Conversely, a prolonged downturn in U.S.-Russian relations could result in either government exercising SORT's permissive withdrawal

clause. Although Putin and other current Russian officials have renounced a need to match the U.S. military buildup missile-for-missile,
expressing confidence that less costly asymmetric responses would prove
adequate for maintaining the credibility of Russia's nuclear deterrent,
their successors might be more concerned about retaining quantitative
strategic parity with the United States. An unexpectedly rapid strengthening of China's strategic nuclear arsenal—which could also trigger a
compensatory U.S. military buildup—might lead Russia to alter its own
nuclear force structure. Concerns about a potential long-term Chinese
challenge to Russian interests have already reinforced Moscow's interest
in retaining a credible nuclear arsenal.[85]

These uncertainties continue to induce caution in Washington, and
militate against major unilateral reductions in the size of America's own
nuclear arsenal. Until a change of government occurs in both countries
in 2008, the prospects for additional bilateral agreements to reduce strategic nuclear weapons, limit destabilizing military operations, jointly
develop ballistic missile defenses, and enhance transparency regarding
tactical nuclear weapons are low. Fortunately, considerable opportunities exist for profitable near-term collaboration in cooperative threat reduction and curbing third-party nonproliferation.[86]

Notes

1. See also his rankings of the MOD's "priority tasks" in his responses during
interviews published in *Izvestia* on February 21, 2006 and March 28, 2006.

2. Viktor Myasnikov, "Starie osnovi novoy doktriny," *Nezavisimaya gazeta*,
December 19, 2006.

3. U.S. Department of State, "START Aggregate Numbers of Strategic Offensive Arms," April 1, 2007, http://www.state.gov/t/vci/rls/prsrl/83132.htm. For
additional information on the numbers of Russia's major nuclear systems see
"Russian Strategic Nuclear Forces," http://Russianforces.org/current.

4. Robert S. Norris and Hans M. Kristensen, "Russia Nuclear Forces, 2007,"
Bulletin of the Atomic Scientists 63 (March/April 2007), 61, 63.

5. This debate is reviewed in Nikolai Sokov, "Modernization of Strategic
Nuclear Weapons in Russia: The Emerging New Posture" (May 1998), http://
www.nti.org/db/nisprofs/over/modern.htm; and Frank Umbach, *Future Military Reform: Russia's Nuclear & Conventional Forces* (Camberley: Conflict Studies Research Centre, Defence Academy of the United Kingdom, August 2002),
11-14.

6. "Transcript of the Press Conference for the Russian and Foreign Media," January 31, 2001, http://www.kremlin.ru/eng/speeches/2006/01/31/0953_type82915type82917_100901.shtml.

In an interview with NBC News, Putin likewise observed: "How can we talk about ensuring global security and address the issues of non-proliferation and disarmament if we do not include Russia, which is one of the biggest nuclear powers?" July 12, 2006, http://kremlin.ru/eng/speeches/2006/07/12/1443_type82916_108525.shtml.

7. Nabi Abdullaev, "Russia Won't Seek Nuclear Parity with West," *Defense News* (April 10, 2006), 12.

8. An English version of the Russian National Security Doctrine is reprinted in the January/ February 2000 issue of *Arms Control Today*, http://www.armscontrol.org/act/2000_01-02/docjf00.asp.

9. An English version of the Russian Military Doctrine is reprinted in the May 2000 issue of *Arms Control Today*, http://www.armscontrol.org/act/2000_05/dc3ma00.asp.

10. Mark Schneider, *The Nuclear Forces and Doctrine of the Russian Federation* (Washington, DC: United States Nuclear Strategy Forum, 2006), 8-9, http://www.nipp.org/Adobe/Russian%20nuclear%20doctrine%20--%20NSF%20for%20print.pdf.

11. For a description of the units involved, see "Russian Defense Ministry to Conduct First Big Military Exercise in 25 years," February 4, 2004, http://english.pravda.ru/main/18/88/351/11962_military.html. See also "Russia Cites U.S. Action for War Exercises," *International Herald Tribune*, February 11, 2004. On the continued preoccupation of Russian military planners with a potential war with the West see Victor Myasnikov, "The Red Army: Still the Scariest of them All," *Nezavisimaya Gazeta*, February 27, 2006.

12. "Russian Strategic Bombers Penetrate Buffer Zone near Alaska Coast," September 30, 2006, http://www.tldm.org/News9/RussianBombersBuzzAlaska.htm.

13. Cited in RIA Novosti, "Russia to Buy 17 ICBMs in 2007—Minister," http://en.rian.ru/russia/20061116/55705839.html.

14. For a probably exaggerated assessment of the U.S. capacity to launch an effective first strike against Russia and China see Kier A. Leiber and Daryl G. Press, "The Rise of U.S. Nuclear Primacy," *Foreign Affairs* 85, no. 2 (March-April 2006), 42-54; and Keir A. Lieber and Daryl G. Press, "The End of MAD? The Nuclear Dimension of U.S. Primacy," *International Security*, vol. 30, no. 4 (Spring 2006), pp. 7-44. Russian responses to their assessment are surveyed in Arthur Blinov and Igor Plugatarev, "Guaranteed Unilateral Destruction," *Nezavisimaya Gazeta*, March 23, 2006; and Pavel K. Baev, "Moscow Puts PR Spin

on its Shrinking Nuclear Arsenal," *Eurasia Daily Monitor*, April 17, 2006. Other critiques appeared in the September-October 2006 issue of *Foreign Affairs*.

15. According to one authoritative source, "De-escalation of aggression" is defined as "forcing the enemy to halt military action by threat to deliver or by actual delivery of strikes of varying intensity with reliance on conventional and (or) nuclear weapons" (Sergey Ivanov, *Priority Tasks of the Development of the Armed Forces of the Russian Federation*, Moscow: Russian Ministry of Defense, October 2, 2003, 70, http://www.pircenter.org/index.php?id=184).

16. Nikolai Sokov, "The 'Tactical Nuclear Weapons Scare' of 2001," *Monterey Institute of International Studies CNS Reports*, January 3, 2001, http://cns.miis.edu/pubs/reports/tnw.htm. The exercise began with a simulated NATO attack on Russia's Kaliningrad Oblast following a conflict between Russia and a Baltic country. It ended with Russian nuclear strikes against U.S. territory.

17. Alexander Golts, "Military Reform in Russia and the Global War against Terrorism," *Journal of Slavic Military Studies*, vol. 17, no. 1 (March 2004), 39.

18. Roger McDermott, "Russian Military 'Modernizing,'" Not Reforming—Ivanov," Eurasia Daily Monitor, vol. 4, no. 32 (February 14, 2007), http://jamestown.org/publications_details.php?volume_id=420&issue_id=4003&article_id=2371909. For a list of the new strategic systems see Alexander Bogatyryov, "Russia Should Renew its Nuclear Arsenal," February 9, 2007, http://en.rian.ru/analysis/20070209/60485906.html.

19. Cited in Vladimir Isachenkov, Associated Press, "Weapons Plan Strives to Beat Soviet Readiness," *Washington Times*, February 8, 2007.

20. For a description of these tests, see Dmitriy Litovkin, "Arkhipelag gotov k yadernym ispytaniyam," *Izvestia*, July 20, 2006; and Viktor Litovkin, "Sergey Ivanov Visits Novaya Zemlya Nuclear Testing Site," July 26, 2006, http://en.rian.ru/analysis/20060726/51869240.html.

21. Interfax, "Russian Nuclear Testing Ground Remains Ready—Ivanov," July 19, 2006, http://www.interfax.ru/e/B/0/28.html?id=11556790.

22. Andrei Frolov, "Putin Meets with Nuclear Industry Chiefs," *Moscow Defense Brief*, no. 2 (2006), 12.

23. See for example the interview with Sergey Kirienko, the head of Russia's Federal Atomic Energy Agency, in Aleksandr Emel'yanenkov, "Sergey Kirienko o tom, kak budet razvivat'sya yadernaya energetika Rossii," *Rossiyskaya Gazeta*, July 1, 2006.

24. Nikolai Sokov, "Moscow Rejects U.S. Authors' Claims of U.S. First-Strike Capability, as Putin Protects Nuclear Weapons Infrastructure," *WMD Insights*, no. 5 (May 2006), 19-20.

25. Norris and Kristensen, "Russian Nuclear Forces, 2007," 61.

26. John B. Wolfsthal and Tom Z. Collina, "Nuclear Terrorism and Warhead Control in Russia," *Survival*, vol. 44, no. 2 (Summer 2002), 74.

27. The structure and standard procedures of Russia's nuclear weapons complex are described in Oleg Bukharin, "Downsizing Russia's Nuclear Warhead Production Infrastructure," *The Nonproliferation Review*, vol. 8, no. 1 (Spring 2001), 116-130.

28. RIA Novosti, "Russian Ballistic Missiles to be Equipped with New Warhead," April 24, 2006, http://en.rian.ru/russia/20060424/46839202.html.

29. Ivan Safronov, "Rossiya skreshchivaet boegolovki," *Kommersant*, April 24, 2006.

30. Cited in RIA Novosti, "Wrap: Russia Prioritizes Strategic Forces on Security Agenda," November 16, 2006, http://en.rian.ru.russia/20061116/55710444.html.

31. RIA Novosti, "Russia Should Make 20-30 Ballistic Missiles a Year—Expert," April 11, 2006, at http://en.rian.ru/russia/20060411/45553177.html. See also Fred Wer, "In Moscow, Buzz Over Arms Race II," *Christian Science Monitor*, April 24, 2006.

32. Pavel Felgenhauer, "A Potemkin Democracy, A Potemkin Free Market, and a Potemkin Arms Race," Eurasia Daily Monitor, vol. 4, no. 12 (February 14, 2007), at http://jamestown.org/publications_details.php?volume_id=420&&issue_id=4003.

33. Simon Saradzhyan, "Russia Prepares for 'Wars of the Future," ISN Security Watch (February 12, 2007).

34. Vladimir Bukhshtab, "Garantiinye Sroki Istekli" ["Warranty Periods Have Expired"], *Nezavisimoe Voennoe Obozrenie*, September 15, 2006.

35. Cited in RIA Novosti, "Topol-M Mobile ICBMs Crucial for National Security—Putin," December 14, 2006, at http://en.rian.ru/russia/20061214/56931286.html.

36. Viktor Myasnikov, "Nepredskazuemoe oruzhie generala balyevskogo," *Nezavisimaya Gazeta*, May 18, 2007.

37. RIA Novosti, "Russia to deploy fixed-site Topol-M ICBMs by 2010--SMF cmdr," May 8, 2007, http://en.rian.ru/russia/20070508/65086382.html.

38. Roman Fomishenko and Vitali Denisov, "PROryv Rossii v Novyi Vek" ["Russia's Breakthrough into the New Century"], *Krasnaya Zvezda*, December 15, 2006.

39. Rose Gottemoeller, "Nuclear Weapons in Current Russian Policy," in *The Russian Military: Power and Policy*, ed by Steven E. Miller and Dmitri V. Trenin (Cambridge, Massachusetts: MIT Press, 2004), 191, 193, 195.

40. Pavel Podvig, "Speaking of Nuclear Primacy," March 10, 2006, at http://russianforces.org/blog/2006/03/speaking_of_nuclear_primacy.shtml.

41. Interfax-AVN, December 5, 2005, cited in "Russia Extends Service Life of ICBMs," Global Security Newswire, December 6, 2005, at http://www.nti.org/d_newswire/issues. See also "Kura vstretilas' s 'Topolem,'" *Krasnaya Zvezda*, November 30, 2005; and the interview with RVSN commander Nikolai Solovtsov in Aleksandr Volk and Aleksandr Dolinin, "'Topolya' zhivut dolgo," *Krasnaya Zvezda*, December 2, 2005.

42. Vladimir Bukhshtab, "Garantiynye sroki istekli," *Nezavisimoe Voennoe Obozrenie*, September 15, 2006.

43. Vadim Koval', "Epokha 'Topoley': Prolog" [interview with RVSN Commander Solovtsov], *Krasnaya Zvezda*, December 15, 2006.

44. Yuri Selznyov, "Russia Builds New Nuclear Sub Equipped With Bulava-M Quasi-Ballistic Missiles," Pravda.ru, http://english.pravda.ru/russia/economics/90091-0/.

45. Roger McDermott, "Russian Military 'Modernizing,'" Not Reforming—Ivanov," Eurasia Daily Monitor, vol. 4, no. 32 (February 14, 2007), at http://jamestown.org/publications_details.php?volume_id=420&issue_id=4003&article_id=2371909.

46. Yuri Seleznyov, "Strategic Submarine of New Generation to be Finished Soon in Russia," *Pravda*, March 27, 2007.

47. See the interview with Solomonov by Igor Korotchenko in *Voenno-Promishlenniy Kur'er* (April 4-10, 2007).

48. RIA Novosti, "Tests of Russia's Newest Ballistic Missile to Continue in Summer," April 15, 2007, at http://en.rian.ru/russia/20070415/63665096.html.

49. RIA Novosti, "Russia Launches New Nuclear Submarine," April 15, 2007, at http://en.rian.ru/russia/20070415/63665437.html

50. Vladimir Putin, "Annual Address to the Federal Assembly of the Russian Federation," May 10, 2006, at http://www.kremlin.ru/eng/speeches/2006/05/10/1823_type70029type82912_105566.shtml.

51. Nabi Abdullaev, "Russia Launches First of 8 New Nuclear Subs," *Defense News* (April 23, 2007), 6.

52. Nikolai Sokov, "New Details on Russian Strategic Subs Emerge, as Keel for Third Borey Class Boat is Laid," *WMD Insights*, no. 4 (April 2006), 28.

53. Viktor Myasnikov, "The Bulava Has Been Quietly Sunk: Defense Ministry Conceals an Unsuccessful ICBM Test," *Nezavisimaya Gazeta*, December 27, 2006.

54. Nikolai Sokov, "New Details on Russian Strategic Subs Emerge, as Keel

for Third Borey Class Boat is Laid," *WMD Insights*, no. 4 (April 2006), 27.

55. Podvig, *Russian Nuclear Arsenal*, 12.

56. "Russian Nuclear Submarine Patrols," *Nuclear Brief*, February 24, 2006, at http://www.nukestrat.com/russia/subpatrols.htm.

57. Pavel K. Baev, "Putin's Ambitions and Russia's Military Feebleness," *Eurasia Daily Monitor*, September 11, 2006.

58. These efforts are discussed in Nikolai Sokov, "Russia's Newest Submarine-Launched Missile Fails in Tests, but Tests of other Systems Succeed: Defense Minister Ivanov Raises Questions on Status of Russian Sea-Based Tactical Nuclear Weapons," *WMD Insights*, no. 10 (November 2006), 30-31.

59. Vladimir Putin, "Annual Address to the Federal Assembly of the Russian Federation," May 10, 2006, at http://www.kremlin.ru/eng/speeches/2006/05/10/1823_type70029type82912_105566.shtml.

60. RIA Novosti, "Russian Air Force to Get Two Strategic Bombers Every Three Years," January 18, 2007, at http://en.rian.ru/russia/20070118/59299841.html.

61. Dmitriy Litovkin, "VVS poluchili bombardirovshchik dlya bor'by s terroristami," *Izvestia*, July 6, 2006.

62. "Russia Completes Upgrade to Strategic Bomber," Global Security Newswire, December 8, 2006, at http://www.nti.org/d_newswire/issues/2006_12_8.html#04F3246A.

63. RIA Novosti, "T-160 Bomber to Remain Core of Russian Long-Range Aviation," December 12, 2006, at http://en.rian.ru/russia/20061212/56823656.html.

64. Simon Saradzhyan, "Military to Get $189Bln Overhaul," *Moscow Times*, February 8, 2007.

65. Keir A. Lieber and Daryl G. Press, "The End of MAD? The Nuclear Dimension of U.S. Primacy," *International Security*, vol. 30, no. 4 (Spring 2006), 15, 16.

66. The Moscow BMD system is described in Robert S. Norris and Hans M. Kristensen, "Russian Nuclear Forces, 2004," *The Bulletin of Atomic Scientists*, vol. 60, no. 4, (July/August 2004), 74; Pavel Podvig, ed., *Russian Strategic Nuclear Forces* (Cambridge, MA: MIT Press, 2001), 413-418; and Vladimir Trendafilovski, "Russian Anti-Ballistic Guided Missile Systems," at http://www.wonderland.org.nz/rusabgm.htm.

67. Alexander Bogatyryov, "Russia to Get New Mobile ICBMs," December 12, 2006, at http://en.rian.ru/analysis/20061215/57001891.html.

68. Interfax, "Ivanov Calls for 5th Generation ABM System," February 27,

2007, at http://www.interfax.ru/e/B/politics/28.html?id_issue=11684868.

69. Cited in Olga Bozhyeva and Andrey Yashlavsky, "Dobroe Utro, Tovarish-chi Kommandos," *Moskovsky Komsomolets*, December 16, 2005. See also An-drey Korbut, "Pyatiletka kosmicheskikh voysk," *Voenno-Promishlenniy Kur'er*, February 8, 2006.

70. Vladimir Popovkin, "Russia's Space Defenses Stage a Revival," October 4, 2006, at http://en.rian.ru/analysis/20061004/54509604.html.

71. RIA Novosti, "Russia to Put New Radar Station on Combat Duty in 2007—Commander," January 22, 2007, at http://en.rian.ru/Russia/20070122/59488562.html.

72. Cited in Interfax, "Russia to Continue Building New Radar Stations—Ivanov," February 7, 2007, at http://www.interfax.ru/e/B/0/28.html?id_issue=11673037.

73. Podvig, *Russian Nuclear Arsenal*, 14.

74. Simon Saradzhyan, "Military to Get $189Bln Overhaul," *Moscow Times*, February 8, 2007:

75. Pavel Podvig, "Reducing the Risk of Accidental Launch: Time for a New Approach?" PONARS Policy Memo 328 (November 2004), at.http://www.csis.org/media/csis/pubs/pm_0328.pdf

76. Norris and Kristensen, "Russian Nuclear Forces, 2007," 61. See also Yuriy Grigor'ev, "Ot gonki vooruzheniy XX veka k rotere yadernogo pariteta v XXI," *Nezavisimaya Gazea*, April 7, 2006.

77. Aleksey Nikol'skiy, "Mutatsiya Topolya," *Vedomosti*, May 8, 2007.

78. These continuing problems are assessed in Matthew Bunn and Anthony Wier, *Securing the Bomb 2005: The New Global Imperatives* (Cambridge: John F. Kennedy School of Government, May 2005).

79. See for example Alexei Arbatov, "Superseding U.S-Russian Nuclear Deterrence," *Arms Control Today* 35, no. 1 (January/February 2005): 14; and George Perkovich, "Bush's Nuclear Revolution: A Regime Change in Nonpro-liferation," *Foreign Affairs* 82, no. 2 (March/April 2003): 8.

80. As of July 2004, the Russian government claimed it had a total of 4,959 deployed strategic warheads according to START counting rules; altogether, observers estimate Russia now possesses some 19,500 nuclear warheads, most of which are in storage or awaiting dismantlement; see the figures compiled from various sources in Wade Boese, "Russia on Key Nuclear Issues," *Arms Control Today* 35, no. 1 (January/February 2005): 13.

81. Andrey Loshschilin, *RIA Novosti*, May 3, 2005, reprinted in *Yaderniy*

Kontrol': *Informatsiya,* April 29–May 5, 2005, at http://www.pircenter/org/data/publications/yki9-2005.html.

82. Defense Science Board Task Force on. Nuclear Capabilities, December 2006, "Report Summary," 17.

83. Vladimir Putin, "Speech at Meeting with the Ambassadors and Permanent Representatives of the Russian Federation," June 27, at http://www.kremlin.ru/eng/speeches/2006/06/27/2040_type82912type82913type82914_107818.shtml.

84. Wade Boese, "U.S., Russia Exploring Post-START Options," *Arms Control Today,* vol. 37, no. 4 (May 2007), http://www.armscontrol.org/act/2007_05/PostSTART.asp.

85. For a discussion of Russian strategists' diverging assessment of a potential future Chinese threat to Russia see Yury E. Fedorov, *'Boffins' and 'Buffoons': Different Strains of Thought in Russia's Strategic Thinking* (London: Royal Institute of International Affairs, March 2006), at http://www.chathamhouse.org.uk/pdf/research/rep/BP0306russia.pdf; and Dmitri Trenin, *Russia's Nuclear Policy in the 21st Century Environment* (Paris: IFRI Security Studies Department, Autumn 2005), 11-12.

86. For possible bilateral and multilateral initiatives in this area see Richard Weitz, *Revitalising US–Russian Security Cooperation: Practical* Measures (London: Routledge for The International Institute for Strategic Studies, 2005); and *Russian-American Security Cooperation after St. Petersburg: Challenges and Opportunities* (Carlisle, PA: Strategic Studies Institute of the US Army War College, 2007).

CHAPTER SIX

PAPER TIGER OR WAKING DRAGON?

CONSIDERING NUCLEAR CHANGE IN CHINA

Dakota S. Rudesill

n moments stolen from the all-consuming question of how to prevent Iraq's collapse, the U.S. foreign policy community is trying to
come to terms with the rise of the People's Republic of China (PRC).
The profound changes underway in the world's most populous nation
have put the China question on the front pages of magazines[1] and best
seller lists,[2] generated dozens of congressional hearings and expert reports,[3] and resulted in a controversial annual Pentagon report on Chinese military power,[4] all fueling an intense debate.[5] Adding to the sense
of alarm in some quarters have been headline-grabbing military moves,
including China's successful test of an anti-satellite (ASAT) missile in
January of this year,[6] approach by a People's Liberation Army (PLA)
Navy submarine to the U.S.S. *Kitty Hawk* battle group in October of last
year,[7] and substantial military budget growth in recent years, including
an announced hike of nearly 18 percent for 2007 alone.[8]

The Pentagon's new *Military Power of the People's Republic of China
2007* report suggests that China will shortly field an improved nuclear
force, in both qualitative and quantitative terms.[9] Yet the report informs
rather than resolves debate about the *nuclear* China question, one complicated by the fact that China has the least transparent program of the
"P-5," the five nations with permanent UN Security Council Seats and
legal nuclear arsenals under the Nuclear Non-proliferation Treaty. Great
uncertainty is, however, more than a function of the emphasis on secrecy and deception in Chinese strategy noted by the Pentagon.[10] Thanks
to galloping economic growth and apparent maturation of the DF-31

missile[11] and its variants, the range of possible PRC nuclear futures is also expanding dramatically. The PRC leadership itself may well regard the question as still pending.

Accordingly, this chapter will avoid prognostication in favor of identifying key trends and questions at the intersection of Chinese capabilities and intentions and changes to U.S. strategic posture. Parts I–III provide a snapshot of PRC nuclear forces and modernization today, identify factors driving and auguring against dramatic change, and posit and briefly evaluate several alternate Chinese nuclear futures. To facilitate analysis of PRC nuclear moves, Part IV suggests a six-point "index of leading Chinese nuclear indicators." The chapter concludes by endorsing efforts to engage Chinese officials on nuclear issues and careful evaluation of potential changes to U.S. strategic capabilities and doctrine—prudent responses to persistent uncertainty amid great change and high stakes.

CHINA'S POSTURE

Against the backdrop of growing concern about Chinese military power, what is most remarkable about China's strategic nuclear forces to date is the PRC's relative restraint and divergence from the approach of the other P-5 powers.

The United States and Russia each have several thousand operationally deployed strategic nuclear warheads on a triad of land, sea, and air platforms of intercontinental range. In contrast, open sources suggest China today has 74 to 112 warheads operationally deployed with land-based missiles,[12] only 18-20 of which—mounted on the liquid-fueled DF-5 ICBM—bring the continental United States (CONUS) within range.[13] Since the late 1960s China has fielded bombers able to reach targets in Russia and since the early 1980s has had a single SSBN, the Type 092 submarine *Xia*. However, China's nuclear bomber capabilities remain relatively limited[14] and in 25-plus years the evidently problem-plagued *Xia* has reportedly gone to sea once and conducted zero deterrent patrols.[15] Therefore, in deployed arsenal size and platform diversity the small, largely "uniad" PRC strategic force has less in common with the two top-tier nuclear powers than it does with second-tier powers France and the United Kingdom, which have small arsenals (of roughly 350 and less than 200 active warheads, respectively) designed around SSBNs (France also has warheads deliverable by air-to-surface missiles carried on fighter aircraft).[16] Although China is thought to have a number of tactical nuclear warheads (in which it has not shown sustained interest),[17] the PRC claimed in 2004 to have "the smallest nuclear arsenal."[18]

China is the only P-5 nation presently without patrolling SSBNs or deployed missiles with multiple re-entry vehicles (MRVs). But China's divergence from its P-5 brethren is deeper. Chinese ICBMs and IRBMs are believed to carry multi-megaton warheads[19] suited for counter-value retaliation against population centers, while the other P-5 powers deploy sub-megaton weapons on their ICBMs and SLBMs and have counter-force capabilities. Furthermore, while the United States and Russia maintain ICBMs on alert, and the United States, Russia, United Kingdom, and France deploy SSBNs at sea (and Russia alternately pierside) in responsive postures, none of the nuclear missiles of the Second Artillery—the PRC's rocket corps—are thought to be on alert. China's ICBMs and associated warheads have been stored separately.[20]

China's non-doctrinaire nuclear force has reflected a traditionally limited view of the utility of nuclear weapons. China went nuclear in 1964 to prevent nuclear intimidation and soon thereafter adopted a relatively simplistic, inflexible retaliatory posture.[21] This decision was reportedly based on the Chinese leadership's conclusion in the wake of the threat of U.S. nuclear use in the Korean War that deterrence from the threat of a counter-value second strike is the bomb's only real utility.[22] Otherwise, Mao warned, the "atom bomb is a paper tiger."[23] PRC nuclear writings depict counter-strikes as coming after a first strike has been absorbed.[24]

Today, the PRC retains a no first use (NFU) declaratory policy, a "minimum credible deterrent" force regarding the United States and Russia (and, arguably, also potential theater adversaries, such as India and Japan),[25] and a "counterattack" doctrine focused on inflicting "a heavy psychological shock" on the enemy to induce war termination.[26] Although Evan Medeiros's review of PRC writings shows a stated desire for "assured retaliation,"[27] the PRC's limited, fixed, vulnerable missile deployments to date suggest that the Beijing leadership has for most of its nuclear history believed that *assured doubt* in Washington or Moscow of a first strike completely eliminating the Second Artillery's retaliatory capability is sufficient.

As RAND's Medeiros writes, PRC leaders "continue to view nuclear weapons as primarily political tools to maintain China's freedom of action while minimizing its vulnerability to coercion by other nuclear-armed states."[28] The current nuclear modernization effort, however, has the PRC's forces on course to look more like those of the other P-5 states. Although retirement of older systems is probable and could offset numerically any new deployments,[29] the U.S. intelligence community believes that China's operational warhead total may rise[30] as the PRC fields three solid-fueled DF-31 variants: the road-mobile DF-31 ICBM (which the Pentagon judges "achieved initial threat availability in 2006" and may be operational "in the near future" if not already), the longer-range silo-based DF-31A ICBM ("expected to reach initial operating capability (IOC) in 2007") and the JL-2 SLBM ("IOC 2007-2010") for new Type 094 *Jin* SSBNs, the operational date of which is not clear.[31] The PRC may deploy MRVs on its missiles (including the DF-5), using a new, smaller, more accurate, sub-megaton warhead that may be deployed with penetration aids intended to foil U.S. ballistic missile defenses (BMD).[32] Cruise missiles that could have nuclear capability are also reportedly in development.[33]

In short, China appears to be seeking a deterrent improved in size, survivability, accuracy, and penetrability. Operational deployment on road- and sea-mobile platforms, with warheads continually mated to missiles, may suggest impending, significant changes to posture and doctrine.

MODERNIZATION

Several PRC motives for modernization are relatively obvious. Along with deterring nuclear attacks and preventing nuclear coercion, signaling great power standing is enumerated as one of the arsenal's stated missions;[34] in this sense, modern nuclear forces function as a P-5 status symbol. The rising economic tide that has made the PRC a great power is also lifting all military boats. In turn, more and better nuclear hardware (including from Russia) makes overwhelming and penetrating U.S. BMD easier.

This four-part atomic harmony of prestige, money, technology, and counter-BMD is discernable in discussions of PRC modernization on both sides of the Pacific. It does not, however, fully account for the mounting pressure for change and growth in nuclear capabilities and doctrine. A fuller explanation begins with but goes beyond the most explosive issue in Sino-American relations, Taiwan.

The "comprehensive transformation" of the PLA is focused on enabling the PRC to prevail in a "local war[] under conditions of informationalization"—a brief, intense, high-technology war to capture Taiwan or at least prevent its independence.[35] While Americans tend to view this capability (years away, according to the Pentagon[36]) in terms of something the PRC seeks to acquire, the Chinese Communist Party (CCP) leadership appears to view it in connection with preventing catastrophic loss. Due in great part to the popular nationalism the CCP has stoked in the place of communist ideology, it is common perception in China that "if the Communist regime allows Taiwan to declare formal independence without putting up a fight, the outraged public will bring down the regime."[37] The CCP might contemplate or threaten nuclear escalation to avoid having to back down, and in any event could be expected to hope that the risk of a Taiwan crisis becoming a nuclear crisis will inject caution into U.S. decision-making.[38] As it seeks to deter the United States from conventionally resisting a PRC conventional attack beyond its current frontier, however, China finds itself with legacy nuclear forces designed primarily for a very different Cold War scenario: deterring the Soviet Union from a nuclear attack on (or a massive ground invasion of) PRC territory.[39] The limited capabilities and simple, NFU-based retaliatory doctrine assumed to work in the latter case likely look to some PRC strategists like small, vulnerable, blunt instruments in the former.

Concern about the vulnerability of China's deterrent, and concomitant pressure for its modernization, appear to have been stoked by the 2002 U.S. Nuclear Posture Review (NPR). As part of a "New Triad," the NPR endorsed BMDs that represent an implicit challenge to China's second strike capability, and doctrinally added conventional weapons to U.S. strategic offensive forces.[40] From the U.S. standpoint, proposed conventional ballistic missile (CBM) systems such as the Conventional Trident Modification (CTM)—rejected to date by Congress but requested again this year by the Pentagon[41]—hold out the promise of "prompt global strike" against terrorists and rogue states. Such systems might also meet strategic targeting requirements with fewer nuclear warheads, or suggest the surgical removal of peer or near-peer nuclear forces during a crisis without crossing the nuclear threshold.[42] But from China's standpoint, that is just the problem: some PRC strategists fear that in a Taiwan crisis the United States might attempt a disarming non-nuclear first strike, believing that BMD or the PRC's own NFU pledge would protect against Chinese nuclear retaliation. IDA's Brad Roberts observes that in this scenario China either backs down or else "China is the first user of nuclear weapons, possibly the second user, but also the loser."[43]

Strong gravitational forces are pulling the PRC toward significant nuclear change but it would be wrong to conclude that they are unopposed. The CCP keeps a firm grip on nuclear forces, to the point of rejecting "the Pentagon's offer to set up a military hotline between the high-level armed forces of the two countries because [the CCP] was reluctant to delegate that much authority to the senior commanders."[44] This consideration can be expected to exert a restraining effect on the numbers and operational posture of road-mobile missiles and SSBNs.

A stronger, multifaceted drag is fiscal. The PRC economy and military budget can support a vastly larger nuclear force but resource competition among domestic and defense priorities remains intense. Furthermore, a nuclear arms race with the United States would not only be against explicit PRC policy (one reflecting concern about being militarily competed into bankruptcy like the USSR,[45] and reiterated in the PRC's 2006 Defense White Paper[46]), but the Sino-American Cold War it would reasonably risk would threaten the PLA's funding source: the Chinese economic expansion fueled in great part by trade with the United States and its allies.

THE FUTURE

The true relative weights of the variables auguring for and against dramatic nuclear change in China in 2007 are, of course, as unknowable to us as the composition of China's forces in 2017. More analytically helpful is positing a range of what Roberts terms "alternative futures" for China's strategic forces. Drawing on the work of several analysts, at least five can be identified.

- 1. "The Minimum Means of Reprisal"—In a new book, Harvard's Jeffrey Lewis presents cautionary evidence: in the 1970s, 1980s, and 1990s, U.S. "intelligence community projections...overestimated both the scope and pace of Chinese ballistic missile deployments."[47] "Chinese internal politics" are more likely to drive policy than "changes in the objective balance of capabilities" internationally, and therefore the PRC will retain a "minimum" deterrent not much larger than 80 operational warheads.[48]

Although plausible, this path would assume transformational change in virtually every major Chinese institution *except* its nuclear force. "[T]he evidence is more mixed than Lewis depicts it."[49]

- **2. Baseline Trajectory**—Although Roberts warns that "the evidence…is not strong enough to lead to confident predictions,"[50] he argues that the PRC will modernize as systems age. Together with increased survivability and penetrability, and development of ASATs and other asymmetric capabilities, a "middle way" scenario sees modest "expansion of the intercontinental component of the missile force" to match and therefore overcome (but not exceed) BMD deployments.[51] Medeiros takes a somewhat more certain view, arguing that when completed the PRC's modernization program "will have revolutionized its nuclear capability, providing it with a highly credible nuclear deterrent against major nuclear powers for the first time since 1964."[52]

Roberts sees two primary alternatives to such a baseline trajectory, involving competition with the United States and Russia, respectively. Both are expensive and risk driving other regional players into American arms.

- **3. Race the New Triad**—"Chinese planners might conclude that they need to race for some fixed period of time…to press [PRC] advantages over Taiwan" before the BMDs and CBMs of the New Triad, and the U.S. conventional "transformation" force, are realized.[53] This might involve responses that are asymmetrical (capabilities to track and strike U.S. forces at sea, ASATs) and symmetrical (a Chinese BMD system, together with some increase in offensive nuclear capability).[54]

- **4. Race Russia**—In the late 1990s some PRC political figures suggested China surge ahead to become the top nuclear power in Eurasia, number two overall.[55]

This expensive latter option gets more remote, however, as Russia accelerates its SSBN and ICBM force modernization[56] and harder to justify as China's economic and political clout in Eurasia grows and relations with Russia improve.[57]

- **5. Sprint to Peerhood**—These concerns, and the collapse of Soviet communism during nuclear competition with the United States,

caution the Chinese Communist Party(CCP) against driving for
U.S. peer or near-peer status. The CCP would, therefore, require
a highly compelling reason to pay peerhood's steep fiscal and political costs. In congressional testimony in 2002, however, then-
Defense Secretary Rumsfeld outlined a scenario that would match
a plausible rationale with various estimates that by 2015 the PRC
may field upwards of 100 to 1,000 warheads.[58] U.S. cuts below the
Moscow Treaty's 1,700 to 2,200 deployed strategic warhead level,
he suggested, could lead the PRC to decide that peer or near-peer
status is but a "sprint up" away.[59]

There are other sprint scenarios. For example, large-scale substitution
of CTM for U.S. nuclear SLBMs (such as suggested by Owen Price in
this volume) might present China an opportunity to sprint to numerical
nuclear near-parity if not in counter-force capability.

Alternatively, significant cuts to or elimination of the U.S. ICBM
force could suggest to China a short dash to a small but viable strategic nuclear counter-force capability, even with BMD in place. America's
three nuclear bomber bases, two SSBN bases, and three primary nuclear command and control centers (Washington, D.C., the U.S. Strategic Command, and NORAD) total just eight CONUS counter-force
targets—down from a practically insurmountable 458 with the nuclear
ICBM force.[60] Such a small CONUS counter-force set might make a
damage limitation first strike begin to look conceivable (or at least a
possible threat) to the PRC in a crisis, or provide a rationale for force
increases and C4ISR improvements in peacetime. If, additionally, the
Trident force had become mostly conventional, and/or China possessed
a robust ASAT capability vis-à-vis U.S. nuclear C4ISR assets, the odds of
dramatically degrading U.S. nuclear capabilities—a very serious "shock"
indeed—might begin to look even better.

From the outside, it is difficult to know whether the PRC leadership
would think along such uncertain and dangerous lines during a nuclear crisis, much less anticipate such brinksmanship and on that basis
change the PRC's nuclear doctrine and modernization trajectory. But
we can recognize that American strategic doctrine and capabilities have
the potential to influence China's nuclear calculus, and that change in
China's capabilities and stated intentions is the best means of charting
its nuclear future.

THE INDICATORS

In *Military Power of the People's Republic of China 2006*, the Pentagon identified six "primary indicators" of whether the PRC would adopt a "sea control" strategy.[61] Similarly, we can identify a six-point (but hardly exhaustive)[62] "index of leading Chinese nuclear indicators" that should aid in gauging nuclear change.

- **1. Missile Production**—The Defense Department estimates that all three DF-31 missile variants could achieve IOC this year. Rapid economic and military budget growth and the 100-plus SRBMs China produces each year[63] suggest how rapidly the PRC could grow its strategic missile forces. Accordingly, actual production will be a bellwether for PRC pursuit of options 2-5 above.

- **2. SSBN Production**—The first of several Type 094 SSBNs was reported to have been launched in 2004, but work on it apparently continues.[64] Successful operationalization of even four SSBNs would in terms of SSBN quantity (but not quality or capability) match France and the United Kingdom, while eight boats would equal the U.S. and exceed the current Russian Pacific fleets (of eight and five active boomers, respectively).[65]

- **3. Force Posture**—One analyst has suggested that when and if the Type 094s and JL-2s become operational China must choose between the blue-water deployment approach of the United States (and United Kingdom and France and Soviet Union) and the defended coastal "bastion" strategy of the USSR in the 1980s.[66] Omitted are at least two other alternatives: the Russian pierside alert posture (which, ironically, would put Russia in range of the JL-2, but not the CONUS), and generally staying in port off alert but rehearsing for other SSBN operations modes to provide crisis contingency options. Deploying Type 094s within JL-2 range of the CONUS (a departure from the PRC's current practice of rarely sending submarines on patrol),[67] plus frequent patrols by road-mobile DF-31s, could suggest realization of a standing survivable second-strike capability against the CONUS.[68] To narrow the gap with the top-tier powers in responsiveness, the PRC could also place its silo-based ICBMs on alert and improve nuclear C4ISR.

- **4. MRVs and Testing**—The PRC may place MRVs on the legacy DF-5. Some analysts believe the PRC can now MRV the DF-31 and JL-2, but that view is not universally shared; a senior U.S. intelligence official testified in 2002 that to certify a warhead small enough to mount in multiples on the DF-31 family, it "would probably require nuclear testing."[69] This politically costly move would strongly signal prioritization of nuclear capabilities.

- **5. Declaratory Doctrine: No First Use (NFU)**—In recent PRC *Military Power* reports the Pentagon has highlighted PRC debate about whether to change its NFU policy (and, additionally, preemption of stronger opponents).[70] A key question is whether the PRC should regard a conventional strike on its nuclear deterrent as tantamount to nuclear first use. "It remains unclear what military actions constitute 'first use' for Chinese leaders, and thus what would trigger nuclear retaliation."[71]

- **6. Asymmetries**—Deploying a robust ASAT capability could suggest PRC interest in racing the New Triad or in parity. Other asymmetric options include use of EMP and emphasis on cruise missiles or theater nuclear forces to counter U.S. strategic superiority.

THE WAY AHEAD

Chinese military strategy emphasizes asymmetries and "disruptive technologies" as a weaker power's key to defeating a stronger one.[72] This approach stands in contrast to the highly symmetrical U.S.-Soviet nuclear competition. A deeper asymmetry, however, is that the United States and China are bound together economically to an extent the United States and USSR never were. Any serious Sino-American confrontation is likely to threaten economic damage the parties may find unwilling to accept, long before unacceptable losses from use of nuclear weapons become a clear and present factor in decision-making.

Nevertheless, military power and nuclear weapons remain foundational and potentially explosive elements of the evolving relationship, particularly in the Taiwan context. China is on course to making significant qualitative and quantitative improvements to its nuclear forces, pulled toward modernization by forces ranging from great power prestige to concern about conventional U.S. strikes on the PRC's nuclear deterrent. Although what we do not know about China's nuclear program vastly exceeds what we do, the PRC likely has a broad range of alternative nuclear directions from which to choose. Because their implications for crisis stability are uncertain and potentially serious—particularly when viewed together with possible U.S. force alternatives—the United States ought to pay particular attention to several key indicators of China's nuclear trajectory. Crisis stability concerns, and in particular avoiding miscalculations, also argue for continued American civilian and military efforts to engage their Chinese counterparts on nuclear issues, and carefully evaluating the potential implications of significant changes in U.S. strategic forces and doctrine.

Notes

1. See, e.g., *The Economist*, May 19, 2007 (cover story: "America's Fear of China").

2. See, e.g., Susan L. Shirk, *China: Fragile Superpower* (2007); Bates Gill, *Rising Star: China's New Security Diplomacy* (2007).

3. See, e.g., Council on Foreign Relations (CFR) Independent Task Force, Carla A. Hills & Dennis C. Blair, Chairs, *U.S.-China Relations: An Affirmative Agenda, a Responsible Course* (New York: CFR, 2007) [hereinafter Hills & Blair]; Anthony H. Cordesman & Martin Kleiber, *Chinese Military Modernization and Force Development* (Washington, D.C.: CSIS, 2006).

4. See Office of the Secretary of Defense, *Military Power of the People's Republic of China 2007* [hereinafter *PRC Military Power 2007*].

5. See, e.g., Hills & Blair, 7, 54 ("Taking stock of U.S.-China relations, the Task Force finds that China's overall trajectory over the past thirty-five years of engagement with the United States is positive" and there is "no evidence" that China will become "a peer military competitor" by 2030); Bill Gertz, "The China Threat is Real, the Solution is Democracy," ABCNews.com, May 14, 2007, http://abcnews.go.com/International/story?id=3157634&page=1 ("The China threat…is real and growing stronger").

6. *PRC Military Power 2007*, 1.

7. Ibid., 2.

8. Alexa Olesen, "China: U.S. Exaggerating Military Threat," *Associated Press*, May 27, 2007.

9. *PRC Military Power 2007*, 18-19.

10. *PRC Military Power 2007*, 14.

11. The DF-31 is also known as the CSS-9. I use DF designations for consistency and simplicity.

12. For low estimate of 74-85 deployed strategic nuclear warheads, see Jeffrey Lewis, *The Minimum Means of Reprisal: China's Search for Security in the*

Nuclear Age (Cambridge: MIT Press, 2007), 30. Another estimate based on DoD numbers is 93 warheads, in Hans M. Kristensen, Robert S. Norris, & Matthew G. McKinzie, *Chinese Nuclear Forces and U.S. Nuclear War Planning* (Washington, D.C.: FAS/NRDC, 2006), 46 [hereinafter FAS/NRDC]. Assuming that only one warhead is operationally deployed for each deployed missile, DoD data suggest up to 112 operationally deployed strategic warheads with land-based missiles. *PRC Military Power 2007*, 42. See ibid., page 19, for missile ranges.

13. DoD puts the number of deployed DF-5s at "approximately 20" (see *PRC Military Power 2007*, 18) but the public discussion includes references to 18 (see, e.g., Lewis, 31). The DF-5 is alternatively known as the CSS-4 and is being upgraded to the DF-5A

14. Cordesman & Kleiber, 85.

15. For General Habiger's reference to a single *Xia* "cruise" and Navy data indicting zero SSBN patrols, see respectively Lewis, 35, and Robert S. Norris & Hans M. Kristensen, "Nuclear Notebook: Chinese Nuclear Forces, 2006," *Bulletin of the Atomic Scientists* (May/June 2006): 61.

16. FAS/NRDC, 37; http://www.globalsecurity.org/wmd/world/france/bomber.htm.

17. See Brad Roberts, "The Nuclear Dimension: How Likely? How Stable?" in Evan Medeiros, Michael D. Swaine, & Andrew Young (eds.), *Assessing the Threat: The Chinese Military and Taiwan Security* (forthcoming) ("Whatever prior interest China might have had in tactical nuclear weapons seems not to have survived that earlier era" in which they were developed and at least one exercise was held), but see also Lewis, 1 (apparently inferring from lack of available evidence of operational tactical warheads with ground, air, and naval units that the "PRC does not maintain tactical nuclear forces of any kind").

18. See FAS/NRDC, 38. The PRC may have 200 to 350 total warheads. See Norris & Kristensen,: 60; Cordesman & Kleiber, 94.

19. See, e.g., FAS/NRDC, 59.

20. See, e.g., Lewis, 1-2. The Second Artillery also operates the conventional SRBMs deployed opposite Taiwan. For discussion, see Evan S. Medeiros, "Minding the Gap: Assessing the Trajectory of the PLA's Second Artillery," paper presented at U.S. Army War College Conference "Exploring the "Right Size" for China's Military: PLA Missions, Functions, and Organization," October 2006, pp. 12-21.

21. Ibid., 2-3.

22. Lewis, 12-14.

23. Quoted in Lewis, 61.

24. Larry M. Wortzel, *China's Nuclear Forces: Operations, Training, Doctrine,*

Command, Control, and Campaign Planning (U.S. Army Strategic Studies Institute, 2007), 16; Medeiros, 9.

25. Brad Roberts writes that there is disagreement on whether the PRC has the same view of theater nuclear forces as it does its strategic forces. See Roberts, "Assessing the Threat," footnote 10.

26. Medeiros, 7.

27. Ibid., 5, 8.

28. Ibid., 5.

29. For this view see FAS/NRDC, 42-44 (also arguing that total deployed megatonnage will decline as smaller yield warheads enter the force).

30. See ibid., 42.

31. *PRC Military Power 2007*, 3; for discussion of the Type 094, see http://www.globalsecurity.org/wmd/world/china/type_94.htm.

32. See Cordesman & Kleiber, 95; FAS/NRDC, 43-44; Lewis, 32, 48-49.

33. *PRC Military Power 2007*, 19.

34. Medeiros, 5.

35. *PRC Military Power 2007*, I.

36. Ibid., 33.

37. See Susan L. Shirk, *China: Fragile Superpower* (Oxford, 2007), 2-3.

38. For discussion of how PRC nuclear capabilities might play in a Taiwan confrontation that starts with conventional forces, see, e.g., Richard C. Bush & Michael E. O'Hanlon, *A War Like No Other: the Truth About China's Challenge to America* (Hoboken: Wiley & Sons, 2007), 153-159.

39. Medeiros, 8.

40. Ibid.; see also http://www.globalsecurity.org/wmd/library/policy/dod/npr.htm. Note that the PRC may one day face a CBM threat from Russia, as well. See Robert S. Norris & Hans M. Kristensen, "Nuclear Notebook: Russian Nuclear Forces, 2007," *Bulletin of the Atomic Scientists* (March / April 2007): 63.

41. For the fiscal year 2008 request for R&D funds, see http://www.finance.hq.navy.mil/fmb/08pres/rdten/RDTEN_BA4_book.pdf.

42. There is a potential legal argument for CBMs. Employing conventional rather than nuclear warheads would better meet obligations under the law of armed conflict to adhere to the requirement of proportionality: avoiding incidental harm to protected persons and property that exceeds the anticipated military benefit, and in any case minimizing such harm to protected persons and property. See Articles 51(5)(b) and 57(2)(a)(ii) of Protocol I Additional

to the Geneva Conventions of 12 August 1949, and Relating to the Protection of Victims of International Armed Conflicts, June 8, 1977, 1125 U.N.T.S. 3. A policy argument against CTM is that until impact a CTM would look the same as a nuclear SLBM and therefore could trigger impulsive, mistaken nuclear retaliation. Overflight route and patrol area adjustments, plus launch notification, have been suggested as remedial measures.

43. Brad Roberts, "Alternative Futures," in Paul Bolt & Al Wilner (eds.), *China's Nuclear Future* (2006), 180.

44. Shirk, 71.

45. For discussion, see Medeiros, 6.

46. *PRC Military Power 2007*, 19.

47. Lewis, 50-51.

48. Ibid., 1-2.

49. Brad Roberts, "Book Review: Nuclear Minimalism" (reviewing Jeffrey Lewis, *The Minimum Means of Reprisal*), *Arms Control Today* (May 2007): 41.

50. Ibid.

51. Roberts, "Alternative Futures," 176.

52. Medeiros, 10-11.

53. Roberts, "Alternative Futures," 181.

54. Ibid.

55. Ibid., 182.

56. See, e.g., Jim Heintz, "Russia Test-Launches New ICBM," *Associated Press*, May 29, 2007.

57. See *PRC Military Power 2007*, 1.

58. See National Intelligence Council, *Foreign Missile Developments and the Ballistic Missile Threat to the United States Through 2015* (1998), 5, and House Select Committee on U.S. National Security and Military/Commercial Concerns with the People's Republic of China, declassified report issued May 25, 1999, cited in Roberts, "Alternative Futures," footnotes 1-2.

59. Rumsfeld was before the Senate Foreign Relations Committee; see Lewis, 144-45.

60. The U.S. Air Force plans to retire 50 of the current 500 Minuteman III ICBMs, for a planned force of 450.

61. *PRC Military Power 2006*, 31.

62. For example, one additional issue meriting attention is the "risk of accidental nuclear conflict" that could result from the Second Artillery loading the same classes of ballistic missiles with conventional and nuclear warheads and

co-locating them—particularly if U.S. C4ISR assets are attacked by PRC ASATs or other asymmetric capabilities. See Wortzel, ix.

63. *PRC Military Power 2006*, 3.

64. Cordesman & Kleiber, 67; *PRC Military Power 2007*, 3 (stating the *Jin* SSBN is "in development").

65. See Norris & Kristensen, "Nuclear Notebook: French Nuclear Forces, 2005," *Bulletin of the Atomic Scientists* (July/August 2005): 73; Robert S. Norris & Hans M. Kristensen, "Nuclear Notebook: British Nuclear Forces, 2007," *Bulletin of the Atomic Scientists* (November / December 2005): 77-78; Robert S. Norris & Hans M. Kristensen, "Nuclear Notebook: Russian Nuclear Forces, 2007," *Bulletin of the Atomic Scientists* (March / April 2007): 63 (all *Delta III* SSBNs are thought deployed in the Pacific); and http://www.navy.mil/navydata/fact_display.asp?cid=4100&tid=200&ct=4.

66. Richard Fisher, Jr., "Developing U.S.-Chinese Nuclear Naval Competition in Asia," International Assessment and Strategy Center, January 16, 2005, http://www.strategycenter.net/research/pubID.60/pub_detail.asp#.

67. Strategic Security Blog, "China's Submarine Fleet Continues Low Patrol Rate" ("China's entire submarine fleet conducted only two patrols in 2006" according to declassified U.S. Navy data).

68. Depending on deployment location, eastern Russia is already in range of the solid-fuel, road-mobile DF-21 (also known as the CSS-5). See *PRC Military Power 2007*, 19; Cordesman & Kleiber, 96. DF-21s, however, may spend most of their days in garrison. See Lewis, 34.

69. Cordesman & Kleiber, 95; FAS/NRDC, 55.

70. *PRC Military Power 2006*, 28, 13-14; *PRC Military Power 2007*, 12, 20.

71. Medeiros, 9; see also Wortzel, 14.

72. *PRC Military Power 2007*, 13.

CHAPTER SEVEN

NUCLEAR DETERRENCE

THE FRENCH PERSPECTIVE

Bruno Tertrais

CURRENT NUCLEAR POLICY: PRINCIPLES AND SCENARIOS

Traditionally, France has had a fairly conservative approach to deterrence—to the point that a senior defense policy official could claim in early 2001 that France was "the last outpost of nuclear fundamentalism in the West."[1] The words "nuclear" and "deterrence" are still very much associated in the nation's strategic culture. The 1994 White Paper expressed considerable reservations about the relevance of "conventional deterrence" as a possible substitute for nuclear weapons.[2] And there is a traditional defiance vis-à-vis missile defense, for strategic and budgetary reasons.

There has been, however, a significant evolution since the end of the Cold War. In particular, Chirac's landmark speeches on nuclear deterrence issued on June 10, 2001 and January 19, 2006 introduced significant new inflexions.

The French defense model, designed in 1996, revolves around four "operational functions:" Deterrence, Prevention, Projection, and Protection. However, in his January 2006 speech, Chirac has reshuffled the cards. He has sought to place nuclear deterrence less as a separate component than as the very foundation of French defense policy. He presented it as the "ultimate expression" of the prevention function and the backup for its conventional military intervention capabilities.[3] He also made it clear that nuclear weapons protected France's ability to project its forces abroad.

The French nuclear deterrence covers "vital interests." Since the end of the Cold War, this notion has been given a broad meaning. The 1994 White Paper defined it as follows: "the integrity of the national territory, including the mainland as well as the overseas departments and territories, the free exercise of our sovereignty and the protection of the population constitute the core [of our vital interests] today."[4]

The limits of vital interests remain vague, to avoid an adversary being able to calculate the risks inherent in his aggression, because the scope of such interests evolves and can change over time, and because it would be up to the President to decide whether or not these interests are at stake. But occasionally, French Presidents drop hints.

In his January 2006 speech, Chirac stated that "the defense of allied countries" could be part of vital interests.[5] The mere mention of "allies" was not new. But it was generally associated in French public discourse with the words "Europe" or "Atlantic Alliance." The use of the word "allies" without any elaboration left open the possibility that non-NATO French defense partners, for instance in the Persian Gulf, could be protected.

Chirac also stated that the "safeguard of strategic supplies" could not be excluded from the scope of vital interests. While this scenario appears farfetched to some, it is not entirely incredible: a hypothetical alliance between Russia and several Middle East oil and gas producers deciding to cut off exports to the European Union would bring Europe to its knees, given its increasing dependency on external imports.[6]

According to French doctrine, an attack on vital interests would bring on a nuclear response in the form of "unacceptable damage" regardless of the nature of the threat, the identity of the State concerned, or the means employed. A noted part of Chirac's January 2006 speech was the strong part that explicitly included the threat of State-sponsored terrorism: "Leaders of States resorting to terrorist means against us, as those who might consider, one way or the other, weapons of mass destruction, must understand that they risk a firm and adapted response from us. And this response can be of a conventional nature. It can also be of another nature."[7] Through this statement, France made it clear that it considers that the use of terrorism or weapons of mass destruction (WMD) would not necessarily represent a threat to the country's vital interests, but at the same time sought to reaffirm that it would not hesitate to use nuclear means should the threshold of vital interests be crossed in the French President's view.

France's nuclear deterrent is for States only. Chirac reaffirmed this a few weeks after the September 11 attacks.[8] Nevertheless, as explained above, he was also keen to emphasize in his January 2006 speech that a State using terrorist means against vital interests would be subject to nuclear reprisals. The country's counter-terrorism policy has been made coherent with this statement. In March 2006, the French government published a White Paper outlining why France has become a target for terrorist attacks and specifying various attack scenarios, including WMD use. In such circumstances, the White Paper states, France must not "exclude any response." It recalls President Chirac's January 2006 speech and takes note of France's right to self-defense under Article 51 of the United Nations (UN) Charter.[9]

Two major rationales are put forward by French leaders to retain and continue to modernize the country's nuclear force.

One is the "life insurance" function. French leaders realize that the world can change rapidly. They believe that it is impossible to exclude the emergence of a new major threat to Europe at the horizon of 15-30 years, and deem it prudent to maintain a national nuclear deterrent. Did we not have no less than two major strategic surprises in little more than a decade, the fall of the Wall and the fall of the Towers? Chirac implicitly referred to potential major power threats by observing that France is "not shielded from an unforeseen reversal of the international system, nor from a strategic surprise."[10] The dismantlement in 1996 of the land-based missiles allowed France to declare in September 1997 that no French nuclear asset was targeted anymore. French nuclear strategy has become again *tous azimuts,* to borrow an expression from the de Gaulle years. The then-Prime Minister indicated in 1999 that French deterrence should be able to counter any threat, "even a distant one."[11] This was interpreted as signifying that the build-up of nuclear arsenals in Asia was deemed a matter of concern for Europe. The rise of China is considered by some analysts as deserving attention. Some in France do believe that the capability to deter China might be needed in the future. Beijing could try to prevent European support for the United States in the course of a crisis in Asia, or European participation in a Western intervention in a region of strategic interest. More broadly, in his January 2006 speech, Chirac emphasized that the rise of nationalism and the competition between poles of power could give rise to new major threats.

A second rationale is to guarantee that no regional power will be in a position to blackmail or pressure France with WMD (for instance at the occasion of a military intervention in the Middle East or in Asia). In this regard, the prevailing opinion in Paris has traditionally been that nuclear deterrence is a better and safer choice than missile defense. Starting with the 1994 White Paper, Paris acknowledged that its vital interests could be threatened by regional powers. France had to "take into account the potential threats to our vital interests from the proliferation of weapons of mass destruction."[12] This evolution was confirmed when Chirac came to power in 1995.[13] The kind of scenario that has French officials worried is one where, for instance, a country tries to block military intervention by threatening to strike the national territory. This concept could be called "counter-deterrence" or "counter-blackmail." No specific countries of concern are identified in French discourse. However, according to Defense Minister Alliot-Marie, examples include North Korea, Iran, and Pakistan.[14]

CURRENT NUCLEAR POLICY: WEAPONS AND PLANNING

France has reduced its nuclear arsenal since the end of the Cold War and dismantled several key nuclear installations, including its nuclear testing site and fissile material production facilities. It maintains its force at a level of "sufficiency" (a French expression equivalent to "minimum deterrent"). It considers that its nuclear policy is consistent with its international legal obligations, including Article VI of the nuclear Non Proliferation Treaty.

The current format of French nuclear forces has been fixed in 1996. It was decided to retain only a "dyad" made of two complementary components, each with its own characteristics. This variety is designed to provide flexibility in planning as well as an insurance against any adverse technical development that could weaken the capabilities of either.[15]

France now has four SSBNs (in 2006, one Le Redoutable-M4 class and three new-generation Le Triomphant-M45 class). Three of them are in the operational cycle, making it possible to maintain continued at-sea deterrence with at least one vessel on patrol at all times, and even two at all times if the President so decides. If the SSBN force were fully generated, with three boats at sea, a total of 48 missiles and 288 warheads would be available assuming that each missile carries six warheads. The

M45 missile has a range of at least 4,000 kilometers and carries six TN75 warheads, each in the 100-150 kiloton range. The fourth and final new-generation SSBN will enter service in 2010. (The first one is scheduled to go into retirement around 2030.)

A new, longer-range SLBM, the M51, will be introduced in 2010, allowing the French deterrent to "go global." Initially, it will be equipped with the same warhead as the M45 (TN75). This M51.1 version will be later supplemented by a M51.2 version, with a new generation warhead (*Tête nucléaire océanique*, TNO). The range of the M51 with a full payload of warheads and penetration aids is said to be about 6,000 kilometers. (Its range with a single warhead may be much greater.[16]) Officials have suggested that the M51 will have in-flight trajectory correction abilities and that the M51.2 version will have a greater range than the M51.1 version. The M51 missile could last until 2040.

France also has three squadrons of Mirage 2000Ns and a small carrier-based fleet of Super-Etendard—a feature that distinguishes the French posture from those of its NATO allies.[17] These aircraft carry the ASMP (*Air-Sol Moyenne Portée*) air-breathing missile. The ASMP, whose range is about 300 kilometers, was designed to carry a 300 kiloton TN81 warhead, but it is possible that adaptations to the system were made since it entered service in 1986. The successor to the ASMP will be the "improved" ASMP (ASMP-A for *ASMP Amélioré*), equipped with TNA (*Tête Nucléaire Aéroportée*) warheads with better performance. The Rafale will replace both the Mirage 2000N and Super-Etendard after 2008. The range of the ASMP-A is reported to be 300 to 400 kilometers, and its precision less than 10 meters. It will include an in-flight trajectory correction mechanism. The air component is considered particularly well suited for the exercise of deterrence vis-à-vis a regional power.

The current total numbers of nuclear weapons is not known. Most public estimates put it around 350. Charts given in official documents suggested that, in 2000, France possessed 48 SLBMs and about 60 nuclear-capable aircraft.[18] The TNA and TNO are not more sophisticated weapons but so-called "robust" warheads: they are less sensitive to variations in parameters resulting, for example, from the ageing of components. The concept for the TNA and TNO was tested during the 1995-1996 final testing campaign. The lumping together of all French nuclear weapons in a single category of "strategic" systems provides for an increased flexibility in nuclear planning and operations. Depending on circumstances, airborne weapons could supplement SSBNs for exerting "unacceptable damage," or perhaps a single SLBM shot could be used as a "final warning." News reports have indicated that re-targeting at sea will be an option. French officials insist that both components are able to participate in all nuclear missions.

French nuclear planning and targeting would be adjusted to the threat. To deter a major power, France would rely on the threat of "unacceptable damage of all kinds."[19] Chirac's use of this phrase deliberately left the threat vague, and this was consistent with the abandonment, since the 1994 White Paper, of France's previous "anti-cities" threats in its declaratory policy.

To deter a regional power, France would rely on the threat of destroying "centers of power." This was announced by Chirac in his June 2001 speech: "the damage to which a possible aggressor would be exposed would be directed above all against his political, economic, and military power centers."[20] Chirac repeated these ideas in his January 2006 speech, and added that France's instrument of deterrence is its increasingly precise and controllable ability to strike the adversary state's "power centers, its capacity to act," with nuclear weapons.[21] In her January 2006 testimony about the President's speech, Minister of Defense Alliot-Marie said,

> In fact, a potential adversary might think that, given its principles and its known respect for human rights, France would hesitate to use the entire yield of its nuclear arsenal against civil populations. The President of the Republic has underlined that our country has made its capabilities for action more flexible and henceforth has the possibility of targeting the decision centers of a potential aggressor, thereby avoiding the excessive general effects capable of making us hesitate.[22]

An original French concept is the "final warning" (*ultime avertissement*), the idea to threaten an adversary who would have misjudged French resolve with a single limited strike on military targets. As devised in the 1970s, the final warning was a compromise between the need to avoid the "all or nothing" dilemma and the equally pressing need, in French minds, to avoid adopting a flexible response-type concept—both options judged not credible. It is also the necessary counterpart to the deliberate uncertainty that exists regarding the scope of vital interests and its evolving limits. The final warning cannot be repeated, and would be followed by an "unacceptable damage" strike if the adversary persisted.

This concept has been judged still valid, and perhaps even more so in the new context, given that a regional or distant adversary might be more prone to misjudge French determination to safeguard its vital interests and would not necessarily understand the exact limits of the vital interests. Chirac reintroduced the expression in the public discourse by stating: "we still maintain, of course, the right to employ a final warning to signify our determination to protect our vital interests."[23] Nonetheless, since 1996 any nuclear planning is considered of a strategic nature. The idea is that *any* nuclear weapons use would be a sea change in the nature of the conflict.

In his January 2006 speech, Chirac mentioned the ability to hold an adversary's "capacity to act" at risk. In a subsequent briefing, the French government explained how an enemy State's capacity to act could be distinct from its "power centers." It was said that France could explode a nuclear weapon at high altitude and thereby create an electromagnetic pulse (EMP) that could cripple non-hardened computers and communications systems.[24] An EMP attack might be particularly well suited to transmit a devastating but theoretically non-lethal final warning message.

Also in 2006, Chirac announced that some French submarine-launched ballistic missiles (SLBMs) could carry a smaller number of warheads than others. This confirmed that France might undertake a "split launch," allowing for greater flexibility in planning and targeting.

While specific weapon adaptations have not been made public, it is widely believed that the French have diversified their yield options in recent years. The option of exploding only the first-stage "primary" may have been exploited, since it is known to be an easy adaptation from a technical point of view.

France has consistently rejected the adoption of a "no first-use" posture. This has been manifested by reservations attached to the Negative Security Assurances conferred in 1995 by France. Paris sees nuclear retaliation as being consistent with the right to self-defense recognized by Article 51 of the UN Charter, thus prevailing in case of aggression over commitments of non-use made in peacetime. France asserts that countries that do not respect their own non-proliferation commitments should not expect that the NSA would apply to them, thus implicitly subscribing to the norms of "belligerent reprisals" that also underpin U.S. and UK doctrines. These reservations to the NSAs were reaffirmed in 2003.[25] Chirac insisted, however, that these changes did not represent "any lowering of the nuclear threshold."[26]

France is traditionally cautious about territorial missile defense, for both conceptual and budgetary reasons. However, it has shown an increasing pragmatism in this domain. In June 2001, Chirac confirmed that the country's forces abroad should be protected against the threat of tactical missiles. To that effect, the *Aster* family of weapons systems developed in cooperation with Italy will provide the basis for short-range ballistic and cruise missile defense.[27] In addition, at the NATO Summit of November 2002, Paris confirmed its participation in feasibility studies for missile defense in Europe to protect "Alliance territory, forces, and population centers against the full range of missile threats."[28] Finally, in 2006 Chirac stated that missile defense could be a *"complement"* to nuclear deterrence "by diminishing our vulnerabilities."[29] This paved the way for French participation in a future NATO missile defense system. In light of France's long-standing reservations about strategic missile defenses, this new tone constitutes a quasi-breakthrough on the conceptual level.

FUTURE PROSPECTS

It is unlikely that France will take major crucial decisions regarding its nuclear deterrence force in the coming decade. The consensus on the continued relevance of possessing nuclear weapons remains fairly strong among politicians and public opinion, and France remains sheltered from the dramatic political debates that affect the United Kingdom about the renewal of its own deterrent. All the more since no decision regarding the future of the French deterrent will be needed before 2020, when the question of replacing the new-generation SSBNs will begin to be raised.

Nevertheless, in the coming years, the French nuclear deterrent will face two broad challenges, one internal and one external.

The first challenge is of a domestic nature. It will be to maintain the nuclear consensus and the budgetary expense needed to maintain the long-term credibility of the French deterrent.

By U.S. standards, the French political lifespan is extremely long. Until 2007 there were still major politicians on the French scene such as former Presidents Jacques Chirac and Valéry Giscard d'Estaing, or former Prime Minister Edouard Balladur who had begun their careers during the Kennedy/Johnson era. However, today a new generation of political leaders is emerging. Nicolas Sarkozy, the new French President elected in May 2007, is the first true "post-Gaullist" generation. Since it is prudent to assume that defense budgets in Europe are now structurally constrained due to high social demands, maintaining the French nuclear consensus will require political leadership as well as good communication skills to explain why the choice that was made in the late 1950s is still valid today. Today nuclear programs make up for about 20 percent of the defense equipment budget. On average, the nuclear budget for the period 2003-2008, as voted by the Parliament in 2002, is €2.82 billion per year. The French nuclear budget has never been so low, in terms of both proportion of the defense expenditure (less than 10 per cent) and share of the national budget and GDP. Still, many in the armed forces and in Parliament criticize the heavy burden of nuclear expenses in the defense budget.

France faces the same problem as other mature nuclear-weapon States in retaining adequate scientific, technical, and operational knowledge in the post-Cold War context. The ability to maintain and adapt France's deterrent is weakening. The *Commissariat à l'énergie atomique* and the *Marine Nationale* have more difficulties than in the past to attract the best scientists, engineers and officers. Around 2012-2013, the CEA will have completed the transition between the "Cold War" generation that conducted nuclear testing and a new generation. France's missile expertise is now in the hands of a private multinational company (European Aeronautic Defense and Space Co., EADS), for whom nuclear deterrence is more a business than a mission.

The second challenge is of an international nature. France will have to take into account the progress made in European integration, as well as the probable deployment of missile defense systems by the Atlantic Alliance.

France's independent nuclear stance will be harder and harder to reconcile with its drive for a more integrated EU. This challenge has been recognized since the early 1990s by successive French governments, and the issue has been a recurring theme in French strategic thinking since former President Mitterrand first raised the question in 1992, at the time the EU was created. However, so far none of them has been able to give a satisfying answer to the tension between nuclear independence on the one hand, and political and defense integration on the other.

French leaders have suggested that the country's nuclear deterrent already plays an implicit role in the protection of Europe. In June 2001, Chirac stated that any decision by France to use nuclear weapons "would naturally take into account the growing solidarity of European Union countries."[30] And in January 2006, he stated that "the development of the European Security and Defense Policy, the growing intermeshing of the interests of European Union countries, the solidarity that now exists between them, make the French nuclear deterrent, by its mere existence, an unavoidable element of the security of the European continent."[31]

But France has fallen short of declaring that its nuclear deterrence explicitly covers its Union partners.[32] If the "mutual security guarantee" that was to be included in the failed EU Constitution is adopted one way or the other in the coming years, France will have to give its interpretation as to what that means for its nuclear policy.

There is the possibility that future British and French leaders deem it useful to reinforce their cooperation. Since the early 1990s, bilateral dialogue and cooperation mechanisms exist between the two countries in the nuclear field. In 1995, through the so-called Chequers Declaration (1995), where John Major and Jacques Chirac stated that they "could not imagine a situation in which the vital interests of either of our two nations, France and the United Kingdom, could be threatened without the vital interests of the other also being threatened."[33] The UK December 2006 decision to renew its nuclear deterrent was seen favorably by Paris. In the short run, nothing would preclude a solemn and explicit affirmation by London and Paris that their two nuclear forces protect the EU countries. However, it is unlikely that things could go very much further in the current strategic context.

France will also have to take into account the coming of missile defense in Europe. The country is a party to the debate on missile defense architectures in NATO; and its geographical location make it impossible to stay entirely out of any future system of defense against long-range ballistic missiles. (A first site is to be set up in Europe in 2011.) French political leaders will face a few problems. The first will be conceptual: the deployment of missile defense in Europe will force the French into rethinking the relative role of nuclear deterrence on the one hand, and of missile defense on the other. Would the threat of a conventional ballistic strike on French territory be covered by nuclear deterrence? Or would France expect a NATO missile defense to cover this risk—and in that case, does Paris have the will and the means to be a significant partner in such a system? The second will be political: what will be the place of Paris in NATO missile defense arrangements? It is dubious that France will not be at least party to the allied early warning system that will be set up. The third problem will be of a budgetary nature; assuming that the defense budget is not increased, any significant "entry cost" into a NATO missile defense architecture will imply savings on other programs.

In fact, both challenges are closely intertwined. Domestic political evolutions and budgetary constraints may lead the French towards revising their concept of independence in the nuclear field.

France's concept of "nuclear independence" is today fairly restrictive. Paris has sought to build and maintain autonomously all the necessary components of its nuclear arsenal. But future French political leaders will perhaps be tempted to ponder options for increased cooperation with London and/or Washington as a possible way to save money.

One possible avenue of cooperation may be the costly French "simulation" program, aimed at maintaining an enduring stockpile without live nuclear testing. The program includes a high-power laser (*Laser Mégajoule*, LMJ), a dual-axis radiography machine (AIRIX[34]), and a massively parallel computer architecture (*Tera* project).[35] The simulation program does not allow for the formation of new designs or development of entirely new types of warheads. In addition, France is not able to independently test nuclear weapons any more even if it wanted to, because it dismantled its facilities in 1997. The only realistic option would be to use another country's test facilities.

Another would be the "pooling" of French and British forces, which would require overcoming two major obstacles. Both countries would have to recognize that their "vital" interests are completely identical, to the point that either of the two could theoretically exercise deterrence in the name of the other. A second potential obstacle would be the existence of U.S./UK agreements that may preclude an increase of technical and/or operational cooperation.

COMPARISON BETWEEN U.S., UK, AND FRENCH POLICIES

French doctrine is much closer to U.S. and UK doctrines than generally thought. London, Paris, and Washington share a common view about the fundamentally political role of nuclear weapons, which are sup-posed to be an instrument of deterrence rather than a war-fighting tool. Nuclear deterrence is relevant whatever the means employed by the adversary in circumstances where essential security interests are at stake. In the current environment, none of them foresees a conventional threat that might warrant exercising nuclear deterrence the same way it was practiced during the Cold War.[36] Nevertheless, all three capitals oppose a "no-first-use doctrine:" they believe it would weaken deterrence by allowing an adversary to calculate the risks inherent in his aggression, and signal that the use of chemical or biological weapons could be considered without a risk of nuclear retaliation. This transatlantic consensus was made clear in the 1999 NATO Strategic Concept.[37]

London, Paris and Washington exercise nuclear deterrence primarily through the threat of inflicting "unacceptable damage" upon an adversary. Targeting would focus on assets held dear by an adversary. All three countries insist that they should have limited nuclear options in addition to massive strike options. They have adapted their respective nuclear arsenals in order to be able to make them relevant to a world of multiple and diverse nuclear deterrence scenarios and thus ensure that deterrence remains credible in the eyes of an adversary in foreseeable scenarios. None of them mentions "counter-city" targeting anymore, at least in public language. All three countries seem to implicitly consider that Russia and China should be treated as potential major threats, and continued at-sea deterrence is seen as an integral part of deterrence, with at least one SSBN on patrol at all times. Nevertheless, all three have "de-targeted" their nuclear forces along with the other two official nuclear weapon States.[38]

Such convergences should not be surprising. The French nuclear mythology does not do justice to the importance of UK and U.S. inputs to the origins of French strategy. The UK government's adoption of a massive retaliation strategy attracted attention in the early years of the French program. In his main book, *Stratégie de l'âge nucléaire*, published in 1960, General Pierre Gallois describes at length the British deterrent and implicitly tells his French readers that Paris could adopt the same posture. Initial French thinking about nuclear strategy also came from NATO. The main French military thinkers such as generals André Beaufre and Pierre Gallois learned about nuclear strategy in an allied context. They also both had numerous interactions with the RAND Corporation, then the intellectual breeding ground of U.S. nuclear strategy. Some specific French expressions come from allied doctrines, such as "unbearable" or "unacceptable" damage. The former expression originated in the UK White Paper of 1962, and the latter was introduced by the United States Government in the early 1960s.[39] It appeared in France in the early 1970s. Another borrowed expression was "sufficiency," which had been introduced by the Nixon administration in 1969.

There are, however, differences. Today, three particular features of French nuclear doctrine differentiate it from the American and British.

France's concept of a "final warning" is different from the U.S./UK concept of "sub-strategic" or "non-strategic" planning and use. As mentioned before, the final warning is the idea to threaten an adversary who might have underestimated French resolve to defend its vital interests, or misjudged the exact limits of these interests, with a single limited strike on military targets. The final warning could not be repeated, and would be followed by a massive strike if the adversary persisted.

A second difference is manifested in the way the legal grounds for nuclear deterrence are expressed in declaratory policies. Washington and London express their willingness to consider the use of nuclear weapons vis-à-vis a regional WMD threat through the threat of unspecified retaliation. (A classic example is the expression "overwhelming and devastating response.") France chooses to center its declaratory policy vis-à-vis such threats by promising a nuclear response to any aggression against its vital interests, whatever the means employed.[40] This reflects a different concept of deterrence and, in particular, of the balance between certainty and uncertainty: Washington and London are clear about the circumstances that would constitute a particular threshold (WMD use), but unclear about the response; Paris is vague about the exact threshold (vital interests), but clear about the response.[41] This also reflects a different legal culture. Both the United States and the United Kingdom are traditionally keen to ensure the compatibility of their doctrines with international law, in particular the compatibility of negative security assurances with their stated nuclear doctrines. France traditionally has a more lenient view of the impact of international legal norms on its policy.[42] It insists on the importance of the right to self-defense enshrined in Article 51 of the UN Charter as a legal basis for nuclear deterrence.[43] But it has never been inclined to emphasize the need for a "proportionate" response as its U.S. and UK allies do.[44] France has been much more vocal than its allies in stating publicly and explicitly the usefulness of nuclear deterrence vis-à-vis regional and WMD threats—including for States sponsoring such attacks. Here the difference may be due to different factors at play in Washington and London: since 1997, the delicate ideological balance within the Labour Party has made British leaders more prudent than previous (Conservative) governments in their support for the relevance of nuclear weapons.

A third area of differentiation is extended deterrence. While Paris has never seen its nuclear arsenal as solely protecting its national territory, and has stated on several occasions since the end of the Cold War that its deterrent also protects common European vital interests, France has never explicitly expressed a concept of "extended deterrence".

Some differences exist between U.S. nuclear policy and those of its two European nuclear allies. Both France and the UK have emphasized the importance of strengthening international legal norms of non-proliferation: they both have ratified the Comprehensive Nuclear Test-Ban Treaty (CTBT) and are keen to see a Fissile Material Cutoff Treaty (FMCT). A major traditional difference is that neither London nor Paris is known to consider "counter-force" nuclear options. Both countries have stated "minimum deterrence" posture (the French concept is called "sufficiency"), which implicitly exclude such options. This is clearly an effect of the limited availability of technical and financial resources, since counterforce is the most demanding of all nuclear missions. Largely for the same reasons, there is no evidence that either France or the United Kingdom has ever considered multiple strategic strikes: "unacceptable damage" would be a single strike option.

The UK December 2006 White Paper has brought British doctrine closer to the French one in at least two regards. France and the United Kingdom both consider that any nuclear use could only be of a "strategic" nature. And both countries refer to "vital interests" as the threshold for nuclear use.

Another difference concerns the place of nuclear deterrence in national security policies. Since the 1960s, the United States has sought to reduce the role of nuclear weapons in its defense strategy. Recent progress in conventional precision munitions and missile defense has made it possible to further downgrade the role of nuclear deterrence. The 2001 Nuclear Posture Review was a milestone in this regard: the new U.S. "Triad" considerably reduces the role of nuclear weapons in the U.S. defense policy. France acknowledged in 2003 that "the improvement of [conventional] capabilities for long-range strikes should constitute a deterrent threat for our potential aggressors."[45] And Paris and London have sought to take advantage of new technologies to develop more efficient long-range precision strike capabilities. But neither France nor the United Kingdom has been willing to recognize a major strategic role for conventional deterrence to the point of making it an equivalent of nuclear deterrence. Likewise, they have never emphasized the notion of "deterrence by denial."

At the same time, U.S. nuclear weapons have two roles that have no real equivalent in French and British official thinking. One of them is what the 2001 NPR calls "Reassurance": U.S. nuclear protection helps avoid nuclear proliferation for those countries that are explicitly protected by such weapons. The other is what the NPR called "Dissuasion," a concept that primarily applies to missile defense, but also to nuclear weapons to some extent: U.S. nuclear weapons are seen as having a role as a disincentive for those countries that could be tempted to match the United States from a military standpoint.

Finally, there are a few areas of convergence between the United States and France that leave the United Kingdom isolated. Paris in recent years has proven much more "conservative" than London in the area of nuclear disarmament, allowing for a French-U.S. convergence at the 2000 and 2005 NPT Review Conferences. France's interpretation of Article VI of the NPT and of the commitments made in 2005 (the "13 Steps") is much closer to that of the Bush administration than of that of the UK government. It intends to retain nuclear weapons as long as it judges it necessary for its security. Also, France maintains a wider range of nuclear options than the United Kingdom through the continued existence of an airborne component, which can be launched from land or from the sea.

The three allied nuclear powers do not have identical conceptions on the role of nuclear weapons in their security policies, and there are some significant differences in their declaratory policies. Those divergences stem from both different strategic cultures and the availability of technical and budgetary resources.

There are, however, enough similarities between the three countries about nuclear weapons, and their concepts of when and how to exercise nuclear deterrence, that there is an "imperfect consensus" among them on nuclear policy. The evolution of French nuclear policy since 2001 tends to make the differences less salient than the points of convergence. Three points deserve being noted: an increasing willingness by France to recognize the usefulness of conventional weapons for deterrence and of missile defense; a clear readiness to affirm the role of nuclear weapons to deter the use of WMD by regional actors, including State sponsors of terrorism; and emerging deterrence statements ("firm and appropriate response") that relate more to U.S. (and British) thinking than to the traditional French approach.

French thinking may be influenced by the strategic debates that take place in the United States. However, it would not be appropriate to call these recent evolutions an "Americanization" of French nuclear policy. As David Yost rightly points out, "What some observers have called "Americanization" would therefore be more accurately termed a de facto convergence of some key features of independently developed U.S. and French policies."[46]

WHY FRENCH NUCLEAR POLICY MATTERS TO THE UNITED STATES

There are five distinct reasons why French nuclear policies and debates matter to the United States.

First, the French intention to maintain an independent nuclear stance for the foreseeable future implies that Paris will continue to be able to challenge U.S. policies when and where it deems appropriate. It is not certain that France would have actively opposed U.S.-UK intervention in Iraq had it not been endowed with nuclear weapons.

A second reason is that French attitudes on nuclear policy issues matter for consensus and political coalition-building in international forums and negotiations. This includes the Conference on Disarmament (CD), the Nuclear Non-Proliferation Treaty Review Conferences, and UN Security Council and General Assembly debates on nuclear issues, as well as NATO.

Third, changes in French nuclear posture might affect technical cooperation between Washington and its allies. There is the possibility that Paris and London may be tempted to deepen their bilateral cooperation, with in turn would have a potential effect on U.S./UK cooperation. But there also exists a significant and less known French-American technical cooperation. The two capitals have generally been discreet about it. Former President Giscard d'Estaing confirmed in his recent memoirs that there was in the 1970s indirect American help for the miniaturization of French nuclear warheads.[47] Later, in the mid-1990s, as both countries respected a moratorium on nuclear testing, Paris made public that there was an increased cooperation on security and safety issues.[48] In particular, French and U.S. experts cooperate on high-powered lasers.[49] Any termination or significant change in French programs would have an impact on such cooperation. Finally, the French 10-year experience in designing so-called "robust" warheads may be of interest to the United States as it implements its "Reliable Replacement Warhead" (RRW) program.

A fourth reason is the fact that France's nuclear weapons contributed to Western nuclear deterrence and the defense of common interests. This contribution was recognized by NATO in 1974 despite France's withdrawal from the integrated military structure in 1967. Today, France openly considers that its nuclear force contributes to the protection of its allies, European and non-European. There is thus a potential interdependence relationship between the U.S. umbrella to Europe and the French nuclear deterrent. Any significant evolution of the NATO defense strategy may have an impact on French defense policy; and evolutions of French policy may have an impact on European security. The withdrawal of U.S. nuclear forces stationed on the continent may lead the French to a more explicit nuclear protection of European Union members. Conversely, a French decision to adopt an explicit "extended deterrence" posture vis-à-vis its EU allies might lead European nations hosting U.S. nuclear weapons to question the relevance of their continued permanent stationing. Also, the deployment of territorial missile defense may lead Paris towards a greater coordination of its deterrence with that of its allies. Finally, a hypothetical future French-British desire to "pool" their respective national nuclear forces might lead to a reexamination of existing U.S.-UK nuclear agreements.

A fifth and final reason is that it is possible to imagine circumstances where Paris and Washington (as well as London) may have to consult and possibly coordinate deterrence statements, and possibly nuclear planning. French abstention from the 2003 Iraq war was an exception rather than a general rule. In many instances, French and U.S. forces fight side by side. Since the end of the Cold War, this has been the case at least in four significant occasions: in Iraq (1991), in Bosnia (1995), in Kosovo (1999), and in Afghanistan (since 2001). It can be assumed that there may be scenarios in which the two countries will face an adversary threatening to use weapons of mass destruction, for instance in the Middle East. Also, one can imagine scenarios where France and other European allies bring support to a U.S. intervention in Asia and a nuclear-armed adversary seeks to dissuade them by reminding them of its nuclear status.

In such scenarios, the question of whether deterrence statements should be coordinated will be raised; and in extreme circumstances common nuclear planning may even be discussed. As stated above, there are some differences in the way the three countries attempt to deter an adversary from using chemical or biological weapons. Depending on the circumstances, such differences in declaratory policies could be either a liability or an asset. They might make it more complex to demonstrate common resolve in the form of a joint statement; but they could also complicate an adversary's calculations, as was the case during the Cold War. The same could be said about nuclear options and planning. The French consider that their "final warning" could not be repeated, whereas the Americans and the British are more flexible. But would this really matter in crisis time? There are good grounds to believe that in the real world there are very few foreseeable circumstances where the U.S. and the UK would consider it relevant to embark on a prolonged nuclear escalation. It is reasonable to assume that any U.S., British or French leader willing to consider the use of nuclear weapons would want even an initial, selective use to be the last. Old NATO concepts of "repeating" limited nuclear strikes are hardly relevant to the current strategic context. *Any* Western leader, if and when contemplating the use of nuclear weapons, would want it to be decisive.

Notes

1. Personal communication.

2. "It is illusory and dangerous to claim that they [advanced conventional military technologies] could prevent war like nuclear weapons. All the lessons of history plead to the contrary. These conceptions enhance the significance of conventional force balances, which are by nature unstable and founded on strategies of use, of the preparation and conduct of war. They suggest the possibility of resolving international problems through the use of force and lead to arms races. They are not compatible with our strategy. Far from substituting for nuclear deterrence, a so-called conventional deterrent would only add to it." "Livre Blanc sur la Défense," 1994 (Paris: Editions 10/18, 1994), 99.

3. "In the face of the crises that shake the world, in the face of new threats, France has always first chosen the road of prevention. It remains, in all its forms, the very basis of our defense policy (..). Such a defense policy relies on the certainty that, whatever happens, our vital interests will be protected. That is the

role assigned to nuclear deterrence, which is directly in keeping with the continuity of our strategy of prevention." Speech of M. Jacques Chirac, Président de la République, lors de sa visite aux forces aérienne et océanique stratégiques, Landivisiau—l'Île Longue (Brest), January 19, 2006.

4. «Livre blanc sur la Défense,» 1994, 4.

5. Speech of M. Jacques Chirac, January 19, 2006.

6. The main external providers of oil and gas to EU countries are the following: for oil, Saudi Arabia, Iran, Iraq and Algeria; for gas, Russia and Algeria. By 2025, Middle East countries will provide about 50% of EU oil needs, while gas imports will come mainly from Russia (60%). Nicole Gnesotto & Giovanni Grevi, "The New Global Puzzle. What World for the EU in 2025?" (Paris: EU Institute for Security Studies, 2006), 64.

7. Speech of M. Jacques Chirac, January 19, 2006.

8. "Of course, these [September 11] attacks do not affect at all the credibility of nuclear deterrence. [Such deterrence] was never aimed at countering individuals or terrorist groups. It concerns States." Speech of M. Jacques Chirac, Président de la République, lors de sa visite de la marine (Toulon), November 8, 2001.

9. Secrétariat Général de la Défense Nationale, "La France face au terrorisme: Livre blanc du Gouvernement sur la sécurité intérieure face au terrorisme" (Paris: La Documentation Française, 2006).

10. Speech of M. Jacques Chirac, January 19, 2006.

11. Speech of M. Lionel Jospin, Premier Ministre, devant l'Institut des Hautes Etudes de Défense Nationale, Paris, 22 October 1999.

12. "Livre blanc sur la Défense," 1994, 97.

13. "Being responsible to the nation for the future and safety of the country, it is my duty to remind French men and women that only its deterrence force shields France from the possible use of weapons of mass destruction of whatever type." Speech of M. Jacques Chirac, Président de la République, à l'occasion de la réunion des ambassadeurs, Paris, August 31, 1995.

14. "At the time when we see countries with non-democratic and sometimes uncontrollable governments—one could mention North Korea, Iran, Pakistan—at the time when we see a whole bunch of countries acquiring nuclear weapons, should we let our guard down?"(France-Inter Radio, November 2, 2003).

15. For sources on data on nuclear forces see Bruno Tertrais, "Nuclear Policy: France Stands Alone", *Bulletin of the Atomic Scientists*, July-August 2004.

16. Jacques Isnard, "La France s'arme face aux puissances régionales 'proliférantes'", *Le Monde* [Internet version], November 7, 2003.

17. U.S. surface ships do not carry nuclear weapons anymore. France has currently only one aircraft carrier, thus this nuclear capability will not be permanent until a second carrier enters service, early in the next decade.

18. See "Arms Control, Disarmament and Non-Proliferation: French Policy" (Paris: La Documentation Française, 2000), 39.

19. Speech of M. Jacques Chirac, January 19, 2006.

20. Speech of M. Jacques Chirac, Président de la République, devant l'Institut des Hautes Etudes de Défense Nationale, Paris, June 8, 2001.

21. Speech of M. Jacques Chirac, January 19, 2006.

22. Michèle Alliot-Marie, Audition devant la Commission de la Défense Nationale et des Forces Armées, Assemblée Nationale, January 25, 2006.

23. Speech of M. Jacques Chirac, January 19, 2006.

24. Jean Guisnel, "Innovation française," Le Point, February 9, 2006. See also Laurent Zecchini, "La guerre nucléaire 'propre'?" Le Monde, March 3, 2006.

25. See "Rapport de la France sur l'application de l'article VI et de l'alinéa C) du paragraphe 4 de la décision de 1995 sur les principes et objectifs de la non-prolifération et du désarmement nucléaires," Deuxième session du comité préparatoire de la conférence d'examen du TNP de 2005, Geneva, April 30, 2003.

26. Chirac quoted in Laurent Zecchini, "Chirac et le nucléaire: l'Europe silencieuse, l'Iran critique," Le Monde, January 26, 2006.

27. An initial capability against missiles of up to 600 km range will be deployed in 2012. It will be based on the SAMP-T Block 1 interceptor (using the Aster 30 missile) and M3R radars.

28. Prague Summit Declaration, Issued by the Heads of State and Government participating in the meeting of the North Atlantic Council in Prague on November 21, 2002, para. 4.

29. Speech of M. Jacques Chirac, January 19, 2006.

30. Speech of M. Jacques Chirac, June 8, 2001.

31. Speech of M. Jacques Chirac, January 19, 2006.

32. Defense Minister Alliot-Marie declared that "our deterrent protects us and protects a large part of Europe" (Interview on France-Inter Radio, November 2, 2003).

33. Agence France-Presse, "Texte de la déclaration commune franco-britannique sur le nucléaire," October 30, 1995.

34. Accélérateur par induction de radiographie par imagerie X.

35. Both the LMJ and AIRIX machine will be fully operational in 2012.

36. India and Israel would probably share that view.

37. The Alliance's Strategic Concept approved by the Heads of State and Government participating in the Meeting of the North Atlantic Council, April 23-24, 1999, para. 62.

38. A P-5 statement was made to that effect in 2000.

39. For instance, "maintaining a clear and convincing capability to inflict unacceptable damage on an attacker," in Senate Armed Services Committee, Military Procurement Authorization, Fiscal Year 1966, Washington, DC: U.S. Government Printing Office, 1965, p. 43. MacNamara also referred from 1962 onwards to "intolerable punishment"; see for instance Statement of Secretary of Defense Robert S. MacNamara before the House Armed Services Committee on the Fiscal Year 1966-1970 Defense Program and 1966 Defense Budget, February 18, 1965, 39.

40. Another difference is that contrary to what the United States and the United Kingdom have done in recent years, France has not sought to deter the use of WMD through the threat of making "personally accountable" those responsible for such use.

41. A noteworthy exception is Chirac's January 2006 speech: "Leaders of States resorting to terrorist means against us, as those who might consider, one way or the other, weapons of mass destruction, must understand that they risk a firm and adapted response from us. And this response can be of a conventional nature. It can also be of another nature." (Speech of M. Jacques Chirac, January 19, 2006).

42. This difference in legal cultures was made clear during the presentation of national arguments to the International Court of Justice in 1995-1996, following the UN General Assembly's request for an advisory opinion on the legality of the use or threat of use of nuclear weapons.

43. Indian thinking is close to French thinking in this regard. See "Draft Report of National Security Advisory Board (NSAB) on Indian Nuclear Doctrine," August 17, 1999.

44. The right to self-defense is based on criteria of necessity and proportionality.

45. Loi no. 2003-73 du 27 janvier 2003 relative à la programmation militaire pour les années 2003 à 2008, section 2.3.1., "Les fonctions stratégiques".

46. David S. Yost, "France's new nuclear doctrine", International Affairs, Vol. 82, no. 4, (2006), 718.

47. See Valéry Giscard d'Estaing, "Le Pouvoir et la Vie," Volume III: Choisir (Paris: Compagnie 12, 2006), pp. 503-504. This U.S. contribution in the form of "negative guidance" had previously been revealed in Richard H. Ullman, "The Covert French Connection," Foreign Policy 75 (Summer 1989): 3–33.

48. Reuters, "France Confirms U.S. Nuclear Data Sharing Pact", June 17, 1996.

49. A MoU on cooperation in megajoule-class solid-state laser technology was signed by DOE and the CEA on November 19, 1994. Ignition for the NIF is currently scheduled for 2010. (LMJ ignition is scheduled for 2012.)

CHAPTER EIGHT

RENEWING TRIDENT

BRITAIN'S NUCLEAR POLITICS

Nick Ritchie and Michael Sulmeyer

Britain's nuclear forces have been gradually reduced since the end of the Cold War and its status as a nuclear weapon power rarely features in domestic or international political debate. However, a 2003 Ministry of Defence (MOD) strategy document brought these issues to the fore by announcing that crucial decisions would be needed in the current parliament (2005-2010) on whether or how to retain its nuclear weapons capability.

This chapter frames the key issues that are likely to mark the public debate following the release of the British government's December 2006 White Paper *The Future of the United Kingdom's Nuclear Deterrent*. What factors will decisively affect the policymaking process? What are the viable options available to Her Majesty's Government to maintain a nuclear deterrent beyond the 2020s? What are the potential implications, both at home and abroad, of a decision to retain a nuclear deterrent? Answering these questions will not only bring greater clarity to the debate over procuring new submarines, but is likely to inform an upcoming debate over whether Britain should develop a next-generation nuclear warhead. We begin with a brief review of Britain's current force posture and the current security environment.

---

* This chapter was written before Parliament voted on Trident in March 2007.

PRELUDE TO THE DEBATE

Although the full four-boat Trident deterrent has been active for only seven years, the British government will soon make preliminary decisions about the future of the British nuclear deterrent. Specifically, the first of Britain's ballistic missile submarines (SSBNs) will near the end of its projected 25-year life span in the early 2020s.[1] According to the government's 17-year procurement schedule, decisions are needed in 2007 to maintain a minimum deterrent nuclear force when the current SSBNs retire.[2]

Indeed, the government's 2003 Defence White Paper provided advance notice that preliminary decisions would likely need to be made during the current government.[3] Though no plans for a successor to the Vanguard-class submarines were on hand when the Strategic Defence Review (SDR) was published in 1998, the government asserted the need to maintain potential design capabilities at the Atomic Weapons Establishment, Britain's nuclear warhead design and production facility.[4]

The post-September 11 follow-on chapter to the SDR affirmed that nuclear weapons "have a continuing role in guaranteeing the ultimate security of the UK."[5] The government argued in 2003 that the UK would need to maintain its minimum nuclear deterrent due to concerns over increased nuclear proliferation and the near-certainty that other states will continue to possess large stocks of nuclear weapons.[6] These arguments were presented again in the December 2006 White Paper. Prime Minister Blair has promised the fullest debate on post-Trident plans, though both he and his likely successor, Gordon Brown, have already voiced support for a replacement system.[7]

Understanding Trident

The British nuclear deterrent, commonly referred to simply as "Trident," is comprised of three components: the platform, the delivery system, and the warhead. The platform for Trident is the Vanguard-class SSBN submarine, built by Vickers Shipbuilding and Engineering Limited (now owned by BAE Systems) in the United Kingdom. Beginning in 1993, four Vanguard-class boats were commissioned: the *Vanguard*, the *Victorious*, the *Vigilant*, and the *Vengeance*. Each of these nuclear-powered submarines has a crew of approximately 140 and is based at Her Majesty's Navy Base Clyde in Scotland.

Each submarine's loading of Trident II submarine-launched ballistic missiles (SLBMs) serves as the strategic delivery system.[8] Designed in the United States by Lockheed Martin, these three-stage solid-fuel missiles have a range of approximately 7,400 kilometers and are accurate to within 90 meters. Under terms of the Polaris Sales Agreement[9] (updated for Trident in 1980 and 1982), the UK owns a pool of 58 missiles from a larger U.S. stock at King's Bay, Georgia—home to many of America's Ohio class SSBN submarines that employ Trident missiles as well.[10] The United States has initiated a life extension program to increase the service life of the missiles from 30 to 45 years.[11] Britain has declared its intent to participate in this life extension program as well.[12]

Each Trident missile can deliver 12 independently targeted warheads, giving each Vanguard-class submarine the capability to deploy 192 warheads.[13] These warheads are manufactured and designed in the UK by the Atomic Weapons Establishment and are believed to be closely based on the 100 kiloton American W76 warhead design.[14]

The current posture of Britain's nuclear deterrent reflects the government's commitment to maintaining a minimum level of deterrence. The UK is the only recognized nuclear state under the NPT to reduce its nuclear arsenal to a single weapon system, as land, air and surface maritime platforms have been withdrawn.[15] The 1998 SDR capped the number of warheads onboard each submarine at 48, or 25% of capacity.[16] Only one submarine is at sea at any given time to fulfill the government's minimum deterrence posture of continuous-at-sea-deterrence. The government also recently committed to restricting its operationally available warhead stockpile to less than 160.[17] Furthermore, the alert status of all Trident missiles has been lowered from minutes to days.[18]

Trident's Utility

Trident provides Britain a strategic nuclear deterrent. During the Cold War, the objective was to deter Soviet aggression by being able to inflict considerable damage on Soviet assets, including the capability to penetrate the Soviet missile defense system around Moscow.[19] Then and now, submarines offer an invulnerable and reliable second-strike capability.[20]

With the end of the Cold War and the withdrawal of other nuclear platforms and delivery systems from the British arsenal, Trident assumed an additional sub-strategic or tactical capability. In an operational setting, this would imply equipping a Trident missile with only a single, lower yield warhead as opposed to the multiple higher yield warheads that would be used in a strategic context. Allowing for lower yield detonations, a sub-strategic Trident weapon could be employed to signal the resolve to use nuclear weapons in a conflict without escalating to major exchanges.

Today, however, the role of Trident in the context of Britain's security is contested. Critics of the government's position focus on the absence of any current strategic military threat, and are confident that none are likely to emerge in the foreseeable future that will require a British nuclear retaliatory threat. Such assertions are indeed supported by the government's own 1998 Strategic Defence Review.[21] Others argue that Trident enables the UK to project power abroad with greater confidence than if the UK lacked nuclear weapons or was merely under the U.S. nuclear umbrella. This is considered by advocates of the government's position to be a crucial capability since confronting regional instability, the proliferation of weapons of mass destruction, and transnational terrorism will likely remain key priorities in the absence of major power conflict.

THE NATURE OF THE DEBATE

In December 2006, the government decided to pursue a new submarine platform to replace the Vanguard-class submarines. The rationale for this decision was detailed in the December 2006 White Paper, *The Future of the United Kingdom's Nuclear Deterrent.* The government's primary argument for retaining nuclear weapons is that they continue to provide an unparalleled deterrent against strategic nuclear threats to Britain's interests.[22] It is an argument primarily of prudence, accepting that the future is hard to predict and that continued proliferation makes today a sub-optimal occasion to abandon nuclear weapons. The government also argues through a comparative analysis that factors such as cost, vulnerability, and capability suggest that submarines remain the best platform for the future.

Sources of Contention

There has been discussion of delaying a decision on replacing the Vanguard submarines by initiating a life-extension program for the current fleet. The government has challenged this suggestion, noting that replacing major components of the submarines, such as the steam generators, is not cost-effective, nor was the capability for such an overhaul intended in the original design.[23] The number of additional years of service might be marginally increased, but operational availability of each submarine would only decrease with age, while support costs would grow.

Some analysts have suggested other platforms to host Britain's deterrent. Alternatives include modifying the new Astute-class nuclear attack submarine to accommodate the Trident missile[24] or procuring a new multipurpose attack submarine capable of launching Trident ballistic and conventional cruise missiles along with the capability to deploy Special Forces.[25] The government dismissed these proposals as either too expensive or vulnerable to attack, opting to continue with an SSBN platform for the Trident missile.[26]

The largest point of contention with the government's proposals challenges the necessity of maintaining any nuclear weapons whatsoever and the impact of retention on efforts to stem the proliferation of nuclear weapons. The Campaign for Nuclear Disarmament, for example, argues that purchasing the next generation of Trident submarines violates Britain's international treaty commitments, specifically Article VI of the Nuclear Non-proliferation Treaty.[27] Many church organizations have also spoken out, including the Right Reverend Alan McDonald who asked, "How can it be right to spend £25bn on a weapon of unimaginable destruction and horror when so many of the 6 billion inhabitants of the earth still exist on less than a dollar a day?"[28] The necessity and utility of the British government's possession of nuclear weapons has emerged as the central topic of debate.

How is the debate likely to be framed, conducted, and decided? A host of strategic, normative, domestic political and economic factors is likely to influence the outcome.

Deterrence

The purpose of Britain's nuclear weapons remains unchanged since their introduction in 1956: to protect Britain's (and NATO's) vital interests, particularly from the threat of nuclear attack. Given the abatement of the Soviet threat and the end of the Cold War, however, the rationale for possessing nuclear weapons has been widely debated. Some argue that Britain has no need for nuclear weapons because there are no longer strategic threats to deter and Britain is unlikely to face such threats in the future.[29] Others maintain that the security environment could evolve to feature a state whose ambitions might be best checked by deterrence with nuclear weapons.

It is prudent to assume that the international strategic environment will change over the next 30-50 years. As such, this 'uncertainty argument' is powerful because it cannot be refuted. Indeed, it is the central plank of the British government's rationale for retaining nuclear weapons. It is important to be clear, however, that uncertainty in this context refers to the risk of the re-emergence of a strategic nuclear threat to the UK and Western Europe for which British nuclear weapons are considered an appropriate response, rather than just the emergence of general security challenges (in which nuclear weapons may play little or no role). The government argues in its 2006 White Paper that the potential for such threats to emerge is sufficient to merit retention of Britain's existing nuclear weapons.

Despite the absence of current or foreseeable strategic military threats to the UK, the belief in the enduring importance of a nuclear deterrent 'just in case' is strong. Given the cases of proliferation in recent years, it is argued that it would be foolish to unilaterally surrender a nuclear arsenal, particularly since such a move would effectively be permanent.[30] That the other declared nuclear powers are not actively pursuing abolition is an argument used by the government to cast additional doubt that the time is right for Britain to abolish its nuclear deterrent.[31] Retention of nuclear weapons therefore appears all but inevitable.[32]

Whilst the "deterrence as a hedge against uncertainty" argument will continue to figure prominently in the public debate surrounding the future of Britain's nuclear weapons, for many thoughtful critics it does not by itself constitute a comprehensive rationale for retention. For them, three additional issues are also at hand.

The Special Relationship with the United States

The Labour government and the wider British political establishment argue that the UK should play a major role in global affairs and that this is important for global stability.[33] In keeping with post-war British tradition, Prime Minister Tony Blair is an ardent Atlanticist and firmly believes that Britain's fortunes on the world stage, particularly its security, necessitate a close relationship with Washington.[34]

Of utmost centrality to the British government's security policies is the relationship with the United States. Britain's defense doctrine is primarily, although not exclusively, designed to support and influence U.S. national security policy as the best means of ensuring British security. From the government's perspective, Britain's military capabilities, their interoperability with U.S. forces, and an enduring political commitment to U.S. national security objectives allow it to maintain its own security, have a degree of influence in Washington, and remain a significant force in shaping international security.[35] The importance of political and military credibility in Washington through interoperability with U.S. armed forces is clear.[36]

Britain views its nuclear capability as an important power projection, deterrent, and potential war-fighting tool that demonstrates and validates Britain's role as a powerful and credible political and military ally.[37] Britain's nuclear-weapons relationship with Washington is therefore considered an important function of the closeness of the broader military and political relationship.[38] In particular, Britain's nuclear weapons arguably facilitate its willingness to support the United States militarily in interventionist activity that Britain believes will enhance international, and therefore British, security. They provide a reassurance that, in the process of interventionist engagement, regional powers will not transgress major UK interests.[39] By facilitating that support, Britain's nuclear weapons serve an indirect role in allowing Britain to remain the United States' primary military ally, thus ensuring Britain's security.

There is an important military and political constituency in Whitehall that sees significant risk to Britain's military credibility in Washington in not replacing Trident.[40] Actions that could conceivably have a negative affect on the relationship with the United States and thereby undermine Britain's security will be studiously avoided. The British military may have a more ambivalent view of the value of retaining nuclear weapons, but these will be political rather than military decisions.

Being viewed as a major and responsible world power and the closest ally of the United States is intrinsic to the defense and wider political establishment's enduring identity. Challenges to that identity are likely to be vigorously resisted. Nuclear decisions can serve important symbolic functions that both reflect and inform a state's identity.[41] This can be discerned in the current debate in Britain.

Economics

Economic factors will have an important impact on if and how the Vanguard system is replaced. To ensure the retention of nuclear submarine design and construction skills and capabilities—a stated MOD objective[42]—Britain's nuclear submarine industry will need to design and build a post-Vanguard submarine by the mid-2010s.[43] The industry has therefore been urging the government to replace the Vanguard fleet with new submarines.

The primary economic issue at stake is the potential impact of the new submarines' approximately £25bn price tag on broader defense spending. An argument against procuring a new fleet of submarines is that such funds could better be spent on other, non-nuclear defense activities. However, the opportunity cost of procuring the new submarines is unlikely to be so clear-cut. Although MOD is likely to argue that since the nuclear force is a national asset, these weapons should not be paid out of the MOD budget, it is unclear that the funds allocated for new submarines—which may indeed involve increased funding—would remain available to fund new conventional capabilities in the absence of Trident's renewal.

Domestic Politics

A final element in the upcoming debate stems from the Labour Party's traumatic history of nuclear weapons decisions. Such decisions during the Polaris and Trident debates in the 1960s and 1980s threatened to tear the Party apart. Labour is therefore likely to guard against repeating this history by asserting a strong posture. Party leaders will see little domestic or international political payoff in being the government that perhaps irreversibly renounces British possession of nuclear weapons. Tony Blair's personal commitment to a strong defense, his considerable sensitivity to defense issues after they became an electoral liability for Labour in the 1980s, and the widespread assumption that he has already made up his mind in favor of retention, make it extremely unlikely that non-replacement will be a serious option.[44]

There is unlikely to be widespread public or parliamentary opposition to retaining nuclear weapons post-Vanguard. It is estimated that there are only 30 anti-nuclear MPs in the Parliamentary Labour Party. This, together with Labour's commitment to retaining a minimum nuclear deterrent, enables Tony Blair or the next Labour leader to carry the majority of the party if they decide to retain nuclear weapons.[45] This will be abetted by Conservative Party commitment to retaining nuclear weapons[46] and the probable absence of a groundswell of public support in favor of relinquishing nuclear weapons.[47]

Summary

Taken together, these factors practically ensure that Britain will retain a submarine-based nuclear weapons capability beyond Vanguard, as proposed in the December 2006 White Paper. Yet it is unlikely that these factors will be debated at length by the British parliament. Despite pressure to debate the issues in full from critics on the Labour back benches, small minority parties, and outside parliament, the government is likely to present a strategic military rationale that asserts the continuing relevance of nuclear deterrence in British defense policy in the context of an uncertain future where the UK might face a nuclear-armed aggressor.

Perhaps the absence of strategic military clarity makes the current debate over Trident more of a *political* decision than the decisions of the late 1970s. As such, factors such as the character of the special relationship and domestic political and economic considerations will have more weight vis-à-vis the strategic military uncertainty factor than they otherwise would in an environment dominated by an obvious strategic threat. Nonetheless, the uncertainty that inspires prudence will be amongst the most compelling arguments within government.

CHARTING THE WAY AHEAD

Historically, the executive has tightly controlled the formulation of nuclear weapons decisions. In keeping with that tradition, the decisions taken in No. 10 will govern the post-Vanguard policy-making process.[48] The historical record suggests that the Prime Minister, advised by a select group of ministers and advisers, will play the dominant role regarding decisions about the future of Britain's nuclear arsenal. Issues of national security policy have generally been developed informally based on meetings and discussions between Blair's senior advisers and defense and foreign affairs officials and ministers. The decision-making processes have been, for the most part, secretive and conducted behind the closed doors of ad hoc Cabinet committees convened by the Prime Minister, with the full Cabinet playing no major role.[49]

The policymaking process on post-Vanguard decisions began in 2002 when study groups were formed in MOD to review the options. The groups studied life extension options, initiated discussions with the defense industry, explored options for new submarine nuclear reactors, and began talks with the United States.[50] The December 2006 White Paper signaled the end of the initial review process. One option has now emerged from the process that would appear to have the full support of the Prime Minster, Chancellor, and defense minister.

A parliamentary vote in 2007 will be followed by a formal decision to proceed with the government's preferred option. This will accommodate the required 17-year procurement window. During the first 5-6 years, there will be little financial outlay, perhaps several million pounds on detailed studies, followed by a period of perhaps two years where a political shift may be possible and alternative decisions made. After this period, billions will have been committed to building the new system, making change or cancellation extremely unlikely.[51]

The British government's decision-making is likely to reflect a strong desire to minimize risk. At a strategic level of analysis, retaining Trident ensures Britain maintains her ultimate guarantor of security. British leaders are also unlikely to risk potentially rocking the boat of the special relationship with the United States. Not renewing Trident also risks upsetting the broad consensus between both the Labour and Conservative parties on the maintenance of a nuclear deterrent. Within the civil service, it is likely that the parameters of the internal debate have excluded the full exploration of non-nuclear or non-deployed nuclear options as politically untenable for the current Labour leadership and therefore politically risky for those seeking to advocate them within the policymaking bureaucracy.[52] Within MOD, the path of minimum organizational risk entails planning to retain a comparable nuclear force after Vanguard, given the challenge a non-nuclear option presents to the British defense establishment's political-military identity and the bureaucratic caution and pragmatism exhibited by most large institutions such as MOD. The political incentives for change, then, seem minimal, and the decision to maintain the British submarine nuclear deterrent all but inevitable.

Though the outcome of the debate may be somewhat over-determined, the timescale for the post-Vanguard policy-making process is long. Blair's predilection for replacement may be formalized in a political decision supported by his likely successor, Chancellor Gordon

Brown, before he leaves office, but policy is seldom set in stone. As options, issues, bureaucratic conflicts, and political differences evolve, there will be a number of opportunities for change.[53] For example, how funding for the submarines impacts the overall budgets of the armed services may be subject to revision over time. A crucial variable in this timeframe is when and if Chancellor Gordon Brown takes over from Tony Blair as leader of the Labour Party, and how the debate on Trident is shaped during and after the transition to a Brown premiership.

Where Downing Street's standard operating practice on nuclear weapons issues is secrecy, a number of parliamentarians have sought to expose the debate to greater scrutiny and accountability, including the House of Commons Defence Committee. Advocacy organizations therefore have an important role to play in supporting active parliamentarians, constructively engaging policymakers, keeping the press and interested public informed and, perhaps most crucially, widening the debate beyond purely anti-nuclear parameters and into the realm of Britain's role in enhancing international security.

CONCLUSION

In its December 2006 White Paper, the British government elected to retain a strategic nuclear weapons capability for the foreseeable future. The government's primary rationale is that the future international security environment is uncertain and, so long as nuclear weapons proliferate and other major powers retain nuclear arsenals, it would be imprudent for Britain to divest itself of its nuclear arsenal. Critics have responded that the government has not articulated a convincing argument as to why these factors compel the UK to retain nuclear weapons in the absence of a current or specific potential strategic nuclear threat. This has led to a growing debate on the necessity of renewing Trident, how, or indeed whether, nuclear weapons and deterrence contribute to Britain's security, and the impact of the British decision on the nuclear Non-Proliferation Treaty. This chapter has explored a number of facets of the debate, including several key factors beyond the strategic 'uncertainty argument' that will affect the policymaking process.

Whilst the renewal of Trident seems inevitable, debate about its necessity and utility are likely to continue in the years ahead. There are no correct or final answers to the questions raised by the British government's decision; rather there are arguments based on strategic and political judgement. An alternative method of examining these issues would be to place the Trident decision in the context of a full review of Britain's strategic security policy. This would build on the 1998 Strategic Defence Review and the subsequent new chapter on the war on terrorism. Such a review would frame decisions regarding the future of the British nuclear arsenal in the context of the broader aims of British foreign and defense policy. This context could include: the long-term strategic threats to Britain; the impact of the relationship with the United States to British security; and the role of nuclear weapons in British defense policy. Such a review would go far beyond the December 2006 White Paper and should include a detailed response to the recommendations put forward by the House of Commons Defence Committee's reports on the future of the UK strategic nuclear deterrent.

Finally, one cannot dismiss the importance of the United States on the future of Britain's nuclear arsenal. The UK is likely to look to the United States for political and technical support for its SSBN replacement program.[54] If, or when, the British government builds a new fleet of submarines to take the Trident D5 missile, it will need that missile to endure until at least 2050. Although the United States only plans to keep the missile in service until 2042, it has assured the British government that the UK will be able to participate in any future American program to replace the Trident D5 missile, and that any such next-generation missile will be compatible with the launch system in Britain's new SSBNs.[55] The long-term viability of Britain's nuclear arsenal therefore remains firmly wedded to enduring U.S. political and technical cooperation for at least the next 30-40 years.

Notes

1. See "Appendix B: The Expected Life the Trident System" in *Memorandum submitted by the Ministry of Defence*, House of Commons Defence Committee Hearing on the UK's Strategic Nuclear Deterrent (London: House of Commons, March 14, 2006). The Memorandum puts the service life of the SSBNs at 25 years. The SDR said that the Trident *system* had an expected service life of 30 years—but a definition of *system* was not made. *Strategic Defence Review* (London: Ministry of Defence, 1998), 17. A 2005 RAND study for MOD (John F. Schank, et al *The United Kingdom's Nuclear Submarine Industrial Base, Volume 1: Sustaining Design and Production Resources* (Arlington: RAND Corporation, 2005) says that "originally the Vanguard-class submarines were to have a life of

25 years, and that plan has not yet officially been changed, but the new reactor cores should permit operation until age 40."

2. "Appendix B: The Expected Life the Trident System" in *Memorandum submitted by the Ministry of Defence*: "it would be imprudent to assume that any successor to the Vanguard-class could be designed procured and deployed within 14 years." The 2006 White Paper gives a figure of 17 years "from the initiation of detailed concept work to achieve the first operational patrol." *The Future of the United Kingdom's Nuclear Deterrent* (London: The Cabinet Office, December 2006), 10.

3. *Delivering Security in a Changing World: Defence White Paper*, (London: Ministry of Defence, 2003), 9.

4. *Strategic Defence Review*, 117-118.

5. *The Strategic Defence Review: A New Chapter,* (London: Ministry of Defence, 2002), 12.

6. *Delivering Security in a Changing World*, 9. For more on how the current "minimum" posture was arrived at, see *Strategic Defence Review*, 112.

7. Gordon Brown, *Speech by the Chancellor of the Exchequer, the Rt Hon Gordon Brown MP at the Mansion House, London* (London: H. M. Treasury, 21 June 2006).

8. The Bulletin of Atomic Scientists states that "the load-out of an SSBN on patrol with strategic and substrategic missions would likely be either 10, 12, or 14 SLBMs loaded with multiple warheads." Robert S. Norris and Hans M. Kristensen, "British Nuclear Forces, 2005," *Bulletin of the Atomic Scientists* 61, no. 6 (November/December 2005), 77-79.

9. For more on the acquisition of Polaris, see Richard E. Neustadt, *Report to JFK: The Skybolt Crisis in Perspective* (Ithaca: Cornell University Press, 1999).

10. Michael Quinlan clarifies this point, noting, "Missiles are periodically serviced at King's Bay on the US Atlantic coast as part of a common U.S./UK stock, but the UK share is fully owned, not leased." See Michael Quinlan, "The Future of United Kingdom Nuclear Weapons: Shaping the Debate" *International Affairs* 82, no. 4 (2006), 628.

11. Ibid., 630.

12. *The Future of the United Kingdom's Nuclear Deterrent*, 26.

13. International Institute for Strategic Studies, *The Military Balance, 2006* (London: Routledge, 2006), 107.

14. Michael Clarke, "Does My Bomb Look Big In This? Britain's Nuclear Choices After Trident," *International Affairs* 80, no. 1 (2004), 50-51.

15. See *Strategic Defence Review*, 112; and Clarke, 51.

16. *Strategic Defence Review*, 25-26.

17. *The Future of the United Kingdom's Nuclear Deterrent*, 13

18. Clarke, 52.

19. Indeed, this particular capability was the purpose for the Chevaline upgrade to the original Polaris system. See Lawrence Freedman, "Britain an Ex-Nuclear Power?" *International Security* 6, no. 2, (Autumn 1981), 82. See, also, *The Future of the UK's Strategic Nuclear Deterrent: the Strategic Context: Government Response to the Committee's Eighth Report of Session 2005–06* (House of Commons Defence Committee, London, July 24, 2006), 4. For another useful review, see Walter C. Ladwig III, "The Future of the British Nuclear Deterrent: An Assessment of Decision Factors," *Strategic Insights* VI, no. 1 (January 2007).

20. See Graham Spinardi, "Trident: Tracing the Course of Nuclear Weapons Technology" *Social Studies of Science* 17, no. 2. (May 1987), 371.

21. *Strategic Defence Review,* 8, notes "there is today no direct military threat to the United Kingdom or Western Europe. Nor do we foresee the re-emergence of such a threat."

22. *The Future of the United Kingdom's Nuclear Deterrent*, 7.

23. *Ibid.*, 10-11.

24. It was reported in April 2006 that MOD was conducting feasibility studies to determine whether the Astute-class SSNs could be re-engineered to accommodate the Trident missile. Tony Skinner, "Nuclear Debate," *Jane's Defence Weekly,* April 12, 2006.

25. A number of commentators have since suggested that the Maritime Underwater Future Capability (MUFC) submarine program could fulfill this role. This program was originally called the Future Attack Submarine (FASM) and was established to replace the fleet of aging Trafalgar class SSNs. Lee Willett of the Royal United Services Institute argues that following the Astute building program, "they [UK Ministry of Defence] will look to have a single generic platform able to conduct land attack, nuclear deterrence and deploy special forces," "UK debates Trident sub replacement," *Defense News*, May 31, 2004.

26. *The Future of the United Kingdom's Nuclear Deterrent*, 34-39.

27. Kate Hudson, "We're Not Simpletons. Trident will Breach the Nuclear Treaty," *The Guardian*, November 29, 2006.

28. "Nuclear Fissions Over Trident," *The Guardian*, November 27, 2006.

29. See, for example, evidence by Professor William Walker, *The Future of the UK's Strategic Nuclear Deterrent: the Strategic Context* (House of Commons Defence Committee: London, June 2006), Ev 132.

30. Quinlan, 634. See also Admiral Sir Raymond Lygo, "Are there realistic security and military rationales for the UK retaining its nuclear weapons?" in Frank Barnaby and Ken Booth, eds., *The Future of Britain's Nuclear Weapons* (Oxford Research Group: Oxford, 2006), 28.

31. Clarke, 61. Britain has formally committed itself to working towards nuclear disarmament under Article 6 of the Nuclear Non-Proliferation Treaty but as part of a global nuclear disarmament process involving the other Nuclear Weapon States. The UK Foreign and Commonwealth Office website states that "we remain committed to securing a world free from nuclear weapons. We value all reductions in nuclear weapons levels whether achieved through unilateral, bilateral, or multilateral means and continue to support multilateral negotiations towards mutual, balanced, and verifiable reductions in nuclear weapons worldwide. When we are satisfied that sufficient progress has been made to allow us to include British nuclear weapons in any negotiations, without endangering our security interests, we shall do so." Foreign and Commonwealth Office, http://www.fco.gov.uk/servlet/Front?pagename=OpenMarket/Xcelerate/ShowPage&c=Page&cid=1087554441356, accessed (November 12, 2006).

32. On Tony Blair see Tim Ripley, "Secret Plans for Trident Replacement," *The Scotsman,* June 9, 2004, and Colin Brown, "Revealed: Blair to upgrade Britain's nuclear weapons," *The Independent,* May 2, 2005. On Gordon Brown see Stephen Fidler, "Brown Fires Only First Shot in Missile Debate," *Financial Times,* June 23, 2006, and Gordon Brown, *Speech by the Chancellor of the Exchequer.* On Defence Secretary Des Browne, see Richard Norton-Taylor and Patrick Wintour, "Defence Minister Backs Nuclear Arms," *The Guardian,* July 8, 2006, 18.

33. See Lawrence Freedman, *Defence,* in Seldon, A., ed., *The Blair Effect: The Blair Government 1997-2001* (Little Brown and Company: London, 2001), 295; Geoff Hoon, "Intervening in the new security environment," Speech to the Foreign Policy Centre, November 12, 2002.

34. See Tony Blair, "Britain's Place in the World," Prime Minister's speech at the Foreign and Commonwealth Office Leadership Conference, January 7, 2003. http://www.pmo.gov.uk/output/Page1765.asp, accessed (March 16, 2006).

35. See *UK International Priorities,* UK Foreign and Commonwealth Office, December 2003. Cited in "UK White Papers on defence and Foreign Policy," *Disarmament Diplomacy,* No. 75 (January/February 2004); *Delivering Security in a Changing World,* 8. Jeremy Stocker argues that an important function of British nuclear weapons has always been to influence the United States as "the ultimate guarantor of Britain's political independence and physical survival." *The Future of the UK's Strategic Nuclear Deterrent: the Strategic Context,* Ev 101.

36. See *Delivering Security in a Changing World*, 8; and Paul Rogers, "Big Boats and Bigger Skimmers: Determining Britain's Role in the Long War," *International Affairs* 82. No. 4 (2006), 651.

37. Lawrence Freedman, *The Politics of British Defence, 1979-98* (Macmillan: Basingstoke, UK, 1999), 98.

38. See remarks by British Army Major General Charles Vyvyan, then Defence Attaché at the British Embassy in Washington, in Charles Heyman, "The Jane's Interview," *Jane's Defence Weekly*, July 2, 1997, 32.

39. See Brad Roberts, *Multipolarity and Stability* (Institute for Defense Analysis, November 2000). Roberts states, "A good argument can be made that the primary function of nuclear weapons here is not deterrence, but self-assurance," 13.

40. Arguments about the influence that being a nuclear weapon state confers Britain in its international relations are ambiguous and open to challenge. Sir Michael Quinlan, Former Permanent Under Secretary at MOD, stated that he did not find the "seat at the top table" argument persuasive or attractive. See *The Future of the UK's Strategic Nuclear Deterrent: the Strategic Context*, 16.

41. Scott Sagan, "Why Do States Build Nuclear Weapons?" *International Security* 21, no. 3 (Winter 1996/97), 73. He goes on to state that "State behavior is determined not by leaders' cold calculations about the national security interests or their parochial bureaucratic interests, but by deeper norms and shared beliefs about what actions are legitimate and appropriate in international relations."

42. Keith Hartley, "The UK Submarine Industrial Base: An Economic Perspective" Centre for Defence Economics, University of York, unpublished, May 1999.

43. Peter Whitehouse, transcript of oral evidence before the House of Commons Defence Committee hearing on the UK's strategic nuclear deterrent, March 28, 2006. On April 4, 2006 the *Financial Times* reported that Peter Whitehouse of DML, the company that owns the Devonport nuclear submarine yard in Plymouth, stated "If we are not to see a very big gap in throughput, Barrow needs to be getting on with the design and build of the submarines [post-Vanguard SSBNs]."

44. See Ripley, "Secret Plans"; Freedman, *Defence*, 289; and Philip Stephens, "Politics Calls the Nuclear Missile Shot," *Financial Times*, June 27, 2006.

45. John Keegan, "Britain needs a nuclear deterrent more than ever," *Sunday Telegraph*, 25 June 2006.

46. For example, see House of Commons Early Day Motion No. 149 of October 12, 2005 led by Michael Ancram MP, then Shadow Secretary of State for

Defence and Deputy Leader of the Conservative Party, which said "this House believes that the United Kingdom should continue to possess a strategic nuclear deterrent as long as other countries have nuclear weapons; and accordingly endorses the principle of preparing to replace the Trident system with a successor generation of the nuclear deterrent."

47. The degree of public support for retaining nuclear weapons is mixed. For example, a survey conducted for the Ministry of Defence in 1998, where the question was "Should Britain keep its nuclear weapons?" found 35 per cent said they should be kept in all circumstances, and a further 35 per cent that they should be kept in some circumstances. Strategic Defence Review, Omnibus Survey Report, prepared by BMRB International Limited, BMRB/JT/SK/1153-344, July 1998, cited in Tom Milne, et al, *An End to UK Nuclear Weapons* (British Pugwash Group: London, 2002), 36.

48. Freedman, *British Defence*, 134.

49. See Nick Ritchie, *Replacing Trident: How will the decision be made and who will make it?* Working Paper (Oxford Research Group: Oxford, November 2004); William Hopkinson, *The Making of British Defence Policy* (London: The Stationery Office Books, 2000), 24.

50. See Geoff Hoon MP, *Hansard,* House of Commons, June 30, 2004, Column 356W and John Reid MP, *Hansard,* House of Commons, April 19, 2006, Column 672W on service life extension; R Scott, "UK Funds Nuclear Propulsion Studies," *Janes Defence Weekly*, September 21, 2005, 13 on nuclear reactors; James Boxell, "MoD Tests Water on Trident Replacement," *The Financial Times*, April 4, 2006 on industry talks; and David Cracknell, "Talks Start With U.S. on Trident's 15bn Successor," *The Sunday Times,* July 17, 2005 and talks with the U.S.

51. Personal communication; and Tim Hare, transcript of oral evidence before the House of Commons Defence Committee hearing on the UK's strategic nuclear deterrent, March 28, 2006.

52. See David Weir and Stuart Beetham, *Political Power and Democratic Control in Britain* (Routledge: London, 1999), 171 on the pre-structuring of options and outcomes civil servants and its near monopoly of ministerial advice and information.

53. William Wallace, *The Foreign Policy Process in Britain* (The Royal Institute of International Affairs: London, 1975), 6.

54. It was reported in July 2005 that Defence Secretary John Reid had authorized officials to begin negotiations with Washington on the nature of Britain's post-Vanguard nuclear force. David Cracknell, "Talks start with U.S. on Trident's 15bn successor," *The Sunday Times,* July 17, 2005.

55. *The Future of the United Kingdom's Nuclear Deterrent*, 31. See letters exchanged by Prime Minister Tony Blair and U.S. President George W. Bush dated December 7, 2006. http://www.number10.gov.uk/files/pdf/letter_Bush.pdf, and http://www.number10.gov.uk/files/pdf/letter_Blair.pdf.

CHAPTER NINE
_____

U.S.-RUSSIAN MISSILE DEFENSE COOPERATION AND NUCLEAR DETERRENCE

Eric A. Miller

O n May 24, 2002, Presidents George Bush and Vladimir Putin signed the Joint Declaration on the New Strategic Relationship and agreed that "the era in which the United States and Russia saw each other as an enemy or strategic threat has ended." The two presidents agreed to cooperate "to advance stability, security, and ... to jointly counter global challenges."[1] For the Bush administration, one of the most pressing challenges was confronting the proliferation of weapons of mass destruction and ballistic missile delivery systems.[2] The nation's vulnerability, especially to long-range missile attack, prompted a drive to develop and deploy a layered ballistic missile defense system of various ground-, sea-, and air-based missile defense capabilities.[3] In this new era, it seemed, the development of missile defenses would neither destabilize international security nor jeopardize the rapprochement between the United States and Russia.

The Bush Administration idea was for missile defense to become a cooperative endeavor. After the U.S. withdrawal from the Anti-Ballistic Missile (ABM) Treaty, the presidents agreed to strengthen confidence and increase transparency in the area of missile defense, examine possibilities for missile defense cooperation, and explore opportunities for practical cooperation on missile defense within the North Atlantic Treaty

_____

The views expressed in this chapter are those of the author and do not necessarily reflect the official policy or position of the U.S. Department of Defense or the U.S. government.

Organization (NATO)-Russia Council.[4] The presidents reaffirmed this intention in a joint statement on June 1, 2003, declaring their "intention to advance concrete joint projects in the area of missile defense which will deepen relations between the United States and Russia."[5] After a September 2003 summit at Camp David, they agreed to intensify the dialogue on missile defense cooperation.[6] The next month at a NATO Informal Meeting of Defense Ministers, U.S. and Russian defense leaders started "immediate practical pragmatic work" to identify concrete measures to achieve near-term missile defense cooperation.[7] Given this high level interest and direction, several compelling questions remain. In what ways has missile defense cooperation been successful between Russia and the United States? How concerned is Moscow about the U.S. missile defense system? How would U.S. missile defenses affect Russian deterrence and nuclear weapons policy?

This chapter examines these questions in three parts. First, it chronicles how Washington and Moscow have pursued cooperation on missile defense issues bilaterally as well as within the NATO-Russia framework. The second section discusses Russian perceptions of U.S. missile defense, especially with the potential for missile defense capabilities in Europe. Finally, it examines the ways in which U.S. missile defense progress is influencing Russian nuclear deterrence and strategy. Russian military thinkers are concerned about the combination of more sophisticated missile defenses and conventional U.S. precision-guided weapons, which they believe could threaten Russia's nuclear deterrent capability in the future. From this perspective, missile defense cooperation could prove detrimental to Russian security in the long run, although in the short term they feel confident in their strategic deterrent. As this chapter concludes, missile defense cooperation is more about rhetoric than the reality underlying the competitive nature of the strategic relationship.

TO COOPERATE OR NOT TO COOPERATE?

The George W. Bush administration's missile defense plans have prompted attention of late, but U.S.-Russian missile defense cooperation is not a new concept. In 1991, President George H. W. Bush proposed a new missile defense system, nicknamed Global Protection against Limited Strikes (GPALS) to refocus President Ronald Reagan's Strategic Defense Initiative (SDI) program. Bush (41) sought a more modest missile defense system to provide protection against accidental, unauthorized, or limited ballistic missile strikes against U.S. deployed forces, U.S. friends and allies, and the United States itself. Understanding the importance of superpower cooperation, in his September 27, 1991 address Bush called upon the Soviet Union to "join [the United States] in taking concrete steps to permit limited deployment of non-nuclear limited defenses."[8]

For their part, Russian leaders reciprocated this cooperative initiative. In an October 1991 address, Soviet Premier Mikhail Gorbachev stated that the Soviet Union was ready to "discuss the U.S. proposal on non-nuclear ABM systems," further suggesting "the possibility of developing joint early warning systems with land- and space-based components."[9] This marked the first time ever a Soviet leader agreed to discuss a system that would violate the ABM Treaty. Similarly, in January 1992 Russian President Boris Yeltsin stated, "[Russia is] ready to develop, then create and jointly operate a global defense system, instead of the SDI system... for the protection of the world community."[10] GPALS met an early end, however, when the incoming Clinton administration adhered strictly to the ABM Treaty and focused program activities on the development of theater missile defense.

Shortly thereafter, the Russian-American Observation Satellite (RA-MOS) program was conceived to build trust between the two nations. RAMOS would have consisted of two co-orbital satellites for imagery of missile launches using Russian satellites with U.S. and Russian payloads. Cost overruns, a failure to conclude a government-to-government agreement, and the perception the program did not enhance U.S. missile defense capabilities consistently plagued the initiative.[11] The United States spent more than $140 million on RAMOS between fiscal years 1992-2004; and at the time of cancellation in February 2004, total costs tripled from the original estimate of $236 million. As Lieutenant General Ronald Kadish, then Director of the U.S. Missile Defense Agency (MDA), stated, "we couldn't, at the government-to-government level, make the agreements allowing us to proceed without worrying about barriers that have to be overcome." As a result, he proposed a less ambitious approach, "If we can be successful in the short run on modest goals, then we will be able to move forward quicker on more ambitious activities."[12]

Other bilateral cooperative initiatives were examined in the U.S.-Russian Missile Defense Working Group, which was the primary policy forum for U.S.-Russian missile defense cooperation and transparency issues. It was created under the auspices of the U.S.-Russian Consultative Group for Strategic Security in 2002, and met seven times before its eventual dissolution in 2005.[13] According to Lieutenant General Trey Obering, MDA's current Director, cooperation with Russia on targets for missile defense testing and radar cooperation for early warning could prove fruitful.[14]

Russian ballistic missiles as targets were desirable for several reasons. Many of the ballistic missiles found throughout the world, especially in countries perceived to be near-term threats, are based on Russian missile technology. Moreover, Russia has converted many of these missile systems to commercial space launch vehicles, such as the Cyclone-3 rocket, which could be used for testing the U.S. missile defense system. This three-stage liquid fuel vehicle resembles other intercontinental ballistic missiles (ICBM), affording opportunities to test against targets more representative of real world threats. As a result, this level of realism cannot be replicated using existing or aging U.S. ballistic missiles traditionally used for testing. Furthermore, the ability to test the system using more realistic threat trajectories is critical.[15] For example, test launches from the Russian-leased Baikonur space facility in Kazakhstan would be highly useful for missile defense testing and enable the system to practice against relevant threat trajectories.

Again, the inability to conclude a government-to-government agreement hindered cooperation, much as it did for RAMOS. For instance, with respect to possible radar cooperation, the Joint Data Exchange Center (JDEC), originally announced by Clinton and Putin in June 2000, was to be completed in 2001 to reduce the risk of accidental nuclear war by sharing early warning information on missile launches.[16] However, failure to resolve issues over taxes and liability stopped the center in its tracks.[17] Despite continued U.S. efforts to find agreement on these issues, Moscow's reluctance to come to an agreement is one indicator of Russian passivity towards missile defense cooperation with the United States. Beyond the legal dimension, the fact that Russian radars are still integrated into the operational ballistic missile early warning system could be problematic to Russia.[18]

At a multilateral level, Russia and NATO have also begun discussions on theater missile defense. In June 2002, the NATO-Russia Council established the Theater Missile Defense Ad-Hoc Working Group (TMD AHWG).[19] The group is examining whether Russian and NATO missile defense forces are interoperable and the benefits of interoperability to include how these forces and systems should interoperate to maximize the benefit. A multi-phased approach has been adopted to look at these issues. The TMD AHWG initially created a common glossary of terminology, and then developed an experimental concept of operations (CONOPS), studied the feasibility and desirability of interoperability, and conducted three command post exercises in 2004, 2005, and 2006 to test elements of the CONOPS. In the future, possibly sometime in 2007, it could begin to focus on the design and development of a prototype TMD system. Finally, if the political decision were to move forward, the group could begin to field, train, and exercise the proposed system.[20]

The Russian rationale for cooperation is straightforward. First, Russia hopes NATO countries will purchase Russian missile defense technologies and weapon systems. Russian leaders have offered to contribute the S-300 and forthcoming S-400 air defense systems to a future European missile defense system, including one directed against cruise missiles.[21] Second, Moscow is undoubtedly interested in information about budding NATO missile defense plans. In mid-2005, the alliance established its Active Layered Theater Ballistic Missile Defense program office, which will be responsible for ensuring connectivity and interoperability for NATO missile defense forces to protect deployed forces in theater. Then in July, the NATO Missile Defense Feasibility Study was concluded; it took a broader strategic approach to missile defense and examined options for protecting alliance territory, population centers, and forces against the full range of missile threats. By continuing discussions with NATO, Russia likely hopes to gain additional insight into NATO missile defense planning. Lastly, despite the noteworthy accomplishments of the first two phases, the difficult political decision as to whether NATO and Russia should actually develop an interoperable force has yet to be taken.[22] This decision will likely be delayed since neither NATO nor Russia would want at this time to be seen as the party that walked away from the program. To date the program has not been particularly costly, as costs have been shared by NATO allies, and it has not forced any major policy decisions. Rather, it has facilitated the exchange of ideas between technical and operational experts.

Ultimately, bilateral missile defense cooperation has failed to produce concrete results despite presidential guidance to do so. Cooperative discussions continue in the NATO-Russia framework, but slowly and with few major inroads. A central factor is that missile defense is increasingly seen as a zero-sum game in Moscow. Russia is likely concerned that the United States could gain insight into Russia military capabilities. As we will see below, concerns that this may assist the United States in its missile defense program, possibly to the detriment of Russian security, fuel Moscow's reluctance. As Chief of the Russian General Staff Yuri Baluyevskiy has pointed out, the key is to find cooperative efforts that benefit both sides equally, "We need to shift from declarative transparency to actual mutually advantageous cooperation. Cooperation in the missile defense sphere should not be a separate problem, but must…ensure strategic stability and security."[23] From the U.S. perspective, cooperation for the sake of cooperation is of little value.[24] And while MDA is still interested in cooperation, the failure to resolve long-standing legal issues over taxes and liability undermines this effort.

RUSSIAN CONCERNS WITH U.S. MISSILE DEFENSE

Missile defense cooperation with Russia has sputtered for myriad reasons. Many Russian leaders believe the United States is pursuing a policy of military supremacy and question U.S. intentions for missile defense deployments to Europe.

In a broader sense, Russia is convinced that the United States is actively seeking military and space dominance, and perhaps more disconcerting, that it is technologically capable of achieving this.[25] Russian officials often point to U.S. space policy as direct evidence. According to the new national space policy of August 31, 2006, one of the main goals is to "develop and deploy space capabilities that sustain U.S. advantage…to ensure freedom of action in space, and if directed, deny such freedom of action to adversaries."[26] More directly, General Lance Lord, then head of U.S. Space Command, stated, "Space superiority is not our birthright, but it is our destiny. Space superiority is our day-to-day mission. Space supremacy is our vision for the future."[27] From a Russian perspective the message is clear.

The primary concern for Russia, though, is not that the United States might pursue programs to dominate space, but that Russia cannot match U.S. efforts. According to scientists from one of the leading Russian defense firms, space threats to Russian security "will qualitatively expand by 2015-2020," adding that the United States is accomplishing the "greatest" amount of research and development in hypersonic technologies. In other leading space industries, the United States is "intensely mastering these technologies," which poses a "growing threat for Russia."[28] Moreover, the type of spiral development the MDA is pursuing allows for the deployment of technologies as they become proven. As with any research and development program, technological breakthroughs occur and can lead to further innovations. In the process, the technological gaps that exist today, especially in the field of space and missile defense, may grow even wider. According to one leading scholar at the Russian Academy of Military Sciences, "we should constantly expect new U.S. breakthroughs in the operational/strategic and (or) military technical spheres, which will ensure the United States military strategic superiority by developing and deploying new strategic weapon systems as it sees fit."[29]

Adding to the situation, U.S. precision-guided weapons have fundamentally altered today's battlefield. Indeed, the evolution of U.S. precision bombing since the first Gulf War, through Kosovo, and now in Afghanistan and Iraq have had a profound impact on how Russian military thinkers view future war fighting. This approach was further solidified when the 2001 U.S. Nuclear Posture Review shifted from the Old Triad of ICBMs, submarine-launched ballistic missiles (SLBM), and bombers to the New Triad, which emphasized nuclear and non-nuclear strike capabilities along with missile defenses and a responsive infrastructure.

Russian strategists acknowledge that the initial phase of a conflict is likely to be the most crucial to victory.[30] And in this regard, the United States has demonstrated since the first Gulf War that it will begin conflicts with precision strikes aimed at crippling an adversary militarily and decapitating command and control centers necessary to conduct military operations. Translating this into a worse case scenario, Russian defense planners undoubtedly believe that any conflict with the United States would begin with precision strikes that could neutralize or at least mitigate Russia's nuclear retaliatory capability. "The United States," in the estimate of one senior Russian scholar, "will be able to ensure the delivery of a disarming strike by precision guided weapons armed with conventional warheads against an adversary's strategic nuclear forces and a reduction in the deterrence capability of strategic nuclear weapons."[31] Missile defenses only strengthen this equation, which some Russian commentators believe "ensure[s] the United States absolute strategic domination."[32]

U.S. plans to arm Trident SLBMs conventionally, as stated in the 2006 Quadrennial Defense Review, are a case in point.[33] The intellectual argument can be made to Russian leaders that a prompt non-nuclear global conventional strike asset is necessary in the war on terrorism. But Russians view the problem differently.[34] They argue that while the technological challenges can be overcome, conventional ballistic missiles can only be assigned a very small set of missions and thus such a capability is not cost effective.[35] To smooth the way, Washington tried to gain Russian support for the idea. As former U.S. Secretary of Defense Donald Rumsfeld stated after meeting Russian Defense Minister Sergey Ivanov in August 2006, we "would like Russia to do the same," adding, "I hope that when my friend Sergey returns to Russia, he will call me and say: Good idea." But as Ivanov replied, these plans "evoke certain questions in Russia."[36] The question is simple: why does the United States, with its proven conventional precision weapons, need such a capability? In Russian defense circles, the long-term answer is discomforting, since such a weapon would be an ideal first strike weapon in the initial phase of a war or potential nuclear exchange.[37]

Similarly, the potential deployment of missile defense capabilities in Central Europe is a stated concern.[38] In July 2006, Chief of the Russian General Staff Baluyevskiy stated that potential deployment of missile defense interceptors to Central Europe caused "special alarm," arguing that such silos could easily be "reconfigured to accommodate ballistic missiles, which are capable of reaching the most remote targets in Russia."[39] He added more recently that Russia "cannot sit back passively" and watch activities that could "threaten strategic stability and security."[40] For Colonel General Nikolai Solovtsov, Commander of Russia's Strategic Missile Forces (SMF), missile defense interceptors "could upset strategic stability," and the "fear that [they] could have a negative effect on the parameters of Russia's nuclear deterrence potential is quite justified."[41] For his part, Ivanov has suggested that any such plans should be developed "with maximum transparency, in order not to provoke a desire to hastily create means of overcoming these missile defense systems."[42]

But the primary concern for Russia apparently is not that it believes the United States intends to deploy offensive ballistic missiles to Europe or that a handful of interceptors could threaten Russia's vast nuclear arsenal, a consideration addressed in the next section. Rather it is a psychological question about the potential military buildup near Russian borders. For example, Polish defense officials stated that the installation of Patriot missiles would be necessary to defend any prospective interceptor sites.[43] Envisioning such a build-up, Lieutenant General Yevgeniy Buzhinskiy, Russia's military lead for missile defense issues, stated that Russia had no illusions the activities would be limited to the initial facilities and that Europe would "become overgrown" with new installations.[44] The Russian Foreign Ministry added that the deployments "cannot be seen as anything but a fundamental reconfiguration of the American military presence in Europe."[45] From Moscow's perspective, this entails yet another strengthening of the NATO alliance, militarily, politically, and psychologically. The deployments, thus, are seen as a harbinger of more things to come. In the end, these developments, along with improvements in U.S. space and missile defense capabilities and conventional precision-guided weapons, are of considerable concern to Russian defense thinkers, especially given Moscow's paranoia over current and future U.S. military superiority. The next questions, though, are how this has influenced Russia's view of nuclear deterrence and how this may affect U.S. policy.

ON THE OTHER SIDE OF MISSILE DEFENSE

U.S. missile defense efforts have heightened Moscow's rhetoric, but has this fundamentally altered how Russia views its nuclear weapons policy and deterrence strategy? The answer to this question is mixed. Russian attitudes toward nuclear weapons have changed little of late, and Moscow continues to focus on nuclear weapon modernization and development as a counter to U.S. missile defenses. Russian leaders believe that missile defenses will enhance U.S. capabilities, but under the current architecture, they will not be capable of defeating a large-scale attack from Russia. Regardless, this has prompted debate within Russian defense circles about how much threatened/achievable damage is enough to deter the United States. In light of new missile systems and advanced countermeasures, Russian leaders appear confident in their ability to deliver a sufficiently powerful nuclear strike to deter the United States.

Nuclear weapons remain essential to Russian defense policy.[46] "The prospects for the future," Putin noted, "oblige Russia to view its nuclear deterrent as a fundamental element guaranteeing its security, which... remains one of the top priorities of Russian Federation policy."[47]

Ivanov concurred, "We understand very well that the state of our nuclear arsenal will remain the key factor determining the country's defense capability for a long time to come."[48] This enduring reliance on nuclear weapons is rooted in several realities. First, nuclear weapons provide a sense of superpower status that cannot be afforded to Russia for any other military reason.[49] The overall weakness of Russia's conventional military forces also necessitates a strong nuclear deterrent, since Russia has fallen far behind the United States and NATO in terms of high technology weaponry. In this context, Moscow has even spoken about the possible first use of nuclear weapons to de-escalate a conflict when facing large-scale conventional attack because of their likely inability to do so successfully with conventional forces.[50] In addition to the shortcomings of Russian conventional forces, much of this rationale rests with lingering Cold War thinking within Russian defense circles. Despite any noticeable tensions or indicators, Russia remains concerned with the threat from the United States and NATO, rumored to be part of a new Military Doctrine, as it faces few other near-term challenges (short of terrorism in the North Caucasus).[51]

While Moscow's reliance on nuclear weapons remains constant, U.S. missile defenses have stimulated discussion as to how robust a Russian nuclear response must be to deter an aggressor.[52] In this regard, Russia counterforce strategies, targeting an adversary's military-industrial infrastructure, may be giving way to more counter value strategies, in which population centers are held at risk. Writing in the Russian Ministry of Defense's journal, *Military Thought*, one senior Russian military thinker writes, "If the combat capabilities of the strategic nuclear forces ensure the delivery to an adversary's territory under attack of at least 10 percent of the maximum level of 400 to 500 warheads, the possible adversary will hardly dare to carry out a preemptive strike against the Russian Federation even if it has a missile defense system."[53] Thus, from the author's perspective, even if only 40 to 50 warheads were detonated over U.S. cities, an adversary (like the United States) would be sufficiently deterred from preemptively striking Russia. Missile defenses may defeat some incoming warheads, but they could not intercept them all, significantly raising the stakes of a preemptive strike. In other Russian modeling, scholars have drawn similar conclusions, notably that deterrence will still work if Russia can successfully deliver even a limited number of nuclear warheads.[54]

Moreover, only a significantly more robust system than the one being developed by the United States today could threaten this deterrent, "To destroy the basic nuclear deterrence mechanism, the U.S. missile defense system would have to acquire capability to effectively neutralize retaliatory action by the Russian Federation Strategic Nuclear Forces. But that would provoke the danger of U.S. preemptive strike in crisis situations."[55] Thus, while Russians understand the utility of U.S. missile defenses, they believe their strategic deterrent is still effective because it could inflict sufficient damage on the United States, even if this only involved a handful of nuclear detonations in major cities. In this regard, U.S. missile defense efforts have not fundamentally altered Russian nuclear deterrence.

Technological advances in Russia's nuclear arsenal are another factor that Russians believe ensures their strategic deterrent. Chief among these are newer ICBMs, like the SS-27 (Topol-M), and advanced countermeasures, such as a new hypersonic glide vehicle. As Putin suggested recently, "ABM systems are simply helpless" to these new asymmetric responses, adding that Russia is "not confining [itself] just to these" and "will have a new generation of systems on which ABM systems will have absolutely no impact."[56] Ivanov offered a similar assessment, stating that Russia is "calm" concerning plans to deploy missile defenses to Europe because the Topol-M "can overcome any ABM defenses."[57] These technological measures "were not needed earlier," noted Russian Deputy Defense Minister Alexei Moskovsky, "but their time has come."[58] Citing these improvements, SMF Commander Colonel General Solovtsov stated, "The global missile defense system, which is to be created by Washington before 2020, will have restricted capabilities for intercepting the warheads of [Russian] strategic missiles. It will be unable to seriously weaken the efficiency of Russians strategic nuclear forces during this period of time."[59] Thus, despite the at times alarmist statements of Russian officials, other senior leaders are confident in Russia's current and future strategic capabilities.

While not strictly related to Russian deterrence thinking, missile defense interceptor deployments to Central Europe could prompt Russia to withdraw from the Intermediate Range Nuclear Force (INF) Treaty, which bans land-based ballistic and cruise missile between 500 and 5,000 km. Russia may want shorter-range missile systems that could effectively counter any missile defense deployments in a crisis situation for which their longer-range strategic weapons are not suited. While Ivanov has stated that Russia is not considering withdrawal from the INF Treaty, he acknowledged that the treaty "is a Cold War relic."[60] Other Russian commentators highlight the additional financial costs associated with new missile production as well as the political ramifications from concerned European governments, as was seen in the 1980s, suggesting the measure would be counterproductive.[61] As the interceptor deployments to Europe unfold, INF challenges could emerge, whether for rhetorical purposes to pressure the United States or for the actual development of missiles that could preemptively strike European missile defense sites.

THE FUTURE OF MISSILE DEFENSE COOPERATION AND NUCLEAR DETERRENCE

U.S.-Russian missile defense cooperation, much like the larger U.S.-Russian strategic relationship, has been fraught with irony over the past few years. As Ivanov stated in October 2003, while the United States is not an enemy, they "are not allies either, that is for sure."[62] This attitude has been an undercurrent as Moscow and Washington have discussed possibilities for missile defense cooperation, and ultimately this sentiment thwarted cooperation. As one Russian observer noted concerning missile defense cooperation, "The brief political rapprochement brought about by President Putin's solidarity stance after September 11 was not sustainable against the deep-running attitudes of distrust within the military and political elites of the two countries."[63] As a result, the technical discussions that some DOD officials eagerly pursued never got beyond higher-level policy and legal considerations. The future of NATO-Russia cooperation is similarly unclear. As the United States continues to enhance its missile defense capabilities into the future, the likelihood for real cooperation with Russia will diminish even further. Russian perceived security interests have forestalled any real achievements.

Ultimately, the Bush administration witnessed the birth and death of post-ABM Treaty missile defense cooperation with Russia. In 2002, when discussions about missile defense cooperation began, the United States was still in the testing, development, and planning phase of its missile defense system. This cooperative impulse was also fueled by post September 11 security cooperation between Washington and Moscow and a feeling of true mutual partnership. But only a few years later that intent was successfully translated into actual deployment of some initial missile defense assets. Moreover, as the U.S. system evolved, the prospects for additional deployment and assets abroad grew as well, with Central Europe possibly the next site for placement of interceptors and sensors. Moscow is a spectator for many of these decisions, and it will likely move forward as long as Washington and its allies (and their publics) agree. Left with few political, military, and diplomatic options, Moscow's increased rhetoric about the destabilizing effect of such deployments is not surprising.

In retrospect, the past few years have been a transition period for larger strategic questions. The cooperative impulse of 2002, and the subsequent realities that followed, have changed the discourse between Russian and U.S. policy makers – a cooperative discourse unlikely to return in the near future. During this transition, U.S. missile defense efforts have not significantly altered Russian deterrence and nuclear weapons policy, despite some political rhetoric to the contrary, which the United States cannot ignore. Russian leaders and strategists continue to grapple with the numerous military challenges and competing priorities facing the country, and countering U.S. missile defenses is one of many with which to contend. However, as many Russian leaders have pointed out, the strategic weapons' modernization already under way is essential to ensuring Russia's nuclear deterrent in the future and simultaneously will ensure that U.S. missile defenses will not pose a threat to Russia's nuclear deterrent. Whether that dynamic changes in the future depends on: how relations between Washington and Moscow unfold, how effective Russia's nuclear weapon modernization and development turn out to be, and how the U.S. missile defense program progresses. Only time (and technology) will tell.

Notes

1. "Joint Declaration on the New Strategic Relationship," May 24, 2002, http://www.whitehouse.gov/news/releases/2002/05/20020524-2.html.

2. The White House, *National Strategy to Combat Weapons of Mass Destruction*, December 2002, 1, http://www.whitehouse.gov/news/releases/2002/12/ WMDStrategy.pdf; The White House, *The National Security Strategy of the United States of America*, September 2002, 16 http://www.whitehouse.gov/nsc/ nss.pdf; and J.D. Crouch, Assistant Secretary of Defense for International Security Policy, "Special Briefing on the Nuclear Posture Review," January 9, 2002, http://www.defenselink.mil/news/Jan2002/t01092002_t0109npr.html.

3. As Bush stated in December 2001: "We know that the terrorists, and some of those who support them, seek the ability to deliver death and destruction to our doorstep via missile. And we must have the freedom and the flexibility to develop effective defenses against those attacks." See "President Discusses National Missile Defense," December 13, 2001, http://www.whitehouse.gov/news/releases/2001/12/20011213-4.html. The mission of the Missile Defense Agency is "to develop an integrated, layered Ballistic Missile Defense System to defend the United States, its deployed forces, allies, and friends from ballistic missiles of all ranges and in all phase of flight." For an overview of the U.S. planned missile defense system, see "A Day in the Life of the BMDS," http://www.mda.mil/mdalink/pdf/bmdsbook.pdf. See also Peppi Debiaso, "Proliferation, Missile Defense, and the Conduct of Modern War," *Comparative Strategy* 25, no. 3 (2006): 157-72.

4. "Joint Declaration on the New Strategic Relationship."

5. "Joint Declaration by President Bush and President Putin," June 1, 2003, http://www.whitehouse.gov/news/releases/2003/06/20030601-1.html.

6. "President Bush Meets with Russian President Putin at Camp David," September 27, 2003, http://www.whitehouse.gov/news/releases/2003/09/20030927-2.html.

7. "Press Briefing by Sergei Ivanov," October 9, 2003, http://www.nato.int/docu/speech/2003/s031009c.htm.

8. Pavel Podvig, "A History of the ABM Treaty in Russia," Project on New Approaches to Russian Security (PONARS) Policy Memo No. 109 (February 2000). For an overview of Bush's views on superpower cooperation see, Eric A. Miller and Steve A. Yetiv, "The New World Order in Theory and Practice: The Bush Administration's Worldview in Transition," *Presidential Studies Quarterly* 31, no.1 (2001): 56-68.

9. Podvig, "A History of the ABM Treaty."

10. Ibid.

11. Andrey Lebedev, "We are Building a BMD System for Every Contingency," *Izvestiya*, November 20, 2003, translated in Open Source Center (OSC), formerly Foreign Broadcast Information Service, Doc ID: CEP20031231000142.

12. Michael Sirak, "New Approach Urged on Shared BMD Strategy by Russia and US," *Jane's Defense Weekly*, July 14, 2004, 7.

13. "Joint Declaration on the New Strategic Relationship."

14. See Public Statement of Lieutenant General Trey Obering, "Missile Defense Program and FY2006 Budget," spring 2005, 20, http://www.mda.mil/mdalink/pdf/spring05.pdf; Jeremy Singer, "MDA Proposals Include Russian-Based Early Warning Radar," *Space News*, June 21, 2004, 8; and Jeremy Singer,

"Weldon Presses Missile Defense Cooperation with Russia," *Space News*, March 7, 2005, 6. At a much lower cooperative level, the Theater Missile Defense Exercise (TMDEX) is an unclassified, computer-based exercise program managed by the Joint Staff. The program began in 1994, and five U.S.-Russian exercises have been conducted. Within the TMDEX framework, the United States and Russia have also conducted technical discussions on developing an unclassified missile defense modeling and simulation capability.

15. MDA has increasingly been trying to conduct more realistic testing to enhance the system's capability. On March 15, 2005, Lieutenant General Obering commented before the House Armed Services Strategic Forces Subcommittee that he will add "new test objectives and [use] more complex scenarios." Before the Senate Armed Forces Strategic Forces Subcommittee on April 7, 2005, David Duma, Department of Defense (DOD) acting director for operational test and evaluation, emphasized the need for more "operational realism" in missile defense testing.

16. Eric Rosenberg, "U.S.-Russian War Center Still Stalled," *Arizona Republic*, April 9, 2006. See also Pavel Podvig, "Reducing the Risk of Accidental Launch: Time for New Approach?" PONARS Policy Memo No. 328 (November 2004).

17. For an overview of the original JDEC mission intent and negotiations see, Alexei Arbatov and Vladimir Dvorkin, *Beyond Nuclear Deterrence: Transforming the U.S.-Russian Equation* (Washington, D.C.: Carnegie Endowment for International Peace, 2006), 143-48.

18. This has not stopped Russian officials from stating that their early warning radars could be useful in the development of a European missile defense system. During a recent interview about possibilities for Russian-European missile defense cooperation, General Vladimir Mikhailov, Commander of the Russian Air Force, stated that "our radar systems for early warning about a missile attack, differing from the American systems, cover the missile-dangerous sectors for the majority of the countries of Europe." See Viktor Ruchkin, "An Anti-Ballistic Missile System for Europe," *Krasnaya Zvezda*, December 1, 2006, translated in OSC, Doc ID: CEP20061201330001. Russia may be concerned that U.S. technical experts could identify shortcomings in the early warning system – a factor they are already sensitive to today. For instance, Russia military and political leaders have reacted strongly to articles by Keir Lieber and Daryl Press, which pointed to the ineffectiveness of the Russian early warning system. See "Replying to Foreign Affairs Article, Expert Mulls Nuclear Arms Programs," *Krasnaya Zvezda*, April 12, 2006, translated in OSC, Doc ID: CEP20060411330004; and "Russian Media See Article on U.S. Nuclear Primacy as Provocation," OSC Analysis, April 3, 2006, in Doc ID: CEF20060403324001. The original articles can be found in Keir A. Lieber and Daryl G. Press, "The

Rise of U.S. Nuclear Primacy," *Foreign Affairs* 85, no. 2 (2006): 42-54; and idem, "The End of MAD? The Nuclear Dimension of U.S. Primacy," *International Security* 30, no. 4 (2006): 7-44.

19. Statement of the NATO-Russia Council at the level of Defense Ministers, June 6, 2002, http://www.nato.int/docu/pr/2002/p020606e.htm.

20. For an overview of this cooperation see, "A NATO-Russia Exercise to Take Place in Moscow," *NATO Press Release*, no. 121, October 12, 2006, http://www.nato.int/docu/pr/2006/p06-121e.htm; "NATO and Russia to Conduct Joint Theater Missile Defense Exercise," *NATO Press Release*, no. 034, March 9, 2005, http://152.152.96.1/docu/pr/2005/p05-034e.htm; and Robert Bell, Chairman of the NATO-Russia Council Ad-Hoc Working Group on Theater Missile Defense, "Ballistic Missile Threats: A NATO-Russia Strategic Challenge," *Krasnaya Zvezda*, February 27, 2003, http:///www.nato.int/docu/articles/2003/a030227a.htm.

21. "Russia Proposes Missile Defense Cooperation with Europe," *Moscow Agentstvo Voyennykh Novostey*, December 5, 2006, translated in OSC, Doc ID: CEP20061205950236; Ruchkin, "An Anti-Ballistic Missile System for Europe"; and Richard Weitz, *Revitalizing US-Russian Security Cooperation: Practice Measures* (London: Routledge, 2005), 70.

22. For an earlier look at this cooperation see, Alla Kassyanova, "Russian-European Cooperation on TMD: Russian Hopes and European Transatlantic Experience," *The Nonproliferation Review* (Fall-Winter 2003): 1-13.

23. Yuriy Baluyevskiy, "About the United States: What's Next? Who Needs a Missile Defense Umbrella and Why?" *Voyenno-Promyshlennyy Kuryer*, July 26, 2006, translated in OSC, Doc ID: CEP20060725436001.

24. As Lieutenant General Kadish stated, "We don't want to invest in it just to do international cooperation. We want to invest in it so that we get the benefit to our allies as well as us." Marc Selinger, "MDA: International Cooperation Must have Tangible Benefits," *Aerospace Daily and Defense Report*, June 25, 2004.

25. Aleksandr Gorshkov, "Exploration of a New Theater of War," *Nezavisimoye Voyennoye Obozreniye*, July 28, 2006, translated in OSC, Doc ID: CEP20060728436004.

26. Office of Science and Technology Policy, "U.S. National Space Policy," August 31, 2006, http://www.ostp.gov/html/US%20National%20Space%20Policy.pdf.

27. Tim Weiner, "Air Force Seeks Bush's Approval for Space Weapons Programs," *The New York Times*, May 18, 2005.

28. V. Fateyev, S. Sukhanov, V. Omelchuk, "The Threats to Russia's Security are Growing," *Vozdushno-Kosmicheskaya Oborona*, translated in OSC, Doc ID: CEP20060822330001.

29. V. V. Korobushin, "Russia's Strategic Deterrence: Security Functions and Development Prospects," *Military Thought* 14, no. 3 (2005): 10.

30. S. A. Bogdanov, "Military Art: Features of the Initial Period of Past and Future Wars," *Voyennaya Mysl*, March 1, 2003, translated in OSC, Doc ID: CEP20030609000350; and A. N. Zakharov, "Desert Fox Operations: Development of Strategy and Operational Art," *Military Thought*, September 1, 1999. Some Russian observers have argued that precision-guided weapons are inherently offensive weapons designed to be used, as their deterrent capability has yet to be proven. See, for example, Vladimir Belous, "High-Precision Weapons: Deterrence or War?" *Nezavisimoye Voyennoye Obozreniye*, March 18, 2005, translated in OSC, Doc ID: CEP20050318000308.

31. Korobushin, "Russia's Strategic Deterrence," 15.

32. V.V. Sukhorutchenko and S.V. Kreydin, "Topical Aspects of Nuclear Deterrence and Strategic Nuclear Sufficiency," *Military Thought* 13, no. 3 (2004): 17.

33. U.S. DOD, *Quadrennial Defense Review Report*, February 6, 2006, 6, http://www.defenselink.mil/pubs/pdfs/QDR20060203.pdf. For an overview of Russian concerns with conventional Trident SLBMs see, Pavel Podvig, "Russia and the Prompt Global Strike Plan," PONARS Policy Memo No.417 (December 2006).

34. Putin in his May 2006 State of the Union Address emphasized the destabilizing effect of non-nuclear ballistic missiles, noting "the launch of such a missile could provoke an inappropriate response from one of the nuclear powers, [and] could provoke a full-scale counterattack using strategic nuclear forces." See his "Annual Address to the Federal Assembly of the Russian Federation," May 10, 2006, http://www.kremlin.ru/eng/speeches/2006/05/10/1823_type70029type82912_105566.shtml.

35. See, for example, Artur Blinov and Vladimir Mukhin, "Missile Haggling in Alaska," *Nezavisimaya Gazeta*, August 29, 2006, translated in OSC, Doc ID: CEP20060829379001; and Vladimir Belous, "They are Not Suitable for Combating Terrorism," *Nezavisimoye Voyennoye Obozreniye*, July 28, 2006, translated in OSC, Doc ID: CEP20060728436002.

36. Dmitriy Litovkin, "Rumsfeld Received Our Full Nuclear Response to the Proposal to Deliver Ballistic Missile Strikes Against Terrorists," *Izvestiya*, August 29, 2006, translated in OSC, Doc ID: CEP20060829380003.

37. Despite Putin's statements, many Russians downplay the destabilizing effect of such weapons, since as one observer noted, "attacking Russian territory with one missile is senseless." In the words of Vladimir Dvorkin, a former head of the Fourth Central Scientific Research Institute, "there will be no 'inadequate' reaction to a single missile launch." See Ibid; and Kseniya Fokina,

"Friendship between Warheads," *Gazeta*, August 29, 2006, translated in OSC, Doc ID: CEP20060829380002.

38. Similar concerns were voiced when the United States and Denmark agreed to upgrade the Thule early warning radar in Greenland. See Alla Kassyanova, "Russia: In Search of Strategy, in Search of Self," *Contemporary Security Policy* 26, no. 3 (2005): 666.

39. Baluyevskiy, "About the United States"; and "Russian Minister Warns of Need to Focus on U.S. Defense Motives," *Moscow Agentstvo Voyennykh Novostey*, June 7, 2006, translated in OSC, Doc ID: CEP20060607950095.

40. "U.S. Base in Czech Republic 'May Threaten' Russia's Strategic Stability," *Prague Pravo*, January 23, 2007, translated in OSC, Doc ID: EUP200701244035002; and "U.S. Plan to Build Missile Defense in Europe A Mistake," *Interfax*, December 13, 2006, translated in OSC, Doc ID: CEP20061213950299.

41. "Russian Missile Commander: U.S. Missile Defense Threatens Russia's Security," *Interfax*, April 22, 2006, translated in OSC, Doc ID: CEP20060422029045.

42. Aleksandr Sadchikov, "Poetry and Missile: U.S. and Russian Defense Ministers Find Topics in Common," *Izvestiya*, August 29, 2005, translated in OSC, Doc ID: CEP20060829035002.

43. Jacek Przybylski, "Poland Needs Patriots," *Rzeczpospolita*, September 5, 2005, translated in OSC, Doc ID: EUP20060905095005. For an overview of Polish thinking on missile defense issues see, Rafal Domisiewicz and Slawomir Kaminski, "Poland: Waiting for Washington," *Contemporary Security Policy* 26, no. 3 (2005): 571-87.

44. "Russia Promises to Adequately Respond to U.S. Missile Defense Efforts in Europe," *Moscow Agentstvo Voyennykh Novostey*, January 16, 2007, translated in OSC, Doc ID: CEP20070116950078; and "Deployment of U.S. Missile Defense System in Europe Seen as a Threat," *Izvestiya*, October 17, 2006, translated in OSC, Doc ID: CEP20061017021009.

45. "U.S. Antimissile Base Will Affect Russian Military Planning," *ITAR-TASS*, January 26, 2007, translated in OSC, Doc ID: CEP20070126950164.

46. According to Russia's April 2000 Military Doctrine, "The Russian Federation reserves the right to use nuclear weapons in response to the use of nuclear and other types of weapons of mass destruction against it and (or) its allies, as well as in response to large-scale aggression utilizing conventional weapons in situations critical to the national security of the Russian Federation." The 2000 Russian Military Doctrine was reprinted in *Arms Control Today* 30, no. 4 (2000).

47. "Russian Nuclear Deterrent a Key Element in Security Policy," *Interfax*, March 29, 2006, translated in OSC, Doc ID: CEP20060330950105.

48. "Russia Developing Unbeatable Strategic Weapons," *ITAR-TASS*, June 20, 2006, translated in OSC, Doc ID: CEP20060620950399.

49. Aleksandr Makayev, "Russia: Debate on Superiority of Liquid-Fuel Strategic Nuclear Ballistic Missiles Continued," *Krasnaya Zvezda*, February 5, 2005, translated in OSC, Doc ID: CEP20050204000315; Oleg Falichev, "Russia: Editorial Remarks for Reprinted Interview with RVSN Commander Solovtsov," *Krasnaya Zvezda*, January 12, 2005, translated in OSC, Doc ID: CEP20050111000292; David Holley, "Russia Seeks Safety in Nuclear Arms," *Los Angeles Times*, December 6, 2004, 1; and Andrey Piontovskiy, "Russian 'Impasse' on NMD Blamed on Putin's Anti-U.S. Policy," *Segodnya*, February 14, 2001, translated in OSC, Doc ID: CEP20010214000117.

50. For an overview see, Mark Schneider, *The Nuclear Forces and Doctrine of the Russian Federation* (Fairfax, VA: National Institute Press, 2006), 19-22.

51. See Aleksey Demyanov, "More Than a Doctrine," *Moscow Lenta.ru*, September 19, 2006, translated in OSC, Doc ID: 20060920330001. Similarly, after the publication of "Urgent Tasks of the Development of the Russian Federation Armed Forces" in October 2003, the first doctrinal publication of the Putin government, Duma Deputy Committee Chairman Aleksei Arbatov noted that "although the main enemy is not named, it is clear from everything said that the main enemy is considered to be the United States and NATO as before. The wars predicted are global and nuclear, and wide-scale combat operations are foreseen." In February 2004, Baluyevksiy also stated clearly that "if one reads between the lines, it says the principal enemy is America and the entire NATO." Cited in Schneider, *The Nuclear Forces and Doctrine of the Russian Federation*, 7.

52. For discussions of possible nuclear reductions and their impact on deterrence see, Stephen J. Cimbala, "Russia and Missile Defenses," *Journal of Slavic Military Studies* 19, no.1 (2006): 1-24; and idem, "Strategic Reassurance in a Proliferation Permissive World: American and Russian Options," *Defense and Security Analysis* 22, no. 3 (2006): 221-40.

53. According to experts at the Russian Federation Academy of Military Sciences, the critical level of damage that is necessary for deterring an adversary can be assumed at up to 30 to 35 percent of its production capacities and up to 20 to 25 percent of its population. This hypothetical level of damage can be inflicted on the adversary should 400 to 500 standard (equivalent) warheads be delivered to its territory. Korobushin, "Russia's Strategic Deterrence," 12-13.

54. See, for example, Sukhorutchenko and Kreydin, "Topical Aspects of Nuclear Deterrence and Strategic Nuclear Sufficiency," 17-19; and G.N. Okhotnikov, "The Normative Approach in Current Deterrence Theory," *Voyennaya Mysl*, December 1, 2005, translated in OSC, Doc ID: CEP20060403330001.

55. Sukhorutchenko and Kreydin, "Topical Aspects of Nuclear Deterrence and Strategic Nuclear Sufficiency," 17.

56. "Putin's News Conference: Response to U.S. Missile Defense," *Moscow Vesti TV*, February 1, 2007, translated in OSC, Doc ID: CEP20070201950290.

57. "U.S. Planned ABM Defense in Europe Not a Threat to Russia," *Interfax*, December 22, 2006, translated in OSC, Doc ID: CEP20061222950169.

58. "Russia Preparing 'Asymmetric Response' to U.S. Missile Defense," *Interfax*, November 3, 2006, translated in OSC, Doc ID: CEO20061103950097.

59. "Russia Will Respond to Deployment of U.S. NMD in East Europe," *Moscow Agentstvo Voyennykh Novostey*, January 10, 2007, translated in OSC, Doc ID: CEP20070110950015.

60. "Russian Minister Sees INF Treaty as 'Cold War Relic' but Withdrawal Not on Cards," *RIA-Novosti*, April 24, 2006, translated in OSC, CEP20060424950170. One Russian defense official stated that Moscow could unilaterally leave the INF Treaty, citing the U.S. precedent of withdrawing from the ABM Treaty. "Defense Ministry Official Not Ruling Out Russian Withdrawal from INF Treaty," *ITAR-TASS*, August 25, 2006, translated in OSC, Doc ID: CEP20060825950140.

61. Vladimir Belous, "Donald Rumsfeld's Strange Proposals," *Nezavisimoye Voyennoye Obozreniye*, September 15, 2006, translated in OSC, Doc ID: CEP20060915436004.

62. Yuliya Kalinina, "National Security Agent: Sergey Ivanov," *Moskovskiy Komsomolets*, October 27, 2003, translated in OSC, Doc ID: CEP20031027000215.

63. Kassyanova, "Russia: In Search of Strategy, in Search of Self," 669.

PART THREE

ISSUES IN OPERATIONALIZING NUCLEAR STRATEGIES

CHAPTER TEN

STRATEGIC CONVENTIONAL TRIDENT MODIFICATION

SIZING AND STRUCTURING THE U.S. STOCKPILE FOR A "MINIMUM COUNTERFORCE" CAPABILITY

Owen C.W. Price

There is little consensus on the purpose or required character, composition, and size of the U.S. nuclear stockpile. This chapter considers potential road maps for the future of the U.S. nuclear deterrent and in particular examines how it could be shaped around a "minimum counterforce" stockpile by the introduction of "Strategic Conventional Trident Modification."

President George W. Bush articulated the U.S. vision for a "credible nuclear deterrent with the lowest possible number of nuclear weapons, consistent with [U.S.] national security needs" in 2001.[1] Subsequently, the administration has reexamined the role of nuclear weapons in U.S. security strategy and set out its strategy to meet this vision.[2] The Bush team sought to deemphasize the overall role of nuclear weapons.[3] The policy was driven by the need to prepare for emerging security threats and attendant inherent uncertainties. Owing to congressional skepticism of the underlying objectives, fear of unintended consequences, and the more immediate pressure of the post-9/11 conflicts in Afghanistan and Iraq, there has been only sporadic progress toward realization of the vision within the context of the "New Triad."[4]

Moreover, it is clear that the U.S. president's vision for the nuclear element of the strategy, which also stated that "we can and will change the size, composition, and character of our nuclear forces...," has yet to be accomplished. Some progress has been made. Specifically, the de-emphasis of nuclear weapons, together with a focus on regional states with "rogue" regimes and WMD ambitions, has been underscored by significant stockpile *size* reduction of the number of operationally deployed warheads. This has achieved rhetorical and political progress. But this has been matched neither by transformation of the *character* and *composition* of U.S. nuclear forces nor by the realization of a responsive infrastructure.[5] A lack of national consensus on the purpose of nuclear weapons is partly to blame. [6]

Focusing on warheads, owing to the infrastructure bottleneck of U.S. plutonium pit production, this chapter examines the potential evolution of the nuclear stockpile and posture.[7] It examines how Bush's vision for the smallest nuclear stockpile consistent with U.S. security needs could be realized.[8] Identifying the significant decisions that are likely to be made in the near future, the chapter first identifies potential road maps for various options for force and infrastructure transformation. One of these options is then developed in more detail to examine how a reduced stockpile could contribute to a "grand bargain" that could be struck to allow the modernization of the U.S. stockpile and nuclear complex.[9] Such a bargain could link deep stockpile size reductions, the modernization of the stockpile—introducing the Reliable Replacement Warhead and Conventional Trident Modification—and modernization of the nuclear infrastructure.[10]

ROAD MAPS

Although the principal barriers to modernization progress are political, there are practical issues—chiefly limited discretionary U.S. government budgets—that constrain the options for the future of an enduring U.S. nuclear stockpile. Therefore, any strategy developed to meet policy goals is likely to embody a degree of incremental transformation that may be regarded as the summation of several key near-term decisions that employ readily available assets and technology.

The decision includes whether to maintain the nuclear triad,[11] whether to field the Reliable Replacement Warhead (RRW) designs, Conventional Trident Modification (CTM) warheads and conventional Intercontinental Ballistic Missiles (ICBMs), and how large to size new plutonium pit production facilities.[12] Also, there are many choices that can theoretically be made in constructing a nuclear deterrence posture.

One example is the potential to place greater emphasis on counter-value ("city-busting") targeting in planning guidance and deterrence doctrine.[13] In turn, some of these decisions would allow other choices to be made, such as whether to retain, reduce, or eliminate the reserve stockpile and how large to size the operationally deployed stockpile. Owing to the nature of interrelationships between these decisions, tradeoffs may be made among them. Also, tradeoffs may be made between the decisions and the overall enterprise characteristics, such as the time to respond to strategic surprise (e.g. a future arms race). Some example roadmaps—combinations of choices—are illustrated in Figure 10.1.

Figure 10.1 U.S. Deterrent Roadmaps Options

Item	Options				
Force Structure	Triad	Dyad (SLBM / ICBM)	Dyad (SLBM / Bomber)	Dyad (ICBM / Bomber)	Monad (SLBM) Monad (ICBM) Monad (Bomber)
Doctrine		Counterforce			Countervalue
CTM and / or Conventional ICBM		No			Yes
Reserve Stockpile		Yes			No
Pit Production		No			Yes
RRW		No			Yes

●——● Baseline   ●－－－● Minimum Counterforce   ●······● Minimum Assured Destruction

Figure 10.1 shows that combinations of near-term decisions, taken together with some strategic decisions about the nuclear force structure and targeting policy, can be viewed as three distinct classes of options, here named "Baseline" (maintaining the status quo for as long as warheads in the stockpile remain certifiable), "Minimum Counterforce" (reduction of the 'strategic' nuclear stockpile to the minimum size to meet the current targeting requirements and guidance), and "Minimum Assured Destruction" (a small stockpile that would rely on "city-busting").[14]

Choices about one element of the nuclear enterprise affect the requirements of other elements. For example, the large size and diversity of the reserve stockpile allows a smaller pit production facility (obviating the need for a large "surge" capacity),[15] and hedges against future uncertainty of warheads' reliability and ageing effects, respectively. The reserve stockpile maintains the ability to respond to strategic surprise by allowing the rapid increase in the size of the operationally deployed stockpile by the upload of warheads onto exiting delivery systems. Alternatively, elimination of the reserve stockpile—facilitated by the introduction of RRW to improve the long-term confidence in stockpile reliability—could have political benefits, but would likely necessitate a larger pit production facility than presently exists in order to provide a sufficiently responsive surge capacity to respond to strategic surprise.[16]

Although this chapter goes on to discuss the roadmap for "Minimum Counterforce" in a little more detail by introducing the concept of "Strategic CTM", it is important to note that, although the current administration has a strategy for only some of the component parts of the nuclear element of the New Triad, an overall plan has yet to be fully agreed with Congress. There is some doubt whether this can realistically be achieved, if the current incremental decision-making process continues.[17] Hence the need for a "grand bargain", where the elected representatives of the American people can see an overall strategy that not only meets the technical needs of the stockpile and the New Triad, but the other dimensions of the nation's nuclear ("strategic") deterrent.[18]

Before detailing the "minimum counterforce" approach to the realization of the U.S. policy vision, the stockpile characteristics—purpose, character, composition, and size—are briefly reviewed. Although the size of the stockpile is not necessarily the best way of characterizing deterrence and nonproliferation effects, it remains an emotive symbol of the U.S. posture and has great bearing on infrastructure modernization. It is therefore the central topic for this chapter.

The introduction of Strategic CTM would help realize two policy objectives which might otherwise be characterized as being in conflict with each other. First, it will appeal to those who believe that fewer nuclear weapons in the world cannot be a bad thing and value overt commitments to article VI of the Nonproliferation Treaty (NPT) and thus its contribution to the current U.S. policy of "the lowest possible number of nuclear weapons..." is attractive. Second, the stockpile reductions could contribute to a political "grand bargain" to allow the necessary modernization of the U.S. nuclear stockpile and infrastructure and reinvigoration of its human capital. Therefore the proposal should also appeal to those who value a strong strategic deterrent.[19]

STOCKPILE CHARACTERISTICS

Purpose and Character

Regardless of any academic debate, it would seem that the purpose of the stockpile will remain unchanged for the foreseeable future. Although the U.S. stockpile has lost its stark Cold War mission, the U.S. national interest and those of its friends and allies demand a minimum-sized, safe, and secure U.S. strategic nuclear deterrent.[20]

To meet the needs articulated in The National Security Strategy[21]— assure, deter, dissuade, defeat—nuclear forces will not act in isolation of other efforts. However, in determining the force size, character and composition, it is necessary to build consensus on the role of nuclear weapons within this national security construct.

Such an enduring role encompasses: large-scale war prevention; existential deterrence (the deterrence of a range of nuclear weapons and WMD threats against the United States and its allies and an uncertain future);[22] assurance of allies against such threats, encouraging restraint from U.S. allies with so called "latent" nuclear weapons capability, through extended deterrence; provision of escalation dominance and control that allows conventional power projection and conventional preemptive strike options while maintaining intrawar deterrence; and deterrence of nuclear (or WMD) coercion–counter-coercion.

Given that nuclear weapons cannot be un-invented, and given that at least some of the facets of their U.S. security role will continue to be seen as legitimate by the majority of the U.S. electorate, it seems reasonable to assume that the United States will continue to maintain a nuclear stockpile for the foreseeable future.

Nuclear deterrence, whether achieved by threat of response with overwhelming force or by denial, require—to a greater or lesser extent—the following: an underpinning political resolve and appropriate communications with adversaries and allies;[23] and the ability—the credibility—to hold certain targets at risk, as part of particular "tailored" deterrence and dissuasion strategies.[24]

Although nuances of the role of U.S. nuclear weapons may change, the underlying purpose and character appear set to be constant for the foreseeable future. The character will remain principally political, but will include the technical credibility to fight a nuclear war if necessary.

Composition

The strategic nuclear stockpile is currently composed of Cold War era designs. Owing to the test moratorium and the current approach to ongoing stockpile certification—through the science-based Stockpile Stewardship Program—the current mixture of high yield designs that makes up most of the stockpile requires a reserve stockpile as a hedge against the uncertainly of warhead aging and strategic surprise.[25] Francis Slakey and Benn Tannenbuam describe in Chapter 14 of this volume the evolving debate about whether Life Extension Programs (LEPs) or the RRW program best addresses the challenges facing the U.S. nuclear stockpile and complex.

Although previous proposals for new nuclear weapon effects (e.g. RNEP and the Advanced Concept Initiative) and for improvements in ballistic missile accuracy have now been defeated in Congress, critics of any nuclear modernization proposals (e.g. RRW) cloud the debate by continued reference to them.[26] Therefore, if only in recognition of political reality, it would seem that the future stockpile should (and likely will) retain a similar range of weapon effects options as the current stockpile, but not necessarily in the Cold War stockpile ratios.[27] Although eventually the introduction of RRW could change the types of warheads in the stockpile, it would seem likely that these *replacement* warheads together with any retained LEP warheads—all within existing weapons—would maintain a sufficient diversity of weapon effects to meet the roles described previously.[28]

Selective retirement of warheads during drawdown toward the Moscow Treaty commitment (or beyond if the Strategic CTM proposal is adopted) from the current stockpile has the potential to change its composition, albeit within the limits of existing weapons designs (and thus existing weapon effects), to meet current security needs. For example, the ratio of W76 to W88 warheads retained in the operationally deployed stockpile could change.

Notwithstanding these observations, it should be noted that there are currently two schools of thought among proponents of stockpile modernization. The first is that the generic stockpile composition of today (although not ideal) is sufficient for deterrence, as the negative implications on nonproliferation of modernization that involves any new design with new military characteristics (e.g. warhead effects) would likely outweigh any potential benefits.[29] The second is that if new designs are to be put into service (e.g. RRW), driven by the safety, reliability and rejuvenation of the intellectual capital imperatives (which also communicates U.S. resolve), negative impact will occur. So the argument goes, the United States might as well include some new—some say necessary[30]—military characteristics in some variants of the designs to better address post-Cold War, post-9/11 threats.

Secretary Rice's 2006 visit to Tokyo created the impression that Japan sees the character and composition of the U.S. stockpile as a secondary issue. During the visit Secretary Rice publicly stated, "I reaffirmed the President's statement of October 9th that the United States has the will and the capability to meet the full range—and I underscore full range—of its deterrent and security commitments to Japan."[31] Japan's reaction was heartening: "we, the Government of Japan, has [sic] no position at all to consider going nuclear."[32] Outside the context of an arms race, as long as the U.S. believes its stockpile to be credible—as part of an overall credible deterrence posture—it is likely that allies and adversaries alike will adopt the same view.[33]

Size

The planned size of the operationally available stockpile (as codified in the Moscow Treaty), of 1700-2200 by December 31, 2012, and the reserve stockpile of around 3500 warheads, is based on a capabilities-based planning approach. This approach is distinct from previous target-based planning that sized and structured the U.S. nuclear force and war plans around a defined target set (and assigned all nuclear warheads to particular targets). It is judged by the U.S. administration that the operationally deployed stockpile is now sized a little smaller than would be required for a response against Russia under current targeting guidance and large enough to dissuade competition from China or other emergent near peers.[34] It should also be noted that the U.S. posture must avoid initiating a nuclear arms race with China—a consideration that must go beyond "dissuasion."

While no longer prompted by antipathy to Russia, the implicit policy of maintaining a stockpile "second to none" and of near numeric parity with Russia, together with limited missile defense and proposals for advanced conventional munitions, risks the misunderstanding by critics and by Russia itself that U.S. planning is still focused on Russia (potentially with a first strike "nuclear primacy" strategy).[35]But this must be balanced against the benefits of maintaining nuclear weapons as a hedge against an uncertain future. Decreased alert levels, de-targeting former adversaries, declaratory language, increased transparency, communication and signaling, and other confidence building measures such as military-to-military dialogue, have the potential to ameliorate such concerns. The size and composition of the U.S. nuclear stockpile could be changed to reinforce the benign U.S. intent; there is clearly no wish to launch a sneak attack.

Although inherently political, noting the capability-based approach to its current sizing plans, the size of the stockpile in 2012 could still cater to the worst-case reference scenario. Such a scenario would be based on the need to deter or, in the event of deterrence failure respond to, a resurgent Russia or massive attack by a resurgent Russia. Such a scenario is considered by the author as worst case, as its magnitude bounds any other reasonably foreseeable nuclear crisis. Other factors that complete the picture will be considerations for the need to maintain intra-war deterrence of the adversary and other potential adversaries—through maintenance of a secure reserve—and targeting policy, doctrine and guidance. Also, many other aspects need to be taken into account, such as the cost of ownership, costs of ownership imposed on potential adversaries, the number of warheads not available owing to maintenance and other logistics activities, confidence in stockpile reliability, production and assembly capacity, and intelligence assessments of the size and production capabilities of potential adversaries' stockpiles.[36] Sizing a stockpile is truly a system issue.

From the near-term choices identified in Figure 10.1, three generic strategic options are identified: "Baseline," "Minimum Counterforce" and "Minimum Assured Destruction." The table below provides indicative stockpile sizes (numbers of warheads) for these.

APPROACHES TO STOCKPILE SIZE REDUCTION

Next, for the sake of completeness, before turning to the "Minimum Counterforce" proposal central to this chapter, it is worth examining how the stockpile (operationally deployed and reserve) could be further reduced to meet the president's vision. The following approaches—in no particular order—are the most obvious candidates, although it is by no means certain that all would yield net benefits:

Table 10.1. Indicative Stockpile Sizing

Options	Operation-ally Deployed Stockpile	Reserve Stockpile	Conven-tional Trident Modification (CTM) Warheads	Notes
Baseline	1700-2200	3536-4036	0	Current CTM proposals are limited to two missiles per boat for the Prompt Global Strike Mission
Minimum counter-force	1190	0	1120	Based on the assumption that 1700 nuclear warheads are sufficient to meet today's stockpile requirements
Minimum assured deterrent (mad)	500	0	?	500 is about the minimum necessary to maintain continuous patrols[1]

[1]For example see, Sidney D. Drell and James E. Goodby, 'What Are Nuclear Weapons For? Recommendations for Restructuring U.S. Strategic Nuclear Forces,' (Arms Control Association, 2005) http://www.armscontrol.org/pdf/USNW_2005_Drell-Goodby.pdf

- Adoption of a counter-value targeting doctrine (or, under current planning guidance, recognition that the "urban withhold" [37] would have to be released early in a nuclear exchange), and a reexamination of the doctrine of nuclear sufficiency, or adequacy;

- Incorporation of conventional munitions into the nuclear war plans, particularly the prompt global strike proposal, Conventional Trident Modification (CTM);

- Improved accuracy for the current stockpile weapons;

- Development and deployment of the Reliable Replacement

Warhead (RRW) design to alleviate fears about long-term reliability;

■ Construction of pit production facilities sufficient to respond to any future increases in tension or strategic surprise—this can be viewed as a system trade. Which is better, a large stockpile and no manufacturing capability (the current position), a small stockpile with a large production capacity, or a modest stockpile and modest production facility?

■ Further engagement in bilateral or multilateral strategic nuclear arms reduction and control, transparency, confidence building measures and nonproliferation, intelligence, etc.

Targeting Doctrine and Weapon Accuracy

The first and third must be dismissed as unrealistic approaches. For some of the reasons George Nagy touches upon in Chapter 11, adoption of a counter-value targeting doctrine or "minimum deterrence" is unthinkable in U.S. civilian and military planning circles. It is not thought that improvements in accuracy would significantly reduce the operationally deployed stockpile size, although proponents argue that certain target types may be better held at risk. However, again, looking at consistent legislative trends, the political reality is that the U.S. Congress is unlikely to authorize accuracy improvements to nuclear weapons in the foreseeable future.

Introduction of the Reliable Replacement Warhead

The introduction of Reliable Replacement Warhead designs into the operationally deployed stockpile should reduce the reliance on the reserve stockpile, which is currently kept, in part, as a hedge against uncertain aging of the Cold War designs and its potential impact on reliability. This, together with a modest pit production capability, could allow for the retirement of part, or all, of the 3500 warhead reserve stockpile. Francis Slakey and Benn Tannenbuam discuss how LEPs are an alternative approach to RRW. However, even with the establishment of pit production capacity, the LEP approach does not seem to offer realistic prospects for deep cuts in the reserve stockpile size.

Construction of pit production facilities

Pit production is only one small aspect of the infrastructure that is necessary to manufacture and integrate nuclear weapons. However, it is the current production bottleneck. The only facility able to produce pits (Technical Area 55 (TA-55) at Los Alamos National Laboratory in New Mexico) is not currently able to make certified pits at its design capacity (reported to be as high as 50 pits per year). Further, is too small to support NNSA stockpile plans at projected stockpile sizes (requiring a rate of over 100 pits per year), assuming that the RRW program proceeds to development and production.[38]

If a pit production facility of any significant size were established it would reduce the reliance on the current reserve stockpile. It could be used to reduce the average age of warheads and to remanufacture existing designs or new (RRW) designs in the event of serious problems with one of the designs in the stockpile or in the event of a strategic surprise that demands a larger stockpile.

Alternatively, if the reserve stockpile can be eliminated and the operational stockpile much reduced, it is possible that the TA-55 facility could have sufficient capacity to maintain the stockpile. If the stockpile size ever proved to be insufficient, the production rate could be stepped up by the addition of a second production shift.

Furthermore, it would likely be more acceptable politically to build a new pit *dismantlement* facility (as part of a consolidated facility)[39] that could process plutonium components from retired and dismantled warheads. Such a facility could be used to support stockpile stewardship and be a contingency for pit production.

Arms Control

With the expiration of the Strategic Arms Reduction Treaty (START) treaty in 2009 and the Moscow Treaty in 2012 there is ample opportunity to consider further cuts in offensive strategic arms. However, it is the view of the U.S. administration that 1700-2200 is a practical minimum to meet the dissuasion (of strategic nuclear competition by China) mission, so any form of agreement offering further reductions would need to involve other parties.

The Way Ahead

The combined introduction of RRW and the operation of pit production facilities offer the prospect of reducing or eliminating the reserve stockpile.

With the exception of the introduction of CTM, the remaining approaches might allow some operationally deployed stockpile reductions, if the marginal advantages are matched by marginal cost increases. However, based on simplistic analysis, the Strategic CTM approach offers the potential to make politically significant reductions in the operational stockpile with more certainty than those introduced above.

MINIMUM COUNTERFORCE STOCKPILE AND STRATEGIC CTM

In order to examine the lowest possible number of nuclear weapons consistent with U.S. national security needs, two studies have been examined to gauge the sufficiency of the Moscow Treaty numbers as a starting assumption. This is necessary as it is generally acknowledged that the Treaty numbers were politically influenced, as previously noted, rather than having been solely generated from a bottom-up assessment of the nuclear war plan needs to meet targeting guidance—target-based planning.[40]

The studies conclude that approximately 1000 warheads are needed for their counterforce Russia scenarios.[41] Moscow Treaty reductions by Russia and a general decline in Russian nuclear forces may reduce the number further. A percentage would need to be added to this for logistics purposes and a few hundred would be needed to deter China—a highly risk averse state with a no first use policy[42]—and other small WMD states following any U.S.-Russian exchange. Finally, it is assumed that a few hundred more for a strategic reserve would need to be retained. Therefore, it is believed that 1700-2200 represents the smallest nuclear-only strategic stockpile (given its present composition) that would support current U.S. nuclear deterrence criteria. Indeed, 1700 could be sufficient. Also, it is worth noting that the modest inventory of tactical[43] nuclear weapons, together with conventional forces, could be used to deter smaller WMD states with rogue regimes. However, this ignores the concerns about the aging stockpile and potential reliability problems in the future and the potential for strategic surprise (or a future nuclear arms race), which led to the creation of the reserve stockpile. As already discussed, the former could be addressed in large part by the introduction of RRW and the latter by the resumptions of pit production.

Given the above, the challenge is how to achieve the same—or enhanced—deterrence and the threat of nuclear war fighting effects, which could be used in the event of deterrence failure, with a significantly smaller operationally deployed nuclear stockpile, without perceptions of lowering the nuclear threshold. Here the potential role of the CTM technology in conjunction with nuclear forces—here termed Strategic CTM—is examined.

INTRODUCING CONVENTIONAL MUNITIONS INTO THE STRATEGIC NUCLEAR STOCKPILE

The 2006/7 CTM proposal

Provision was made in the 2007 and 2008 president's budgets for the CTM program.[44] Deployment of the CTM technology—two missiles of non-nuclear warheads per ballistic submarine (SSBN)—was proposed to provide a conventional Prompt Global Strike (PGS) capability.[45] This would give the National Command Authority the ability to strike a few targets anywhere on the globe within about 30 minutes. PGS was aimed at deterring and, if necessary, defeating high value targets—such as WMD missiles being prepared for launch or terrorist leaders—that could not otherwise be struck and for which a U.S. preemptive nuclear strike is not credible.[46]

Strategic CTM

However, by applying this in greater numbers of conventional warheads deployed on submarine launched ballistic missiles (SLBMs), the proposed conventional warheads are capable of defeating at least 30 percent of the traditional nuclear target set. For illustrative purposes, it is assumed that 1700 nuclear warheads are sufficient for the current nuclear war plans. The addition of CTM warheads into the existing Ohio Class Trident SLBM submarine fleet, without any change of doctrine and targeting guidance, could reduce the stockpile size to 1190 nuclear warheads if complemented by 1020 CTM warheads (see the calculation below). This ignores much targeting detail and subtlety not available to the author, but the implication of such issues could be addressed by increasing the number of CTM warheads up to the maximum capacity per missile and the potential of fielding conventional ICBMs.[47] If the ICBM leg of the nuclear triad were to be retained in the case of Strategic CTM deployment, at least a further 450 spaces would be available on SLBMs for CTM warheads.[48] Alternatively, 900-1350 conventional warheads of a different design could be uploaded to the existing fleet of 450 ICBMs to augment the strategic nuclear mission.

ILLUSTRATIVE STRATEGIC CTM UPLOAD CALCULATION

- SLBM capacity
  - 14 ballistic submarines (SSBNs) less 2 in overhaul = 12 SSBNs
  - 24 Trident II D5 missiles per boat = 288 operationally deployed missiles
  - 8 warheads per missile (START counting rules)
  - Maximum capacity of 2688 operationally deployed warheads under START counting rules, 2304 operationally available
- Impact of CTM warheads to augment the strategic strike
  - Assume 1700 nuclear warheads (NW's) needed to deter (hold at risk) the worst case 'reference scenario' (targets)
  - 30% of targets can be held at risk using CTM, but assume that all the NW's can defeat up to 2 targets (and 2 CTM warheads are needed to destroy some targets)
  - 30% of 1700 = 510 NW targets. 510 x 2 = 1020 CTM targets
- Therefore same counter force effect could be achieved with 1190 nuclear and 1020 CTM warheads. A total of 2210 warheads (average of 6.6 warheads per missile) would be required.

Use of CTM (and / or ICBMs) for a non-nuclear element of this strategic mission would have the additional benefit of making good use of existing military platforms and missiles that have a projected service life well into the 2040s. Keeping such systems in service would, in itself, be a hedge against an uncertain future.

In addition to facilitating a near 50 percent reduction in the operationally deployed nuclear stockpile, the introduction of Strategic CTM together with deployment of RRW into the operational stockpile could eliminate the need to construct large, expensive new pit production facilities. Making only modest assumptions about warhead life (30 years), surveillance activities (4 per year) and starting with the current stockpile size, a 50 pits per year facility based on the TA-55 facility at Los Alamos is a credible alternative to a larger new facility. However, this does not take dismantlement requirements for retired warheads into account.

Prompt Global Strike with Strategic CTM

In addition to augmenting the strategic strike role of nuclear forces, the introduction of CTM warheads into the SLBM force *could* be used for the PGS mission, similar to the 2006/7 proposed deployment plans for CTM, in a way that would bolster deterrence and dissuasion strategies. Some critics will, of course, observe that such a move would lend credibility to "nuclear primacy" accusations, saying that this lowers the nuclear threshold as it make nuclear war seem less unthinkable.[49] But, to the author, a nuclear war where the world has to live with the aftermath of an exchange of 1000-2000 warheads rather than 1700 or 4400 warheads is no less horrific. And something short of mutual assured annihilation—where some sort of society has to live with the horrific results of such an exchange—might prove a better deterrence in the post-Soviet era. Also, the availability of a PGS option would obviate the need to consider U.S. nuclear use in some scenarios (e.g. preemptive strike against well-located WMD targets). Therefore, the addition of CTM—whether in small or large numbers—would raise the nuclear threshold, especially if U.S. strategic deterrence doctrine were to remain essentially unaltered.

Likely Criticism of Strategic CTM

If CTM were to be integrated in larger numbers than the 2006/7 administration proposal, some of the current criticisms of the administration's CTM proposal would need to be addressed. These are principally the issues of "ambiguity" and "recklessness." For the former, it is argued that launch of CTM warheads in small numbers for a PGS mission (and not part of a nuclear strategic response) would risk accidental misinterpretation by Russia, which could lead to an inadvertent nuclear war. Launch notification and other forms of cooperation could address this.[50] It could also be potentially addressed by (legally required) segregation of CTM and nuclear ballistic submarines. CTM submarines could be operated *openly* in different patrol areas—to address the PGS mission—and only be tasked to operate in strategic deterrent patrol areas *clandestinely* in times of increased tension.[51] Alternatively, legislation could mandate that CTM warheads be mingled on the same missiles as nuclear warheads to eliminate the PGS role and remove the potential for ambiguity. In this case, Strategic CTM would only have the role of augmenting a strategic (massive) nuclear strike. This could either be achieved by mixing the CTM warheads on the same SLBMs as nuclear warheads, leaving no missile with only CTM warheads, or by placing 900 conventional warheads on the current 450 nuclear ICBMs.[52] This would eliminate the PGS role as, 1) each ICBM would retain a nuclear warhead, and 2) the minuteman missile silos are sited inappropriately for the PGS mission.

The likely Russian and Chinese responses to any Strategic CTM force structure and doctrine would need to be assessed and handled carefully, prior to any such proposal by the U.S. administration. Some sort of transparency might need to be considered. However, although these nations might not fully trust the United States, they are likely to view the United States as scrupulous to a fault for declared activities. Therefore, for example, legislating the mixture (or separation) of nuclear and CTM warheads (as discussed above) could mitigate their concerns without the need for extensive transparency activities. A net assessment would need to be made to ascertain whether any such negative impact would outweigh the security and nonproliferation (NPT Article VI) benefits. Consultation with allies would also be important. "Recklessness"—fear that the president may be tempted to use conventional PGS assets too readily—is a political issue associated with Congress's relationship with President George W. Bush. And therefore it is transitory and unlikely to endure beyond this administration. If necessary, this could be addressed by abandoning the option to use CTM for the PGS mission through legislated upload requirements.

CONCLUSIONS AND RECOMMENDATIONS

Integration of large numbers of conventional warheads into the current SLBM fleet (and/or ICBMs) has the potential to reduce the operationally available strategic nuclear stockpile by approximately 50 percent, while maintaining the military capability to meet existing deterrence requirements. The technology, which was proposed for the Conventional Trident Modification (CTM), is already available and could be rapidly deployed at a modest cost. Strategic CTM could also serve to provide a Prompt Global Strike (PGS) capability and make good use of existing military assets and technologies. Alternatively, Strategic CTM could be introduced in a manner to prevent it from being used for the PGS role, if this became politically unacceptable. If implemented together with the RRW program, this Strategic CTM proposal could realize a "minimum counterforce" nuclear stockpile, which could significantly reduce the infrastructure needs and costs by allowing a much smaller plutonium pit production complex to be maintained; this could center on an existing facility.

Whether simply motivated by a desire to meet the U.S. president's policy of achieving the smallest operationally deployed stockpile consistent with national security requirements or as part of a larger systems approach to nuclear modernization—offering demonstrable commitments to the Nonproliferation Treaty Article VI without relaxing (or otherwise changing) deterrence requirements—this Strategic CTM proposal and its potential variants should be investigated in a classified study to examine whether it stands up to scrutiny in a detail that cannot be achieved in unclassified form.

Last, it is noted that this proposal will have its critics. However, the questions before the U.S. administration and Congress will require political judgments, weighing tangible benefits against costs and risks. Issues that have dogged the 2006 and 2007 CTM proposals are to some extent shared with this Strategic CTM proposal. However, the issues in either case are not insurmountable. This paper offers some potential solutions. It is the judgment of the author that the proposals in this chapter, considered along with introduction of the Reliable Replacement Warhead (RRW) program, could productively contribute to the debate and perhaps facilitate a "grand bargain" to allow appropriate and overdue modernization of the U.S. nuclear force and complex.

Notes

The author acknowledges and thanks Jenifer Mackby and Drs. Clark Murdock, Benn Tannebaum, and Richard Weitz and the Senior Editors for their help and advice in writing this chapter and editing the volume.

1. National Defense University, May 1, 2001

2. Much of the Bush administration's national security strategy was well articulated by Condoleezza Rice in , 'Campaign 2000: Promoting the National Interest', Foreign Affairs, January/February 2000 http://www.foreignaffairs.org/20000101faessay5/condoleezza-rice/campaign-2000-promoting-the-national-interest.html?mode=print The National Security Strategy, 2001 Nuclear Posture Review and Quadrennial Defense Reviews have built on such foundations. There has been much policy development since the 2001 Nuclear Posture Review, which has for the most part articulated through top-level policy

documents such as the 2006 Quadrennial Defense Review and congressional testimony. For example, see Statement of Admiral James O. Ellis, Jr., USN Commander in Chief U.S. Strategic Command before the Strategic Forces Subcommittee Senate Armed Services Committee on the Nuclear Posture Review, http://fas.org/irp/congress/2002_hr/021402ellis.pdf and subsequent testimony, for example, the Statement of Admiral James O. Ellis, Jr., USN Commander U.S. Strategic Command before the Strategic Forces Subcommittee Senate Armed Services Committee on Strategic Deterrence and Strategic Capabilities March 24, 2004, http://www.dod.mil/dodgc/olc/docs/test04-03-24Ellis.doc and Testimony of Amb. Linton Brooks to the same hearing, http://www.nnsa.doe.gov/docs/Congressional/2004/2004-Mar-24_SASC_testimony-19Mar04.pdf.

3. It is clear that there is no consensus on whether the NPR set out a policy that actually reduced the salience of nuclear weapons. See George Farfour, "Deterrence: Cold War to Tailored, It is time To Think Differently," *High Frontier*, Vol. 2, No. 4, 32, http://www.afspc.af.mil/shared/media/document/AFD-060912-044.pdf.

4. It is acknowledged that much effort and expenditure has been made on missile defense and C3I.

5. The administration's plan for the RRW and Complex 2030 offer a strategy to meet these aspects of the vision, but it is clear that neither has yet achieved sufficient political traction to receive sustained Congressional support and funding. These are discussed in other chapters.

6. There has been considerable criticism of the previous plans for new nuclear weapons, for example see Roger Speed and Michael May, "Assessing the United States' Nuclear Posture," 248-296, George Bunn and Christopher Chyba, ed. *U.S. Nuclear Weapons Policy* (Washington, D.C.: Brookings, 2006). Continued reference to long-abandoned administration proposals detracts from the debate on current proposals risking entrenchment of a chronically declining 'status quo'.

7. It is assumed that if there is a codified (treaty or written) agreement to follow the START Treaty, which expires in 2009 and the Moscow Treaty, which expires in 2012, owing to comparatively small stockpiles and overcapacity for deployment systems (e.g. ICBMs could be MIRV'd, if necessary), the focus of such a treaty and its verification protocols would be focused on warheads. The START Treaty verification protocols focus on strategic platforms. The Moscow Treaty has no specific verification protocol. The Cold War pit (the plutonium 'primary' component of a nuclear weapon) production plant, Rocky Flats closed in 1989 after having been stormed by the FBI after concerns about its environmental performance.

8. This reality need not be incompatible with expressing a commitment to Article VI of the Nonproliferation Treaty and thus visions and practical steps

toward disarmament, for example those identified by George Schultz, William Perry, Henry Kissinger and Sam Nun, "A World Free of Nuclear Weapons", *Wall Street Journal*, January 15, 2007 and Joseph March, see "Los Alamos scientist criticizes federal approach to arsenal," *sfgate.com*, February 13, 2007, need not be dismissed as utopian.

9. The author is not alone in this suggestion. For example, see Walter Pincus, "Bush Urged to Develop Overall Nuclear Arms Policy," *Washington Post*, March 18, 2007, A05

10. Rep. Ellen Tauscher has made it clear that the RRW program will need to be coupled with a continued commitment to the U.S. nuclear test moratorium, but it is not yet clear that this 'horse trade' will be sufficient political compromise to allow the RRW program to proceed to full development and deployment. Rep. Tauscher summarized the congressional review process for the RRW program in a congressional Strategic Forces Subcommittee hearing held on March 8, 2007, http://hascaudio.house.gov/Strat030807.wma.

11. The nuclear triad, although replaced conceptually by the new triad, retains nuclear bombers, submarine launched ballistic missiles (SLBMs), and land based intercontinental ballistic missiles (ICBMs). It is argued that the three elements provide unique characteristics and the necessary redundancy to mitigate potential system reliability risks and strategic surprise. Some critics suggest that retirement of the ICBM leg could be beneficial to security—contributing to strategic stability—by eliminating the need for a rapid (at worst 'hair-trigger' response), although there are others that point out that U.S. unilateral leadership in this respect would not likely motivate Russia to respond likewise.

12. The evolution of proposals for these and related technologies and the issues facing lawmakers—in the context of Prompt Global Strike—are summarized in Amy F. Wolf, *Conventional Warheads for Long Range Ballistic Missiles* (Washington, D.C.: CRS, February 9, 2007) http://fpc.state.gov/documents/organization/81935.pdf and Todd C. Shull, *Conventional Prompt Global Strike: Valuable Military Option or Threat to Global Stability?*(Monterey: Naval Post Graduate School, September 2005), http://www.ccc.nps.navy.mil/research/theses/shull05.pdf.

13. If adopted, owing to ambiguities in interpretation of the terms and deeply held views in the Whitehouse and Office of Secretary of Defense (for targeting policy and guidance) over successive administrations (and its likely continuation into the future), this should be interpreted as a recognition that any nuclear response against a peer adversary would arrive at the Presidential decision of whether to release the "urban withhold" to allow targets near population centers to be struck sooner than for previous nuclear postures. For a good summary of the evolution of U.S. strategic nuclear doctrine, see Charles H. Fairbanks, Jr., "MAD and U.S. Strategy," in Henry D. Sokolski (ed.), *Getting*

MAD: Nuclear Mutual Assured Destruction, Its Origin and Practice (Carlisle, PA: Strategic Studies Institute, 2004), 137-147.

14. It is considered axiomatic that any deterrent posture and stockpile of any size would need to remain credible (e.g. retain the command and control, planning and targeting functions for use if necessary) to be an effective deterrent. But a) how large does that need to be, and b) what of the deterrent value of conventional forces? Also a small stockpile can conceivable be used to underpin explicit or implicit extended deterrence—the assurance of allies—as demonstrated by the British and French. By necessity the figure has been simplified. For example, a "Minimum Counterforce" posture could include a small number of bombers, which might be retained for signaling purposes. Equally, it is not certain that a "Minimum Assured Destruction" force would require CTM or conventional ICBM's.

15. See Chapter 14, "The Nuclear Weapons Production Complex and the Reliable Replacement Warhead," in this volume.

16. The size of facilities for the dismantlement of retired warheads also needs to be considered. Strategic surprise, by definition, cannot be forecast; common examples include a resurgent Russia and an arms race with China.

17. Walter Pincus "Bush Urged to Develop Overall Nuclear Arms Policy," *Washington Post,* March 18, 2007, A05.

18. It is the author's view that no such bargain can be struck until the next administration takes office, although much groundwork can be laid.

19. For a good summary of "entrenched views" and "alternate views" about nuclear weapons matters see, *Report of the Defense Science Board Task Force on Nuclear Capabilities*, Report Summary, December 2006, 3, http://www.acq.osd.mil/dsb/reports/2006-12-Nuclear_Capabilities.pdf.

20. The deterrent is much more than the stockpile. For examples of other elements of a credible deterrent, see Dean Wilkening and Kenneth Watman, *Nuclear Deterrence in a Regional Context* (Santa Monica: RAND, 1995), 14.

21. *The National Security Strategy of the United States of America*, September 2002, http://www.whitehouse.gov/nsc/nss.pdf

22. Such a justification was well articulated by Prime Minister Tony Blair and the British Defence White Paper, see http://www.pm.gov.uk/output/Page10532.asp and http://www.mod.uk/DefenceInternet/AboutDefence/CorporatePublications/PolicyStrategyandPlanning/DefenceWhitePaper2006Cm6994.htm.

23. For a good deterrence model, see Dean Wilkening and Kenneth Watman, *Nuclear Deterrence in a Regional Context* (Santa Monica: RAND, 1995), 14. The *Global Deterrence Joint Operating Concept,* http://www.dtic.mil/futurejointwarfare/concepts/do_joc_v20.doc reflects how the U.S. military (or at least

U.S. Strategic Command) thinks about and operationalizes (or is beginning to think and operationalize) deterrence.

24. See the U.S. *National Security Strategy*.

25. Some designs, e.g. B61 free fall bombs, are reported to provide lower yield options and other military characteristics, such as limited earth penetration capability. These designs are believed to be retained in relatively small numbers at low states of readiness.

26. Such proposals allowed misinterpretation of U.S. intent leading to accusation of the United States seeking nuclear (first strike) primacy over Russia. The administration needs to set out a clear policy that reassures critics and Russia that this is not its strategic aim.

27. It is recognized that the continued reference to what Speed and May refer to as the Bush Doctrine is technically valid as there has been no formal revision of the 2001 / 2002 Nuclear Posture Review and therefore even when proposals are not pursuing the contentious (and now debunked) elements of the policy, they get tarred with the same brush and critics remain skeptical of the administration's motives. It is also noted that reported developments such as W76-1 have addressed some of the new NPR missions in a way much more acceptable than the previously proposed low yield bunker busters.

28. The RRW program proposal would not change the military effects of the weapons into which it may be integrated. This was confirmed in congressional Strategic Forces Subcommittee testimony on March 8, 2007 by Gen. James Cartwright, USSTRATCOM Commander, http://hascaudio.house.gov/Strat030807.wma.

29. *Report of the Defense Science Board Task Force on Nuclear Capabilities*, Report Summary, December 2006, 5 http://www.acq.osd.mil/dsb/reports/2006-12-Nuclear_Capabilities.pdf.

30. Ibid.

31. Secretary Condoleezza Rice, *Remarks With Japanese Foreign Minister Taro Aso After Their Meeting*, (transcript). Tokyo, Japan, October 18, 2006 http://www.state.gov/secretary/rm/2006/74669.htm.

32. Foreign Minister Taro Aso, *Remarks With Japanese Foreign Minister Taro Aso After Their Meeting*, (transcript). Tokyo, Japan, October 18, 2006, http://www.state.gov/secretary/rm/2006/74669.htm.

33. Such empirical evidence has been challenged by a recent DTRA/SAIC study, *Foreign Perspectives on U.S. Nuclear Policy and Posture*, December 2006.

34. Explicit decoupling of the stockpile size and the (traditional) Russian target base was necessary, as President Bush had stated that Russia was no longer an enemy of the United States.

35. The Russian reaction to suggestion of a U.S. strategy of nuclear primacy and the potential role of CTM for PGS was twofold. The first impulse was to be dismissive and technically discredit the notion of U.S. nuclear primacy and the second, seeing U.S. provocation, was to capitalize upon for domestic political reasons—an excuse to modernization of Russian nuclear and nuclear related assets. For examples of how Russia responded to proposed U.S. weapon developments, see President Putin's state of the union speech: http://www.mosnews. com/column/2006/05/11/PutinAddress.shtml. Another example is a retired General's reaction to suggestions of first strike primacy, "There is no fundamental difference in the fact that the United States is capable of destroying Russia several times over whereas Russia can destroy the United States once or twice... likelihood of a world or large-scale nuclear war is infinitesimal... [the United States] is already predominant... and will undoubtedly be willing to put its well being at risk [through nuclear preemption]," Viktor Yesin, "Replying to Foreign Affairs Article, Expert Mulls Nuclear Arms Programs," Krasnaya Zvezda, April 12, 2006, translated in OSC, Doc ID: CEP20060411330004; and "Russian Media See Article on U.S. Nuclear Primacy as Provocation," OSC Analysis, April 3, 2006, in Doc ID: CEF20060403324001.

36. The historical evolution of the U.S. thinking about some of these issues is discussed by Sidney D. Drell and James E. Goodby, 'What Are Nuclear Weapons For? Recommendations for Restructuring U.S. Strategic Nuclear Forces,' (Arms Control Association, 2005), http://www.armscontrol.org/pdf/USNW_2005_Drell-Goodby.pdf. They conclude that only 500 operationally deployed warheads (with 500 in a reserve stockpile) are required for foreseeable nuclear missions.

37. It is understood by the author that further presidential authority is required to launch nuclear attacks against targets in or near population centers after initial authority for a nuclear (counterforce) strike is given. Authority is withheld until released by the President.

38. See, *Plutonium Pit Production — LANL's Pivotal New Mission*, Los Alamos Study Group, http://www.lasg.org/campaigns/PUPitProd.htm.

39. Stemming from the Overeski Report there is Congressional pressure to consolidate all fissile material operation in a single location within the U.S. nuclear complex. Realization of such a vision seems impractical with NNSA budgets, while maintaining warhead production and dismantlement schedules. This issue has become politically entangled with the RRW program proposal.

40. Personal communication.

41. Matthew G. McKinzie, Thomas B. Cochran, Robert S. Norris and William M. Arkin, *The Nuclear War Plan: A Time for Change* (Natural Resources Defense Council, June 2001); and Michele Flournoy and Clark A. Murdock,

Revitalizing the U.S. Nuclear Deterrent (Center for Strategic and International Studies, July 2002).

42. This of course could change and the actions and strategic posture of the United States will do much to influence China's strategic choices during its "peaceful rise."

43. Although the author believes that there is a role for small numbers of nuclear weapons for tactical platforms—so-called tactical nuclear weapons—especially to deter regional rogue regimes, such a need is considered inconsequential for the purposes of this study.

44. Congress expressed concerns about the proposals that are discussed later in the text. As a result, at the time of writing, it is not clear whether the CTM proposals will progress to deployment or not.

45. Kathleen McInnis and Owen Price, "Iran Claims Nuclear Rights; U.S. Seeks Safer Stockpile", *Defense News*, March 6, 2006 http://www.defensenews.com/story.php?F=1578923&C=commentary

46. Amy F. Wolf, *Conventional Warheads for Long Range Ballistic Missiles*, 3

47. START counting rules limit U.S. SLBMs to a maximum of eight warheads.

48. Conventional ICBM warhead used for the augmentation of the strategic nuclear stockpile rather than the proposed "Strategic CTM" SLBM based approach, especially if one nuclear warhead were retained on each minuteman missile, would eliminate the *ambiguity* issue, which has also dogged the CTM proposal, as such weapons could not be used for the Prompt Global Strike mission. However, it is the author's preference that the Strategic CTM be investigated first, as 1) the technology is currently available, 2) PGS remains a mission requiring such assets, and 3) Strategic CTM provides the potential to retire the ICBM leg of the old nuclear triad—further cost savings and contribution to a modernization "grand bargain."

49. For example Keir A. Lieber and Daryl G. Press, "The Rise of U.S. Nuclear Primacy", *Foreign Affairs* (March/April 2006) and David S. McDonough, *Nuclear Superiority, The 'new triad' and the evolution of nuclear strategy*, Adelphi Paper 383 (London: IISS, 2006), 63 argue that modernization proposals are sought to underpin a nuclear first strike strategy.

50. Scholars such as Theodore Postol and Pavel Podvig question this assertion, often citing the Russia reaction to the Norwegian sounding rocket incident. See, Joseph Poznanski, *Refit of Trident debated*, http://media.www.avionnewspaper.com/media/storage/paper798/news/2006/10/17/Aeronautica/Refit.Of.Trident.Debated-2352394.shtml Theodore Postol and Nikolai Sokov voiced such concerns at a seminar entitled, "Conventional Missiles and Early

Warning Systems" held on October 6, 2006 at Rayburn House Office Building Washington, DC. For other examples of criticism see, *Russia and the Prompt Global Strike Plan,* http://www.csis.org/media/csis/pubs/pm_0417.pdf Dennis Shorts offers an alternative view of the evidence presented by the sounding rocket event in his chapter. Nonetheless, it is acknowledged that such criticisms have influenced the U.S. Congress on CTM proposals and therefore this counter to "ambiguity" is insufficient.

51. It is noted, however, that the very act of changing the patrol patter could either be an effective signal or risk exacerbating an escalating crisis.

52. Further variations that should be considered include (1) uploading three conventional warheads per existing ICBM in place nuclear warheads, as the non-nuclear component of the strategic force, and (2) a combination of mixed nuclear and CTM warheads on SLBMs and ICBMs. Both would eliminate ambiguity and preclude the use of the technology for the PGS mission.

CHAPTER ELEVEN

NUCLEAR DETERRENCE AND THE AMERICAN WAY OF WAR

A NEW LOOK FOR THE POST-9/11 ERA?

Lieutenant Colonel (select) George Nagy, USAF

Since the dawn of the nuclear age in 1945, U.S. military officers have struggled over how best to integrate nuclear weapons into this country's defense posture. While many politicians, public officials, academics, and ordinary citizens debate the consequences of nuclear weapons, few outside the military planning community fully understand how U.S. military culture influences the detailed planning and targeting for their potential use. Old habits die hard, and any attempt to change how nuclear weapons are integrated into U.S. defense policy must consider this cultural environment, even though U.S. nuclear weapons are explicitly under civilian (presidential) control to a level far beyond that of most military matters.[1] Despite the assertion by some in the policy community that U.S. nuclear weapons planning today is driven solely by the President, Secretary of Defense, and their supporting staffs, this has not always been the case and may, again, prove untrue in the future. For this reason, it is crucial to understand how U.S. military culture influences decisions regarding the use of particular weapon technologies in wartime.

This military culture is commonly referred to as "The American Way of War" after Russell Weigley's 1973 book of the same name.[2] While never explicitly defined by Weigley, the American Way of War suggests a uniquely U.S. approach to combat emphasizing: 1) conflict waged as a last resort; 2) the massive use of firepower in combination with other technological enablers; 3) a preference for total victory or unconditional surrender; 4) the complete destruction of an enemy through the annihilation of his military forces, and; 5) the presumption that such destruction would force the enemy to capitulate, thereby ensuring victory for the United States.

In her 1993 award-winning essay, U.S. Air Force Lieutenant Colonel Anita Arms identified the following values as historically having the greatest impact on U.S. political and military establishments:[3]

- The tendency towards isolationism based on North American geography
- The adherence to an ideology based on individual rights and freedom
- The purely political (rather than ethnic) interpretation of what it means to be American
- The balance between education, the Protestant work ethic and capitalism
- The moralistic approach to politics and affairs of state
- An ethnocentric belief that Americans occupy the moral high ground
- The chauvinistic opinion that the entire world aspires to be American
- The belief in the extremely high value of human life
- The overwhelming need for immediate action and gratification
- The use of force to accomplish national security objectives as a last resort; but once committed, war is to be won by methods as brash as necessary without regard to style, subtlety, or logic

This last point is particularly illuminating and points to the paradoxical role of firepower and the means of violence employed throughout U.S. military campaigns. Historically, the U.S. military has relied upon precision and technology to make up for limited numbers of troops on the battlefield—the experience of settling the American wilderness manifesting itself through the Industrial Revolution and substitution of capital for labor. In civilian terms, technological innovation expressed itself through inventions such as the steam engine and the cotton gin; in military terms, this same preference led to the rifled musket, steam-powered ships, and precision aerial bombardment.

In execution, however, U.S. battlefield experience with technology has been decidedly mixed. Limited application of force has often given way to a strategy of total annihilation when faced with seemingly insurmountable odds. Ulysses S. Grant's unsuccessful attempts to destroy the Confederate Army outright ultimately gave way to Sherman's burning of Atlanta; precision bombing of Japan during World War II was superseded by the firebombing of Tokyo and other major industrial centers—ending in the use of nuclear weapons on Hiroshima and Nagasaki. To quote Weigley on this paradox:

> If the total submission of the enemy had to become an object of war, Sherman's design for pursuing the object by attacking the enemy's resources and will could well appear preferable to Grant's method of destroying the enemy armies by direct means, a process almost certain to cost heavy casualties among one's own soldiers. When a new technology of war, offered by the internal combustion engine in the airplane and the tank, seemed to promise new ways of invoking Sherman's strategy, then its appeal rose especially high. If Sherman had had the airplane, then he might indeed have been able to deprive the Confederate armies of the economic resources they needed to continue the fight, while destroying popular morale as well.[4]

One might just as easily believe, however, that any new technology could be equally applied to Grant's strategy of attacking enemy forces directly. This is particularly true if a technology offers the promise of success while saving American and noncombatant lives. This is the U.S. military's unstated preference for many reasons, in particular because it views itself as a force for moral good. When precision has proved inadequate, however, American generals and admirals have shown little hesitation in resorting to the massive application of force.

To understand the American experience with nuclear weapons since World War II, it is important to put these weapons in the context of the preceding historical discussion. It is also important to understand the military *planning* culture central to the U.S. defense establishment. This planning culture drives U.S. military operations in ways that are most often unseen by the general public and misunderstood by many except for, perhaps, those individuals in government most closely connected to the process. Some government civilians have argued that, in the case of nuclear weapons, policy considerations trump military considerations almost exclusively, and that military culture plays no part in the planning and target selection process.[5] This assertion, while perhaps true today, neglects both the early history of U.S. nuclear planning as well as its indirect influence on subsequent events. As described in Fred Kaplan's seminal history of the U.S. nuclear community, *The Wizards of Armageddon*, no civilian (including the President and the Secretary of Defense) had seen the military's own nuclear planning guidance until 1960, fifteen years after the introduction of nuclear weapons.[6] The subsequent thirty-plus years of the Cold War saw occasional (but noteworthy) differences of professional opinion between senior military and civilian leadership on a variety of defense topics, nuclear weapons foremost among them. During the 1980s, military historian John Keegan went so far as to refer to the demands of supreme (i.e. civilian) command as the "post-heroic" model: decision-making focused on inaction and preservation of the status quo, with prudence and rationality triumphant over all other political considerations in order to prevent nuclear holocaust.[7] Another observer similarly suggested that "the first duty of the U.S. government is to avoid defeat, not to enforce defeat upon the enemy."[8] No single phrase better captures this philosophical difference between politicians, whose principle aim to is avoid defeat and preserve future political options, and military officers, who are charged with defeating adversaries when directed by their civilian masters.

THE U.S. MILITARY PLANNING PROCESS

The U.S. military planning process is complex and highly stylized. The basic outputs of the process are informally known as "war plans," or more formally Operations Plans (OPLANs), and other plans of lesser scope (OPLANs in concept form, Functional Plans, etc.). The purpose of these plans is to provide for the orderly translation of national political and military objectives under postulated threat scenarios into concrete military actions that achieve these objectives in peace, crisis, and war. Although administrative details have changed over the decades, the basic process for creating U.S. war plans has not changed significantly since World War II and is derived from the Prussian General Staff model.[9] War plan development falls primarily on the staffs of the 4-star geographic and functional combatant commanders responsible for their execution. These plans outline the commander's strategic intent and operational focus, identify enemy and friendly centers of gravity, and describe the general phasing of operations, including the commander's intent for each phase. A full OPLAN, including annexes, might easily be several hundred pages in length. This top-level plan, however, is still insufficient to support the actual accomplishment of large-scale military operations. Subordinate units complete additional plans for accomplishing assigned tasks, including weaponeering, logistics, and support activities at the tactical level. The time and effort expended in planning activities is enormous—the document that describes the process itself is currently 104 single-spaced pages in length—yet generally remain unrecognized by the public, academia, Congress, and others.[10] Historically, the bulk of U.S. war plans have focused on traditional full-scale conflict between nation states. When U.S. military forces enter combat, their actions are most likely scripted (in whole or in part) by either a deliberate military plan or a crisis-action plan modified on short notice from an existing deliberate plan.

While most military observers have heard the aphorism, "no plan survives first contact with the enemy intact," fewer acknowledge the warning that "failure to plan is planning to fail." The outcomes of military planning are much more than the war plans themselves; they include standard operating procedures, organizational relationships, planner familiarity with regional issues, lines of communication, etc., that allow for military operations to proceed despite the fog and friction of actual combat. Through planning, military staffs try to reduce the likelihood that unforeseen events will occur in wartime, while at the same time recognizing that military force is a blunt instrument whose outcome cannot be predicted with certainty; nor can its violence be controlled with infinite precision. Additionally, war plans explicitly account for the limited force structure (ships, divisions, air wings, etc.) available to planners at any given time.

Although the basic war plan development process includes flexibility to accommodate a wide variety of military strategies (such as blockades/ quarantines, punitive raids/strikes, or counterinsurgency methods), in practice the U.S. military has structured its war plans very traditionally. A "typical" regional OPLAN most often resembles the large-scale combined arms style of war fighting perfected during World War II. It includes phases devoted to pre-crisis (general) deterrence and mobilization, halting enemy forces, offensive operations, and post-conflict rebuilding.[11] Why this is true is open to debate; arguably, today's joint doctrine represents the services' consensus on proper roles and missions based on the last fully satisfying application of the American Way of War over 60 years ago.

Several assumptions are often made for planning purposes: 1) mobilization will not precipitate a crisis by itself, yet pre-conflict deterrence will fail; 2) planning for either the "most threatening" or "most likely" adversary responses will bind the scope of U.S. military activities once hostilities commence; 3) "major combat" offensive operations constitute the bulk of the U.S. military effort, since the enemy's war-making potential is usually the center of gravity which must be neutralized. These assumptions drive a series of planning decisions that are almost entirely predictable: the mobilization of crisis-response forces constitutes the bulk of escalatory deterrence efforts (deterrence presumed to be a by-product of the mobilization itself); the enemy will capitulate when their fielded forces or defense infrastructure are destroyed; mobilized U.S. forces are precisely those optimized for destroying the enemy's major combat units (army divisions, ships, aircraft, etc.). The overall result is a war plan that is very tidy in conceptual terms and wholly consonant with the American Way of War and corresponding value structure.

U.S. NUCLEAR PLANNING

U.S. nuclear planning has historically followed a different, sometimes disconnected path from the rest of conventional military planning, but is nonetheless shaped by the services' general planning culture and military perspective. The introduction of nuclear weapons in 1945 ushered in new possibilities for advancing this American Way of War—namely, the potential to devastate a country's military power rapidly (within hours or days) without the need for a large standing army or navy. Airpower finally had at its disposal a weapon that might fulfill the promises of strategic bombing advocates in the manner predicted by Giulio Douhet in the 1920s.[12] Nuclear weapons drove new requirements for improved planning processes and support activities such as intelligence collection and target development. The newly created U.S. Air Force (acting through its Strategic Air Command (SAC)) concentrated on planning for independent air campaigns to be conducted against the Soviet Union. In 1950 the Joint Chiefs of Staff designated three basic target categories for nuclear weapons in order of priority: 1) BRAVO (blunting) targets—those targets affecting the [Soviet] capability to deliver atomic bombs; 2) ROMEO (or retardation) targets—targets intended to stop the advance of conventional forces into Western Europe; and 3) DELTA (disruption) targets—characterized as vital elements of Soviet industrial war-making capacity.[13] These target categories represented a traditional approach to U.S. military strategies by placing emphasis first on the enemy's military capabilities—Grant's approach—and only then on the industrial infrastructure required to sustain it (Sherman). In the early 1950s, however, the SAC's ability to destroy BRAVO targets was considerably weaker when compared to its ability to attack DELTA targets. This shortfall was a result of the limited intelligence available behind the Iron Curtain, the moderate navigation and bombing accuracy of then-current technology, the limited promptness of bomber-delivered weapons, and the inherent biases of SAC leadership based on their wartime experiences in World War II. Nuclear counterforce capabilities developed slowly through the 1950s and 1960s, relying first on advances in nuclear weapons technology to produce increased explosive yields, but subsequently giving way to improved accuracy (particularly with later generations of Intercontinental Ballistic Missiles (ICBMs) and increased responsiveness (both ICBMs and Submarine-Launched Ballistic Missiles (SLBMs)).

It is important to understand how fundamental this "counterforce" targeting bias is to the American Way of War (both nuclear and conventional).[14] The basic assumption that destruction of an enemy's military might is the core activity of military planning is so ingrained in U.S. military thinking that it generally goes unquestioned throughout the planning process. Targeting requirements typically drive the size and number of military forces required to execute a particular plan. Nevertheless, a basic outcome of even the earliest nuclear war plans was that the large-scale use of nuclear weapons would utterly devastate a country such that other military operations would be superfluous to achieving total victory. It is this second point that politicians, academics, and laypeople most often focus on when discussing nuclear deterrence—the horror accompanying nuclear use that would surely give rational leaders pause. In creating military war plans that are consistent with presidential guidance military leaders propose "Grant" strategies that many civilians perceive as "Shermanesque." Given the enormous destructive power of nuclear weapons, this is not an unreasonable conclusion. The differing institutional viewpoints also help explain many differences in policy regarding U.S. nuclear weapons strategy and force structure during the past sixty years. For example, while the demonstrative use of nuclear weapons to indicate political resolve may be an attractive concept to civilians, it makes little sense to a military officer charged with providing planning options for the prompt destruction of offensive military forces.

It is useful to consider a concrete example of the counterforce bias shown during the early phase of the Korean War. In July 1950, both the Army and Air Force staffs examined the feasibility of using nuclear weapons to halt the North Korean offensive. The Air Force staff concluded that their use would be militarily ineffective and place the United States in the untenable propaganda position of "a butcher discarding his morals and killing his friends in order to achieve his end."[15] The Army staff study concluded that "at the present time, the use of atomic bombs in Korea is unwarranted from the military point of view, and questionable from the political and psychological point of view," but that eventual use of the weapon might be necessary "to avert impending disaster."[16] Importantly, the first consideration by both staffs was the *military utility* of nuclear use rather than their psychological impact or consequences of collateral damage.

THE SIOP

As the number of nuclear weapons increased dramatically during the 1950s (including deployments by the Army and Navy in quantity), planning for their effective employment became a major undertaking. In particular, the development of the long-range Polaris SLBM required the deconfliction of U.S. Air Force and U.S. Navy plans to prevent fratricide; this deconfliction would eventually extend to NATO forces as well.[17] The Single Integrated Operational Plan (SIOP) became the primary focus of U.S. nuclear planning efforts with the creation of the Joint Strategic Target Planning Staff (JSTPS) in 1960.[18] At the outset, the SIOP represented an all-out general war plan designed to deter the Soviet Union by threatening massive nuclear retaliation. Its design was colored by the experiences of World War II and represented the ultimate expression of the American Way of War. Interestingly, the SIOP represented an entirely new type of military planning effort organized through JSTPS and distinctly separate from the traditional activities of the regional military planning staffs (although regional staffs retained the ability to plan short-range "tactical" nuclear weapons). Creation of the SIOP was driven primarily by civilian policy makers, although the idea originated with the Air Force (presumably for reasons of organizational politics—to keep the Navy in line by preventing SLBMs from competing with tasks of bombers and ICBMs).[19] The SIOP was an exceedingly centralized approach to planning, and its execution represented the execution of *national* capabilities in a manner previously unheard of in U.S. military planning and operations. The resources and personnel required for SIOP development were enormous, requiring hundreds of individuals working full-time in a never-ending cycle of intelligence analysis, target updating, and plan rework. Ironically, these JSTPS preparations were in many ways the best example of "jointness" (i.e., the deliberate coordination of two or more military service activities by an integrated staff) prior to the enactment of the 1986 Goldwater-Nichols legislation.

With the development of the SIOP and the massive growth in nuclear arsenals during the 1960s (including the emergence of nuclear weapons states in addition to the United States and Soviet Union), a conflict arose between lay and military opinions on the ultimate utility of nuclear weapons. Many concluded that vast Cold War arsenals somehow made war obsolete—that Mutual Assured Destruction (relying upon the ultimate vulnerability of both sides) represented a Mexican standoff from which neither side could escape. Others, including many in the U.S. military, disagreed with this assessment. War in the era of nuclear weapons was still an extension of policy by other means, even if their primary role was to prevent a general superpower conflict by threatening the vital centers of both sides. However, the belief that conflict could be successfully waged by the Soviet Union "below" the nuclear threshold (while their nuclear arsenal held U.S. leadership in check) drove the U.S. defense establishment to consider fighting conventional wars that could achieve U.S. political and military objectives while avoiding massive societal destruction on both sides.

CONVENTIONAL VS. NUCLEAR PLANNING— THE PENDULUM SHIFTS

The U.S. military's institutional desire to reduce its reliance on the threat of nuclear retaliation was the result of many factors, including the U.S.

failure in Vietnam and the perception of decreased U.S. military strength during the 1970s. While the NATO strategy of Flexible Response adopted in 1967 explicitly linked *both* conventional and nuclear responses to a Soviet/Warsaw Pact invasion of Western Europe, many senior U.S. military leaders (particularly within the U.S. Army) were wary of embracing this "political" solution to the exclusion of more traditional military approaches.[20] Tactical nuclear weapons might prevent the Soviet Union from successfully invading Western Europe, but they were by no means capable of doing so without unleashing a devastating nuclear retaliation on the United States or the rest of the Western Alliance in response. Consequently, the overall Soviet/Warsaw Pact advantage in conventional armaments might cause Western leaders to capitulate in the face of Soviet aggression rather than risk igniting an all-out global war (this calculation no doubt played a part in the British and French political decisions to maintain independent nuclear forces).

At roughly the same time, senior U.S. political leaders demanded greater planning flexibility for strategic nuclear forces to counter perceived challenges to American credibility. The so-called "Schlesinger Doctrine," named after President Nixon's Secretary of Defense James R. Schlesinger and announced in 1974, called for limited nuclear options. In theory these options provided "escalation control," e.g., an allowance for a negotiated pause after the limited use of nuclear weapons in conflict. However, at least one senior military advisor to the President during this period has stated that "precisely how limited nuclear options were to work was never made clear."[21] While counterforce standing alone might make sense as a military strategy, its viability as a political strategy was less obvious.

These developments had two important outcomes for the U.S. military. First, the U.S. armed forces began a concerted effort in the 1980s to decrease their reliance on nuclear weapons. Doctrinal concepts such as AirLand Battle, the Maritime Strategy, and the Warden "5 Rings" air campaign model—authored primarily by senior U.S. military officers— implicitly rejected nuclear weapons as a cornerstone of their execution, instead focusing on conventional maneuver warfare conducted "below" the nuclear threshold.[22] These plans were heavily focused on regional objectives and relied upon the conventional military capabilities of U.S. theater commanders for their success. To implement these new concepts, non-nuclear weapons were required that could defeat Soviet/ Warsaw Pact military forces while limiting damage to their immediate

surroundings (including both Western and Eastern European population centers). The U.S. military rejuvenated its conventional capabilities with a new generation of technologically reliant precision weapons
(laser-guided bombs, non-nuclear cruise missiles, stealth aircraft, etc.)
capable of achieving significant military objectives while limiting collateral damage. With the development of precision non-nuclear weapons
(and better target acquisition, geolocation, and communications), the
U.S. military by the 1990s had developed an unparalleled conventional
war fighting capability.

Coincidentally, the development of this conventional war-fighting
juggernaut occurred at exactly the same time that the Soviet Union and
Warsaw Pact disintegrated from within. Rather than being used against
the adversaries for which they were intended, the new advanced con-
ventional weapons saw their baptism by fire in Operation Desert Storm
against Iraq in 1991. Subsequent actions in both the Middle East and
Southern Europe (Operation Deliberate Force in Bosnia and Operation
Allied Force in Kosovo) validated the value of these new technologies.
Of particular note, none of the adversaries engaged in conflict with the
United States during this period possessed nuclear weapons (although
Iraq was seeking them and possessed chemical and biological weapons). With the threat of superpower conflict greatly diminished in the
1990s, nuclear weapons planning took on a reduced role within the
U.S. military. A major restructuring of the Air Force in 1992 resulted
in the dissolution of the SAC and the creation of a new unified command headquarters, U.S. Strategic Command (USSTRATCOM), which
replaced JSTPS and assumed the majority of nuclear planning functions
across the Department of Defense. Cold War arsenals shrank as a result
of arms control treaties and the number of military officers with nuclear
weapons experience decreased dramatically. By the beginning of the
new millennium, some political and military leaders dared to entertain
the belief that the nuclear era was finally over—or at least reduced to
the point that the declared nuclear powers needed only a handful of
weapons in reserve to prevent the outbreak of full-scale war between
nations.[23]

TODAY'S PLANNING LANDSCAPE

In 2007, the view of the global strategic/political landscape looks decidedly less optimistic than it did less than a decade ago. The emergence of

the Global War on Terrorism following 9/11 presents several challenges to the traditional American Way of War. Foremost among them is the lack of a clear mechanism for "victory," at least in the traditional sense (a trait shared, ironically, with nuclear war). Previously, the defeat of a nation state's armed forces or conquest of their territory was believed to lead inexorably to capitulation. Today's potential adversaries may not agree with this conclusion. Although "traditional" nation-state threats still exist, a growing number of adversaries are of the non-state actor variety—either widely dispersed across friendly, adversarial, neutral, or ungoverned spaces (e.g., al Qaeda) or parasitically embedded within a host nation (e.g., Hezbollah). These adversaries do not have the traditional dependencies of nation states that can be defeated through large-scale combat in a Grant or Sherman mode; instead, these groups must be defeated or neutralized in a highly dispersed manner, sometimes at the level of finding and eliminating specific individuals. Additionally, the destruction of these organizations must often be accomplished while simultaneously preserving the support of the host nation or rebuilding the weakened infrastructure of a failed nation. The U.S. counterinsurgency experience to date in Iraq and Afghanistan suggests that the U.S. military has been slow in effectively planning for and defeating these threats. Indeed, the major U.S. military response to Vietnam was to ignore the primary lessons of that conflict and instead focus on the kinds of conflict it preferred to fight (e.g., major combat operations) and for which the American Way of War was best suited. Now, almost forty years later, this weakness is reemerging as an Achilles heel. Resources for managing this type of conflict are scarce within the Department of Defense and the military services are struggling to adapt.

Correspondingly, the current crop of adversaries appears acutely aware that they do not have to decisively defeat the U.S. military in traditional combat. Instead, they undermine U.S. political support for military intervention through attritional attacks against U.S. fielded forces and non-combatants, combined with the use of modern communications (including television, digital imagery and the Internet). This is deliberately aimed against the American perception of the value of human life in an attempt to sap U.S. resolve. So-called "rogue" nations, such as Iran or North Korea, could leverage these terrorist movements to threaten allied interests around the world while advancing their national political interests. These same nations appear to be developing and acquiring nuclear weapons to prevent the successful application of conventional U.S. military power as accomplished in Iraq, Bosnia, and Kosovo. Far from being a "weapon of the weak" as characterized by many anti-nuclear activists, nuclear weapons are clearly weapons of the strong—since their presence may prevent the unfettered application of conventional military power.

PLANNING FOR THE FUTURE

What does all this imply for the future of nuclear weapons planning within the U.S. military? Since 2001, the Department of Defense completed two Quadrennial Defense Reviews and one Nuclear Posture Review with a renewed emphasis on broadening the U.S. approach to strategic deterrence generally and modernizing U.S. nuclear capabilities in particular. The realignment of several combatant commands in 2002 (including the establishment of U.S. Northern Command (USNORTH-COM) and the reorganization of USSTRATCOM) and their subsequent publication of the Homeland Security and Strategic Deterrence Joint Operating Concepts suggest a major shift is underway in the approach of these organizations to their future military planning activities.[24]

Current U.S. defense initiatives are intended to better integrate the entire spectrum of U.S. military force against current and projected threats. Increasing emphasis has been placed on improving the United States' ability to deter via the denial of "rogue state" military capabilities.[25] Active missile defense, long-range conventional counterforce missiles, and improved homeland security mechanisms all contribute to damage-limitation for the U.S. and its allies. Additionally, new methods of inflicting unacceptable punishment on adversaries may include computer network attacks or directed-energy weapons. The emphasis on both the "New Triad" and "tailored deterrence" provides a wider portfolio of defense options for countering the entire range of potential adversaries—from terrorists, other non-state actors, "rogue states," and traditional nation-state threats.[26] Nuclear weapons remain a cornerstone of the New Triad, but their role is downplayed in many respects when compared to the other elements of the force construct (defenses, advanced conventional weapons, infrastructure, and integrating command and control). Public debate, however, has remained focused on the nuclear aspects of policy guidance, presumably since nuclear weapons generate more discussion than other subjects.[27]

Inherent in these new approaches is an understanding that the unconditional surrender of a conventional military force may not signal victory in conflict. Coinciding with these technical developments are changes in the military planning process, specifically an increased focus on adversary behavior and motivation (particularly in cultural and cognitive terms), as well as better integration of military plans across regional boundaries in a manner not seen since the end of the Cold War.[28] The difficulty of meshing the planning efforts of regional and functional commands should not be underestimated. For example, if a missile was launched from North Korea against the United States, it would require a coordinated response from at least three major combatant commands (U.S. Pacific Command, USNORTHCOM, and USSTRATCOM) to address all defensive and offensive options currently available. Although the military planning process allows for staff coordination across command lines, this process has traditionally been quite cumbersome. Future military command and control mechanisms require significant attention, since vertically stovepiped organizations designed for industrial age warfare are likely to prove inappropriate in a networked world. In all cases, these planning initiatives are intended to better link political objectives to military actions. A broader set of strategic response options beyond simple fixed-target retaliation is needed for this approach to succeed.

For offensive operations, the American Way of War has tilted towards a clear preference for precision conventional weapons to achieve battlefield results. These weapons are able to swiftly destroy fielded military forces while limiting damage to non-combatants, consistent with the prevailing American morality and military culture (Grant's approach). Additionally, these weapons could provide the distributed operations and fractionated application of firepower necessary for the likely skirmishes in the global war on terrorism. Planning for counterinsurgency campaigns will be difficult, since success will require a persistence not normally found in U.S. military culture. If the U.S. Army's 19th Century experiences in the American West and the Philippine-American War are any indicator, the pressure to apply Sherman's tactics in search of a quick military solution will be enormous. "Winning" will be measured in very subjective terms and extended military campaigns will require long-term support from both the U.S. Congress and the American public.

However, for traditional nation-state threats and those terrorist targets which conventional weapons are incapable of defeating, nuclear weapons remain available to ensure the success of our military efforts, while protecting the citizens of the United States and our allies. The employment of nuclear weapons in these situations will be given serious consideration undoubtedly only under the gravest of circumstances. With current and projected conventional capabilities, the major foreseeable role for U.S. nuclear weapons remains as a damage limitation option, when no other recourse is available. The types of targets or scenarios that might drive nuclear planning would include adversary WMD threats (nuclear, biological, or chemical) for which no other military option would suffice—targets very much in the mold of the BRAVO category of the 1950s.

Except for a possible conflict with a major nuclear power such as Russia or China, it is not clear that planning for nuclear weapons use should involve more than a handful of actual weapons employed selectively against critical targets. For purposes of military planning, it may be useful to discern (and, in some instances, make known to others the scope and purpose of) damage limitation plans where military effectiveness outweighs all other considerations. An example of this situation might be the destruction of a confirmed terrorist WMD facility. Alternatively, military plans intended for preserving or restoring the status quo might not require the same level of military planning detail, yet they would still be *politically* effective if viewed as credible by adversaries.

DETERRENCE

Deliberate deterrence planning for these targets will be essential, since the United States will wish to refrain from actual nuclear employment, except in the most dire circumstances. A detailed understanding of adversary leadership is essential for the U.S. to effectively communicate both the rewards of "good" behavior (i.e., complying with courses of action consistent with U.S. goals) as well as the certainty of failure and subsequent punishment, should the adversary remain unpersuaded. This approach requires a parallel change in the military planning culture, with less emphasis placed on plans that "service" large numbers of targets and a correspondingly greater effort placed on understanding the cultural, sociological, and cognitive aspects of the adversary's decisionmaking.

This change will not be easy, as the U.S. military must forgo decades of established doctrine to successfully implement these new approaches. Rather than simply allocating weapons against prescribed target categories and determining the physical destructiveness of their planned actions, military planners must now consider the extended military, political, economic, and social effects of military operations. They must also shift their concepts of operation according to the stated objectives of U.S. civilian leadership. For nuclear weapons planning, this might include more deliberate peacetime political signaling (shows of force and restraint) than has been the case since the end of the Cold War. Unlike the Cold War nuclear alerts, however, these actions must be taken with a greater understanding of how particular exercises or planning options are likely to be perceived by their intended target. For example, former Soviet military leaders interviewed in the early 1990s consistently stated their *perception* that U.S. actions throughout the Cold War were actually preparations for a surprise nuclear first strike.[29] These deep-rooted fears came from Russia's historical experiences with Napoleon and Hitler and failed to recognize the U.S. military's institutional biases on how to execute the American Way of War. Given the increased likelihood of post-9/11 conflict with unfamiliar cultures, U.S. military planners must explicitly consider these reaction dynamics when developing specific military plans or actions.

Additionally, an enhanced level of integration between U.S. nuclear and conventional weapons planning is increasingly needed. In the post-9/11 networked world, the antiseptic "spectrum of conflict" conceived during the Cold War does not adequately describe the strategic impact of state-sponsored terrorism on regional conflicts, the possession of deadly biological weapons by millennialist cults, or the use of computer connections to wage worldwide psychological "hearts and minds" campaigns. Correspondingly, military plans will be delineated more by their functionality (e.g., counterforce, damage-limitation, countervalue, counter-economic, etc.) and less by the types of weapons planned or available for employment.

It is not clear that current U.S. nuclear capabilities are particularly well suited for the most likely types of future targets. Current U.S. nuclear weapons lack precision guidance and consequently have much greater yields than would be required if such guidance were retrofitted. Even the newest designs in the U.S. arsenal date back to the 1980s, when maximizing explosive yield (while minimizing mass and volume) produced nuclear weapons with reliability, safety, and security features that are dated by today's demanding standards. During the Cold War, planners could account for reliability issues and the desired probability of destruction by simply allocating extra weapons against a target, the so-called "overkill" factor. By comparison, a future U.S. military planner might need only a single nuclear weapon in the entire war plan to target a specific biological weapons bunker; but that weapon must detonate with the correct yield exactly as planned. If adversaries have reason to question our promised nuclear capabilities, then our deterrence credibility may be weakened immeasurably.

Critics may deride such improvements as preparations for nuclear "war fighting," which, indeed, they are in some sense. However, it is anathema to the American Way of War for the United States to limit itself to retaliatory courses of action solely reliant upon destruction not clearly tied to military purposes. Although a single nuclear strike might well kill tens or hundreds of thousands dependent on target location, it is against U.S. policy to systematically target nuclear weapons against civilians. Despite the views of those who claim that nuclear strategy relies solely on maintaining vulnerability between civilian populations, the U.S. military remains wedded to the Clausewitzian doctrine that war is the continuation of politics by other means. Therefore, military actions must have a clear and logical connection to achieving military objectives in support of overarching political goals. When the United States resorted to widespread attacks against urban industrial centers in Germany and Japan during World War II, it recognized the limits of the military technology and believed that ending the conflict more rapidly would save lives in the long term.. LeMay's methods, however bloody, served their purpose just like Sherman's had a hundred years earlier.

In the twenty-first century, the role of nuclear weapons may not change greatly when deterring traditional nation-state conflict. However, the same doctrine, if applied to terrorists or "rogue-state" dictators (who, some would argue, are supported by "enslaved" populations) might well lead to disaster. Against these adversaries, deterrence by threat of punishment is a dubious proposition at best. The United States would be better served in these cases by concentrating on deterrence by denial—with nuclear weapons, if need be—and on other methods of inducing adversary restraint. This capability must mesh with the ability to conduct extensive coalition ground operations that can secure an enduring result, should deterrence fail.

While the future of U.S. nuclear deterrence still may not be clear in the post-9/11 world, changes are emerging that suggest the American Way of War and the corresponding role of nuclear weapons are indeed evolving. Advanced conventional technologies now allow the U.S. military to defeat opposing armies with only a modicum of effort; therefore, the need to maintain thousands of strategic nuclear weapons is doubtful. Paradoxically, industrial base requirements (or the desire to dissuade other nuclear powers from increasing the size of their current arsenals), rather than targeting considerations, may drive the size and shape of U.S. nuclear force structure. As with the SIOP, planning for the strategic dismemberment of whole nations might well be accomplished with a combination of advanced conventional, cyber, and other non-nuclear methods, with only a small number of nuclear weapons held in reserve to influence political (rather than military) calculations. Given the disposition of U.S. military planning towards counterforce targeting, it is interesting to hypothesize that future military leaders might advocate an even greater proportion of non-nuclear weapons in the arsenal, based on their perceived military utility, while politicians would cling to greater numbers of nuclear weapons.[30] A two-tiered nuclear force structure might emerge: "slow" (second-strike) counterforce weapons in larger quantities for stabilizing great power relations, and robust damage limitation capabilities available in small numbers for "rogue state" confrontations.[31] The crux of the debate is not so much about nuclear weapons as it is about a differing perspective on the role of force in politics: for military officers peace is viewed as an outgrowth of military superiority; for many politicians it is seen as a result of shared military vulnerability. Despite popular perceptions on the matter, the U.S. military is institutionally less wedded to maintaining large numbers of nuclear weapons than it is to maintaining the American Way of War by whatever means most effective.

The greatest emerging threats to U.S. security appear to be not from regional powers, but from so-called "non-state" actors, including transnational terrorists. These threats are so dispersed both geographically and organizationally that their total destruction seems unlikely when compared to defeating a traditional nation-state. Nuclear weapons probably offer little in the way of a direct solution against these threats, except perhaps in taking out the adversary's WMD (through destruction in storage or transit) or deterring the nation-state transfer of WMD to terrorist groups. In these cases, U.S. nuclear planning, though small-scale, must be exceedingly robust, with an eye towards how the political and military landscape will change when the next nuclear weapon explodes in anger.

CONCLUSION

The noted observer Colin S. Gray once remarked that:

> U.S. military power, like American society, is a powerful but blunt instrument. U.S. strategic culture performs certain military enterprises admirably. Fortunately, those enterprises include virtually all of the larger, more orthodox tasks that bear upon war and peace between states and coalitions. Planning and execution of a D-Day landing, of nuclear deterrence, of SIOP-level nuclear war, or of large-scale non-nuclear war all exploit America's strengths and avoid the worst of America's weaknesses. The larger and more violent the endeavor, the more effectively the United States is likely to perform.[32]

This observation clearly extends to the American Way of War and the U.S. military's experience with nuclear weapons over the last sixty years. The challenge for the U.S. military will be how well it can adapt to the changed post-9/11 era, where the kinds of threats it has countered successfully in the past are perhaps the least likely to be encountered in the future. If current trends continue, warfare in the twenty-first century is likely to be increasingly small-scale, decentralized, and violent on an individual level. Agility, rather than mass and firepower, will be the most important trait of U.S. military forces. This change portends fundamental adjustments to the American Way of War if the U.S. military is to remain successful in future conflict. If nuclear weapons are to continue as a useful tool for deterrence and defense of the United States, then the planning for their potential use must reflect the changed security environment in which they exist. More effort must be given to understanding the scenario-specific requirements for deterring particular adversaries from taking specific actions, since "generalized" deterrence (both nuclear and non-nuclear) will likely be less effective against terrorists and "rogue states" than during the Cold War. The dual requirements for greater accuracy and minimized collateral damage will drive U.S. military planners to either seek improved nuclear weapons capable of meeting military needs, or abandoning them in favor of advanced conventional weapons that can do the job instead. In either case, the total numbers of nuclear weapons required to fulfill U.S. military planning requirements will continue to decrease, at least until U.S. policy makers feel so uncomfortable that they believe regional powers might challenge U.S. nuclear superiority for political gain.

Many nuclear policy debates during the Cold War hinged on a common understanding of nuclear weapons colored by the institutional biases of those involved in the discussion: politicians, academics, scholars, etc. These groups would be well advised to also consider the institutional biases of those called upon to execute U.S. nuclear weapons policy, the U.S. military and its uniquely American Way of War. Only by understanding this strategic culture can an informed policy discussion regarding the present and future roles of nuclear weapons take place. Political leaders can then decide whether their subordinates' planning is worthy of Ulysses S. Grant—or perhaps William Tecumseh Sherman— and appropriate to the task.

Notes

1. "The decision to employ nuclear weapons at any level requires the explicit decision of the President." Chairman of the Joint Chiefs of Staff, "Joint Pub 3-12, Doctrine for Joint Nuclear Operations," 18 December 1995, vi.

2. Russell F. Weigley, *The American Way of War: A History of United States Military Strategy and Policy* (Bloomington: Indiana University Press, 1973).

3. Lt Col Anita M. Arms, USAF, "Strategic Culture—The American Mind," *Essays on Strategy*, vol. 9 (1993): 3-32.

4. Weigley, 152.

5. Franklin C. Miller, former Special Assistant to President George W. Bush, communication with the author, 2007.

6. Fred Kaplan, *The Wizards of Armageddon* (New York: Simon and Schuster, 1983), 277.

7. John Keegan, *The Mask of Command* (New York: Penguin Books, 1987), 330-351.

8. Colin S. Gray, "Presidential Directive 59: Flawed but Useful," *The Nuclear Arms Race Debated* (New York: McGraw-Hill, Inc., 1986), 271.

9. Col Christopher R. Paparone, USA, "U.S. Army Decisionmaking: Past, Present and Future," *Military Review* (July-August 2001): 45-46.

10. Chairman of the Joint Chiefs of Staff, "Joint Pub 5-0, Doctrine for Planning Joint Operations," 13 April 1995, http://www.dtic.mil/doctrine/jel/new_pubs/jp5_0.pdf.

11. Chairman of the Joint Chiefs of Staff, "Joint Pub 5-00.1, Joint Doctrine for Campaign Planning," 25 January 2002, http://www.dtic.mil/doctrine/jel/new_pubs/jp5_00_1.pdf.

12. Giulio Douhet (English translation by Dino Ferrari of the 1921 original text), *The Command of the Air* (Washington, D.C.: U.S. Government Printing Office (reprint), 1983).

13. David M. Kunsman and Douglas B. Lawson, *A Primer on U.S. Strategic Nuclear Policy* (Albuquerque: Sandia National Laboratories, 2001), 29-30.

14. "Counterforce targeting is a strategy to employ forces to destroy, or render impotent, military capabilities of an enemy force. Typical counterforce targets include bomber bases, ballistic missile submarine bases, ICBM silos, antiballistic and air defense installations, C2 centers, and WMD storage facilities (Joint Pub 3-12 Chap. 2 para. 3b)." This is contrasted in the same paragraph with countervalue targeting, "Countervalue targeting strategy directs the destruction or neutralization of selected enemy military and military-related activities, such as industries, resources, and/or institutions that contribute to the enemy's ability to wage war. In general, weapons required to implement this strategy need not be as numerous or accurate as those required to implement a counterforce targeting strategy, because countervalue targets generally tend to be softer and unprotected in relation to counterforce targets."

15. Conrad C. Crane, *American Airpower Strategy in Korea (1950-1953)* (Lawrence: University Press of Kansas, 2000), 37.

16. Ibid

17. Jerry Miller, *Nuclear Weapons and Aircraft Carriers* (Washington, D.C.: Smithsonian Institution Press, 2001), 206-227.

18. Charles K. Hopkins, "Unclassified History of the Joint Strategic Target Planning Staff (JSTPS)" (pamphlet produced by the Staff Historian of the JSTPS, Offutt AFB, Nebraska, June 1990).

19. Kaplan, 263.

20. Major Paul H. Herbert, USA, "Deciding What Has to Be Done: General William E. DePuy and the 1976 Edition of FM 100-5, Operations," *Leavenworth Paper #16* (Ft. Leavenworth, KS: U.S. Army Command and General Staff College, 1988): 90-91.

21. Lt Gen William E. Odom, USA (ret.), "The Origins and Design of Presidential Decision-59: A Memoir," in *Getting MAD: Nuclear Mutual Assured Destruction, Its Origins and Practice (Henry D. Sokolski, ed.)* (Carlisle Barracks, PA: Strategic Studies Institute, 2004): 177.

22. Dept. of the Army, "FM 100-5, Operations," May 1986. U.S. Naval Institute, "The Maritime Strategy," January 1986. Col John A. Warden III,

USAF, *The Air Campaign: Planning for Combat* (Washington, D.C.: NDU Press, 1988).

23. Michael J. Mazarr, "Nuclear Weapons After the Cold War," *The Washington Quarterly*, vol. 15 no. 3 (Summer 1992): 185-201.

24. Department of Defense, "Homeland Security Joint Operating Concept," and "Strategic Deterrence Joint Operating Concept," February 2004. http://www.dtic.mil/futurejointwarfare/joc.htm. In December 2006 a revised version of the latter document (primarily incorporating greater discussion of terrorism and non-state actors) was approved by then-Secretary of Defense Donald Rumsfeld and published on the website with the title "Deterrence Operations Joint Operating Concept – Version 2.0."

25. Deterrence Operations Joint Operating Concept – Version 2.0, 26.

26. Department of Defense, "Quadrennial Defense Review Report," 6 February 2006. http://www.defenselink.mil/qdr/report/Report20060203.pdf. 49-51.

27. Kurt Guthe, "The Nuclear Posture Review: How Is the 'New Triad' New?" (Washington, D.C.: Center for Strategic and Budgetary Assessments, 2002). http://www.csbaonline.org/4Publications/Archive/R.20020729.Nuclear_Posture_Review/R.20020729.Nuclear_Posture_Review.pdf

28. The latest version of the Deterrence Operations Joint Operating Concept identifies a five-step process for deterrence planning: 1) Specify the deterrence objective(s) and strategic context; 2) assess the decision calculus of adversary decision-makers; 3) Identify desired deterrence effects on adversary decision calculus; 4) Develop and assess tailored courses of action (COAs) designed to achieve desired deterrence effects; 5) Execute deterrence COAs and monitor and assess adversary responses. The deterrence planning process is intended to be integrated into the current military planning process, which primarily takes into account only U.S. military objectives.

29. John A. Battilega, "Soviet Views of Nuclear Warfare: The Post-Cold War Interviews," in *Getting MAD: Nuclear Mutual Assured Destruction, Its Origins and Practice*, 157-164.

30. It appears this trend is already occurring. In his annual statement to the House Armed Services Committee on March 8, 2007, the Commander of U.S. Strategic Command, USMC General James E. Cartwright, included the following remarks: "We have a prompt delivery capability on alert today, but it is configured with nuclear weapons, which limits the options available to our decision-makers and may reduce the credibility of our deterrence. The capability we lack is the means to deliver prompt, precise, conventional kinetic effects at inter-continental ranges." Testimony accessed online at http://armedservices.house.gov/pdfs/Strat030807/Cartwright_Testimony030807.pdf

31. Scott D. Sagan, *Moving Targets: Nuclear Strategy and National Security* (Princeton, NJ: Princeton University Press, 1989), 90-93.

32. Colin S. Gray, "Strategy in the nuclear age: The United States, 1945-1991," in *The Making of Strategy: Rulers, States, and War (Williamson Murray, MacGregor Knox, and Alvin Bernstein, eds.)* (Cambridge: Cambridge University Press, 1994): 613.

CHAPTER TWELVE

NUCLEAR COMMAND AND CONTROL IN THE TWENTY-FIRST CENTURY

TRENDS, DISPARITIES AND THE IMPACT ON STABILITY

Jerome M. Conley

With the turn of the twenty-first century a renewed interest has arrived in the role of nuclear weapons as symbols of national power as well as tools for strategic posturing. The 1998 nuclear tests in South Asia, the 2002 U.S. Nuclear Posture Review (NPR), the British debate over Trident replacement, and the overt pursuit of nuclear capabilities by Iran and North Korea represent key examples of an overall shift in the number of states with nuclear capabilities, nuclear aspirations, and legacy systems that require modernization. However, the 2001 attacks on the United States with airplanes and anthrax underscore a changing security environment in which asymmetric risks created by non-state actors may alter and/or diminish the degree of security afforded by nuclear deterrence.

As discussed in the previous chapters, these multifarious factors converge to provide a rich forum for assessing the future utility of nuclear weapons and the transformation of nuclear deterrence. These assessments and projections, however, focus almost exclusively on the quantity and quality of warheads and delivery systems and seldom broach the equally critical topic of the command and control (C^2) systems that define nuclear operations. As the design and robustness of C^2 systems impact the safety, security and reliability of nuclear weapons during peacetime, crises, and wartime, an adequate and balanced assessment of nuclear deterrence and stability in the twenty-first century must simultaneously explore the quantity and quality of nuclear weapon systems as well as the systems and processes that control them. In an era when the true strategic intentions of existing and aspiring nuclear nations grow more opaque, an analysis of the command and control trends within these states can serve to clarify the role of nuclear weapons for these actors.

KEY ASPECTS OF NUCLEAR COMMAND AND CONTROL

This chapter explores the technical and procedural aspects of nuclear safety, security, and reliability, the ongoing changes in global and regional security dynamics, and the implications of these factors on nuclear deterrence and stability in the twenty-first century. Overall, nuclear command and control[1] involves the designation of select personnel who have the authority to determine the disposition and employment of nuclear weapons; it also involves the creation of systems and processes to ensure that the intentions and decisions of these authorities are properly executed. The U.S. Department of Defense defines nuclear command and control as:

> The exercise of authority and direction by the President, as Commander in Chief, through established command lines, over nuclear weapon operations of military forces; as Chief Executive over all Government activities that support those operations; and, as Head of State over required multinational actions that support those operations. The [nuclear command and control] structure supports the exercise of authority and direction by the President.[2]

The means through which this presidential authority is executed is the nuclear command and control system and includes the "combination of facilities, equipment, communications, procedures, and personnel essential for planning, directing, and controlling nuclear weapons, weapons systems, and associated operations."[3] Though the names and authorities may vary, all C^2 programs involve the same attributes of a human decisionmaker(s) and the employment of technical and procedural control measures to ensure the safe, secure, and reliable execution of these decisions. Differences occur, however, in the types of control measures emphasized by these actors and the ability of their command and control systems to ensure consistent and balanced safety, security and reliability during times of peace, crisis, and hostility (nuclear or otherwise).

The "Always-Never" Challenge and the Role of Positive and Negative Controls

A core challenge in the design and development of a C^2 system is the need to strike a balance between having a process that ensures nuclear weapons are always employed when proper authorization is provided, and ensuring they are never employed (or detonated) in the absence of proper authorization. From a system design perspective, this "always-never" challenge is addressed through the development of positive controls (measures that ensure nuclear employment when properly authorized) and negative controls (measures that prevent accidental or unauthorized nuclear employment).[4] In mature C^2 systems, these positive and negative controls are applied in a layered and redundant manner in order to achieve six primary functions:

1. Maintain the technical conditions and combat readiness of the strategic systems;
2. Prevent the accidental or unauthorized use of nuclear weapons;
3. Facilitate routine operations among staff and subordinate forces;
4. Provide inter-service and interagency coordination on all aspects of the nuclear mission, to include ballistic missile defense, early warning, reconnaissance, etc.;
5. Develop and update nuclear war plans; and
6. Enable the combat use of nuclear weapons.[5]

As detailed below in Figure 12.1, two general approaches are applied when developing the negative and positive controls necessary for achieving these six functions: the use of procedural and technical measures.

Procedural Approaches to Negative and Positive Controls

Procedurally, operational plans, doctrine, and training can dictate varying degrees of safety, security, and reliability as the strategic forces transition from a peacetime posture through a crisis, and toward employment. Procedural measures in support of negative controls can include: the use of a two-person rule that makes it impossible for a single person to initiate a launch; the separation of special nuclear material (SNM) from the high-explosive assembly of a warhead; the separation of a warhead from its delivery vehicle; or restricting access to launch codes. In addition, a strategic doctrine that espouses no-first use (NFU) or delayed retaliation posture can be considered a negative control. These postures seek to provide a cushion of time for strategic decision-makers who may be subject to stress and "the fog of war" during a crisis and potentially face the unintended use of nuclear weapons due to the inadvertent escalation of a crisis.[6] In this context, nuclear use is authorized by the appropriate command authority, but "unauthorized" in the context of inaccurate and incomplete knowledge or not meeting the original, pre-crisis intent of the strategic authority.

Figure 12.1. Procedural and Technical Approaches to Negative and Positive Controls

	Negative Controls (-)	Positive Controls (+)
Procedural Controls	• Delayed retaliation posture • No-first use or Launch on Warning • Two-person rule • Restricted access to launch codes • Separation of warhead components • Separation of warheads & vehicles • Other	• Airborne alert status • Launch on Warning (LOW) posture • Strip alert for strategic bombers • Pre-delegation of launch authority • Final assembly of warhead • Mating warhead with delivery vehicle • Other
Technical Controls	• One-point safety warhead design • Mechanical / electrical locks • Fail safe weapon designs • Electrical exclusion regions • Weak-link designs • Environmental sensing devices • Other	• Fully automated launch system • Frequency diversity • Hardened communication systems • Sea-based delivery vehicles • Mobile command systems / posts • Jam / interference resistance • Other

Examples of procedural measures that promote positive control over nuclear forces include the delegation of launch authority to subordinate or field commanders, the final assembly of warhead components, the mating of warheads with their delivery vehicles, the initiation of airborne alert status for bombers and the deployment of mobile missile forces. These measures provide for the rapid execution of authorized launch orders and an assurance of nuclear use. From a doctrinal perspective, a launch-on-warning (LOW) posture (sometimes referred to as a "hair-trigger" posture) can also provide rapid and assured nuclear use.[7]

Technical Approaches to Negative and Positive Controls

A broad array of technical measures for providing negative and positive controls have been developed and fielded over the past sixty years, though the availability and use of these measures vary among the spectrum of nuclear nations. Technical measures include "one-point safety" designs for weapons that ensure the accidental detonation of a weapon's high-explosive assembly does not provide an adequate impulse for detonation of the nuclear core. Other negative controls include mechanical and electronic locks (to include Permissive Acton Links - PALs), fail safe designs, weak links, electric exclusion zones, and other technical measures that prevent unauthorized or accidental use. Technical measures that provide positive nuclear controls include hardened communications systems, frequency diversity, mobile command posts, interference resistant communications, and environmental sensing devices for warhead arming.[8] An additional technical positive control measure is a fully automatic launch system, such as the Dead Hand ("Mertvaya Ruka") system explored but never deployed by the Soviet Union.[9] This type of automatic system, however, may be considered destabilizing as it removes the human decisionmaker from the response cycle and does not allow for a strategic pause if de-escalation is desired.

General Impressions on Strategic Stability and Negative and Positive Controls

Figure 12.2 provides a summary graphic of the general implications and trends associated with the procedural and technical measures of negative and positive control. As this overall analysis centers on the role of command and control within strategic stability, it is important to note that certain C^2 trends may bias a system toward use, but this bias does not predetermine actual use. From a strategic stability perspective, the maintenance of negative controls during peacetime, crisis, and conflict ensures that nuclear assets are only employed when properly authorized by the designated authority(s). In many cases, however, the procedural aspects of negative controls rely on the proper and disciplined execution of these measures by people within the command and control system. For this reason, Personnel Reliability Programs (PRPs)[10] are critical in established as well as emerging nuclear programs.

Figure 12.2 also underscores the critical procedural transition that can occur during a crisis when the negative control measures of having warheads disassembled and unmated with delivery vehicles change to positive control measures of fully assembled warheads being mated to delivery vehicles and deployed to the field. This "either-or" aspect of negative/positive controls poses significant risk for countries lacking mature technical negative controls, as the decision to cross into positive procedural controls eliminates the primary negative controls provided by weapon disassembly.[11]

Figure 12. 2. Balancing the "Always-Never" Challenge

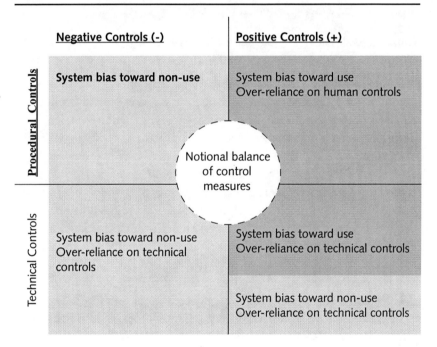

The role of technical approaches to negative and positive controls is perhaps the most significant and destabilizing aspect of C^2 disparity in the twenty-first century, as new and emerging nuclear custodians rely heavily on procedural measures, due to their limited expertise and financial resources for developing robust technological measures. Moreover, unlike positive procedural controls that foster a bias toward use, most positive technical controls (with the exception of fully automated launch systems) foster a bias toward non-use during crises. This is because the robustness and assurances provided by these technologies can allow adequate guarantees against the complete loss of nuclear forces and/or C^2 in the case of an adversary's first strike. In this respect, a balanced mix of positive technical controls and negative controls (both procedural and technical) and the limitation/avoidance of positive procedural controls can provide a sufficiently robust C^2 system to ensure a safe, secure, and reliable nuclear arsenal. Stated differently, the promotion of a C^2 posture that continuously maintains positive and negative controls within the left side and bottom right portion of Figure 12.2 will meet the requirements of the "always-never" challenge for a nuclear custodian while simultaneously assuring a credible deterrent to potential adversaries.

Cuba 1962: Historical Example of the Role of C^2 within the "Always-Never" Challenge

The Cuban missile crisis of October 1962 is the most cited case of the potential risks created when two nuclear nations enter into a crisis. Analysis of the Soviet records of this event show that heavy reliance on negative controls (primarily procedural) provided a sufficient C^2 bias toward non-use and that the actual approach toward the nuclear brink was perhaps less precipitous than often cited. Central to this assertion is the fact that General Issa Pliyev, commander of Soviet forces in Cuba, did not have full authority to employ nuclear forces. In addition, procedural safeguards were enacted to ensure that the nuclear weapons on the island were stored separately from their delivery vehicles and required authorization directly from Moscow (instead of General Pliyev) to remove them from storage.[12] Figure 12.3 captures the resultant non-use bias created by these procedural negative controls.

As stated above, however, heavy reliance on procedural measures during a crisis places significant emphasis on the personnel within the C^2 structure and their ability (and willingness) to execute the orders of the national command authority. During the Cuban crisis, General Pliyev made repeated requests to Moscow to remove the warheads for the medium-range Frog missiles from storage. Though these requests were all denied, as commander of all Soviet forces on the island, he could theoretically have forced the officer in charge of the nuclear storage site to release the weapons to him, at which point General Pliyev had the technical capability to launch the nuclear-armed missiles without final authorization from Moscow. Due to the strict Soviet command structure, General Pliyev did not violate his orders from Moscow and the negative procedural controls remained intact. This potential loss of negative controls unnerved the Soviet leadership and as Mark Kramer recently observed, "After the Cuban missile crisis, however, the option of relying solely on the physical separation of warheads and delivery vehicles was deemed inadequate."[13]

Figure 12. 3. Cuba, 1962: Historical Example of C^2 System Bias Toward Non-Use

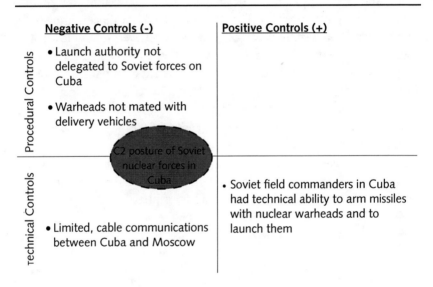

TWENTY-FIRST CENTURY NUCLEAR ACTORS AND THEIR C^2 POSTURES

Given the previous discussion on the key concepts and aspects of negative and positive controls, it is appropriate to explore these issues within the context of the international actors that currently possess or are pursuing nuclear capabilities. Though certain limitations exist on the availability and quality of open source data for some actors, sufficient information exists to identify trends and potential biases within their C^2 postures.

The P5 Nations

China, France, Russia, the United Kingdom, and the United States are all custodians of legacy nuclear capabilities and their associated command and control systems. In the sixteen years since the end of the Cold War, each nation has explored the future structure and posture of their strategic arsenals in the context of the changing global security environment.[14]

The specific design and construct of the Chinese nuclear command and control system is believed to be based on an assertive, centralized command structure with the Chairman of the Central Military Commission, currently President Jiang Zemin, as the national authority for nuclear use. For negative controls, China is believed to employ a "two man rule," as well as the separate storage of warheads and delivery vehicles. Positive technical controls include hardened command and control facilities, redundant, flexible and EMP-hardened communication networks, and the pursuit of new digital microwave communication systems for all weather and encrypted capabilities. China is not believed to employ permissive action link (PAL) technologies but maintains a sufficient land-based and sea-based ballistic missile capability to meet the survivability requirements of its minimal nuclear deterrent posture.[15]

France has recently placed considerable emphasis on the need to have a tailored deterrent that goes beyond its large, cold war posture of "deterrence by the weak of the strong."[16] This desire to develop flexibility through smaller, more accurate warheads on its submarine-launched ballistic missiles (SLBMs) is a departure from France's cold war policy of executing a complete sixteen-missile retaliatory response from its ballistic missile submarines[17] and will require enhanced communication procedures and C^2 planning. France also employs procedural negative controls such as the two-person rule, technical negative controls that include a locking system similar to PALs, and redundant, hardened command and control facilities. France's nuclear launch authority is expected to remain firmly centralized and under presidential control.[18]

Russia has a long history of utilizing a broad range of negative and positive controls for ensuring the safety, security and reliability of its nuclear deterrent. However, recent Russian emphasis on the development and deployment of new Project 955 Borey class submarines, Bulava SLBMs and Topol-M mobile ICBMs, and the 1999 abandonment of its no first use doctrine were seen by some observers as a shift toward a preemptive strike posture.[19] In response to these assertions, a leading Russian strategic analyst remarked that the development of survivable strategic systems, at a much greater cost than silo-based systems, represents a significant investment by Russia in an assured retaliatory strike capability. These investments in new delivery vehicles are also accompanied by the enhancement of certain aspects of the Russian command and control system.[20] Similar to the United States, however, Russia has significant negative control procedures, including the use of the two-person rule, employment of feedback loops that allow senior commands to monitor subordinate commands, electronic systems that allow higher echelons to remotely disable missile launchers, and the use of blocking devices to physically prevent unauthorized use of weapons.[21] From a C^2 perspective, therefore, these efforts to enhance the survivability of delivery vehicles and communications networks, coupled with a strong Russian/Soviet history of negative controls, promote an overall Russian C^2 bias toward non-use under crisis conditions.[22]

The nuclear arsenal of the United Kingdom is centered on a sea-based nuclear deterrent with current discussions exploring the modernization of this single-legged capability. The warhead currently employed on the British Trident missile is similar to the U.S. W76 warhead and is presumed to have similar technical positive and negative control measures, since the Arming, Fusing and Firing System (AF&F) is reported to be designed by Sandia National Laboratory in the United States.[23] The United Kingdom has a centralized strategic release structure, with the prime minister maintaining launch authority. In addition, the United Kingdom relies heavily on procedural measures such as two-person rules, as well as authentication codes to prevent unauthorized nuclear use aboard its submarines.[24]

The United States employs many of the technical and procedural aspects of negative and positive controls discussed at the beginning of this chapter, including the two-person rule and use of PALs.[25] For negative controls within the U.S. SSBN fleet, a "Use Control" system was installed during the summer of 1997 that requires the receipt of an external code in order to unlock a critical component of the SSBN system (the Captain's Indicator Panel Key) which is stored in a safe onboard the submarine. Without this component, the system is unable to launch.[26] In 2001, the Department of Defense initiated an "End-to-End Review of the U.S. Nuclear Command and Control System." Though many of the findings from the review were classified, some of them included: the need to enhance system survivability and hardness due to degradation since the end of the cold war; a decline in the number of people who have expertise in nuclear command and control; challenges associated with incorporating a vertical, hierarchical C^2 structure with the new broad, dispersed mission space of U.S. Strategic Command; and the integration of nuclear and conventional capabilities within the new U.S. strategic triad.[27] A central challenge posed by this C^2 modernization is the maintenance of nuclear positive and negative controls if certain components and delivery vehicles of the nuclear system are simultaneously conducting conventional operations. This challenge is discussed below.

Though not a declared nuclear weapon state, Israel is believed to maintain up to 300 nuclear warheads of various types that can be delivered by aircraft, ballistic missiles, and, potentially, artillery. Israel is also pursuing an assured second-strike capability through the acquisition of three Dolphin-class submarines from Germany. The authority to employ nuclear weapons rests with the Israeli prime minister and physical control of the weapons falls under the defense minister. For negative controls, Israel is believed to store its weapons disassembled, with the capability to rapidly assemble them and mate the warheads with their delivery vehicles.[28] Due to the opaque nature of its nuclear deterrent, further details about the technical control measures for Israeli nuclear weapons are not openly published.

Following the 1998 nuclear tests in India and Pakistan, both countries forfeited the luxury they previously had of not having to discuss their strategic command and control procedures. India released its draft nuclear doctrine in the summer of 1999 and began to discuss more openly some of the positive and negative controls that it was enacting. These included the creation of a Nuclear Command Authority (NCA), maintaining civilian control of nuclear weapons, the declaration of an NFU doctrine, keeping warheads unmated from delivery vehicles, keeping weapon components disassembled with separate custody organizations, and pursuing a retaliatory strike capability through hardened command bunkers and a sea-based leg of the deterrent.[29] Some concern remains, however, over the chain of succession in the case of the demise of the prime minister, the sole authority over nuclear use, as well as operational challenges for the military units who are tasked with nuclear employment responsibilities during war but are unfamiliar with the weapons for training purposes. In certain circumstances, India is expected to pre-delegate nuclear authority to military leaders to ensure a retaliatory strike capability.[30]

Pakistan has also recently increased its public discourse on its nuclear command and control structure and processes. These include an announcement about separation of the authorities to use nuclear weapons from the authorities responsible for executing use,[31] establishment of an organization dedicated to weapon security, and not mating warheads with delivery vehicles. Unlike India, however, Pakistan retains the right to first use in its nuclear doctrine. In addition, Pakistan relies heavily on negative procedural controls that are slowly degraded during a crisis in favor of positive procedural controls (such as assembling warheads or mating warheads with delivery vehicles), thus creating a potential C^2 bias toward nuclear use.[32] The implications of this degradation are discussed below.

The final two nuclear actors to be explored in this chapter are North Korea and Iran. Due to the nascent and secretive nature of both programs, limited information is readily available through open sources about any negative and positive controls measures that may exist, though it is expected that both nations maintain a tight, centralized control over their limited nuclear stockpiles. On 9 October 2006, North Korea openly stated its nuclear intentions by conducting a nuclear test. The technical challenges apparently experienced during the test underscore the early stages of the North Korean program and the likelihood that any negative control measures currently in place, such as storing weapon components disassembled, will be primarily procedural. North Korea is expected to rely initially on aircraft delivery for any nuclear devices it develops for operational purposes, with positive controls restricted to procedural measures related to the forward deployment of assembled weapons at airfields and possibly the mating of assembled weapons with the aircraft. In addition, the authoritarian nature of the North Korean regime raises concern over the chain of custody for nuclear devices if Kim Jong Il dies.[33] One U.S. expert who visited North Korea shortly after the October 2006 test remarked, "The officials we met appeared to have little appreciation for the new challenges they faced for nuclear weapons safety and security that results from the possession of nuclear weapons."[34]

Similar to North Korea's secrecy regarding its nuclear program, Iran continues to claim that its nuclear aspirations are strictly peaceful and serve no military purpose. Due to the lack of transparency, analysis of

Iranian nuclear C^2 is limited to the current understanding of civilian-military authorities within Iran and its previous command and control procedures for its chemical weapons program. Central to the development and potential deployment of Iranian nuclear capabilities is the role of the Islamic Revolutionary Guard Corps (IRCG). Iran maintains a dual military structure, with the regular armed forces responsible for the defense of Iran's territory and political integrity, while the IRGC is responsible for preserving the Islamic revolution. The IRGC is believed to be developing nuclear weapons through four military organizations in Iran and operates at a much higher strategic level than the regular armed forces. Due to the immaturity of Iran's nuclear program, safety and security procedures for the initial nuclear devices will primarily involve procedural measures such as the separation of warhead components for storage; but these procedural negative controls will be forfeited if warheads are assembled and mated to delivery vehicles during a crisis (i.e. a transition to procedural positive controls). In addition, it is possible that an internal security organization may be created specifically to ensure the security of Iran's nuclear weapons.[35]

C^2 STABILITY DYNAMICS IN THE TWENTY-FIRST CENTURY AND IMPLICATIONS FOR POLICY

The preceding discussion explores the stability dynamics associated with a variety of negative and positive nuclear control measures. This assessment highlights the potential stability provided by a non-use bias during a crisis when procedural negative controls (such as two-person rules, restricted access to launch codes, or a delayed response posture) are maintained simultaneously with technical negative controls incorporated in the weapon design and positive technical controls that ensure system robustness and survivability during combat operations. The overview above of existing nuclear C^2 postures highlights four key areas, depicted graphically in figure 12.4, where existing command and control systems risk transitioning toward a use bias during a crisis:

1. Procedural chain of custody measures (negative controls) in Iran, North Korea, and Pakistan that potentially exist without complimentary negative technical controls;
2. South Asian security dynamics and the degradation of Pakistani negative control procedures during crisis escalation;

3. U.S.-Russian crisis management during conventional SLBM and BMD engagements against third party threats; and

4. Deliberate asymmetric threats against existing C^2 systems.

Though Iran and North Korea maintain a greater shroud of secrecy around their nuclear weapons programs than Pakistan, all three nations appear to rely on negative procedural controls and the associated personnel reliability procedures as the primary means of ensuring the safety and security of the nuclear capabilities. With its totalitarian organizational structure, North Korea may have adequate security for its nuclear devices as long as they remain in a non-deployed and disassembled status. The safety of North Korea's devices, however, is most likely lacking since technical measures such as one-point safety, weak links and electrical exclusion zones are probably inadequately incorporated in their weapon designs. For this reason, policy efforts should focus on not provoking any nuclear posturing from North Korea that may include the final assembly and potential deployment of their nuclear devices.

Iran poses a significant challenge in that its negative procedural controls appear inadequate if the forces transition into a deployed status. Even if they remain under the control of the authorized nuclear command structure, it would be the IRGC, which is the more bellicose branch of the Iranian armed forces. The end result is a challenge similar to North Korea in that external pressures may have limited ability to prevent the acquisition and development of nuclear weapons, but ill-considered external pressures may result in a deployed nuclear posture and a potential C^2 instability bias toward use.

Pakistan, a more advanced nuclear state than Iran and North Korea, can leverage the influence of external actors to assist in dampening regional crisis escalation involving India, which is the most likely reason for a Pakistani transition from negative to positive procedural controls. South Asian security dynamics highlight an Indian C^2 posture that is biased toward non-use and a Pakistani C^2 posture biased toward use.[36] The geography of the region provides India with sufficient strategic depth to assure some level of retaliatory strike capability, an advantage that simultaneously creates an almost immediate requirement for Pakistan to transition toward a use bias in order to present a credible deterrent. Pakistani confidence in the survivability of its nuclear deterrent can decrease the perceived need for positive procedural controls and reduce crisis instability and escalation. Potential bilateral measures that can contribute to a non-use bias during a crisis include the avoidance of counter-force targeting—including C^2 networks and command posts—by conventional as well as nuclear forces, and the declaration of a no first use posture.[37] Overall, the criticality of C^2 stability in South Asia is captured well by one expert who noted, "A peacetime environment in the region will pay the dividend of keeping arsenals non-deployed and the safety and security coefficient will remain high. This situation would change, however, if regional strategic dynamics lead to formal nuclear deployments..."[38] Finally, Pakistan may be willing to receive information and assistance on negative technical controls as long as this level of cooperation does not threaten the security of its nuclear stockpile.[39] This type of assistance can provide safety during regional crises as well as scenarios involving theft of a device where negative procedural controls are insufficient.

U.S.-Russia

The ongoing transformation in U.S. and Russian strategic postures poses a unique challenge and has global implications. Though both countries have stated policies that they are no longer adversaries and do not target each other with strategic systems, the adaptation of legacy weapon systems and legacy command and control processes to address new and emerging threats can still place these two nations at strategic odds during a crisis. The pursuit of global strike and global missile defense capabilities by the United States significantly increases the need for transparency between the two countries, as misperceptions may result during the employment of conventionally armed ballistic missiles (especially submarine-launched) or interceptor flight paths that broach Russian airspace. The U.S. Congress identified some of these risks in the *National Defense Authorization Act for Fiscal Year 2007* in which Congress calls upon the Secretary of Defense to provide:

- a report on the capabilities of other countries to discriminate between the launch of a conventional or nuclear sea-launched ballistic missile;

- an assessment of the notification and other protocols that would have to be in place before using any conventional sea-launched ballistic missile and a plan for entering into such protocols; and

- a joint statement by the Secretary of Defense and the Secretary of State on how to ensure that the use of a conventional sea-launched ballistic missile will not result in an intentional, inadvertent, mistaken, or accidental reciprocal or responsive launch of a nuclear strike by any other country.[40]

Some of these concerns and requirements can be addressed through the execution of the June 2000 "Memorandum of Agreement Between the Government of the United States and Government of the Russian Federation on the Establishment of a Joint Center for the Exchange of Data from Early Warning Systems and Notifications of Missile Launches."[41] This agreement, commonly referred to as the Joint Data Exchange Center (JDEC), is held up by legal wrangling between the two countries over personal tax and liability issues for U.S. personnel working in the proposed Moscow-based center.[42]

Figure 12.4. C² Stability Dynamics and Policy Implications

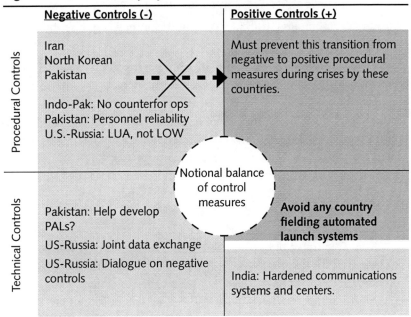

An additional bilateral concern involving the United States and Russia is their maintenance of launch on warning (LOW) postures despite their stated non-adversarial relationship. This perceived "hair trigger" environment was tested during the 25 January 1995 launch of a Norwegian sounding rocket from an island off the northwest coast of Norway, a perceived area for U.S. Trident submarine patrol routes.[43] A senior

Russian general who served in the Strategic Rocket Forces (SRF) command center during the event asserts that the negative procedural controls in place adequately diffused the situation and Russian forces were never prepared for launch. The launch commands associated with the Russian strategic systems involve four stages:

- *preliminary command*—after the identification of a potential threat from EW systems;

- *permission command*—upon confirmation of a missile attack against Russia, preparation by the president, minister of defense and chief of the General Staff of authorization for nuclear use, and delegation of use to the three military commanders in chief;

- *direct command*—submission of launch commands with special unblocking code values and the number of the operational plan to launch crews at the operational level; and

- *launch command*—the execution of the launch order by the missile crews.[44]

According to the Russian General, only the first level of launch command was initiated during the Norwegian incident as command center personnel recognized the launch as an anomaly and considered it very unlikely that the United States would engage Russia with a single submarine-launched ballistic missile (SLBM). American officials have also stated that their perception of the incident was that the Russian system "worked" and no launch authorization was issued over a misinterpreted threat.[45] Despite these assurances, however, experts from the Russian and American strategic communities agree on the need to enhance bilateral transparency in the areas of early warning and data exchange.

A final area for exploration in C^2 stability dynamics is the potential risks created by deliberate, asymmetric attacks against the command and control system of a nuclear nation in order to generate false warnings or unauthorized procedures. These attack profiles may involve the degradation of negative control procedures or the manipulation of positive control procedures and center on taking remote control of command systems rather than physical control of the actual nuclear weapons. In the investigations following the September 11 attacks in the United States, intelligence officials discovered that one of the plots discussed in an Al Qaeda training camp was the hijacking of a Russian ICBM launcher and forcing the crew to launch their missile against the United States.[46] Though much more technically challenging (if not impossible), this asymmetric attack profile represents a scenario that merits further consideration and consultation: the intentional manipulation of nuclear command and control procedures in order to execute nuclear release.[47] Of particular concern is the assurance that negative control procedures are adequately robust from a security perspective (and safety perspective) to prevent all possible avenues for initiating nuclear release. Moreover, the joint exploration of negative controls can be conducted without posing a risk to the positive control measures or degrading the efficacy of the negative controls.[48] Finally, joint discussions on negative controls can also cover potential insider threats emerging from underpaid nuclear scientists and military personnel serving in nuclear duties, a cause of concern in the West.[49]

This chapter highlights the role of nuclear command and control systems in promoting strategic stability during a crisis. The previous discussion underscores the importance of promoting a non-use bias through sustained procedural and technical negative controls and assured system robustness and survivability through positive technical control measures. The end result of this balanced mix of control measures is that command and control systems are sufficiently safe, secure, and reliable during the transition from peace to crisis, and into wartime, that nuclear use never occurs as a result of unauthorized or accidental events, and that nuclear authorization is less likely to occur as a result of the fog of war.

Notes

1. This chapter uses the term "command and control" to represent all aspects of the system developed by a state to conduct its nuclear operations and provide safety, security and reliability to its arsenal. Included in this discussion are the communication processes that are part of the command and control system but not the supporting intelligence capabilities. As such, this discussion of nuclear command and control also explores the topic of nuclear command, control, and communications (C3) but not command, control, communications, and intelligence (C3I).

2. "U.S. Nuclear Command and Control System Support Staff," Department of Defense Directive 3150.06 (dated August 25, 2006). Available online: www.fas.org/irp/doddir/dod/d3150_06.pdf.

3. Ibid, 2.

4. See for example John D. Steinbruner, "Choices and Trade-offs" in Ashton B. Carter, John D. Steinbruner, and Charles A. Zraket, *Managing Nuclear Oper-*

ations (Washington, D.C, Brookings Institution, 1987), 539-541; and Bruce G. Blair, *Strategic Command and Control: Redefining the Nuclear Threat* (Washington, D.C, Brookings Institution, 1985), 68-69. It should be noted that positive controls are different from "positive measures" which the U.S. Department of Defense defines as "design features, safety rules, procedures, accident prevention or mitigation measures, or other controls including physical security and coded systems, used collectively or individually, to enhance safety and to reduce the likelihood, severity, or consequences of an accident, unauthorized act, or deliberate threat." Source: DOD 3150.2-M, *DOD Nuclear Weapon System Safety Program Manual* (December 1996).

5. The six functions are based on a list provided in Valery E. Yarynich, *C3: Nuclear Command, Control Cooperation* (Washington, DC: Center for Defense Information, 2003), 17.

6. Inadvertent escalation refers to scenarios where conventional operations may result in the unintended targeting of an adversary's strategic assets and the potential triggering of a nuclear response by the adversary who perceives the conventional strike as a decapitation or counter-force attack. This type of scenario is commonly mentioned in the need for escalation control in South Asia. On "inadvertent escalation," see Barry R. Posen, "Inadvertent Nuclear War? Escalation and NATO's Northern Flank," *International Security* Vol. 7, No. 2 (Fall 1982), 28-54. For a theoretical discussion on inadvertent escalation in South Asia, see Rajesh Rajagopalan, "The Threat of Unintended Use of Nuclear Weapons in South Asia," *India Review* Vol. 4, No. 2 (April 2005), 214-232. Concerning the limited time available for executing strategic decisions, Dr. Zbigniew Brzezinski has stated his training indicated he had "roughly three minutes in which to verify the nature of the attack and its scale, which would involve several progressive steps. The President, once I reached him, would have four minutes to decide how to respond depending on the scale of the attack. Then the execution would be set in motion." The Atlantic Council of the United States, Christopher J. Makins Lecture given by Dr. Zbigniew Brzezinski on 31 May 2006 at the British Ambassador's Residence in Washington, DC (transcript page 3). Former Soviet President Mikhail Gorbachev stated in a 14 July 2006 interview on radio station Echo in Moscow that when conducting exercises to simulate a strategic attack from China, "they suddenly report to me that missiles are flying from a certain direction, I give a command, I receive proposals [for action], I give my agreement…and it all takes 10-15 minutes…" Available in Russian at: http://www.echo.msk.ru/programs/razvorot/44851/index.phtml (Translation provided by Dr. Mikhail Tsypkin). The September 11, 2001 attacks in the United States highlight, however, that unplanned, real-time communications cannot always be achieved for national leaders. President Bush was unable to conduct critical communications with key strategic advisors in the White House while he was

aboard Air Force One. Kimberly Weisul, "How Air Force One Let Bush Down," *Business Week* (4 November 2002). Available online: http://www.businessweek. com/magazine/content/02_44/c3806015.htm

7. Further discussion on the operational risks associated with no first use (NFU), launch under attack (LUA), and launch on warning (LOW) postures are discussed in the final section of this chapter.

8. For a detailed discussion on the technical aspects of positive and negative nuclear controls, see Chuck Hansen, *The Swords of Armageddon: U.S. Nuclear Weapons Development Since 1945*, Volume VIII (1995); Donald R. Cotter, "Peacetime Operations: Safety and Security," in Ashton B. Carter, John D. Steinbruner, and Charles A. Zraket, *Managing Nuclear Operations* (Washington, D.C, Brookings Institution, 1987), 42-55; and Chris Burroughs, "Tiny 'Micro Guardian' Promises to Safeguard Nuclear Weapons in Big Way, *Sandia Lab News* Vol. 51, No. 1 (15 January 1999).

9. Some confusion exists over whether the Soviet Union ever fielded Dead Hand and the misidentification of this system with the Soviet Perimetr system. A recently declassified top secret memorandum drafted in 1985 for the Soviet Politburo by Oleg Belyakov (titled "On Shortcomings in the Organization for Work to Increase the Effectiveness of Strategic Armaments") states that "no attention at all has been given to an extremely important military-political proposal to create a fully automated system for retaliatory strike operations that could be activated by the highest command levels during a threatening period." The implications of this memorandum and the known Soviet emphasis on centralized, assertive control seem to indicate that Dead Hand never went beyond the proposal stage. Correspondence with Mark Kramer, 1 March 2007. For a discussion on the Perimetr system that employs rocket-borne transponders to communicate launch orders to Russian ICBM crews when landlines are severed, see Valery E. Yarynich, 156-159. Perimetr concepts appear to mirror those of the U.S. Emergency Rocket Communication System (ERCS).

10. Personnel Reliability Program refers to the screening of military and civilian personnel before they are assigned to nuclear duty positions. Nuclear duty positions are generally divided into two categories: a critical nuclear duty position (where the person has served in a command and control position, has technical knowledge of the system, or has access to nuclear weapons under the two-person rule), or a controlled nuclear duty position (where the person has access to nuclear weapons but does not require technical knowledge). Critical nuclear duty positions include personnel who perform maintenance and/or modifications on nuclear weapons or serve in critical command and control positions such as PAL teams, delivery and warhead support units, or emergency action message authentication and employment responsibilities. Controlled nuclear duty positions include personnel who handle nuclear weapons, such

as vehicle, equipment and aircraft operators, and members of nuclear weapon storage site security forces. See Donald R. Cotter, "Peacetime Operations: Safety and Security," 60-61; and "DODD 5210.42 Nuclear Weapon Personnel Reliability Program (PRP)" (15 December 1995). Available at: www.fas.org/nuke/guide/usa/doctrine/dod/dodd-5210_42.htm

11. This point is explored in the final section during the discussion on South Asian stability dynamics.

12. Soviet operational procedures in the early 1960s specifically required that theater commanders receive approval prior to using tactical nuclear weapons in a war. General Anatolii Gribkov, whose comments at a U.S.-Russian meeting in Havana in 1992 initiated some of the rumors about Soviet delegation of launch authority to General Pliyev, later retracted his comments to state Pliyev "was *categorically forbidden* to use nuclear weapons of any type" during the Cuban crisis. Quoted in Mark Kramer, "Tactical Nuclear Weapons, Soviet Command Authority, and the Cuban Missile Crisis." Colonel Nikolai Beloborodov, who commanded the storage site for the Soviet nuclear weapons in Cuba, stated in an interview, "No nuclear munitions of any type, whether for the medium-range or the tactical weapons, were ever moved out of storage during the crisis. Nor could they have been moved without my knowledge." Quoted in Mark Kramer, "'Lessons' of the Cuban Missile Crisis," 353, footnote 17.

13. Mark Kramer, "'Lessons' of the Cuban Missile Crisis for Warsaw Pact Operations," Cold War International History Project Bulletin, 352.

14. As the space constraints of this chapter do not allow for a detailed discussion on the warheads and delivery vehicles employed by each of the nuclear actors, this section focuses on general trends as they impact command and control requirements.

15. "Command and Control—China Nuclear Forces." Federation of American Scientists. Available at: http://www.fas.org. While trying to improve its strategic communications capabilities, China has openly admitted that the Second Artillery Corps continues to be challenged when conducting field exercises. See Hans M. Kristensen, Robert S. Norris, and Matthew G. McKinzie, *Chinese Nuclear Forces and U.S. Nuclear War Planning.* Federation of American Scientists & The Natural Resources Defense Council (Washington, DC, November 2006), 47-52.

16. David S. Yost, "France's Evolving Nuclear Strategy," *Survival* Vol. 47, No. 3 (Autumn 2005), 122.

17. David Yost, "France's New Nuclear Doctrine," *International Affairs* Vol. 82, No. 4 (2006), 704. Dr. Yost also highlights French discussions on possibly reducing the yield of existing weapons to only a detonation of the "primary" warhead stage ("amorce") thus reducing collateral damage. See also Bruno Ter-

trais, "Nuclear Policy: France Stands Alone," *Bulletin of the Atomic Scientists* (July/August 2004), 48-55.

18. David Yost, "France's New Nuclear Doctrine," Bruno Tertrais, "Nuclear Policy: France Stands Alone," as well as a discussion on French nuclear command and control in Gurmeet Kanwal, "Command and Control of Nuclear Weapons in India," *Strategic Analysis* Vol. 13, No. 10).

19. Mark Schneider, "The Nuclear Forces and Doctrine of the Russian Federation." A Publication of the United States Nuclear Strategy Forum (Washington, DC, National Institute Press, 2006).

20. Vladimir Dvorkin, "On Strategic Relations between Russia and the U.S.: An Analysis of Mark Schneider's paper titled 'The Nuclear Forces and Doctrine of the Russian Federation,'" (September 2006). General Dvorkin also observed that the Russian abandonment of its no first use doctrine mirrored the postures of France, Great Britain and the United States (Dvorkin, 13-18).

21. Valery Yarynich, 206-209.

22. The final section of this chapter includes a more detailed discussion of Russian procedural negative controls in the context of the January 1995 launch of a Norwegian sounding rocket and Russian response to this event.

23. Paul Robinson of Sandia National Laboratory is reported to have stated in 1994 that "Sandia also designs the arming-fusing-firing mechanisms for the British nuclear weapons programme." Included in these design features would be two strong links and one weak link component. See John Ainslie, "The Future of the British Bomb," WMD Awareness Programme (Glasgow, UK, Clydeside Press, 19 October 2006).

24. Robert S. Norris and Hans M. Kristensen, "British Nuclear Forces, 2005," *Bulletin of the Atomic Scientists* Vol. 61, No. 6 (November/December 2005), 77-79.

25. An extensive discussion of U.S. command and control procedures and technologies can be found in Bruce G. Blair, *Strategic Command and Control: Redefining the Nuclear Threat* (Washington, DC: Brookings Institution, 1985); Ashton B. Carter, John D. Steinbruner, and Charles A. Zraket, *Managing Nuclear Operations*; and Valery E. Yarynich, *C3: Nuclear Command, Control Cooperation.*

26. Mel Lyman, "Crimson Tide: They Got It All Wrong," *The Submarine Review* (April 1999).

27. Robert D. Critchlow, "Nuclear Command and Control: Current Programs and Issues," CRS Report to Congress (3 May 2006).

28. Seth Elan et al, "Open-Source Research on Nuclear Doctrine and Strategy, Command and Control, and Delivery Systems in Iran and Israel," Library

of Congress (December 2005). "Israel Nuclear Overview." Center for Nonproliferation Studies (September 2004). Available at: www.nti.org; and Warner D. Farr, "The Third Temple's Holy of Holies: Israel's Nuclear Weapons," The Counterproliferation Papers, Future Warfare Series No. 2 (Maxwell Air Force Base, Alabama, September 1999).

29. Ashley J. Tellis, "Toward a 'Force-in-Being': The Logic, Structure, and Utility of India's Emerging Nuclear Posture"; Feroz Hassan Khan, "Nuclear Command-and-Control in South Asia during Peace, Crisis and War," *Contemporary South Asia* Vol. 14, No. 2 (June 2005), 163-174; Peter R. Lavoy and Christopher Clary, "Strategic Stability in South Asia: Conference Summary," (29 June–1 July 2004), available at: http://www.ccc.nps.navy.mil/events/recent/jul04southasia.pdf; and Harsh V. Pant, "India's Nuclear doctrine and Command Structure: Implications for India and the World," *Comparative Strategy* Vol. 24 (2005), 277-293.

30. Peter R. Lavoy and Christopher Clary, "Strategic Stability in South Asia: Conference Summary."

31. Though some observers believe key people in Pakistan have both use and execution authorities.

32. Feroz Hassan Khan, "Nuclear Command-and-Control in South Asia during Peace, Crisis and War" and Peter R. Lavoy and Christopher Clary, "Strategic Stability in South Asia: Conference Summary."

33. Robert S. Norris and Hans M. Kristensen, "North Korea's Nuclear Program, 2005," *Bulletin of Atomic Scientists* (May/June 2005), 64-67.

34. Siegfried S. Hecker, "Report on North Korean Nuclear Program," Center for International Security and Cooperation, Stanford University (15 November 2006). Available at: www.fas.org.

35. Gregory F. Giles, "The Islamic Republic of Iran and Nuclear, Biological, and Chemical Weapons," in Peter R. Lavoy, Scott D. Sagan, and James J. Wirtz, eds., *Planning the Unthinkable. How New Powers Will Use Nuclear, Biological, and Chemical Weapons* (Ithaca: Cornell University Press, 2000), 79–103; Seth Elan et al, "Open-Source Research on Nuclear Doctrine and Strategy, Command and Control, and Delivery Systems in Iran and Israel;" and Jack Boureston and Charles D. Ferguson, "Schooling Iran's Atom Squad," *Bulletin of the Atomic Scientists* (May/June 2004), 31-35.

36. Peter R. Lavoy and Christopher Clary, "Strategic Stability in South Asia: Conference Summary."

37. Though India already has a no first use policy and is believed to have a counter-value targeting strategy, the inability to verify/enforce these policies makes it difficult for Pakistani officials to be comfortable accepting these Indian declarations at face value. For conventional operations, India can avoid

offensive actions against known weapon and vehicle storage sites and known command and control networks and posts.

38. Feroz Hassan Khan, "Nuclear Command-and-Control in South Asia during Peace, Crisis and War," *Contemporary South Asia* Vol. 14, No. 2 (June 2005), 170-171.

39. The sharing of PAL technology and other negative controls is viewed by many observers as a violation of the nuclear non-proliferation treaty (NPT) since it would be a de facto acceptance of Pakistan as a nuclear weapons state. Similar discussions surround the sharing of civilian nuclear energy technologies with India by the United States. From a policy perspective, therefore, the crux of the issue is that negative controls prevent unauthorized use but can be perceived as enhancing Pakistani nuclear capabilities and increase the risks they might be able to take during a crisis. From a nuclear safety and security perspective, however, negative controls can also prevent the use of a nuclear device due to theft or diversion by an insider.

40. Section 219, paragraph b (5), (6) and (14).

41. "Agreement on the Establishment of a Joint Warning Center for the Exchange of Information on Missile Launches and Early Warning." White House Fact Sheet, Office of the Press Secretary (4 June 2000).

42. Wade Boese, "Joint Data Exchange Center on Hold," *Arms Control Today* (June 2006). Available at http://www.armscontrol.org/act/2006_06/CartwrightInterview.asp#Sidebar

43. Pavel Podvig, "If It's Broke, Don't Fix It," *Bulletin of the American Scientists* (July/August 2005), 21-22. Despite some reporting, this launch of a Black Brant XII was not an unannounced event but part of a series of three rocket launches scheduled for the period of 15 January–10 February 1995 from the Andoya Rocket Range. See "Royal Ministry of Foreign Affairs (Oslo) letter to The Heads of Mission," Number 21776/VII/94 (dated 21 December 1994).

44. Valery E. Yarynich, 152-153.

45. Interview with Russian and American officials directly involved in the incident (July 2002).

46. Faye Bowers and Peter Grier, "9/11 Panel Details Plots of Al Qaeda," *Christian Science Monitor* (17 June 2004).

47. Valery E. Yarynich, "The Ultimate Terrorism," *Washington Post* (30 April 2004), A29.

48. For an extensive discussion on this topic, see Valery E. Yarynich, *C3: Nuclear Command, Control Cooperation.*

49. There was a highly publicized incident in September 1998 in which a sailor killed a guard and seven crew members aboard an Akula-class SSN at the

Northern Fleet's Gadzhiyevo Base and then attempted to detonate the submarine's torpedoes (resulting in his own death). Western experts often cite this as
an example of potential vulnerabilities created by poor living conditions and
low pay for Russian service members. See James Clay Moltz and Tamara C.
Robinson, "Dismantling Russia's Nuclear Subs: New Challenges to Non-proliferation," *Arms Control Today* (June 1999). For a discussion on Russian efforts
concerning nuclear security, see Yevgeny Maslin, "Security of Nuclear Arsenals
in the Russian Federation," *Yaderny Kontrol Digest* Vol. 9, No. 3-4 (Summer/Fall
2004), 6-13; and Vladimir Verkhovtsev, "Nuclear Weapons Security—Russia's
Top Priority in the Long Term," *Yaderny Kontrol Digest* Vol. 10, No. 1-2 (Win-
ter/Spring 2005), 38-45.

CHAPTER THIRTEEN

TRANSFORMATION OF THE NUCLEAR WEAPONS COMPLEX

OVERCOMING THE LEGACY OF A SPRAWLING ENTERPRISE

Lani Miyoshi Sanders

The Nuclear Weapons Complex (Complex) began as a geographically sprawling enterprise, peppering the country with the physical underpinnings of the nuclear age. Today, a buzzword for the Complex is consolidation, reflecting the paradigm shift from the original Manhattan Engineering District and Atomic Energy Commission (AEC) siting strategies to the current strategies for creating a more sustainable and affordable future Complex.[1] That this future Complex cannot be constructed *de novo*, but must emerge from a physical foundation largely misaligned with today's environment, is the challenge of transformation.[2]

The physical foundation of the current Complex can be simplistically summarized as eight major sites in seven states operated (singly or in partnership) by almost a dozen different entities. From one vantage point, this geographic dispersal and relative independence creates a Complex that "does not operate as an integrated enterprise with a shared purpose...resulting in redundant programs and facilities, increasing costs and reducing productivity."[3] Yet, from the point of view of the Complex's original architects, geographic separation, independent operations, and duplication of missions of the sites was a conscious strategy, intended in part to meet three key drivers continuing to have top priority today: security, safety, and responsiveness.

SECURITY AND SAFETY: IN THE EYE OF THE BEHOLDER

Designing for security and safety held a vastly different meaning in the 1940s and 1950s, when the majority of the Complex was sited and constructed. At that time, security centered on secrecy, compartmentalizing knowledge, and the ability to sustain capabilities, even if a site was compromised by an attack; this was the "policy of strategic dispersion."[4] As a result, the AEC sometimes duplicated missions at separate sites, often far from the first location of the mission (e.g., Hanford and Savannah River). Note, almost 60 per cent of the states had a nuclear weapons site resident in them at one time or another.[5]

Security and safety were also intimately linked with remoteness of sites. Remoteness provided secrecy, an utmost concern, as well as protection of the public if there was an accident.[6] The first production facilities for the Manhattan Project, constructed in Tennessee (Y-12 and K-25, for electromagnetic separation and gaseous diffusion of U-235, respectively; and X-10, for the experimental plutonium pile and separation facilities), were "located in valleys away from the town...provid[ing] security and containment in case of explosions."[7] The choice of Hanford (a half-million acre site) as the full-scale plutonium facility reflected the need for greater isolation than what Oak Ridge could provide.[8]

Today, threats to the security of the Complex stand in stark contrast to those at the time of its inception. Clearly, the September 11 terrorist attacks epitomized that change. The siting and design of the Complex reflected the security concerns of the day—more on the order of Soviet long-range bombing or keeping the Manhattan Project secret than terrorists on suicide missions. In short, "no threat of the current nature was envisioned."[9] For example, the location of production facilities in isolated valleys may have been a reasonable choice when security was synonymous with secrecy, but is a very poor choice in today's environment, where those with the high ground enjoy a huge tactical advantage in a conflict.

Safety is also a very different business today.[10] Note that it took not one, but two deaths, utilizing the same plutonium core, to end hands-on criticality work at Los Alamos in 1946.[11] In this same year, the Atomic Energy Act was passed, and "its major safety concern, other than national security, was protection of the public and property."[12] In other words, worker safety, while important, was not the highest priority. Today, remoteness remains important in mitigating consequences of accidents to surrounding populations, and worker safety is viewed as critically important.

Yet, an effective balance between productivity (from a program stand-point) and safety and security performance has yet to be struck. In 1997, the "120-Day Study" noted that "the largest single problem uncovered is that…DOE's practices for managing environmental, safety, and health concerns are constipating the system."[13] In 2005, the "Overskei Task Force" noted that "the DOE has burdened the Complex with rules and regulations that focus on process rather than mission safety…resulting in a risk-averse posture at all management levels."[14] That safety and security can still wield such power in the Complex, yet mean something quite different to the infrastructure and its operation than in the past, illustrates the profound importance of considering a variety of potential futures when shaping an infrastructure to meet multiple decades to come.

CONSOLIDATION AND RESPONSIVE INFRASTRUCTURE: FRIENDS OR FOES

Although the safety and security needs of the Complex have changed as the world has changed, the meaning of responsiveness has remained deeply tied to what the Complex can do—and in what timeframes. Responsive infrastructure is currently defined with temporal criteria (for example, time to fix, adapt, prototype, produce, or dismantle weapons) or by "the resilience of the nuclear enterprise to unanticipated events or emerging threats and the ability to anticipate innovations by an adversary and to counter them before our deterrent is degraded."[15] Although the specific temporal criteria (i.e., number of months) have evolved, the meaning and intent underlying responsiveness have not evolved as dramatically as the safety and security landscapes, for example. What has changed is the willingness to pay the cost. In other words, using today's lens, a hedge for deterring a resurgent Russia appears expensive (through the lens of the Cold War, the costs looked quite different).

For example, the duplication of capabilities, originally intended to provide strategic redundancy for responsiveness, still provides that redundancy in some cases, but is now often perceived as wasted resources. In recent years, the pressure on the National Nuclear Security Administration (NNSA) to reduce duplication has increased measurably. Yet, reduction in strategic redundancy can have a cost: increased risk and reduced innovation and creativity. A study examining options for "reconfiguring" the Complex in the early 1990s (Complex-21) put it this way: "The thrusts to downsize, consolidate, and privatize must be balanced with a level of prudent redundancy in selected key capabilities, which, if lost, would cause significant and rapid degradation of overall Complex effectiveness."[16] In other words, the responsiveness functions of surge capacity, redundancy, and intellectual capital can be degraded by consolidation and elimination of duplication.

Note that even in the early days of consolidation, the government sometimes chose to pay for responsiveness. For example, in 1963, the AEC decided not to begin shutting down all the reactor operations at either Savannah River or Hanford, but to alternate closings back and forth between sites, although the former made more economic sense. Acting AEC chairman Robert E. Wilson justified this decision to President Kennedy based on the need to maintain surge capacity and strategic redundancy.[17] Minimizing local economic impacts was also given as justification, indicating that politics played an important role then, as it does now.

From a security standpoint, consolidation versus the high expense of a "policy of strategic dispersion" remains a subject of debate. The recent Task Force on Nuclear Weapons Complex Infrastructure stated "the broad distribution of special nuclear materials (SNM)...increases the number of potential terrorist targets within this country...With physical security costs approaching 15 percent of the budget, the benefits of SNM consolidation are substantial, both in terms of reducing capital and operating costs as well as reducing risk to adjacent populations."[18] The opposing viewpoint was captured by Admiral Henry G. Chiles, Jr., USN (Ret.): "We should disperse the facilities that undertake nuclear weapons infrastructure design and manufacturing activities...If these facilities were located in a single site, that location would offer an attractive target to an adversary, who would then be able to cripple our capability for maintaining our present and future stockpile."[19]

This contrast in perspectives hints at a larger question about the role of consolidation in realizing a responsive infrastructure. Consolidation, at its core, is about economics—reducing the fixed costs of the Complex. Although economics certainly play a role in the sustainability of the enterprise as a whole, the explicit tie between responsive infrastructure and consolidation deserves closer scrutiny. Conceptually, a responsive infrastructure could be achieved independent of a geographically consolidated enterprise, if cost was not a central factor. And, indeed, it has been.

THE MANHATTAN PROJECT: FROM SCRATCH, WITH DEEP POCKETS, IN A UNIQUE MOMENT

When discussing the lack of responsiveness of today's Complex, the Manhattan Project is often held up as evidence of what the Complex (and indeed, the nation) could be capable of accomplishing under specific world conditions (a crisis or strategic surprise). It stands as an enduring benchmark for responsiveness—and an obvious antithesis of consolidation. There can be little disagreement that the journey from "laboratory research [to] design, construction, operation, and product delivery in two-and-a-half years (from early 1943 to Hiroshima) [was] a major industrial achievement."[20] The Manhattan Project can be understood as a paragon of responsive infrastructure, even as defined today.

The Manhattan Project had three pivotal responsive infrastructure enablers lacking today: (1) starting from scratch, (2) deep pockets, and (3) a unique world environment. History reveals insights about how necessary and/or sufficient these three enablers can be in creating a responsive infrastructure, and their relevance to consolidation.

The Manhattan Project had the distinct advantage of starting from scratch—a chance to create its own infrastructure to fit the needs of the day, rather than transform an aging infrastructure ill-suited to the needs of the day. The benefits are obvious: no legacy facilities, no contamination, no outdated technology, and clean sheet designs tailored to the needs.

It also had the benefit of deep pockets. With "AAA Priority," top procurement priority obtained by General Leslie Groves from the War Production Board, new and expansive facilities (peopled by some of the best minds in the world with whole new communities to support them) were rapidly constructed for the Manhattan Project.[21] For example, in 30 months, 554 non-residential buildings (including B, D, and F Reactors, and T, B, and U Processing Canyons), 64 underground high level waste tanks, 544 miles of road/railways, and the "government city" of Richland (housing 17,500 people) were constructed at Hanford.[22]

Despite what the Manhattan Project was able to accomplish, it is difficult to argue that starting from scratch is either necessary or sufficient for pursuit of a responsive infrastructure. In essence, it is simpler—it is creation, rather than transformation. The primary option that would mimic starting from scratch today would arise out of consolidation of current facilities at a greenfield site. In other words, consolidation, perhaps more than any other infrastructure transformation strategy, holds the promise of releasing the Complex from the shackles of an infrastructure born out of another time—a chance to start anew, with smaller, highly modernized facilities that reflect the needs of today and what is imagined for tomorrow.

However, consolidation to new infrastructure incurs significant up-front costs. The theory is that these costs are an investment ultimately recouped by the reduction of fixed costs that come from shutting down weapons operations at legacy facilities. This was the argument used to accomplish the one, arguably transformational[23] consolidation of the past few decades, Nonnuclear Reconfiguration, which consolidated missions from Mound and Pinellas primarily to the Kansas City Plant. The up-front cost of this consolidation was around $440M, with an estimated savings of $250M per year hence.[24] However, Nonuclear Reconfiguration consolidated nonnuclear missions to existing sites. The up-front costs of relocating nuclear missions to a new facility would be expected to be significantly more.[25]

Clearly, consolidation is about more than just reducing the fixed costs of the Complex and starting from scratch with modernized facilities. It can be argued that a consolidated Complex provides increased efficiencies (reduced transportation burdens, leveraged interdependencies, such as those between design and production, minimization of duplication, reduced safety and security burdens, etc.). In other words, consolidation can be understood as a potential pathway to responsive infrastructure, due to the efficiencies discussed above.

However, other methods exist for creating efficiencies that can be independent of consolidation. The Reliable Replacement Warhead (RRW) program seeks to create efficiencies in existing facilities through the types of materials and manufacturing techniques employed, the inherent safety features of the warhead, and other characteristics which have led it to be called "the enabler for transformation" of the Complex.[26] It can be argued that these types of efficiencies could come to fruition with or without accompanying Complex consolidation. Indeed, the connection between the RRW program and consolidation is more about politics than strict interdependencies. Representative David Hobson, former chair of the Energy and Water Development Appropriations Subcommittee, put it this way: "RRW is a deal with Congress, but the deal requires a serious effort by the Department to modernize, consolidate, and downsize the weapons complex."[27]

In summary, the primary, tangible (vs. political) link between responsive infrastructure and consolidation is cost. From a business standpoint, consolidation is a way to achieve a return on investment for new facilities (i.e., starting from scratch). Consolidation can also be a way to pay for increased efficiencies. In other words, if cost is an issue and starting from scratch desirable, consolidation is a strategy for a return on investment for new facilities and efficiencies.

The caveat is that it can take a very significant up-front investment, which can lead to a very long payback period.

SECRECY: THE SILVER BULLET FOR RESPONSIVENESS

Holding up the Manhattan Project as evidence of how responsive the Complex (and indeed, the nation) could be must also be examined in the light of the third responsive infrastructure "enabler" discussed above—a unique world environment. In particular, the world environment created a national environment (wartime, a simple, coherent national vision) allowing a secrecy surrounding the Manhattan Project that entirely transformed the timescale for progress. Secrecy lent enormous freedom and latitude for decisionmaking. Secrecy allowed the acceptance of tremendous risk.

A primary result of the exhaustive secrecy was the ability to make and execute decisions rapidly. "Groves told me many times that [the Manhattan Project] would not be possible in peacetime... many urgent decisions he had to take could not be made by committees, or by consent, or by asking permission each time."[28] Put another way: "secrecy made it possible to make decisions with little regard for normal peacetime political considerations."[29]

It is questionable that the nation could ever resuscitate such a tolerance for secrecy in the future. For example, the tolerance for even perceived secrecy in more recent times was strikingly captured during Nonnuclear Reconfiguration in the Congressional Record, in a record titled *Unbelievably Arrogant Conduct by the Department of Energy*: "Mr. Speaker, the Energy Department announced plans to consolidate the nonnuclear manufacturing activities of the weapons complex...I submit an editorial...which expresses the outrage which is felt when an agency of the U.S. Government tries to make major decisions in secrecy."[30]

Even with the knowledge of the different world conditions and the contrasting culture that existed during the Manhattan Project, it is striking to imagine the kinds of decisions that were executed, and their timescales. It is striking to imagine that the government "could throw people off their land with little explanation...fifteen hundred indignant residents of the Richland, Hanford, and White Bluffs areas...refused to believe that in democratic United States, peaceful, law-abiding citizens could be chased from their homes. But very quickly they came to realize that opposition was useless."[31] Although one can imagine a future where those same fifteen hundred indignant residents end up being displaced to support a war effort, it is much more difficult to imagine the process being resolved in a 30-day period. One need look no further than the National Environmental Policy Act of 1969, to understand the vastly different landscape a Manhattan Project could face today.

The acceptance of meaningful risk also accelerated timescales profoundly. For example, pilot plants for many of the new, sometimes speculative, processes were skipped; some processes were simply implemented full scale. "The usual practice with a new process is to test it out...in a pilot plant, and only then to proceed to the full-scale plant. The plants Groves had to build were so novel that in normal times this procedure would have been regarded as doubly necessary."[32] Although one can envision a world environment where available funding increases dramatically or new facilities are on the table, it is more difficult to imagine that the culture of acceptance for risk (especially for safety) or extreme secrecy could ever be fully "reset."

THE DESTINATION OR THE JOURNEY

The preceding discussion proposes that consolidation and responsive infrastructure are primarily linked through cost. Unfortunately, these two are primarily linked in the end state, and a very steep price must be paid to realize that end state. In other words, only after the consolidation has occurred, and only after the responsive infrastructure has been achieved, can the cost savings begin to be realized. Therein lies the dilemma. Given that the consolidated end state is reached, the savings tend to be the primary subject of current debate. Yet this debate is secondary to whether nuclear consolidation is possible on an acceptable timescale, even given the assumption of a compelling future return on investment.[33]

No events in recent history indicate that the nation is capable of getting over this mountain, despite strong and comprehensive efforts to do so over time. Virtually all of the more recent nuclear consolidation, such as the transition of Rocky Flats, Hanford, and Fernald out of the Complex in the late 1980s and early 1990s, was catalyzed by external events. Rather than transformational—designed and executed according to a larger vision—these changes were largely evolutionary.[34] The Complex did indeed become smaller, but at the loss of significant capabilities, such as pit production.

In the early 1990s, the massive "Complex-21" attempt to reconfigure the Complex resulted in the consolidation of only the non-nuclear portion of the Complex. In the end, the nuclear portion was "consolidated in-place." In other words, downsizing was completed within the footprint of the existing sites—making them smaller without eliminating any sites. In the mid-1990s, the Stockpile Stewardship and Management Programmatic Environmental Impact Statement (SSM PEIS) again evaluated consolidation of the nuclear portion of the Complex. In the end, the decision was to "rightsize in place." Today, NNSA's plan for transforming to a "more modern, cost-effective nuclear weapons complex," Complex 2030, is to continue to rightsize in place, consolidating special nuclear material where possible, but within the existing footprint of the current eight sites.[35] Because this "rightsizing" does not include a decrease in the number of sites, this proposal has been interpreted by some to have written off true consolidation.

The effectiveness or responsiveness of the Complex as measured in terms of number of sites is distracting at best, destructive at worst. Much criticism has been dispensed over the failure of past efforts to consolidate the Complex. These criticisms have largely overshadowed thoughtful dialogue on more elusive, but grave, intangible costs incurred with each and every dance towards and away from consolidation. One example is the degradation of trust within the Complex and the relationships between sites. Unlike a corporation considering downsizing, discussion and evaluation of elimination of sites in the Complex—sites that are operated independently, with different developmental histories, cultures, skill sets, and allegiances—can lead to protective behavior that destroys synergy, understanding, and cooperation. Although this may be the price of shutting down sites, it is a high price to pay if such consolidation does not ultimately happen.

An alternative to criticizing past efforts is recognizing that the inability of the nation to consolidate the nuclear missions of the Complex may simply reflect the significant strength of the barriers. These barriers are many, reflect far more than simple economics, and are not new.

BARRIERS TO CHANGE

First and foremost is the legacy argument. The sites of the Complex have fed the economic engines of their communities and their respective States for over half a century. The personnel of these sites represent meaningful constituencies in the political landscape. This is not a new dilemma. Consolidation of the Complex began as early as 1952, and even at that time the social implications of downsizing were a major factor in decisionmaking. The stated goals were to reduce cost while balancing the need for strategic redundancies and minimizing "negative social consequences" accompanying closures.[36]

Even in the early days of the Complex, political sensitivities to siting and consolidating missions in the Complex were paramount. Many lessons were learned the hard way. For example, prior to the decision to site the Reactor Testing Station in Pocatello, Idaho, another site in another state heard that it would be chosen. This led to congressional hearings, placing the entire siting process under intense public scrutiny.[37]

On the other hand, barriers also exist for expanding or siting new missions at existing or new sites. This is the "not in my backyard" argument, and it is neither new nor unique to the nuclear weapons business. For example, in 1952, although Portsmouth was a less attractive choice than Louisville on the basis of siting criteria for a gaseous diffusion plant, the local population was "vehemently opposed to the construction of an 'atomic plant' in the area," and Portsmouth was ultimately chosen.[38]

The skilled workforces cultivated over many decades that fuel the existing sites also represent a major piece of the legacy argument. These workforces cannot be developed (or be relocated from one state to another) overnight—even under conditions like the Manhattan Project. For example, at Hanford in 1943, despite a "relative labor surplus in the Pacific Northwest, shortages plagued the project."[39] Even more recent "rightsize-in-place" strategies (Complex-21 and SSM PEIS) were found to create "demographic distortions in the Complex...skew[ing] the age profile of the workforce, increasing the average age, and reducing the experience level."[40]

Moreover, a vast quantity of dollars has already been invested in existing sites. This was one of the primary arguments used in the Stockpile Stewardship and Management Record of Decision to justify the decision to "rightsize in place" versus consolidate the missions at the plants to the weapons laboratories and the Nevada Test Site.[41]

Most important, nuclear consolidation as a long term cost-saving strategy requires a near term investment on the order of billions of dollars. Having the credibility to make this kind of investment and capital project delivery requires a track record for cost estimating and budgeting that has rarely existed in the nuclear enterprise. For example, in 1942, the estimated cost for the Manhattan Project was approximately $148M ($1.85B 2006 dollars). The costs of the project through the end of 1945 have been estimated at $1.9B ($21.5B 2006 dollars)—roughly an order of magnitude off the original estimate.[42]

Even assuming adequate credibility could be established that the expenditure of billions of dollars in up-front investment for nuclear consolidation could be paid back in a reasonable time period, with commensurate savings thereafter, the yearly reality of the budgetary process by which decisions about government spending are made—yielding scarce power to arguments regarding future return on investment—could dwarf all the other barriers discussed above.

LEARNING FROM THE PAST

The Nuclear Weapons Complex today faces an opportunity called transformation. While releasing the Complex from the shackles of an aging, ill-fitting infrastructure, it must also confront a largely unknowable future. It must stimulate, revitalize, and inspire the intellectual capital of a new generation in the absence of underground tests, important manufacturing capabilities, and a vibrant debate or consensus on the role of nuclear weapons in our national security. The Manhattan Project created an infrastructure from scratch to confront its own, unknowable future, without the benefit of hindsight. In essence, this is where transformation has a leg up on creation—the ability to learn from the past.

Thus, looking back at the events that brought the Complex to its current configuration yields four important conclusions. First, consolidation can reduce the fixed costs of the Complex in the end state. Second, unfortunately this fundamental cost argument has been proven many times to be overwhelmed by the powerful, yet often underestimated, barriers against nuclear consolidation. Third, consolidation is not synonymous with responsive infrastructure, and the linkage between consolidation and responsive infrastructure depends on the perspective. Finally, the rationale and plan for a responsive infrastructure should be decoupled from the rationale and plan for consolidation, lest the barriers that thwart consolidation needlessly bar the chance for a future responsive Complex.

Notes

1. In 2004, the House Energy and Water Appropriations Committee, led by Representative David Hobson, requested an independent review of the Nuclear Weapons Complex by a team of outside experts. One of the primary motivations was to "evaluate options for the consolidation of special nuclear materials, facilities, and operations across the complex to minimize security requirements and the environmental impact of continuing operations." (108th Congress, House of Representatives Report 108-554, Energy and Water Development Appropriations Bill, June 18, 2004.)

2. Note that an analogous argument applies to stockpile transformation.

3. David O. Overskei, Chairman of the Nuclear Weapons Complex Infrastructure Task Force of the Secretary of Energy Advisory Board, Statement to the Strategic Forces Subcommittee of the House Committee on Armed Services hearing on the topic of the National Nuclear Security Administration's Future Plans for the Nuclear Weapons Complex Infrastructure, April 4, 2006. (Note: this work was the response to the request noted in note 1.)

4. William F. Burgess, Jo Anne McCormick, and Eileen Pingatore, *History of the Production Complex: The Methods of Site Selection* (Washington, D.C.: U.S. Department of Energy, 1987), ii-iii, vi-vii.

5. U.S. Department of Energy Office of Environmental Management, *Linking Legacies*, DOE/EM-0319 (Washington, D.C.: U.S. Department of Energy, 1997), 16-17.

6. Burgess et al, *History of the Production Complex*, i.

7. F.C. Gosling, *The Manhattan Project: Making the Atomic Bomb*, DOE/HR-0096 (Washington, D.C.: United States Department of Energy Office of Administration and Human Resources Development, 1994), 20.

8. Ibid., 28.

9. Linton Brooks, Under Secretary for Nuclear Security and Administrator, National Nuclear Security Administration, Testimony to the Committee on Government Reform, Subcommittee on National Security, Emerging Threats, and International Relations, Hearing on Nuclear Security, "Can DOE Meet Physical Security Requirements," April 27, 2004.

10. John May, *The Greenpeace book of the nuclear age: the hidden history, the human cost* (New York: Pantheon Books, 1989).

11. Note that the first accident, which resulted in the death of Harry Daghlian, occurred on August 21, 1945, and the second accident, which resulted in the death of Louis Slotin, occurred on May 30, 1946. Martin Zeilig, "Louis Slotin and the Invisible Killer," *The Beaver* 75, no. 4 (August/September 1995).

12. Joseph DiNunno, *Integrated Safety Management*, DNFSB TECH-16 (Washington, D.C.: Defense Nuclear Facilities Safety Board, 1997), 1-1.

13. P.H. Richanbach, D.R. Graham, J.P. Bell, and J.D. Silk, *The Organization and Management of the Nuclear Weapons Program* (Washington, D.C.: Institute for Defense Analyses, March 1997, ES-1).

14. D.Overskei, J.Crawford, H. Grunder, D. Kaczynski, R. Nickell, D. Trost, *Recommendations for the Nuclear Weapons Complex of the Future* (Washington, D.C.: Department of Energy Secretary of Energy Advisory Board, 2005), vi.

15. Thomas P. D'Agostino, Deputy Administrator for Defense Programs, National Nuclear Security Administration, Testimony for the House Armed Services Committee Subcommittee on Strategic Forces, April 5, 2006.

16. U.S. Department of Energy, *Nuclear Weapons Complex Reconfiguration Study (Complex-21)*, DOE/DP-0083 (Springfield: National Technical Information Service, 1991).

17. Burgess et al., *History of the Production Complex*, 33-34.

18. Overskei et al., *Recommendations for the Complex*, 2.

19. Henry G. Chiles, Jr., "Providing Responsive Infrastructure for Updating and Maintaining the Nuclear Stockpile," Final Report of the 36th Annual IFPA-Fletcher Conference on National Security and Policy, *Implementing the New Triad: Nuclear and Non-Nuclear Forces in 21st Century Deterrence* (The Institute for Foreign Policy Analysis and The Fletcher School, Tufts University, 2005), 85.

20. Gosling, *The Manhattan Project*, 19.

21. Stephane Groueff, *Manhattan Project: The Untold Story of the Making of the Atomic Bomb* (Boston: Little, Brown and Company, 1967), 14.

22. M.S. Gerber, *Legend and Legacy: Fifty Years of Defense Production at the Hanford Site*, WHC-MR-0293, Rev. 2 (Richland: U.S. Department of Energy Office of Environmental Restoration and Waste Management Westinghouse

Hanford Company, 1992), 6.

23. Lani Miyoshi Sanders and Linda J. Branstetter, *Change and the Nuclear Weapons Complex: Key Studies and Outcomes in the Final Decades of the 20th Century*, SAND2005-3505 (Albuquerque: Sandia National Laboratories, 2005).

24. Charles R. Loeber, *Building the Bombs: A History of the Nuclear Weapons Complex*, SAND2002-0307P (Albuquerque: Sandia National Laboratories, 2002), 221

25. Note that the recent Secretary of Energy Advisory Board Nuclear Weapons Complex Infrastructure Task Force estimated ~$10B up-front investment (over a period of ten years) for such a consolidation, with ~six-year payback period after the new consolidated nuclear production facility was operating.

26. Linton F. Brooks, Administrator, National Nuclear Security Administration, U.S. Department of Energy, Testimony before the Senate Armed Services Committee, Subcommittee on Strategic Forces, April 4, 2005. Also see Benn Tannenbaum's and Francis Slakey's chapter in this book.

27. Letter from Representative David L. Hobson to Secretary of Energy Samuel W. Bodman, November 16, 2006.

28. Stephane Groueff, "The Manhattan Project: An Extraordinary Achievement of the 'American Way,'" *Remembering the Manhattan Project: Perspectives on the Making of the Atomic Bomb and its Legacy*, Cynthia C. Kelly, ed. (New Jersey: World Scientific, 2004), 34.

29. Gosling, *The Manhattan Project*, 19.

30. Tony P. Hall, "Unbelievably Arrogant Conduct by the Department of Energy—Hon. Tony P. Hall," *Congressional Record*, Friday, March 20, 1992:

31. Groueff, *Untold Story*, 137.

32. Alwyn McKay, *The Making of the Atomic Age* (Oxford: Oxford University Press, 1984), 71

33. That the current infrastructure is incomplete (missing large-scale pit production, for example) compounds the argument.

34. Sanders and Branstetter, *Change and the Nuclear Weapons Complex*, 35.

35. Linton Brooks, "Notice of Intent to Prepare a Supplement to the Stockpile Stewardship and Management Programmatic Environmental Impact Statement—Complex 2030," *Federal Register* 71, no.202 (October 19, 2006): 61731-61736.

36. Burgess et al, *History of the Production Complex*, iii.

37. Burgess et al., *History of the Production Complex*, v.

38. Burgess et al, *History of the Production Complex*, vi.

39. Gosling, *The Manhattan Project*, 32.

40. Commission on Maintaining United States Nuclear Weapons Expertise (Chiles Commission), *Report to the Congress and Secretary of Energy*, March 1, 1999, D-1.

41. Hazel O'Leary, "Record of Decision Programmatic Environmental Impact Statement for Stockpile Stewardship and Management," *Federal Register* 61, no. 249 (December 26, 1996): 68014-68026.

42. Stephen I. Schwartz, ed., *Atomic Audit: The Costs and Consequences of U.S. Nuclear Weapons Since 1940* (Washington, D.C.: Brookings Institution, 1998), 55-60.

CHAPTER FOURTEEN

THE NUCLEAR WEAPONS PRODUCTION COMPLEX AND THE RELIABLE REPLACEMENT WARHEAD

Francis Slakey and Benn Tannenbaum

A fundamental question in developing a long-range plan for the nation's nuclear weapons complex is: what is the long-term stockpile required by the Department of Defense and how should the Department of Energy size the capability of its complex to match those requirements? This question has not yet been addressed by Congress, DOD, or DOE. Indeed, the Defense Science Board highlighted the "need for a national consensus on the nature of the need for and the role of nuclear weapons."[1] Absent a consensus, the long range plans for the nuclear weapons complex are being based on an arsenal size in the range of 1,700 to 2,200 deployed warheads, as detailed in the terms of the Moscow Treaty.[2]

This default stockpile size places high demands on the nuclear weapons complex. Consider a potential stockpile of 3000 total weapons (counting both reserve and deployed weapons) and assume a functional lifetime of 30 years per warhead, at which time the warhead either needs to undergo life extension or replacement by a new warhead. If only life extension is pursued, this requires processing 100 weapons per year on average. For a new stockpile, this corresponds to a greater workload because every new warhead will be accompanied by the dismantlement of an old warhead, so the steady state throughput in the complex would need to be roughly two hundred weapons per year.[3]

Several groups and individuals have stated that these production and dismantlement numbers present a significant problem: they are in excess of what is currently practical.[4] Consequently, either the production complex needs to be substantially refurbished, or the arsenal size needs to be reassessed. This chapter considers the refurbishment of the complex in light of the proposed Reliable Replacement Warhead (RRW). Chapter ten of this volume assesses the potential for reductions in the size of the arsenal.

THE PROBLEM

Currently, the nation's nuclear arsenal is maintained through a combination of surveillance, assessments, and refurbishments known as the Stockpile Stewardship Program (SSP)[5] that was established in the mid 1990s. Several groups are reviewing the SSP, to determine whether it is providing a safe and reliable stockpile of nuclear weapons that is affordable, sustainable and can maintain the necessary skill base.[6] The preliminary assessment is that SSP is doing well for now, but there are inadequacies in the production complex. In particular, the nuclear weapons production infrastructure needs to be "transformed" into one that can dismantle, refurbish, or build new weapons in a timely and affordable manner.

According to these groups, some capabilities have been effectively restored, but the uranium work at Y-12, the throughput at Pantex, and the pit production at Los Alamos have not yet reached necessary levels to maintain the arsenal.[7] Many factors contribute to this, including: aging facilities that in many instances are more than 50 years old; lack of money for capital investment to replace or modernize those facilities; more stringent safety and security requirements that have doubled or tripled the cost of doing business; closure of the Rocky Flats plutonium processing facility due to safety violations; and manufacturing with "legacy" materials and processes that are technologically obsolete.

TWO PROPOSED SOLUTIONS

Reducing the arsenal below the size established in the Moscow Treaty could ease the demands on the production complex. Absent a consensus on reductions, there are essentially two proposed paths for solving the problem. Either the production complex can be refurbished as part of the existing SSP Life Extension Program (LEP), or a new program can be developed.[8] The new program that has been proposed is the Reliable Replacement Warhead (RRW).

Under the SSP LEP, the production infrastructure will refurbish war-heads and sustain the capability to design, manufacture, and certify warheads. Successful refurbishment would extend a warhead's life by 30 years or more and revitalize the production complex. As a proof of concept, the NNSA recently completed a life extension refurbishment program for the W87 warhead. LEPs are currently planned for the B61 and the W76 and could be extended to all warheads in the arsenal.[9]

Under a RRW program, a new warhead (and subsequent generations of RRWs) would be designed and manufactured to replace one or more weapons in the current stockpile. The RRW would be specifically de-signed for ease of manufacture, and would have upgraded safety and security features. Thus, in the end, it might be a "better" warhead: safer and more secure, potentially provide more flexibility in performance characteristics, and possibly lead to a reduction in the costs needed to maintain an RRW-based stockpile.[10] RRW could transform the complex by modernizing and consolidating manufacturing at a few sites that no longer have to retain legacy practices.

In principle, both the SSP path and the RRW path could be used to revitalize the decaying production complex.[11] However, under either approach, the modernization is projected to require billions of dollars and take until 2030 to fully implement.[12] Given the large budget and long timetable, there is an associated political challenge that must be ad-dressed regardless of the path taken: both require a budgetary commit-ment that must be sustained over 12 Congressional terms and at least three Administrations.

In general, there are two strong, non-partisan arguments that could sustain a decision to pursue one path over the other:

- **Cost**: One path offers a cheaper means of maintaining the nuclear deterrent over the long term.
- **Technical Challenges**: One path presents fewer technical challenges for maintaining the nuclear deterrent over the long term.

At this time, neither argument can be persuasively used to argue for one path over the other, as discussed below.

COST

To date there are limited budget details from NNSA for the transforma-tion plan. A Secretary of Energy Advisory Board Task Force did a very rough approximation of long-term costs for three different program options, but not at a level of detail that can be considered a rigorous estimate. In part, this is because the overall plan requires a number of major new investments (such as a pit facility) and activities (such as conjectured surety savings at some sites) whose budgets have yet to be vetted by an extensive professional process. More important, however, is the development and promulgation of the DOD requirements that will dictate the stockpile size and diversity. How many warheads of what kind will be needed, and how much reserve capacity[13] and surge capability[14] will satisfy the DOD? With an RRW program, this question becomes even more complicated, because the willingness of the DOD to reduce numbers may not occur until the RRW program has been proven feasible, which may not be authorized until the DOD can accept lower numbers. Consequently, the DOE/NNSA budget is strongly dependent on the DOD stockpile requirements. In addition, the RRW would require flight-testing,[15] at an additional cost, before the DOD would accept it.

What is certain, however, is that there will be very little discretionary flexibility in the NNSA budget.[16] The ability to design and manufacture an RRW (and future RRWs) depends on the knowledge gained in the SSP program, so reducing the SSP expenditures would eliminate an essential source of data for the RRW program. It is difficult to reduce safety and security costs until major consolidation in the complex has completely taken place. Modernization of existing sites and clean-up of former sites will entail significant new expenditures, even if the eventual operating costs may decrease. Consequently, under a constant purchasing power budget, one of the few budgetary areas available for RRW development is in the LEP funding.[17] If some of these LEPs can be delayed, stretched out, or cancelled because of a change in stockpile requirements, then some funds could be freed for new investments. It is then a matter of whether these "savings" might be applied to dismantlement or production of RRWs, or made available for building new facilities. However, delaying or curtailing LEPs might then require the introduction of more RRWs at an accelerated pace, possible further increasing the cost.

Given such limited flexibility in a constant NNSA budget scenario, even with a reduction in the LEPs, significant new funds will be needed to produce a responsive production complex. The introduction of RRWs is unlikely to lead to operational savings until all of these investments have been made and amortized. Consequently, an RRW program would likely add to costs in the near term and it is not yet possible to determine whether or when the RRW could lead to savings in the long term.

Given these uncertainties, cost issues have not been sufficiently developed to persuasively drive a decision in favor or against RRW.

TECHNICAL CHALLENGES

A Weibull Curve, or "bathtub curve," characterizes the rate of defects over time for a typical manufactured system (e.g. cars, DVD players, nuclear weapons).[18] The curve has three distinct parts: 1) 'birth' defects that gradually decrease over the early period of the systems life; 2) a quiescent period when the system is relatively trouble free; and 3) an aging period marked by increasing appearance of defects in which various parts begin to wear out and need to be fixed or replaced.

In the nuclear weapons design and maintenance community, the defects are referred to as "findings" and the more serious among them are referred to as "significant findings" or "SFIs." As part of the surveillance activity within the SSP program, the SFIs are closely monitored. Most of these "findings" are due to aging in the non-nuclear part of the warhead system and are relatively easily fixed, but some are potentially more serious and could require cycling through the full production complex for remediation, or involve the refinement of a warhead design.

To date, plutonium aging data has not revealed indications of any significant nuclear physics problems related to aging. Indeed, recent reports suggest that the plutonium lifetime may be more than 100 years.[19] Nevertheless, there are aging issues associated with a plutonium pit (such as corrosion) that are independent of plutonium lifetime. Consequently, there will be a time when significant aging effects begin to emerge and the number of SFIs for each nuclear warhead system begins to rise upwards on the Weibull Curve and enter the end of life phase.

Nuclear warheads have a projected minimum design lifetime of 20-25 years,[20] which means that the oldest systems are beyond the age when a rise in defects might begin to occur. However, while aging defects are present, the defects are not emerging at a rate that is a significant statistical departure from previous years.[21] Consequently, there is no indication to date that any deployed weapons system is reaching the end of life phase on the Weibull Curve. In fact, according to the most recent information, the SFIs have actually *decreased* for one of the oldest systems, though this falls within expected statistical variation.[22] Consequently, at this time, aging defects do not argue for an RRW.

In fact, even after aging defects do emerge, there would not necessarily be an associated technical benefit to switching to an RRW. As a new system, the RRW itself would be expected to follow some version of the Weibull Curve; the RRW will have birth defects of its own. While the RRW is intended to have design features to effectively manage the birth defect problem,[23] it is not known with any certainty whether those defects would present a greater or lesser technical challenge than managing the aging defects of the legacy weapons or even if they would occur at a greater or lesser rate than currently seen in the legacy systems.

BUILDING CONSENSUS

The non-partisan arguments of cost and technical challenges are not yet sufficient to drive a decision toward RRW at this time. Consequently, if a decision is made to pursue RRW, then developing a long-term bipartisan consensus might require combining various arguments. Such a consensus has been developed in the past to support programs, including the current SSP. The consensus for SSP was built on two points: 1) sustaining a strong nuclear deterrent; and 2) providing demonstrable arms control benefits. An RRW program could be developed in precisely this manner.[24]

By any measure, the current nuclear arsenal is a Cold War stockpile designed to maximize the yield to weight ratio in the warheads and to act as a deterrent to the Soviet Union. Although the actual numbers of weapons have gradually been reduced in accord with arms control agreements, the existing stockpile is increasingly disconnected from most national security debates because of its focus on massive firepower. Accordingly, there is a desire on the part of some military planners to develop nuclear options that could play a more active role in national security discussions. No military or congressional consensus has emerged on developing such options.[25] Indeed, these options are available in the existing stockpile, as many of the warheads can be used in a much lower yield mode than their nominal deployment. A critical question that has not yet been addressed by Congress, NNSA, DOD or any other group is one of priorities: what is the long-term stockpile required by the DOD and how should the DOE size the capability of its complex to match those requirements?[26]

Absent debates to clarify those questions, the RRW could still be developed in a manner that advances non-proliferation goals.

In debates about the RRW, the arms control topic is usually raised in the context of the destabilizing effect of "new" nuclear weapons. Ignoring semantic issues, it is hard to see how a warhead designed to do the same mission with the same general characteristics introduces any important differences of "newness" from its predecessor. There is a legitimate concern that the infrastructure necessary to build an RRW—or LEPs for that matter—would be capable of producing new weapons with new missions. However, if the RRW program leads to reduced total stockpile size (by reduction of the reserve stockpile or reduction of the actively deployed stockpile) and if it is congressionally constrained to require legislative approval for new missions, then it could be perceived as an overall arms control benefit.[27]

Such assurances can be built into the RRW program in several ways. The earliest RRW concepts can put a transparent and strong emphasis on test pedigree to alleviate any worries about trusting computers to an unnecessary extent.[28] The closer the RRW adheres to tested analogs, the more likely it is that RRW can be deployed without testing. Consequently, by designing conservatively, a clear statement can be delivered that the U.S. will abide by the testing moratorium under an RRW. An even stronger assurance could be delivered legislatively if the RRW program were coupled to the ratification of the Comprehensive Nuclear Test-Ban Treaty.[29]

A further assurance would emerge by more clearly linking the RRW program to arsenal reductions. To date, these have not been rigorously or even formally coupled and a clearer argument can be made that a responsive infrastructure can lead to significant reductions in the reserve arsenal. The "manufacture on demand" concept behind the RRW responsive infrastructure relieves the need for a warehouse of reserve nuclear warheads. However, maintaining legacy weapons does require a large reserve - and thus requires excess warheads - until the RRW would be substantially introduced into the arsenal. Clarifying the amount and time over which the reserve arsenal can be reduced under an RRW would demonstrate a net arms control gain.

There may also be a possibility to couple the RRW to emerging discussions over the role of nuclear weapons in global strike options. In particular, STRATCOM has proposed that under some scenarios it may be possible to shift from nuclear weapons to non-nuclear kinetic weapons.[30] If an RRW could be shown to enable this shift, then it would clearly demonstrate objective arms control benefits.

SUMMARY

A number of groups have determined that maintaining a nuclear weapons arsenal of the size established in the Moscow Treaty will require refurbishing the production complex. There are two proposed paths to refurbishing the infrastructure: SSP/LEP and RRW. While either path can, in principle, address the infrastructure problems, it is too early in the RRW planning process to determine whether RRW would offer a cheaper long-term solution with fewer technical problems. In fact, RRW planners believe that the RRW path will be more expensive than SSP/LEP in the near term.

Refurbishing the production complex will require a sustained budgetary commitment that must last over 12 Congresses and at least three Administrations. That long term bi-partisan consensus can be built on two distinct points: 1) sustaining a strong and serviceable nuclear deterrent; and 2) providing demonstrable arms control benefits. To overcome inevitable criticisms of near term cost increases, the RRW program would need to make a clearer connection to arms control benefits such as arsenal reductions, the nuclear testing moratorium, and possibly the enabling of a new global strike configuration.

Notes

This paper is based in part on work done in preparation for the AAAS Nuclear Weapons Complex Assessment Committee. [31]

1. Report of the Defense Science Board Task Force on Nuclear Capabilities, December 2006.

2. State Department fact sheet on the Moscow Treaty: http://www.state.gov/t/ac/trt/18016.htm

3. These numbers decrease for a smaller arsenal and/or a longer weapon lifetime and thus are only an upper limit to guide thinking.

4. "Sustaining the Nuclear Enterprise - A New Approach", O'Brien et al, May 2005; Secretary of Energy Advisory Board (SEAB) report "Recommendations for the Nuclear Weapons Complex of the Future"; Testimony of Thomas D'Agostino before the House Armed Services Committee, April 2006; Testimony of Linton Brooks before the Senate Armed Services Committee, April 2005.

5. For a full description of the Stockpile Stewardship program, see http://www.llnl.gov/annual02/pdfs/stockpile.pdf.

6. These include its proprietor, the NNSA/DOE, the authorizing and appropriating committees of the Congress, and its direct customer, the DOD (OSD, STRATCOM, and the involved services [the Navy and the Air Force]). It also includes a number of outside reviews such as those done by the GAO, the CRS, the TRAC, the JASONs, the DSB, and the AAAS Nuclear Weapons Complex Assessment Committee.

7. In general, the identified problems are in the major nodes of the complex: Y-12 (uranium processing), Pantex (warhead dismantlement and refurbishment), and TA-55 (planned plutonium pit production). A major component of the complex is, naturally, the skilled and trained workforce that operates the complex.

8. This either/or approach is a simplified but useful way of framing the problem and long term solutions. Indeed, the NNSA planning document suggests a future arsenal made up exclusively of RRWs: "Complex 2030 An Infrastructure Planning Scenario" October 23, 2006. The either/or approach was also used by the Congressional Research Service in the Report "Nuclear Warheads: The Reliable Replacement Warhead Program and the Life Extension Program" December 13, 2006.

9. Currently there are nine systems in the combined deployed and reserve stockpile, two SLBMS (the W76 and the W88), three ICBMS (the W62 [scheduled for retirement], the W78, and the W87), two aircraft delivered bombs (the B61 [various versions] and the B83) and two cruise missiles (the W80 and the W84 [reserve only]).

10. As currently proposed, the RRW would not have new military characteristics (e.g. yield and effects). Instead, the RRW would replace the yield-to-weight criterion as a measure of merit by a set of criteria that include adequate yield-to-weight, greater reliability of the nuclear part of the warhead, easier manufacturability using modern materials and processes, improved safety and security (collectively called surety) warhead features, and greater flexibility in design to meet the future needs of military planners. As stated in Public Law 109-163, Section 3111: (b) Objectives- The objectives of the Reliable Replacement Warhead program shall be (1) to increase the reliability, safety, and security of the United States nuclear weapons stockpile; (2) to further reduce the likelihood of the resumption of nuclear testing; (3) to remain consistent with basic design parameters by using, to the extent practicable, components that are well understood or are certifiable without the need to resume underground nuclear testing; (4) to ensure that the United States develops a nuclear weapons infrastructure that can respond to unforeseen problems, to include the ability

to produce replacement warheads that are safer to manufacture, more cost-effective to produce, and less costly to maintain than existing warheads; (5) to achieve reductions in the future size of the nuclear weapons stockpile based on increased reliability of the reliable replacement warheads; (6) to use the design, certification, and production expertise resident in the nuclear complex to develop reliable replacement components to fulfill current mission requirements of the existing stockpile; and (7) to serve as a complement to, and potentially a more cost-effective and reliable long-term replacement for, the current Stockpile Life Extension Programs. In addition, Congressman David Hobson (R-OH), Chair of the House Energy and Water Development Appropriations Subcommittee, has stated that he will seek to constrain DOD from pursuing new nuclear missions.

11. George Miller, Director, LLNL, briefing to the AAAS Nuclear Weapons Complex Assessment Committee, August 10, 2006. The House Armed Services committee requested the Nuclear Weapons Council to submit a report by March 2007 that explains the relationship of RRW within SSP and its impact on LEPs.

12. Complex 2030, National Nuclear Security Administration, October 2006.

13. *Reserve capacity* indicates the number of warheads, not necessarily connected to a delivery system, that are maintained as a hedge against a failure of a particular type or class of weapon. This gives the military additional confidence that some nuclear deterrent will always be available.

14. *Surge capability* is the capacity of the nuclear weapons complex to drastically increase the production rate of weapons if needed for a particular crisis. Others suggest as examples of such a crisis a resurgent Russia or a dramatic increase in the size of China's nuclear arsenal.

15. While it is possible to engineer new warheads to the same shape and total mass as existing warheads, producing new warheads with identical mass distribution is highly unlikely. These new weapons must be flight tested to ensure proper targeting capabilities, etc.

16. The General Accounting Office projected that "flexibility will decline drastically" in future budgets. It has identified transformation of the nuclear complex as a key topic for Congressional oversight: GAO-07-235R.

17. The Secretary of Energy Advisory Board proposed consolidating the weapons labs to generate savings: SEAB report "Recommendations for the Nuclear Weapons Complex of the Future."

18. For a detailed discussion of the Weibull curve: http://www.weibull.com/hotwire/issue21/hottopics21.htm

19. JASON panel report, "Pit Lifetime," JSR 06-335, November 20, 2006. The NNSA response to this report is available in the NNSA Press Release "Studies Show Plutonium Degradation in U.S. Nuclear Weapons Will Not Affect Reliability Soon", November 29, 2006.

20. Department of Energy, "Analysis of Stockpile Management Alternatives," July 1996.

21. Gene Schroeder, Senior Technical Director, Global Strike Capabilities Division, STRATCOM in a briefing to the AAAS Nuclear Weapons Complex Assessment Committee, October 24, 2006.

22. Ibid.

23. For example, condition monitoring and lower marginality.

24. Some would add the notion of preserving "human capital," i.e. the capturing of knowledge and experience from soon-to-be-retired experts. However, the RRW program is far from the only way to retain this knowledge. In fact, programs dedicated to doing just this already exist and may be more cost effective than an entirely new program such as the RRW.

25. A Robust Nuclear Earth Penetrator was proposed by NNSA but was opposed in Congress. For details on the debate see: http://www7.nationalacademies.org/cisac/Medalia_Presentation.pdf

26. This question is examined in another chapter in this book.

27. For those for whom the goal of arms control is to immediately eliminate nuclear weapons, such an RRW program would represent a backward step.

28. While it is not expected that the U.S. release detailed design specifications, it would be possible to release statements to the effect that "RRW1 is based on design components which were thoroughly tested at the Nevada Test Site."

29. The "Supreme National Interest Clause" allowing for testing would be critically necessary for achieving consensus on coupling RRW and CTBT.

30. Brian Green, Deputy Assistant Secretary of Defense, http://www.ifpaf-letcherconference.com/oldtranscripts/2005/Brian_Green.ppt. This issue is examined by Owen Price in chapter ten of this book.

31. http://cstsp.aaas.org/content.html?contentid=899

PART FOUR

NONPROLIFERATION IN A NUCLEAR AGE

CHAPTER FIFTEEN
_____

BEYOND THE NPT

THE EMERGING NONPROLIFERATION ENVIRONMENT

Whitney Raas

In 1963, President John F. Kennedy famously envisioned "a world in which fifteen or twenty or twenty-five" states would possess nuclear weapons, possibly even as early as the 1970s.[1] Although today there are now up to five more states with nuclear weapons than at the time President Kennedy made his dire prediction, there are many fewer than were predicted or even expected. The Treaty on the Non-Proliferation of Nuclear Weapons (NPT) is widely credited with slowing the worldwide spread of nuclear weapons since its entry into force in 1970.[2] Since the earliest days of the NPT, however, proliferators have found devious ways to develop nuclear weapons programs while signatories to the NPT, calling into question the lasting efficacy of the treaty and the possible collapse of the non-proliferation regime.[3]

The NPT mandates that nuclear-weapon states refrain from assisting non-nuclear weapon states with the acquisition of nuclear weapons, while non-nuclear signatories to the treaty must declare nuclear material to the International Atomic Energy Agency (IAEA), accept safeguards on peaceful nuclear facilities and refrain from seeking the acquisition of nuclear weapons or receiving nuclear weapon technology. In return, non-nuclear weapon states are promised access to peaceful nuclear energy. This agreement allows states to develop indigenous uranium enrichment facilities and plutonium reprocessing facilities legally under international observation (safeguards), setting the scene for a number of nascent nuclear-weapon states. As more states gain the ability to produce fissile material, either legally through the NPT or illegally through the black market, the question that the nonproliferation regime must address is: what means do the United States and the international community have to combat the spread of nuclear weapons and encourage states to refrain from developing nuclear weapons programs?

The answer is a multi-pronged nonproliferation regime consisting of both a diplomatic and control structure and a more active counterproliferation arm. For the purposes of this chapter, nonproliferation refers to the international arms control regime, while counterproliferation indicates those procedures used to actively prevent the spread of nuclear-related items, information, and material. In other words, nonproliferation is the process by which states are persuaded not to attempt a nuclear weapons program, while counterproliferation is intended to prevent a state involved in proliferation activities from developing a weapons capability.

Since the NPT entered into force, a number of international agreements on arms control have augmented its capabilities, including the Additional Protocol, which establishes a baseline for intrusive inspections and monitoring of NPT signatories' nuclear and non-nuclear facilities, and the provisions on exports set by the Nuclear Suppliers Group (NSG), as well as multiple agreements on weapons testing and the control of delivery system technology. Counterproliferation tools, in contrast to the international monitoring system, are not limited to international diplomacy and agreements and include active involvement by states to oppose proliferation. These approaches include withholding aid, sanctions, the Proliferation Security Initiative (PSI), clandestine efforts (for example to uncover and stop transfers of knowledge and technology), and ultimately, military pre-emption to disrupt emerging nuclear programs.

There are distinct conceptual differences between the two branches. International norms and agreements regarding nuclear nonproliferation are intended to urge countries to refrain from undertaking proliferation activities. The NPT provides an incentive to avoid the development of nuclear weapons: the exchange of civilian nuclear information and benefits as well as international support. Bilateral and multilateral agreements among countries (such as the Treaty of Tlatelolco) bind states to a common goal of using nuclear energy for peaceful purposes only. States are encouraged and legally bound not to attempt to build nuclear weapons by the diplomatic side of the nonproliferation regime. Counterproliferation refers to the actions that states (or international bodies) can take once proliferation has begun. Once a state decides to begin a nuclear weapons program and takes active steps towards that goal, diplomatic efforts must be combined with counterproliferation measures both to halt progress towards a nuclear weapon and to encourage the proliferant to end its program.

This chapter will focus on the interaction of the two approaches to nonproliferation. The first section summarizes key international agreements, especially the NPT and the Additional Protocol (AP). The second section will focus on interdiction and enforcement mechanisms, and the third will discuss the seven steps the George W. Bush administration has put forth to address proliferation. The fourth section will focus on future diplomatic action that can be taken to address nuclear proliferation fears. Finally, a brief discussion on the role of nonproliferation efforts with respect to the threat posed by terrorist groups will be addressed.

INTERNATIONAL AGREEMENTS

International agreements form the foundation of the non-proliferation regime, and will likely continue to do so well into the future. However, there are some who believe the NPT has failed, citing the ongoing North Korean nuclear program and Iran's stubborn refusal to abide by IAEA requests. This prophecy is not only at risk of being self-fulfilling, but would remove the legal norms (and perceived consequential improved security context) that may be constraining some states from nuclear weapons acquisition. Binding multilateral agreements such as the NPT—often called the cornerstone of nonproliferation—have worked well to stigmatize nuclear weapons and halt a rapid spread in the number of nuclear-capable nations.[4] Since the implementation of the NPT, only one signatory to the treaty has developed nuclear weapons, although all three non-signatories are *de facto* nuclear powers.[5]

To be sure, there are nonetheless states that have, or are believed to have, attempted to circumvent the letter and spirit of the treaty by developing secret nuclear weapons programs under the guise of civilian programs or entirely clandestinely. In the last two decades, three states were found or suspected to be developing clandestine nuclear programs within the confines of the "peaceful uses" clause of the NPT, namely Iraq, Libya, and potentially Iran. Iraq admitted to its nuclear ambitions following the 1991 Gulf War, while Libya formally renounced its nuclear weapons program in 2003. While other states (such as Japan, South Korea, Germany, and Brazil) are widely regarded to have the latent indigenous capabilities and the finances necessary to acquire nuclear weapons, several "rollback" states have a variety of such latent capabilities.[6] However, the NPT and the inspection regime have been fundamental to ensuring that these latent capabilities have not evolved into full-scale nuclear weapon programs.

While stated commitments to nuclear proliferation are important, one should always "trust, but verify." A primary criticism of the nonproliferation regime is the lack of enforcement of the NPT and the nonproliferation agreements of the member states. The NPT allows all signatories access to "peaceful" nuclear technology under international safeguards, but some states have used their uranium enrichment facilities, nuclear reactors, and plutonium reprocessing facilities to try to produce nuclear weapons.[7] It is estimated that up to forty states currently have the infrastructure needed to produce the material for nuclear weapons, all operating legally under the NPT in accordance with IAEA safeguards. Determining the final use of these facilities and ensuring their peaceful nature falls to the inspectors of the IAEA, although it is assumed that national intelligence assessments have a significant role to play. Due to the difficulties in inspections and the ability of states to hide facilities, a recurring theme among proliferation pessimists is that the IAEA is failing in its inspection regime and enforcement of nonproliferation agreements is failing.

The inspections regime to enforce Article III of the NPT was established to ensure that civilian nuclear programs were not diverted to weapons development; however, these inspections put into place proved to be insufficient. Following the first Gulf War in 1991, IAEA inspectors in Iraq found evidence that Iraq had undertaken significant work on a clandestine nuclear weapons program. The world was shocked to discover the extent of Iraq's nuclear program, especially given Baghdad's history of relative compliance with the IAEA. This violation of international agreements led the international community to strengthen the IAEA inspection and safeguard mandate by adding an Additional

Protocol agreement. States that sign an Additional Protocol agreement with the IAEA consent to more robust inspections, allow inspectors access to undeclared nuclear facilities on short notice, and must disclose significantly more information to the IAEA than previous safeguards have required.[8]

In addition to the NPT and the safeguards that are its enforcing mechanism, there are a number of bilateral and multilateral agreements to address regional proliferation concerts. These agreements include, among others, the Argentinean and Brazilian nuclear agreements and the recent cooperative efforts on behalf of the Gulf States in the Middle East to form a joint civilian nuclear program. Argentina and Brazil, two long-time nuclear rivals, signed a bilateral agreement in 1991 providing for safeguards on all nuclear activities and establishing a joint monitoring system to account for all nuclear material.[9] At the time, neither state was a signatory to the NPT, and this agreement allowed for previously absent robust safeguards and a commitment to a nuclear-weapons-free South America.

The newly announced agreement among the six Gulf Cooperation Council states (Saudi Arabia, the UAE, Kuwait, Oman, Qatar, and Bahrain), rather than focusing on security concerns, has addressed the economic and political considerations of nuclear power.[10] The proposed agreement would create a common nuclear energy infrastructure, obviating the need for any individual nuclear programs, such as enrichment or reprocessing, that could be diverted for use in a nuclear weapons program. The common interests of all involved would increase barriers to nuclear weapons development.

An example of bilateral nuclear cooperation is the U.S.-India nuclear deal, in which the United States has offered aid to India's civilian program (among other aid offers) in return for India placing its civilian nuclear sites under safeguards and pledging not to export nuclear technologies.[11] These examples of bilateral and regional agreements work well to address the concerns of states who wish to develop nuclear energy programs while satisfying the desires of the United States and others who would like to reduce proliferation. Whether multilateral, bilateral, or regional treaties, formal commitment to use nuclear technology only for peaceful purposes is the common thread that runs through all nonproliferation agreements.

INFORMAL AGREEMENTS

Other informal agreements have also been crucial to the success of the nonproliferation regime. The Nuclear Suppliers Group (NSG), a collection of countries that supply nuclear-related material, promotes nuclear nonproliferation by further regulating the items that can be sold or transferred to non-nuclear countries, and the Zangger Committee placed the first export controls on "trigger list" items related to nuclear power and proliferation.[12] The states cooperating under the guidelines of the NSG and Zangger Committees agree to enforce export controls over nuclear or dual use items, updated when needed to address the spread of technology. This has obvious limitations: participating countries must have control over exports and be willing to take action to halt those sales that do not adhere to NSG guidelines. This is an area where strong oversight, including additional monetary and personnel resources devoted to export control, could make a large difference in nuclear proliferation. Including other countries with the ability to export nuclear-related technology and information, such as Pakistan and India, will improve the nonproliferation environment.

The combination of diplomatic agreements, inspections to enforce those agreements, and voluntary commercial controls over dual-use and prohibited items related to nuclear weapons has served well to slow the spread of nuclear technology to nuclear-weapon programs. Although there have been instances of proliferation among signatories of the NPT, these instances have been few. Moreover, the result of these breaches was a strengthening and expansion of safeguards, export controls, and attention to nonproliferation, rather than the dissolution of the NPT. Since the Treaty came into force, only one state has withdrawn—North Korea in 2003—and has since announced its intention to allow inspectors to return.[13] There is no reason to expect this trend not to continue, and although challenges to the NPT are sure to arise in the future, it is more likely that the end result will be stronger safeguards, not a collapse of the nonproliferation regime itself.[14]

ENFORCEMENT OF NONPROLIFERATION GOALS

Enforcement of nonproliferation goals after states have begun nuclear weapons programs is the next layer of defense following diplomatic activities. These steps, referred to here broadly as counterproliferation, include sanctions, among other activities. Sanctions and withholding of trade or material aid have been commonly used in the past both to punish states for attempting to produce nuclear weapons and to impede their progress.[15] The goal of these activities is to make the cost of continuing a nuclear program prohibitive, thereby encouraging proliferants to end their programs.

Sanctions have been used many times in the past, for varying reasons, with varying degrees of success.[16] Sanctions were imposed by the United States on India and Pakistan in 1998 following their May nuclear tests, but were lifted in 2001 in response to cooperation received after the September 11 terrorist attacks. Similarly, sanctions were imposed on Iraq and Libya for reasons not directly related to those states' suspected nuclear programs, but a side effect was to reduce funds available for nuclear activities. In addition to directly affecting nuclear programs, the financial hardships imposed by sanctions can have such an affect on the overall health of a nation that they may respond by doing what they can to have the sanctions lifted.[17] This, of course, is what sanctions are meant to achieve, but the circumstances in which this result can be attained may vary. However, it is advantageous for those nations closely aligned with proliferants and those who are adversaries to adhere to a "carrot and stick" approach. Offers of aid, combined with threats of sanctions, may prove to be instrumental in curbing proliferation.

Other than sanctions and similar high-level approaches to halting proliferation, there has not been a formal means of interdicting international trade in nuclear technologies beyond the export controls of a given country. The Proliferation Security Initiative (PSI) is a strong first step in providing state enforcement of nonproliferation efforts, and has been noted for its success in stopping a shipment of centrifuge parts to Libya in 2003, helping to bring an end to that country's nuclear ambitions.[18] The PSI is an agreement among states that allows for boarding of vessels with the agreement of the host country.[19] The PSI is intended to deter or interdict shipments of material related to WMD, within current laws governing shipping and the seas.[20] Currently, fifteen states are members of the PSI, including Russia, a key exporter; however, many important providers of WMD and related materials, such as China, remain outside the PSI. Constructive discussions to bring these states into the PSI and actively engage them in stopping shipments of WMD are crucial to the success of the PSI and similar agreements.

Enforcement of nonproliferation agreements is the most difficult aspect of nonproliferation efforts, and the most important. Effective monitoring, enhanced cooperation and information sharing, and strengthened, standardized rules regarding nuclear material and information is necessary to address the difficulties inherent in a secretive subject. With the increase in technical knowledge and the increasing number of dual-use technologies, it is ever more important to identify distinct, or at least the most important, technologies related to nuclear weapons development. By narrowing the export controls to focus on these more specific targets, less confusion and more oversight among governments over the end use of the equipment can be realized. Further, informal agreements that seek to provide a means to *act* against proliferators, such as the PSI, should be encouraged and augmented. For example, one important change to the PSI would be an agreement among states that offer "flags of convenience" to shippers that would allow interdiction in international waters on the open sea.

The international community should embrace the concept that the goal of nonproliferation is just that—no new nuclear weapon states. Thus, action to prevent states from developing nuclear weapons—whether by offers of aid and matériel, sanctions, or forceful interdiction—should be tailored to the specific weaknesses of the proliferator, and may involve compromise and sacrifice on the part of those states that desire to curb proliferation. The synthesis of these tools has convinced at least two states to renounce their nuclear programs, and more can do so in the future.

THE RISE OF MILITARY COUNTERPROLIFERATION

The start of the 21st century has seen the rise of military action as a means of countering nuclear proliferation and the proliferation of other weapons of mass destruction. The Bush Administration's 2002 National Security Strategy is based on the premise that nuclear proliferation in the case of certain states is irreversible and unstoppable, and thus the United States must act militarily when possible to pre-empt or prevent the use of nuclear weapons and keep other nations from gaining access to nuclear weapons technology.[21] Some other countries have accepted this premise, as a "coalition of the willing" joined the United States in a campaign of regime change in Iraq in 2003 with the stated goal of removing Saddam Hussein's suspected nuclear capability.[22] Those who advocate military action in the form of precision strikes against nuclear facilities or regime change generally believe that the role of multilateral and bilateral agreements for curbing nuclear proliferation have failed, and the best way to stop the spread of nuclear weapons is to destroy the means of producing them.[23]

A military strategy to curb nuclear proliferation is not new. The United States contemplated military action against Chinese nuclear facilities and North Korean nuclear facilities to prevent those two countries from becoming nuclear powers, and the Israelis conducted a militarily successful raid against the Iraqi Osirak nuclear reactor in 1981 to keep Iraq from producing plutonium.[24] Currently, the United States and Israel are publicly denying they have plans to attack Iran's nuclear facilities, but many news reports are focusing on the possibility that either country may conclude that military action is the only means of curbing Iran's suspected nuclear ambitions in light of the stalled diplomatic efforts.[25]

Military action may, in some very select cases, be the appropriate response to nuclearization by some countries. However, in many cases, a military role in nonproliferation efforts may very well encourage those same countries to increase their proliferation efforts. For example, following the 1981 Israeli raid on Osirak (which destroyed the reactor), Iraq turned to uranium enrichment as a means of developing nuclear weapons. The extent of Iraq's uranium enrichment program was kept hidden from the IAEA until after the 1991 Gulf War, when it was revealed that the program was significantly more advanced than previously assumed. Similarly, although an attack on Iran's nuclear infrastructure is possible, the effect on any nuclear weapons program could be small if any unknown facilities exist,[26] and Iran's retaliatory capabilities are numerous. Military action should be considered only as a last resort, and only then with full understanding that the consequences may be worse than diplomatic compromise.

ADDRESSING NUCLEAR TERRORISM

The rise of terrorism early in the 21st century and its subsequent high profile in international affairs has led to increasing worry over nuclear terrorism—the stated desire of terrorists to acquire weapons of mass destruction, especially nuclear weapons. In the 2004 U.S. presidential debate, both President George Bush and Senator John Kerry stated that the greatest threat to the United States was nuclear weapons in the hands of terrorists. A significant amount of effort has been devoted to reducing this threat by denying terrorists access to fissile material and assembled nuclear weapons.

Other than appropriate security activities tailored to civilian research reactors, these efforts have been focused primarily on securing fissile material in Russia and other former Soviet states and down-blending highly enriched uranium. With the collapse of the Soviet Union, thousands of nuclear weapons and huge amounts of fissile material were left unsecured. Multiple policy initiatives were established by the Departments of Energy and State and the U.S. Congress, among others, to reduce the threat posed by former Soviet weapons and nuclear material. These cooperative policies have worked very well. For example, thousands of weapons were removed from Ukraine, Belarus, and Kazakhstan and these countries joined the NPT as non-nuclear states.

Denying terrorists access to nuclear weapons or weapons-grade material is largely an exercise in reducing the amount of nuclear material available.[27] In other words, the fewer states with nuclear weapons that can be sold or stolen, and the fewer states with facilities that can produce highly enriched uranium or weapons-grade plutonium, the fewer access points terrorists will have to nuclear weapons and material. Thus, cooperative threat reduction measures that can be implemented with states are increasingly a "non-proliferation" measure against terrorists as well. While this may be an emotionally unfulfilling means of preventing nuclear proliferation to terrorists, given its passivity, it cannot be denied that deterrence by denial is effective.[28]

Active means of denying terrorists access to nuclear material and weapons have also been proposed, including manipulation of the black market with undercover buyers and sellers, disinformation campaigns, and increased monitoring of nuclear traffic.[29] Terrorists groups such as al Qaeda and Aum Shinrikyo have attempted to buy nuclear materials off the black market. As far as we know from reports, these efforts have been unsuccessful: al Qaeda operatives were duped into purchasing harmless materials believed to be nuclear-related, while Aum Shinrikyo, despite close ties to former Soviet nuclear experts, were unable to obtain nuclear materials.[30] Other attempts, however, have been somewhat more successful. Thefts of small amounts (microgram or milligram quantities) of radioactive material are periodically reported by various monitoring agencies or seized by police and other law enforcement or intelligence personnel, but the small amounts and types of material are generally of no value for nuclear weapons.[31]

More serious are the proliferation "networks" such as the A. Q. Khan nuclear network that have quasi-official backing.[32] These networks are more dangerous than the simple black market, as highly enriched uranium and weapons-grade plutonium seems to be available. Given the high level of the officials involved in such networks, the information exchanged or sold is deemed to be fairly accurate and can lead to significant advances in nuclear expertise on the part of the receiver. Libya, for example, admitted to receiving assistance with its centrifuge program, and it is suspected that Iran has obtained a great deal of information regarding P-1 and P-2 centrifuges from A. Q. Khan.

The great fear is that terrorist will be able to take advantage of these sophisticated networks and procure nuclear material, an assembled weapon (or its components), or less likely, the technology for producing nuclear material. Infiltrating nuclear networks and the nuclear black market is key to preventing the transfer of nuclear expertise to terrorist groups. Greater cooperation with other countries to secure nuclear arsenals, material, and technical knowledge will protect nuclear material and information to begin with, and manipulation of the black market can increase the cost to terrorists and force them to divert their energy elsewhere. Finally, the United States and others have worked to develop forensic "attribution" tools to determine the origin of nuclear material used in a nuclear weapon, but there is work to be done to establish the necessary international cooperation.[33] Convincing other countries of the effectiveness of nuclear forensics and the willingness of the U.S. to respond to a nuclear terrorist attack will provide a considerable deterrent effect on would-be sponsors of terrorists.[34]

Nuclear terrorism is a grave concern, and will remain a threat as long as states have unsafeguarded nuclear material or are willing to assist terrorists. Terrorists are highly unlikely to achieve the capability to produce their own weapons-grade uranium or plutonium; the most likely pathway for acquisition of these materials is through the sale or theft of nuclear weapons or material, or coercion of states with nuclear weapons. This can be avoided by striving to secure nuclear facilities, material, and weapons in other nuclear capable states, reducing the number of states that can produce fissile material or nuclear weapons, and ensuring that those facilities that remain operating are monitored under comprehensive international safeguards (including the Additional Protocol and appropriate international security standards). Adequately securing nuclear material, infiltrating the nuclear black market, shutting down nuclear networks, and convincing potential suppliers of retaliatory action will go far towards denying terrorists an opportunity to procure nuclear weapons.

A PATH FORWARD

Nuclear proliferation continues to be problematic more than sixty years after the first nuclear weapon was used in 1945. Nuclear technology has spread across the globe. While the great majority of countries that maintain active nuclear power plants, enrichment facilities and reprocessing plants act in accordance with the NPT and IAEA safeguards, a few manipulate the safeguards agreements to create nascent nuclear weapons programs or secretly engage in activities that could be used to develop nuclear weapons without informing the IAEA. As the technology needed to produce fissile material and build nuclear weapons becomes ever more available, the international community must shift its efforts towards enforcement of international agreements and bilateral and multilateral cooperation to prevent and interdict transfers of nuclear-related technology. While promising new efforts have been made and many proposals have been put forth to combat the spread of nuclear weapons, they do not address some concrete steps that can be taken to help curb proliferation. This section will suggest some additional steps to dissuade states from pursuing nuclear weapons and discuss some of the difficulties of proposed actions.

The Bush Administration proposed in 2004 seven steps towards reducing nuclear proliferation: expand the PSI; strengthen international nonproliferation controls; expand the Nunn-Lugar programs to keep nuclear material out of the hands of terrorists and "rogue states;" strengthen the requirements for use of peaceful nuclear technologies; require ratification of the Additional Protocol; strengthen the IAEA's safeguards and verification division; and, finally, prevent those states accused of violating nonproliferation controls from serving on the IAEA Board of Governors.[35] Assuming these ideas are fully funded and implemented, the proposals can go far towards improving proliferation efforts. However, they are primarily concentrated on enforcing existing international agreements and laws and are designed to force states into compliance with nonproliferation goals.

To create a lasting reduction in nuclear nonproliferation, policies must encourage states not to pursue nuclear weapons in the first place. Counterproliferation tactics may not compel a state to renounce nuclear weapons; a truly determined state may decide that nuclear weapons are so important that the consequence of noncompliance with international laws is worth the benefit of nuclear weapons. Law enforcement and additional safeguards may delay a "rogue" state's nuclear program, compel leaders to implement even more secrecy, and make it more difficult to purchase items for a nuclear program, but without a genuine desire on the behalf of a leader to forgo nuclear weapons, proliferation will continue despite best efforts to stop it.

For many years, the NPT provided a framework within which states could receive assistance with peaceful nuclear power while refraining from nuclear weapons. The international environment during the Cold War encouraged weaker states to secure nuclear guarantees from the great powers, i.e., the Soviet Union and the United States, while renouncing nuclear weapons under the NPT. With the collapse of the Soviet Union, the security fears of many states may not be conducive to seeking a nuclear umbrella, and the retaliation promised by the United States (or Russia) may not be as believable. The reasons that states pursue nuclear weapons must be addressed when searching for nonproliferation tactics. Many of these reasons have little to do with security per se, but are the result of a desire for prestige and domestic pressures both for and against nuclear weapons.[36]

The international nature of nonproliferation agreements does not satisfy the security and economic needs or the desire for prestige of many states. Bilateral and regional agreements among states must be utilized to a greater extent to satisfy the needs of any given country. For the United States and other nuclear powers, the need is to reduce the number of states with nuclear weapons and encourage states to forgo the nuclear option. For non-nuclear states, however, needs vary along with the reasons that states decide to build nuclear weapons. A single international agreement cannot hope to satisfy the diverse needs or desires of all states, but bilateral and regional agreements can. These agreements can take the form of bilateral security arrangements, trade negotiations, or regional security and economic pacts.

There is ample evidence that indicates this approach will be successful and easily realized. The most recent positive indication that bilateral agreements can be successful in reversing proliferation is the 2003 decision by Libya's Muammar Qaddafi to disband his country's nuclear program. This decision was likely brought about due to the diplomatic work of Britain and the United States, resulting in increased economic trade with Libya, removal of sanctions, and reintegration of Libya into the international community. Financial hardship resulting from sanctions, strenuous efforts in reducing nuclear transactions, and the enforcement activities of the PSI undoubtedly played a role in Qaddafi's decision to renounce nuclear weapons; however, the final decision was due largely to diplomatic agreements.[37]

In future arrangements, the United States or others may have to concede more than they wish or have had to do in the past, but the final goal is to have states without nuclear weapons. North Korea, for example, apparently decided that the repercussions of its October 2006 nuclear test were unacceptable. In the face of economic and political pressure from China, economic sanctions from the UN, and significant concessions on behalf of the United States, North Korea agreed to shut down its plutonium-producing reactor and accept intrusive inspections.[38] Some critics in the United States thought this deal gave too much to a "rogue" regime,[39] but others support the engagement. Although in its infancy, this deal may end North Korea's nuclear program by providing the regime with the aid and security assurances it wanted. In return, the United States and the world contend with one fewer nuclear state and lose relatively little in the bargain.[40] Future nonproliferation efforts should follow the model of Libya and North Korea, with positive inducements offered in exchange for nuclear disarmament.

A POSITIVE OUTLOOK

Any changes to the nonproliferation regime will be difficult to implement and will require sustained effort and diplomacy. In spite of many who claim that the nonproliferation regime is crumbling, the reality is much brighter: the NPT has prevented a significant number of states from becoming nuclear powers and will continue to do so. The 2006 North Korean nuclear test and the difficulties in resolving the situation over Iran's nuclear program are tests of the nonproliferation regime, but they also offer opportunities. In 1991, the extent of Saddam Hussein's nuclear weapons program prompted positive changes to the nonproliferation regime. The Additional Protocol strengthened international weapons inspectors' abilities and allowed the IAEA oversight of previously inaccessible facilities, while the disclosure of Iraq's delinquency helped to drive multinational cooperation in curbing the spread of nuclear technology. Similarly, the challenges to the NPT and the nonproliferation regime today present a chance to improve upon the current standards for nonproliferation. First, with the NPT as the fundamental binding agreement on the vast majority of states, the international community can work towards strengthening enforcement of oversight and providing the IAEA with more information and more resources to combat proliferation among states. Second, outside of formal UN agreements, states should improve upon the Nuclear Suppliers Group and Zanggar Committee guidelines to identify the key components of nuclear technology and increase the emphasis on keeping the most important tools and information away from states of concern. Third, the U.S. should work with other countries to strengthen bilateral interdiction and enforcement agreements which have proven to work well to combat proliferation efforts (for example, by enacting a United Nations Security Council (UNSC) resolution that legalizes interdiction on the high seas). Fourth, emphasizing cooperation and enforcement of international agreements, rather than military action, is paramount, as military action often involves unforeseen consequences and is frequently not supported by key UNSC members and U.S. allies. Finally, these actions to reduce proliferation should be supplemented with terrorist targeted infiltration of the nuclear black market, improved nuclear forensics, intelligence sharing, and a renewed effort to convince potential terrorist suppliers of the capability and willingness of the U.S. to retaliate following nuclear attack by state-sponsored terrorists.

Reducing the spread of nuclear weapons will require greater effort and attention as nuclear technology becomes more available to a greater number of states and organizations. Those countries that currently are considered nuclear powers must realize that in some cases compromises must be made to ensure safety and security. Given the rather exciting beginning of the 21st century with the North Korean nuclear test and the controversy over Iran's nuclear program, it would be easy to conclude that the nonproliferation regime has failed. However, these events provide a unique opportunity for the international community to recognize the failings of the current nonproliferation regime, undertake action to remedy the deficiencies, and work towards dramatically strengthening the underpinnings of nonproliferation in the future.

NOTES

1. *Public Papers of the Presidents of the United States: John F. Kennedy, 1963* (Washington, DC, US Government Printing Office, 1964), 280.

2. The exact number of states with nuclear weapons is somewhat opaque: Israel is widely believed to have a nuclear arsenal but has not officially admitted it; and North Korea conducted a nuclear test in October 2006 that was reported by Western agencies to have been less successful than expected..

3. An entire book could likely be written on the success or failure of the NPT. For a relatively brief discussion of its successes, see Jim Walsh, "Learning from Past Success: The NPT and the Future of Nonproliferation," Report for the Weapons of Mass Destruction (WMD) Commission No. 41, September 2006, http://www.wmdcommission.org. For the opposite view, see William C. Martel, "The End of Non-proliferation?" *Strategic Review*, 28:4 (Fall 2000), 16-21.

4. See Nina Tannenwald, "Stigmatizing the Bomb: Origins of the Nuclear Taboo," *International Security*, Vol. 29, No. 4 (Spring 2005), 5-49 for an example of how international structures have constrained or encouraged states to adopt cultural norms and ideas.

5. Only a maximum of five states have developed nuclear weapons since the NPT entered into force—India, Pakistan, Israel (widely assumed to possess nuclear weapons), and North Korea, assuming the October 2006 event to be evidence of an embryonic nuclear weapon capability. South Africa also developed nuclear weapons, but Pretoria unilaterally destroyed its small nuclear arsenal and signed the NPT in 1991.

6. "Rollback" refers to those states that have dismantled their nuclear weapons. South Africa is an example, as is Ukraine.

7. Examples are Iraq, North Korea, and potentially Iran.

8. Additional information on the Additional Protocol, including a model agreement, can be found at

http://www.iaea.org/OurWork/SV/Safeguards/sg_protocol.html.

9. Michael Z. Wise, "Argentina, Brazil Sign Nuclear Accord," *The Washington Post*, December 14, 1991, A19.

10. Ed Blanche, "GCC Pursues Nuclear Energy Programme," *Jane's Defence Weekly*, December 20, 2006.

11. The influence of nuclear cooperation between India and the United States on nuclear proliferation is not yet clear, and a primary criticism of the India deal is the lack of control for New Delhi's nuclear weapons facilities. See Chapter 16 in this volume.

12. For detailed information on the NSG, including participating governments, guidelines, and reports, see http://www.nuclearsuppliersgroup.org.

13. Edward Cody, "Tentative Nuclear Deal Struck With North Korea," *The Washington Post*, February 13, 2007, A1

14. It is important to note that the same dire predictions given today about the demise of the NPT and the failure of the nonproliferation regime were also heard after India's 1974 nuclear test, the revelations of Iraq's nuclear program in 1991, and again following India and Pakistan's 1998 tests. In all these cases, the NPT was further strengthened. See Joseph F. Pilat, "Iraq and the Future of Nuclear Non-proliferation: The Roles of Inspections and Treaties," *Science*, Vol. 255, March 1992, 1224-1229.

15. Sanctions for violating the terms of the NPT or for having been found "noncompliant" have been imposed on North Korea and Iran via UN Security Council Resolutions 1718 and 1737, respectively. There is also evidence that comprehensive sanctions levied against Libya and Iraq played a significant role in undermining those countries' ability to finance a nuclear weapons program.

16. For arguments for and against sanctions, see Robert A. Pape, "Why Economic Sanctions Do Not Work," *International Security*, Vol. 22, No. 2 (Autumn, 1997), p.. 90-136; George Tsebelis, "Are Sanctions Effective? A Game-Theoretic Analysis," *The Journal of Conflict Resolution*, Vol. 34, No. 1 (March 1990), 3-28; and Kimberly Ann Elliot, "The Sanctions Glass: Half Full or Completely Empty?" *International Security*, Vol. 23, No. 1 (Summer 1998), 50-65.

17. There is some evidence that the effect of sanctions imposed on North Korea following its nuclear test significantly hurt the DPRK. There is also reporting that indicates that a desire to have sanctions lifted and normal trade resumed was a factor in Libya's decision to renounce nuclear weapons. On North Korea, see David Sanger, "Outside Pressures Snapped Korean Deadlock," *The New York Times*, February 14, 2007, 1; for information on Libya, see Bruce W. Jentleson and Christopher A. Whytock, "Who "Won" Libya? The Force-Diplomacy Debate and Its Implications for Theory and Policy," *International Security*, Vol. 30, No. 3 (Winter 2005/2006), 47-86.

18. Andrew C. Winner, "The Proliferation Security Initiative: The New Face of Interdiction," *The Washington Quarterly*, 28:2 (Spring 2005), 129-143.

19. Office of the Press Secretary, The White House, "Proliferation Security Initiative: Statement of Interdiction Principles," September 4, 2003, http://www.state.gove/t/np/rls/fs/23764.htm.

20. In practice, this means that maritime interdiction will likely occur within sovereign waters with the cooperation of the appropriate domestic authorities.

21. See The National Security Strategy of the United States of America, Section V, September 2002, http://www.whitehouse.gov/nsc/nss.html.

22. Nuclear disarmament was not the sole reason for the 2003 Iraq war: concerns of other forms of WMD and Saddam Hussein's suspected ties to terrorists were also cited.

23. See Jason D. Ellis, "The Best Defense: Counterproliferation and U.S. National Security," *The Washington Quarterly*, (Spring 2003) 26:2 115-133.

24. For details on the 1981 raid, see Rodger W. Claire, *Raid on the Sun*, (New York: Broadway Books, 2004) and Shelomoh Nakdimon, *First Strike: The Exclusive Story of How Israel Foiled Iraq's Attempt to Get the Bomb*, (New York: Summit Books, 1987). For details on U.S. concerns over China, see Jeffrey T. Richelson, *Spying on the Bomb: American Nuclear Intelligence from Nazi Germany to Iran and North Korea*, (New York: W. W. Norton & Co., Ltd., 1996).

25. One widely cited example is Seymour M. Hersh, "The Iran Plans," *The New Yorker*, April 17, 2006. See also Uzi Mahnaimi and Sarah Baxter, "Israel readies forces for strike on nuclear Iran," *The Sunday Times* (online), December 11, 2005, http://www.timesonline.co.uk/article/0,,2089-1920074,00.html; Ian Bruce, "Israelis plan pre-emptive strike on Iran," *The Herald* (online), January 10, 2006; http://www.theherald.co.uk/news/53948.html; and Josef Federman, "Israeli Hints at Preparation to Stop Iran," *The Washington Post*, January 22, 2006.

26. See Whitney Raas and Austin Long, "Osirak Redux? Assessing Israeli Capabilities to Destroy Iranian Nuclear Facilities," *International Security*, Vol. 31, No. 4 (Spring 2007), pp. 7-33. For one widely cited example of the potential of a secondary secret Iranian nuclear program see Graham Allison, "How Good Is American Intelligence on Iran's Bomb?" YaleGlobal Online, 13 June 2006, http://yaleglobal.yale.edu, accessed 12 November 2006.

27. William Langewiesche, "How to Get a Nuclear Bomb," *The Atlantic Monthly*, December 2006, Vol. 298, No. 5, 80-99.

28. The United States is making contingency plans to deal with the situation of a "failed state" possessing nuclear weapons, as could occur in the event of a coup in Pakistan. See Rebecca K. C. Hersman and Todd M. Koca, "Eliminating Adversary WMD: Lessons for Future Conflicts," October 2004, National Defense University, *Strategic Forum* No. 211.

29. Michael V. Hynes, John E. Peters, and Joel Kvitky, "Denying Armageddon: Preventing Terrorist Use of Nuclear Weapons," *Annals*, AAPSS, 607, September 2006, 150-161.

30. Sara Daly, John Parachini, and William Rosenau, "Aum Shinrikyo, al Qa-

eda, and the Kinshasa Reactor: Implications of Three Case Studies for Combating Nuclear Terrorism," Santa Monica, CA: RAND Corporation, DB-458-AF, 2005, http://www.rand.org/pubs/documented _briefings/DB458/

31. Most seizures have not been highly enriched uranium or plutonium, but rather other nuclear material that could be used in radiological dispersal devices ("dirty bombs").

32. Michael V. Hynes, John E. Peters, and Joel Kvitky, *Denying Armageddon.*

33. For example see, Michael May, Jay Davis, "Preparing for the worst," *Nature* 443, 907 - 908 (25 Oct 2006).

34. Caitlin Talmadge, "Deterring a Nuclear 9/11," *The Washington Quarterly*, Spring 2007, 30:2, the Center for Strategic and International Studies and the Massachusetts Institute of Technology.

35. See "Remarks by the President on Weapons of Mass Destruction Proliferation," Fort Lesley J. McNair—National Defense University, Washington, D.C., February 11, 2004, http://www.whitehouse.gov/news/releases/2004/02/20040211-4.html, accessed 31 December 2006.

36. Widely cited on reasons for proliferation is Scott Sagan, "Why Do States Build Nuclear Weapons? Three Models in Search of a Bomb," *International Security*, Vol. 21, No. 3 (Winter 1996-1997), 54-86.

37. See Bruce W. Jentleson and Christopher A. Whytock, "Who "Won" Libya? The Force-Diplomacy Debate and Its Implications for Theory and Policy," *International Security*, Vol. 30, No. 3 (Winter 2005/2006), 47-86.

38. Whether or not this deal lives up to expectations and succeeds in the future remains to be seen.

39. John Bolton, former Ambassador to the UN, was quoted as denouncing the agreement as a "bad deal." See Glenn Kessler, "Conservatives Assail North Korea Accord," *The Washington Post*, February 15, 2007, A1.

40. This agreement is arguably very similar to previous agreements with North Korea such as the Agreed Framework, which did not succeed. However, the price paid for the attempt is small, and the return could conceivably be large.

CHAPTER SIXTEEN

THE INDIA DEAL AND ITS IMPLICATIONS

Mary Beth Nikitin

"For many years, the United States and India were kept apart by the rivalries that divided the world. That's changed. Our two great democracies are now united by opportunities that can lift our people, and by threats that can bring down all our progress. The United States and India, separated by half the globe, are closer than ever before, and the partnership between our free nations has the power to transform the world."—*President George W. Bush, New Delhi, March 3, 2006*

The U.S.-India announcement of cooperation on civilian nuclear energy technology, announced in March 2006 and approved in principle by Congress in December 2006, was hailed as the centerpiece of President Bush and Prime Minister Singh's New Delhi summit, and touted as the key to moving the bilateral relationship forward on all fronts. President Bush has cited the agreement as a major nonproliferation victory. While it focuses on opening up India's access to civilian nuclear technologies, the "nuclear deal" has implications for India's strategic nuclear program, and gives insights into Washington's changing perspective toward the Indian nuclear arsenal. Furthermore, agreement on this issue was reached in the context of a broadening cooperative security relationship between the United States and India. Its conclusion entails costs and benefits for India's own nuclear program and has implications for the global nonproliferation system.

President Bush has characterized the shift in U.S. policy toward India as a reward for its good nonproliferation behavior, although it is not a party to the Nuclear Nonroliferation Treaty. However, the agreement has broader meaning as part of a developing bilateral strategic partnership: it is a recognition of common goals, that "both our countries are linked by … a desire to increase mutual security against the common threats posed by intolerance, terrorism, and the spread of weapons of mass destruction." The Bush administration sent a clear message that curbing vertical proliferation of India's arsenal is no longer a policy goal. Moving the bilateral relationship forward was prioritized over any potential costs that breaking the civil nuclear trade barrier might have for global nonproliferation goals. Furthermore, it will test whether states that are not parties to the Nuclear Nonproliferation Treaty (NPT) can be brought into the nuclear nonproliferation regime and nuclear supply regime to net positive advantage. While these effects are yet to be fully seen, the proposed agreement sets a precedent and tests the effectiveness of making case-by-case nonproliferation policy.

EVOLVING U.S.-INDIA RELATIONS

The transforming moment in U.S.-India relations may have come much earlier than March 2006. In the words of former Indian Foreign Minister Jaswant Singh, when President Clinton visited India in 2000, "the U.S. helped India cross the bridge to the rest of the world." [1] This visit followed two years of intense shuttle diplomacy after the 1998 Indian nuclear tests, led by U.S. Under Secretary of State Strobe Talbott. [2] These talks began the process of broadening the context for dialogue on security, ending the "cold war" between the U.S. and India. [3] Besides nuclear proliferation questions, the two sides discussed a wide range of geopolitical questions.

Another jump forward in relations occurred when India immediately offered its support to the United States following the September 11 attacks in the war against terror—250 Indian citizens died in the attack on the World Trade Center. [4] President Bush waived U.S. economic sanctions against India and Pakistan that were imposed after their nuclear tests, due to the new defining policy priority of defeating Al Qaeda in Afghanistan, and in December 2001 military-to-military contacts were resumed with India through the Defense Policy Group that had been suspended for three years. [5]

The Bush administration continued the bilateral security dialogue in the intervening years and in January 2004 the two countries agreed on the "Next Steps in Strategic Partnership (NSSP)." The NSSP stated the countries' intention to expand cooperation in the areas of civilian nuclear activities, civilian space programs, and high technology trade, and to expand dialogue on missile defense.[6]

In June 2005 at the Pentagon, U.S. Secretary of Defense Donald Rumsfeld and Indian Minister of Defense Pranab Mukherjee signed the "New Framework for the U.S.-India Defense Relationship."[7] Declaring that the United States and India have "entered a new era" in which the two countries will build a strategic relationship, the document sets out goals for the partnership over the next ten years. The Framework pledges to: conduct joint and combined exercises and exchanges, collaborate in multinational operations, strengthen capabilities to defeat terrorism, expand interaction with other nations to promote stability, enhance capabilities to combat weapons of mass destruction proliferation, expand "two-way defense trade" as a means of strengthening the strategic partnership, increase technology transfer and R&D collaboration, expand collaboration relating to missile defense, strengthen abilities to respond quickly to disasters, work to build worldwide capacity for peacekeeping operations, conduct exchanges on defense strategy and defense transformation, increase intelligence exchanges, and continue high-level strategic dialogue.

Language in the U.S. National Security Strategy (NSS) of 2006 compared to the NSS of 1998 also highlights the dramatic change in bilateral relations. In 1998, India and Pakistan were treated in similar fashion. The document emphasized a freeze on nuclear weapons development and promotion of confidence building measures, and stated that, "India and Pakistan are contributing to a self-defeating cycle of escalation that does not add to the security of either country." In contrast, while relations with Pakistan have improved but the major disputes are not yet resolved, the 2006 NSS treats India and Pakistan distinctly and differently. It emphasizes that the United States is seeking good relations with both and recognizes an improvement in India-Pakistan relations, but it makes no reference to their nuclear weapon programs. Indeed, it focuses on U.S.-India bilateral relations as such: "We have set aside decades of mistrust and put relations with India, the world's most populous democracy, on a new and fruitful path," and states that India is now "poised to shoulder global obligations in cooperation with the United States in a way befitting a major power."

Strong statements by the U.S. military leadership further highlight the extent to which this partnership has developed. For example, General Peter Pace, chairman of the Joint Chiefs of Staff said in a briefing with his Indian counterpart, Admiral Arun Prakash in New Delhi on June 5, 2006, "Our way forward is to... find ways that our two militaries can interact that will reinforce to our friends that we are capable of defending ourselves and our friends, and to reinforce to any potential enemy that India as a sovereign nation and the United States as a sovereign nation, and together as partners, are going to protect our citizens against harm."[8] Indeed, U.S. military cooperation involves significant conventional arms purchases as well.[9] Cooperation following the tsunami in December 2004 also played a role in solidifying these ties. The emphasis on deterring common enemies and combating weapons of mass destruction proliferation reveals that the United States does not see any threat from an Indian nuclear weapon arsenal itself.

The U.S.-India "Strategic Partnership" was further detailed in a July 18, 2005 summit statement. President Bush characterized the partnership as such, "[The] relationship is based increasingly on common values and common interests. We are working together to promote global peace and prosperity. We are partners in the war on terrorism and we are partners in controlling the proliferation of weapons of mass destruction and the means to deliver them." This is part of the shift in rhetoric in U.S. policy from addressing India as part of the proliferation problem to emphasizing its role as partner in preventing further weapons of mass destruction (WMD) proliferation. The partnership based on "our shared values" that was further developed is part of a scientific, military, and economic package that includes cooperation in energy, agriculture, science and technology, trade and investment, high technology, health and a clean environment. The outcome of the March 2, 2006 Summit in New Delhi solidified the July 18 pledges.[10]

THE NUCLEAR "DEAL"

It is in this broadened context of cooperation that the so-called 'nuclear deal' was born. The agreement to establish civilian nuclear cooperation between the United States and India was viewed by the Bush administration as a key to progress on other strategic issues. The linkage between nuclear cooperation and cooperation in other areas was highlighted by

Secretary Rice in congressional testimony in April 2006: "in order to fully realize the potential of this vision for India, we do have to deal with the longstanding impediments associated with civil nuclear cooperation and we need to resolve them once and for all. We believe that this initiative will unlock the progress of our expanding relationship in other areas."[11] Under Secretary of State Nicholas Burns, who was and is closely involved in every step of the negotiations, has said that the civil nuclear accord is the "symbolic centerpiece" of bilateral engagement.[12] The agreement is meant to politically cement the U.S.-India strategic relationship, viewed as critical for ensuring America's strategic and economic strength in the region in the years ahead.

Even with the will on both sides to leave the past dynamic behind, until the last moment it was not clear that they would be able to reach agreement on this most controversial of the July 18 pledges—agreement on the terms of negotiation for a civil nuclear cooperation agreement. When agreement on basic terms was announced by the two leaders at the March 2006 summit, it was greeted with a mixed reaction in both the United States and India.[13]

In effect, the inclusion of civilian nuclear cooperation in the strategic partnership means that the United States has clearly recognized India as a *de facto* nuclear weapon state and implies that it will not seek Indian disarmament until India itself is ready for this. This is especially significant since it not only gives India *de facto* recognition of its nuclear weapons but could in effect give it standing akin to *de jure* status without any commitment to pursue nuclear disarmament in good faith, as the other *de jure* Nuclear Weapon States of the NPT committed to under Article VI.[14] In the eyes of the deal's supporters, this shift is justified since India is seen as a "responsible" nuclear weapons power that does not proliferate to other programs. The terms announced at the March 2006 summit explicitly set no limits to Indian nuclear arsenal development.

Nevertheless, summit statements promising civil nuclear cooperation with India were only a first step. The U.S. administration next needed to obtain authorization from Congress to negotiate a civil nuclear cooperation agreement with India, under section 123 of the U.S. Atomic Energy Act of 1954.[15] Since India is not a member of the Nuclear NPT, express permission was required by Congress under U.S. law. This enabling legislation was passed as the Henry Hyde United States-India Peaceful Atomic Energy Cooperation Act on December 18, 2006.[16]

Further changes to the export rules of the multilateral Nuclear Suppliers Group (NSG) are also required for cooperation to take place. Nuclear trade between India and other countries would then be permitted, as was recognized in the March 2006 statement, "This historic accomplishment will permit our countries to move forward towards our common objective of full civil nuclear energy cooperation between India and the United States and between India and the international community as a whole." This access is intended to improve the safety of Indian nuclear facilities, as well as the ability of India to provide energy for its advancing economy, with residual benefits for the United States and others. India will be invited to join research consortia on future reactor technologies.

In return, India has promised to add IAEA safeguards for more existing power reactors that are not relevant for weapons production and to put future reactors that India determines are for civil use under IAEA safeguards. India has recommitted itself to its informal moratorium on nuclear testing. This does help reinforce the global norm against nuclear testing.

However, India avoided any commitment not to be the first to break the moratorium and successfully resisted U.S. requests that it adopt a moratorium on the production of nuclear materials for weapons, despite U.S. negotiators' attempts to include this in the early phases of the negotiations in the summer of 2005. The five NPT Nuclear Weapon States (U.S., Russia, France, Britain and China) are all currently under informal unilateral moratoria on the production of fissile material. There are also no calls for India to join the Comprehensive Nuclear Test-Ban Treaty or sign up to the Additional Protocol of IAEA safeguards, long part of the U.S. position towards India's military nuclear program. Thus, in the end, India has retained the freedom to expand and advance its nuclear weapon program in exchange for placing a portion of its energy producing reactors under international safeguards.

To make the deal a reality, the U.S. administration is working to carve out a legal exception for India in both domestic law and the international export control regime. This case solidifies a trend toward a selective approach to the problems of proliferation, and ultimately sends the message that it is acceptable for some countries to have nuclear weapons and for others not to. This is perhaps an honest and clear reflection of current U.S. policy. How it affects others' view of the value of nuclear nonproliferation itself, as well as what other exceptions will be made for other states, are yet to be seen.

DEBATE & CONTROVERSY

Internationally, the March 2006 announcement was welcomed by IAEA Director General Mohamed El Baradei, along with UK Prime Minister Tony Blair and French President Jacques Chirac.[17] All emphasized the positive sides of bringing India more closely into the nonproliferation framework through safeguards, improving safety for future power reactors in India and cooperating to prevent nuclear terrorism. "The agreement would assure India of reliable access to nuclear technology and nuclear fuel. It would also be a step forward towards universalisation of the international safeguards regime," Dr. El Baradei said. "This agreement would serve the interests of both India and the international community."[18]

For many, opening up civil nuclear cooperation with India is simply a practical step forward in light of existing realities, namely that India does not intend to give up its nuclear weapons any time soon, yet it needs energy security for its growing population. It was seen by some in the United States and abroad as a relief—the irritant of India's nuclear weapons status could be put aside and their friend no longer would have to be ostracized. Others saw it as a confirmation of their view that the United States held its friends up to a different nonproliferation standard.

In the United States, the reaction to the news was mixed. Nonproliferation experts sounded the alarm that carving out an exception for India--with limited actions requested in return--at a time when the United States was working to decrease incentives for countries to gain nuclear weapons, was shortsighted at best. The timing was particularly criticized, as the United States is working to halt the spread of enrichment and reprocessing technologies, in particular in Iran. The NPT[19] is also at a fragile point in its history. Debate centers on whether civilian nuclear cooperation would enhance or assist India in building up its nuclear weapons arsenal. While experts seemed to agree that a closer relationship with India on a variety of fronts was desirable and welcome, the so-called nuclear "deal" was seen as going too far toward accommodating India and lacking any long-term vision on how this would impact U.S. nonproliferation policies. There was also little accountability created on how India should improve its own nuclear security and export control practices. In fact, many quiet non-governmental efforts to move India closer to the nonproliferation regime and construct confidence-building measures with Pakistan on these issues were derailed when it became clear to India that the U.S. government was changing its position dramatically.

Just as after the 1998 Indian nuclear test, the United States' concern over Indian nuclear weapon development has overridingly centered on the effect of this program on other countries and the nonproliferation regime more generally, rather than a threat from Indian nuclear weapons themselves.

When this debate played out on Capitol Hill, another focus of attention was India's business dealings with Iran and its diplomatic actions toward that country in its stand-off with the Security Council. Some of these concerns were included in final language of the Hyde Act.[20] Congress has fundamentally said that the United States recognizes India's right to have the nuclear arsenal it now has, but civilian nuclear transfers should not include any enrichment, reprocessing, or heavy water technologies and all cooperation would be stopped if India conducted a nuclear test.

In addition to arguments based on economic development and environmentally sound energy expansion, outside experts in support of the deal point to the advantages of India having a robust nuclear arsenal to the extent that this is a balance to China's growing military strength.[21] U.S. deterrence of China would therefore be strengthened with India as a military partner.

In India, the controversy has centered on those not wanting any limits whatsoever on the nuclear activities in the country and those who oppose a closer security and foreign policy relationship with the United States. The latter fear a threat to India's independent foreign policy. The former are concerned that any leverage the United States held over India in the nuclear area could threaten energy supplies in the future should India decide, for example, that it needed to conduct a nuclear-weapon test.

IMPLICATIONS

It can be argued that the pursuit of a civil nuclear cooperation agreement with India reveals several trends in U.S. foreign policy, and nonproliferation policy in particular: rewarding India for 'good' nonproliferation behavior outside its borders, creating incentives for these nonproliferation actions beyond 'virtue as its own reward,' exceptionalism for the friendly, democratic country with a nuclear arsenal, and inclusion of nuclear issues in part of a security package.

Ultimately, it is not at all clear that this deal was necessary to advance bilateral partnership, although many argue that this issue was symbolically a pressure point in bilateral relations that needed to be removed. In many ways the de-prioritization of nuclear nonproliferation issues to the wider question of strategic partnership and sustainable development for India was a conciliatory gift to India. Unfortunately, for many others, especially non-nuclear weapon states, it only enhances the perception that U.S. nonproliferation policies are full of double standards that break the "deal" of the NPT—that those states that agree not to develop nuclear weapons will have preferential access to civilian nuclear technology and that the five official nuclear-weapon states will work to reduce nuclear weapons in the world. Instead, they see the United States abandoning one of the key principles of its foreign policy (no nuclear cooperation with states outside the NPT) and cannot help but reconsider their own country's place in this bargain.

Additionally, opening up civilian cooperation with India —if this allows India more nuclear material for its nuclear weapons program — may affect and accelerate strategic development in Pakistan and China, both of which might feel they need to respond to a more robust Indian nuclear weapons posture. It would therefore be tougher for the United States to argue for limits to those programs. Herein lies the difficulty in carving out an exception for one country, an issue that the Nuclear Suppliers Group is debating. The deal may already have set a precedent, and it may be more difficult than expected to create a one-country exception to NSG rules. China and Pakistan, for example have already discussed concluding a similar civilian nuclear cooperation agreement.[22] The United States thus far has refused to do so, citing the proliferation problems from Pakistan posed by the A.Q. Khan network.

There are clear benefits from tying India more closely to the international nonproliferation regime. It is critical that all states with significant nuclear capabilities place a maximum number of their facilities under safeguards and ensure that nuclear materials under their control are adequately protected. However, this agreement does not place any constraints on India's growing nuclear weapon program or reduce pressure among other states in the region to limit their own nuclear weapon programs.

A build-up of nuclear weapons material anywhere in the world is clearly against U.S. efforts, joined by other like-minded states, to reduce and consolidate this material worldwide to prevent nuclear terrorism.

Thus, in moving forward with the agreement, the ultimate outcome of the net positive versus negative impact on the nonproliferation regime depends greatly on holding India accountable for its nonproliferation promises and maximizing its contribution to the global system against the spread of nuclear weapons to new states or to non-state actors. These steps should be taken regardless of civil nuclear "deal" status.

There is also a continued role for other countries—especially the non-nuclear states of the NPT—to encourage further Indian nuclear restraint, commitments to arms control (limits on stockpile growth and modernization), confidence-building measures and transparency (especially with Pakistan and China) and long-term multilateral disarmament commitments. India has again begun to emphasize its desire to achieve a nuclear-free world "through global, verifiable, and non-discriminatory disarmament."[23] It is time that India be held to account for this rhetoric and also asked what it is doing to advance its professed goals.

Between the United States and India, maintaining a positive nonproliferation outcome for a civil nuclear cooperation agreement will take continued dedication to a security partnership and constant attention to nuclear stewardship cooperation, such as material security best practices and counterterrorism measures. Counterproliferation and counterterrorism cooperation will require intelligence sharing and military ties. True cooperation on these fronts, even more than in the civil nuclear arena, is the real key to a stability-building relationship between the United States and India and is essential for India to become a nonproliferation partner.

Notes

1. Jaswant Singh, remarks to the Johns Hopkins School of Advanced International Studies, November 1, 2006, http://www.sais-jhu.edu/.

2. For a detailed account, see Strobe Talbott, *Engaging India: Diplomacy, Democracy, and the Bomb*, Brookings Institution Press, Washington, 2004, and Jaswant Singh, "A Call to Honor,"

3. Strobe Talbott, remarks to the Johns Hopkins School of Advanced International Studies, November 1, 2006, http://www.sais-jhu.edu/.

4. Statement by Shri Jaswant Singh, Minister of External Affairs and Defence on attacks on World Trade Center and Pentagon, New Delhi, September 11, 2001, http://www.indianembassy.org/press_release/2001/sep/sep_11.htm

5. India Nuclear Milestones, The Wisconsin Project website, http://www.wisconsinproject.org/countries/india/india-nuclear-miles.html

6. U.S. President's Statement on Strategic Partnership with India, January 12, 2004, http://www.whitehouse.gov/news/releases/2004/01/20040112-1.html

7. "New Framework for the U.S.-India Defense Relationship," signed June 28, 2005, http://newdelhi.usembassy.gov/ipr062805.html

8. http://newdelhi.usembassy.gov/pr060706.html

9. Ashish Kumar Sen, "Nuclear Battle Lines Drawn," *Asia Times*, August 12, 2005, http://www.atimes.com/atimes/South_Asia/GH12Df01.html

10. U.S.-India Joint Statement, New Delhi, March 2, 2006, http://www.whitehouse.gov/news/releases/2006/03/20060302-5.html

11. Secretary Condoleezza Rice, Opening Remarks Before the Senate Foreign Relations Committee, Washington, DC, April 5, 2006, http://www.state.gov/secretary/rm/2006/64136.htm

12. R. Nicholas Burns , Under Secretary for Political Affairs and Indian Foreign Secretary Shiv Shankar Menon Remarks at the Carnegie Endowment for International Peace, Washington, DC, February 22, 2007, http://www.state.gov/p/us/rm/2007/81207.htm

13. William Potter, "India and the New Look of U.S. Nonproliferation Policy," CNS Research Story, August 25, 2005; Robert J. Einhorn, "U.S.-India Nuclear Deal Falls Short," *San Francisco Chronicle*, March 17, 2006; Sam Nunn, "Nuclear Pig in a Poke," *Wall Street Journal*, May 24, 2006; Ashley Tellis, "Atoms for War? U.S.-Indian Civilian Nuclear Cooperation and India's Nuclear Arsenal," Carnegie Report, June 2006;

14. Article VI of the NPT states, "Each of the Parties to the Treaty undertakes to pursue negotiations in good faith on effective measures relating to cessation of the nuclear arms race at an early date and to nuclear disarmament, and on a Treaty on general and complete disarmament under strict and effective international control."

15. http://epw.senate.gov/envlaws/atomic54.pdf

16. http://www.whitehouse.gov/news/releases/2006/12/20061218-1.html

17. France had concluded a similar nuclear cooperation agreement with India during President Chirac's visit to New Delhi in February 2006. http://news.bbc.co.uk/2/hi/south_asia/4768422.stm

18. IAEA Press Release 2006/05, "IAEA Director General Welcomes U.S. and India Nuclear Deal," March 2, 2006.

19. Article 1 of the NPT commits the nuclear-weapon state parties "not to transfer to any recipient whatsoever nuclear weapons or other nuclear explosive devices or control over such weapons or explosive devices directly, or indirectly; and not in any way to assist, encourage, or induce any non-nuclear weapon State to manufacture or otherwise acquire nuclear weapons or other nuclear explosive devices, or control over such weapons or explosive devices."

20. Congressional Research Service Summary of H.R. 5682 [109th]: Henry Hyde United States-India Peaceful Atomic Energy Cooperation Act of 2006, December 18, 2006, http://thomas.loc.gov/cgi-bin/bdquery/z?d109:HR05682:@@@D&summ2=m&

21. See Robert D. Blackwill, "The India Imperative," National Interest, Summer 2005.

22. Sudha Ramachandran, "Good deals, but no nukes for Pakistan," Asia Times, November 28, 2006, http://www.atimes.com/atimes/South_Asia/HK28Df01.html

23. Statement of Nuclear Disarmament by Ambassador Jayant Prasad, Permanent Representative of India to the Conference on Disarmament, Geneva, February 13, 2007, http://meaindia.nic.in/speech/2007/02/21ss01.htm ; also see http://www.indianembassy.org/policy/Disarmament/note_india_disarmament.htm

ABOUT THE EDITORS AND AUTHORS

Jerome M. Conley

Jerome Conley is the director of research for Operational Concepts, LLC and a senior research scientist in the Institute for Crisis, Disaster and Risk Management, George Washington University. After eleven years of service in the United States Marine Corps, Mr. Conley served as an advisor in the Advanced Systems and Concepts Office of the Defense Threat Reduction Agency, where he conducted analysis on global and regional trends in nuclear proliferation, U.S.-Russian cooperation in strategic crisis management, and risk management approaches to WMD threats. Ongoing research includes the analysis of factors contributing to situational awareness in a tactical environment. He is the author of *Indo-Russian Military and Nuclear Cooperation: Lessons and Options for U.S. Policy in South Asia* (Lexington Books, 2001). Mr. Conley received his undergraduate degree from the College of the Holy Cross, his M.A. from the Naval Postgraduate School, and is completing his doctorate at the George Washington University.

Jonathan Hagood

Jonathan Hagood is a Ph.D. candidate in the Department of History at the University of California, Davis and is a member of the National Science Foundation's Graduate Research Fellowship Program. He has participated in the CSIS Project on Nuclear Issues since 2004 and is an associate of the Institute on Global Conflict and Cooperation's Public

Policy and Nuclear Threats program. Mr. Hagood has an M.A. in history from U.C. Davis, and he has published articles on topics such as nuclear dissuasion, post-Second World War nuclear research in Latin America, and technology transfer in the twentieth century.

Jenifer Mackby

Jenifer Mackby is a fellow in the CSIS International Security Program. She has worked on the Strengthening the Global Partnership project, a Russian-European project on bioterrorism, the Project on Nuclear Issues, and a number of European projects. She was a contributor to *The Nuclear Tipping Point: Why States Reconsider their Nuclear Choices* (Brookings, 2004) and has written articles for the *New York Times*, *Newsweek*, and the *Bulletin of the Atomic Scientists*, among other publications. Ms. Mackby served as a senior political affairs officer in the Conference on Disarmament in Geneva, where she worked on negotiations for the Comprehensive Nuclear Test-Ban Treaty and then on the verification of the treaty in Vienna.

Eric A. Miller

Eric A. Miller is a research associate at the Institute of European, Russian, and Eurasian Studies at George Washington University in Washington D.C. He previously worked at the U.S. Missile Defense Agency, where he specialized in Russian and Ukrainian affairs. He has served as a consultant and international affairs analyst for the Office of the Secretary of Defense, Joint Forces Staff College, and U.S. Coast Guard and held teaching positions at Old Dominion University and Christopher Newport University. His articles have appeared in *Defense News*, *Jane's Intelligence Review*, *Problems of Post-Communism*, and *Security Studies*, among others. He is also the author of *To Balance or Not to Balance: Alignment Theory and the Commonwealth of Independent States* (Ashgate, 2006). He holds a B.A. in political science from the University of Florida and an M.A. and Ph.D. in international studies from Old Dominion University.

Lieutenant Colonel (select) George R. Nagy, USAF

George R. Nagy is a career space and missile officer with the United States Air Force. He was commissioned in 1992 through the Reserve Officer Training Corps at the Massachusetts Institute of Technology and was assigned from 1993-1997 as a Minuteman III missile launch crew member with the 91st Missile Wing, Minot AFB, North Dakota. His assignments include experience in missile warning and space surveillance test and evaluation as well as serving as a strategy/policy officer from 2002-2005 at Headquarters, United States Strategic Command, Offutt AFB, Nebraska. In 2003 Major Nagy coauthored the Strategic Deterrence Joint Operating Concept at the direction of the secretary of sefense. Major Nagy holds separate master's degrees in space studies, space operations, and applied physics from the University of North Dakota and the Air Force Institute of Technology and is a fully qualified joint specialty officer. He currently serves as the chief of Spaceflight Mission Design, DOD Space Test Program, Kirtland AFB, New Mexico.

Mary Beth Nikitin

Mary Beth Nikitin is a fellow in the CSIS International Security Program, where she concentrates on issues related to preventing weapons of mass destruction proliferation and terrorism. She is coordinator of the Strengthening the Global Partnership project, a consortium of 23 research institutes in 18 European, Asian, and North American countries working to build political and financial support for G-8 efforts to reduce the spread of nuclear, biological, and chemical materials. She has worked at the UN Department for Disarmament Affairs in New York and at the Center for Nonproliferation Studies in Monterey. She regularly publishes and presents her research at international conferences. She received her master's degree at the Monterey Institute of International Studies and her bachelor's degree from Dartmouth College.

David D. Palkki

David Palkki worked as a defense analyst for the U.S. government from 2002 through 2006. He is currently an associate fellow for Public Policy and Nuclear Threats at the Institute on Global Conflict and Cooperation, a PONI Young Nuclear Scholar, and a Ph.D. candidate at the University of California, Los Angeles. His dissertation is on the efficacy of coercive disarmament.

Owen C.W. Price

Owen C.W. Price was a visiting fellow in residence at the CSIS from 2006 through early 2007, on leave from the UK Atomic Weapons Establishment (AWE), where he worked for 12 years. He recently returned to AWE, where he leads warhead capability programs. From 2000 to 2003, he led the AWE Verification Research Program, was a technical adviser to the British Foreign and Commonwealth Office, and was a member of the UK delegation to the Nonproliferation Treaty Preparatory Committee Meetings in 2003 and 2004. Mr. Price has published articles on nuclear matters in *Defense News, The Washington Times* and specialist publications. Mr. Price holds an M.A. in engineering from the University of Cambridge, England, and an M.B.A. in engineering management from the University of Bradford, England. He is currently reading (part time) for an M.Sc. in systems engineering at the UK Defence Academy, Cranfield University, Shrivenham, England.

Whitney Raas

Whitney Raas is a research analyst at the Center for Naval Analyses in Alexandria, VA. She has previously worked on the research staff at MIT Lincoln Laboratory. Her recent publications include "Osirak Redux? Assessing Israeli Capabilities to Destroy Iranian Nuclear Facilities," *International Security*, Spring 2007 (co-authored with Austin Long), "Design and Testing of a High Pressure Gas Target for Fast Neutron Resonance Radiography" and "Neutron Resonance Radiography for Explosives Detection: Technical Challenges," both in *Proceedings of the IEEE* (October 2005). Her primary research interests are nuclear weapons, nuclear proliferation, and energy. She recently received a Ph.D. in nuclear engineering and an M.S. in political science (with a focus on security studies) from MIT. Dr. Rass also holds a B.S. in physics from the University of California, Los Angeles.

Nick Ritchie

Nick Ritchie is completing his Ph.D. at the Department of Peace Studies, University of Bradford, United Kingdom on the evolution of U.S. nuclear weapons policy since the end of the Cold War. He has worked for the Oxford Research Group, a UK think-tank involved in research and advocacy on global security issues, particularly nuclear proliferation and disarmament, since 1999. Recent publications include *The Political Road to War with Iraq* with Paul Rogers (Routledge, 2007) and "Replacing Trident: Who Will Make the Decisions and How?" (Oxford Research Group report, August 2006).

Lawrence Rubin

Lawrence Rubin is a fellow for Public Policy and Nuclear Threats at the Institute on Global Conflict and Cooperation, a PONI Young Nuclear Scholar, and a Ph.D. candidate at the University of California, Los Angeles. Mr. Rubin also serves as the assistant editor of the journal *Terrorism and Political Violence*. Mr. Rubin has worked at the RAND Corporation and has been a visiting research fellow at NDU's Near East South Asia Center for Strategic Studies. He has conducted field work in Yemen, Morocco, Egypt, and Israel, and he speaks both Arabic and Hebrew. Mr. Rubin's dissertation focuses on threat perception and foreign policy decision-making of Middle East states.

Dakota S. Rudesill

Dakota Rudesill is a visiting fellow at CSIS. He served as national security advisor to Senator Kent Conrad and senior defense, intelligence, and international affairs analyst for the Senate Budget Committee. Mr. Rudesill has been a member of PONI since its inception, is a term member of the Council on Foreign Relations, and is a member of the Brady-Johnson Program in Grand Strategy at Yale University. He has consulted on strategic programs for the private sector and briefed on nuclear issues at the U.S. Strategic Command and UK Ministry of Defence. Mr. Rudesill received his B.A. in foreign policy from St. Olaf College and his J.D. from Yale Law School, where he was executive editor of the Yale Journal of International Law.

Lani Miyoshi Sanders

Lani Miyoshi Sanders is a principal member of the technical staff at Sandia National Laboratories. Prior to Sandia, Dr. Sanders worked for the Defense Nuclear Facilities Safety Board at its headquarters in Washington, D.C. and on assignment at the Savannah River Site. Dr. Sanders holds a B.S. from Rice University, an M.S. from Stanford University in civil engineering, and a Ph.D. from the University of New Mexico in chemical engineering.

Dennis Shorts

Dennis Shorts is currently a consultant at Booz Allen Hamilton working within the Operations Directorate (J3), U.S. Forces-Korea (USFK). Previously, he conducted research and taught on a Fulbright grant in South

Korea. He has also served on the research staff at the National Defense University in Washington, D.C. A former Army officer, he holds a double B.A. degree from Texas Christian University and a M.S. in foreign service from Georgetown University.

Francis Slakey

Francis Slakey holds an endowed position at Georgetown University where he is the Cooper/Upjohn Professor of Science and Public Policy and the co-director of the Program on Science in the Public Interest. His technical publications have received more than 500 citations. He has also written widely on science policy issues, publishing more than fifty articles for the popular press including *The New York Times, The Washington Post,* and *Scientific American.* He has served in advisory positions for a diverse set of organizations, including the Council on Foreign Relations, the National Geographic and the Creative Coalition. He is a fellow of the APS, a MacArthur scholar, and currently a Lemelson Research Associate of the Smithsonian Institution. He is also the associate director of public affairs for the American Physical Society. Dr. Slakey received his Ph.D. in physics from the University of Illinois, Urbana-Champaign.

Michael Sulmeyer

Michael Sulmeyer is a Ph.D. candidate in the Department of Politics and International Relations at Oxford University, where he writes about the termination of major weapon systems under development. From 2003-2004 he was special assistant to the principal deputy under-secretary of defense for policy. Previously, he was a research assistant at the Center for Strategic and International Studies. As a Marshall scholar he received his master's from the War Studies Department at King's College, London. Mr. Sulmeyer earned a B.A. in political science from Stanford University.

Benn Tannenbaum

Benn Tannenbaum is currently project director of the Center for Science, Technology and Security Policy at the American Association for the Advancement of Science, focusing on connecting scientists with government on security matters. He has testified before the U.S. House of Representatives Committee on Homeland Security about radiation portal monitors. Dr. Tannenbaum also serves on the American Physical Society's Panel on Public Affairs and on the board of directors of The Triple Helix. Dr. Tannenbaum was the 2002-2003 American Physical Society Congressional Science Fellow, during which time he worked for Representative Edward J. Markey (D-MA) on nonproliferation issues. He has authored or co-authored over 150 papers on technical matters and has published widely on science policy and advising. Dr. Tannenbaum holds B.A., M.S., and Ph.D. degrees in physics from Grinnell College, Michigan State University, and the University of New Mexico, respectively.

Bruno Tertrais

Bruno Tertrais is a senior research fellow at the Fondation pour la Recherche Stratégique (FRS), as well as an associate researcher at the Centres d'études et de recherches internationales (CERI). Between 1990 and 1993 he was the director of the Civilian Affairs Committee, NATO Assembly, Brussels. In 1993 he joined the Délégation aux Affaires stratégiques (Policy Division) of the French Ministry of Defense. In 1995-1996, he was a visiting fellow at the RAND Corporation, Santa Monica. From October 1996 until August 2001 he was special assistant to the director of strategic affairs at the French Ministry of Defense. He is a member of the International Institute for Strategic Studies (IISS), a contributing editor to *Survival*, and a member of the editorial board of *The Washington Quarterly*. His latest book in English is *War Without End* (New-York: The New Press, 2005). Dr. Tertrais graduated from the Institut d'études politiques de Paris in 1984. He also holds a master's degree in public law from the University of Paris (1985) and a doctorate in political science from the Institut d'études politiques de Paris (1994).

Michael Tkacik

Michael Tkacik is an associate professor of political science at Stephen F. Austin State University in Nacogdoches, Texas. His book, *The Future of U.S. Nuclear Operational Doctrine* (The Edwin Mellen Press), was published in 2003. He also writes on security issues, including nuclear weapons, terrorism, democratic transitions, and ethnic conflict. Dr. Tkacik has been a Fulbright scholar. He is currently involved in westernizing the education systems of former Soviet republics. Dr. Tkacik holds a Ph.D. in political science from the University of Maryland, an M.A. in political science from Columbia University and a J.D. from Duke University School of Law.

Richard Weitz

Richard Weitz is a senior fellow and director of program management at the Hudson Institute. By employing scenario-based planning and other techniques, he analyzes mid- and long-term national and international political-military issues. His current areas of research include U.S. foreign policy, Eurasia, defense reform, and homeland security. He also has contributed articles to journals such as *The National Interest, The Washington Quarterly, NATO Review, Studies in Conflict and Terrorism,* and *The Journal of Strategic Studies.* His commentaries have appeared in *Washington Post.com, The Washington Times, Wall Street Journal* (Europe), *Aviation Week & Space Technology,* and many Internet-based publications. He has appeared on the BBC, CNN, ABC, MSNBC, CBC, CTV, Al-Hurra, Al-Jazeera, VOA, Pacifica Radio, and additional broadcast media. He has been a PONI member since 2003. Dr. Weitz is a graduate of Harvard College (B.A. with highest honors in government), the London School of Economics (M.Sc. in international relations), Oxford University (M. Phil. in politics), and Harvard University (Ph.D. in political science).